Operating Systems:
Principles and Practice

Operating Systems: Principles and Practice

Edited by
Reid Barnes

Larsen & Keller
www.larsen-keller.com

Operating Systems: Principles and Practice
Edited by Reid Barnes
ISBN: 978-1-63549-204-0 (Hardback)

 Larsen & Keller

Published by Larsen and Keller Education,
5 Penn Plaza,
19th Floor,
New York, NY 10001, USA

Cataloging-in-Publication Data

Operating systems : principles and practice / edited by Reid Barnes.
    p. cm.
Includes bibliographical references and index.
ISBN 978-1-63549-204-0
1. Operating systems (Computers). 2. Computer software.
I. Barnes, Reid.
QA76.77 .O64 2017
005.43--dc23

The publisher's policy is to use permanent paper from mills that operate a sustainable forestry policy. Furthermore, the publisher ensures that the text paper and cover boards used have met acceptable environmental accreditation standards.

Printed and bound in the United States of America.

For more information regarding Larsen and Keller Education and its products, please visit the publisher's website www.larsen-keller.com

Table of Contents

Preface

Operating systems are one of the most important inventions after the internet. They refer to the system software that manages the program and hardware components of the computers. The most common and famous operating systems are Unix, Microsoft Windows, etc. This book outlines the processes and applications of operating systems in detail. It picks up individual branches and explains their need and contribution in the context of the growth of the subject. Some of the diverse topics covered in this text address the varied branches that fall under this category. This textbook is a complete source of knowledge on the present status of this important field. It will serve as a reference to a broad spectrum of readers.

To facilitate a deeper understanding of the contents of this book a short introduction of every chapter is written below:

Chapter 1- Operating systems help in the management of computer hardware and software resources. Every computer program requires an operating system to function. This chapter is an overview of the subject matter incorporating all the major aspects of operating system.

Chapter 2- Operating systems are best understood in confluence with the major types listed in the following section. Some of the types of operating systems elucidated in the chapter are mobile operating system, network operating system, embedded operating system, distributed operating system, Microsoft windows etc. Mobile operating system is the operating system used in mobile devices. The operating systems used in mobiles are android, iOS, colorOS, HTC Sense and cyanogenMod. This section strategically encompasses and incorporates the major types of operating systems, providing a complete understanding.

Chapter 3- The components of an operating system are vital for the different parts of a computer to work together. The different components of an operating system are kernel, process, interrupt, protected mode, virtual memory, device driver etc. The topics discussed in the chapter are of great importance to broaden the existing knowledge on operating systems.

Chapter 4- A game console operating system is a computer device or a digital device that is particularly used to display a video game. The operating systems of gaming that have been stated in this chapter are Linux for PlayStation 2, Wii U system software, Wii system software, Xbox One system software and otherOS. This section has been carefully written to provide an easy understanding of game console operating systems.

Chapter 5- The computers that were created initially did not have an operating system. Since the computers did not have an operating system, every program required full hardware specification to run properly and to perform tasks correctly. This section helps the readers in understanding the progress operating systems have made over a period of years.

I would like to share the credit of this book with my editorial team who worked tirelessly on this book. I owe the completion of this book to the never-ending support of my family, who supported me throughout the project.

Editor

Introduction to Operating Systems

Operating systems help in the management of computer hardware and software resources. Every computer program requires an operating system to function. This chapter is an overview of the subject matter incorporating all the major aspects of operating system.

An operating system (OS) is system software that manages computer hardware and software resources and provides common services for computer programs. All computer programs, excluding firmware, require an operating system to function.

Time-sharing operating systems schedule tasks for efficient use of the system and may also include accounting software for cost allocation of processor time, mass storage, printing, and other resources.

For hardware functions such as input and output and memory allocation, the operating system acts as an intermediary between programs and the computer hardware, although the application code is usually executed directly by the hardware and frequently makes system calls to an OS function or is interrupted by it. Operating systems are found on many devices that contain a computer – from cellular phones and video game consoles to web servers and supercomputers.

The dominant desktop operating system is Microsoft Windows with a market share of around 82%. OS X by Apple Inc. is in second place (9.8%), and Linux is in third position (1.5%). In the mobile (smartphone and tablet combined) sector, based on Strategy Analytics Q3 2016 data, Android by Google is dominant with 87.5 percent or growth by 10.3 percent in one year and iOS by Apple is placed second with 12.1 percent or decrease by 5.2 percent in one year, while other operating systems amount to just 0.3 percent. Linux is dominant in the server and supercomputing sectors. Other specialized classes of operating systems, such as embedded and real-time systems, exist for many applications.

Types of Operating Systems

Single-and multi-tasking

A single-tasking system can only run one program at a time, while a multi-tasking operating system allows more than one program to be running in concurrency. This is achieved by time-sharing, dividing the available processor time between multiple processes that are each interrupted repeatedly in time slices by a task-scheduling subsystem of the operating system. Multi-tasking may be characterized in preemptive and co-operative types. In preemptive multitasking, the operating system slices the CPU time and dedicates a slot to each of the programs. Unix-like operating systems, e.g., Solaris, Linux, as well as AmigaOS support preemptive multitasking. Cooperative multitasking is achieved by relying on each process to provide time to the other processes in a defined manner. 16-bit versions of Microsoft Windows used cooperative multi-tasking. 32-bit versions of both Windows NT and Win9x, used preemptive multi-tasking.

Single-and multi-user

Single-user operating systems have no facilities to distinguish users, but may allow multiple programs to run in tandem. A multi-user operating system extends the basic concept of multi-tasking with facilities that identify processes and resources, such as disk space, belonging to multiple users, and the system permits multiple users to interact with the system at the same time. Time-sharing operating systems schedule tasks for efficient use of the system and may also include accounting software for cost allocation of processor time, mass storage, printing, and other resources to multiple users.

Distributed

A distributed operating system manages a group of distinct computers and makes them appear to be a single computer. The development of networked computers that could be linked and communicate with each other gave rise to distributed computing. Distributed computations are carried out on more than one machine. When computers in a group work in cooperation, they form a distributed system.

Templated

In an OS, distributed and cloud computing context, templating refers to creating a single virtual machine image as a guest operating system, then saving it as a tool for multiple running virtual machines. The technique is used both in virtualization and cloud computing management, and is common in large server warehouses.

Embedded

Embedded operating systems are designed to be used in embedded computer systems. They are designed to operate on small machines like PDAs with less autonomy. They are able to operate with a limited number of resources. They are very compact and extremely efficient by design. Windows CE and Minix 3 are some examples of embedded operating systems.

Real-time

A real-time operating system is an operating system that guarantees to process events or data by a specific moment in time. A real-time operating system may be single- or multi-tasking, but when multitasking, it uses specialized scheduling algorithms so that a deterministic nature of behavior is achieved. An event-driven system switches between tasks based on their priorities or external events while time-sharing operating systems switch tasks based on clock interrupts

Library

A library operating system is one in which the services that a typical operating system provides, such as networking, are provided in the form of libraries. These libraries are composed with the application and configuration code to construct unikernels – which are specialized, single address space, machine images that can be deployed to cloud or embedded environments.

History

Early computers were built to perform a series of single tasks, like a calculator. Basic operating system features were developed in the 1950s, such as resident monitor functions that could automatically run different programs in succession to speed up processing. Operating systems did not exist in their modern and more complex forms until the early 1960s. Hardware features were added, that enabled use of runtime libraries, interrupts, and parallel processing. When personal computers became popular in the 1980s, operating systems were made for them similar in concept to those used on larger computers.

In the 1940s, the earliest electronic digital systems had no operating systems. Electronic systems of this time were programmed on rows of mechanical switches or by jumper wires on plug boards. These were special-purpose systems that, for example, generated ballistics tables for the military or controlled the printing of payroll checks from data on punched paper cards. After programmable general purpose computers were invented, machine languages (consisting of strings of the binary digits 0 and 1 on punched paper tape) were introduced that sped up the programming process (Stern, 1981).

OS/360 was used on most IBM mainframe computers beginning in 1966, including computers used by the Apollo program.

In the early 1950s, a computer could execute only one program at a time. Each user had sole use of the computer for a limited period of time and would arrive at a scheduled time with program and data on punched paper cards or punched tape. The program would be loaded into the machine, and the machine would be set to work until the program completed or crashed. Programs could generally be debugged via a front panel using toggle switches and panel lights. It is said that Alan Turing was a master of this on the early Manchester Mark 1 machine, and he was already deriving the primitive conception of an operating system from the principles of the universal Turing machine.

Later machines came with libraries of programs, which would be linked to a user's program to assist in operations such as input and output and generating computer code from human-readable symbolic code. This was the genesis of the modern-day operating system. However, machines still ran a single job at a time. At Cambridge University in England the job queue was at one time a washing line (clothes line) from which tapes were hung with different colored clothes-pegs to indicate job-priority.

An improvement was the Atlas Supervisor introduced with the Manchester Atlas commissioned in 1962, "considered by many to be the first recognisable modern operating system". Brinch Hansen described it as "the most significant breakthrough in the history of operating systems."

Mainframes

Through the 1950s, many major features were pioneered in the field of operating systems, including batch processing, input/output interrupt, buffering, multitasking, spooling, runtime libraries, link-loading, and programs for sorting records in files. These features were included or not included in application software at the option of application programmers, rather than in a separate operating system used by all applications. In 1959, the SHARE Operating System was released as an integrated utility for the IBM 704, and later in the 709 and 7090 mainframes, although it was quickly supplanted by IBSYS/IBJOB on the 709, 7090 and 7094.

During the 1960s, IBM's OS/360 introduced the concept of a single OS spanning an entire product line, which was crucial for the success of the System/360 machines. IBM's current mainframe operating systems are distant descendants of this original system and applications written for OS/360 can still be run on modern machines.

OS/360 also pioneered the concept that the operating system keeps track of all of the system resources that are used, including program and data space allocation in main memory and file space in secondary storage, and file locking during update. When the process is terminated for any reason, all of these resources are re-claimed by the operating system.

The alternative CP-67 system for the S/360-67 started a whole line of IBM operating systems focused on the concept of virtual machines. Other operating systems used on IBM S/360 series mainframes included systems developed by IBM: COS/360 (Compatibility Operating System), DOS/360 (Disk Operating System), TSS/360 (Time Sharing System), TOS/360 (Tape Operating System), BOS/360 (Basic Operating System), and ACP (Airline Control Program), as well as a few non-IBM systems: MTS (Michigan Terminal System), MUSIC (Multi-User System for Interactive Computing), and ORVYL (Stanford Timesharing System).

Control Data Corporation developed the SCOPE operating system in the 1960s, for batch processing. In cooperation with the University of Minnesota, the Kronos and later the NOS operating systems were developed during the 1970s, which supported simultaneous batch and timesharing use. Like many commercial timesharing systems, its interface was an extension of the Dartmouth BASIC operating systems, one of the pioneering efforts in timesharing and programming languages. In the late 1970s, Control Data and the University of Illinois developed the PLATO operating system, which used plasma panel displays and long-distance time sharing networks. Plato was remarkably innovative for its time, featuring real-time chat, and multi-user graphical games.

In 1961, Burroughs Corporation introduced the B5000 with the MCP, (Master Control Program) operating system. The B5000 was a stack machine designed to exclusively support high-level languages with no machine language or assembler, and indeed the MCP was the first OS to be written exclusively in a high-level language – ESPOL, a dialect of ALGOL. MCP also introduced many other ground-breaking innovations, such as being the first commercial implementation of virtual memory. During development of the AS/400, IBM made an approach to Burroughs to licence MCP to run on the AS/400 hardware. This proposal was declined by Burroughs management to protect its existing hardware production. MCP is still in use today in the Unisys ClearPath/MCP line of computers.

UNIVAC, the first commercial computer manufacturer, produced a series of EXEC operating systems . Like all early main-frame systems, this batch-oriented system managed magnetic drums, disks, card readers and line printers. In the 1970s, UNIVAC produced the Real-Time Basic (RTB) system to support large-scale time sharing, also patterned after the Dartmouth BC system.

General Electric and MIT developed General Electric Comprehensive Operating Supervisor (GECOS), which introduced the concept of ringed security privilege levels. After acquisition by Honeywell it was renamed General Comprehensive Operating System (GCOS).

Digital Equipment Corporation developed many operating systems for its various computer lines, including TOPS-10 and TOPS-20 time sharing systems for the 36-bit PDP-10 class systems. Before the widespread use of UNIX, TOPS-10 was a particularly popular system in universities, and in the early ARPANET community.

From the late 1960s through the late 1970s, several hardware capabilities evolved that allowed similar or ported software to run on more than one system. Early systems had utilized microprogramming to implement features on their systems in order to permit different underlying computer architectures to appear to be the same as others in a series. In fact, most 360s after the 360/40 (except the 360/165 and 360/168) were microprogrammed implementations.

The enormous investment in software for these systems made since the 1960s caused most of the original computer manufacturers to continue to develop compatible operating systems along with the hardware. Notable supported mainframe operating systems include:

- Burroughs MCP – B5000, 1961 to Unisys Clearpath/MCP, present

- IBM OS/360 – IBM System/360, 1966 to IBM z/OS, present

- IBM CP-67 – IBM System/360, 1967 to IBM z/VM

- UNIVAC EXEC 8 – UNIVAC 1108, 1967, to OS 2200 Unisys Clearpath Dorado, present

Microcomputers

The first microcomputers did not have the capacity or need for the elaborate operating systems that had been developed for mainframes and minis; minimalistic operating systems were developed, often loaded from ROM and known as *monitors*. One notable early disk operating system was CP/M, which was supported on many early microcomputers and was closely imitated by Microsoft's MS-DOS, which became widely popular as the operating system chosen for the IBM PC (IBM's version of it was called IBM DOS or PC DOS). In the 1980s, Apple Computer Inc. (now Apple Inc.) abandoned its popular Apple II series of microcomputers to introduce the Apple Macintosh computer with an innovative graphical user interface (GUI) to the Mac OS.

```
Current date is Tue  1-01-1980
Enter new date:
Current time is  7:48:27.13
Enter new time:

The IBM Personal Computer DOS
Version 1.10 (C)Copyright IBM Corp 1981, 1982

A>dir/w
COMMAND   COM      FORMAT    COM      CHKDSK    COM      SYS       COM      DISKCOPY COM
DISKCOMP COM       COMP      COM      EXE2BIN   EXE      MODE      COM      EDLIN    COM
DEBUG     COM      LINK      EXE      BASIC     COM      BASICA    COM      ART      BAS
SAMPLES   BAS      MORTGAGE BAS      COLORBAR BAS      CALENDAR BAS      MUSIC    BAS
DONKEY    BAS      CIRCLE    BAS      PIECHART BAS      SPACE     BAS      BALL     BAS
COMM      BAS
         26 File(s)
A>dir command.com
COMMAND   COM        4959   5-07-82   12:00p
          1 File(s)
A>
```

PC DOS was an early personal computer OS that featured a command line interface.

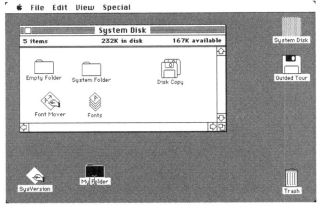

Mac OS by Apple Computer became the first widespread OS to feature a graphical user interface. Many of its features such as windows and icons would later become commonplace in GUIs.

The introduction of the Intel 80386 CPU chip in October 1985, with 32-bit architecture and paging capabilities, provided personal computers with the ability to run multitasking operating systems like those of earlier minicomputers and mainframes. Microsoft responded to this progress by hiring Dave Cutler, who had developed the VMS operating system for Digital Equipment Corporation. He would lead the development of the Windows NT operating system, which continues to serve as the basis for Microsoft's operating systems line. Steve Jobs, a co-founder of Apple Inc., started NeXT Computer Inc., which developed the NEXTSTEP operating system. NEXTSTEP would later be acquired by Apple Inc. and used, along with code from FreeBSD as the core of Mac OS X.

The GNU Project was started by activist and programmer Richard Stallman with the goal of creating a complete free software replacement to the proprietary UNIX operating system. While the project was highly successful in duplicating the functionality of various parts of UNIX, development of the GNU Hurd kernel proved to be unproductive. In 1991, Finnish computer science student Linus Torvalds, with cooperation from volunteers collaborating over the Internet, released the first version of the Linux kernel. It was soon merged with the GNU user space components and system software to form a complete operating system. Since then, the combination of the two major components has usually been referred to as simply "Linux" by the software industry, a naming convention that Stallman and the Free Software Foundation remain opposed to, preferring the name GNU/Linux. The Berkeley Software Distribution, known as BSD, is the UNIX derivative distributed by the University of California, Berkeley, starting in the 1970s. Freely distributed and ported to many minicomputers, it eventually also gained a following for use on PCs, mainly as FreeBSD, NetBSD and OpenBSD.

Examples of Operating Systems

Unix and Unix-like Operating Systems

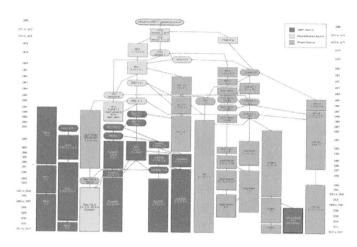

Evolution of Unix systems

Unix was originally written in assembly language. Ken Thompson wrote B, mainly based on BCPL, based on his experience in the MULTICS project. B was replaced by C, and Unix, rewritten in C, developed into a large, complex family of inter-related operating systems which have been influential in every modern operating system.

The *Unix-like* family is a diverse group of operating systems, with several major sub-categories including System V, BSD, and Linux. The name "UNIX" is a trademark of The Open Group which licenses it for use with any operating system that has been shown to conform to their definitions. "UNIX-like" is commonly used to refer to the large set of operating systems which resemble the original UNIX.

Unix-like systems run on a wide variety of computer architectures. They are used heavily for servers in business, as well as workstations in academic and engineering environments. Free UNIX variants, such as Linux and BSD, are popular in these areas.

Four operating systems are certified by The Open Group (holder of the Unix trademark) as Unix. HP's HP-UX and IBM's AIX are both descendants of the original System V Unix and are designed to run only on their respective vendor's hardware. In contrast, Sun Microsystems's Solaris can run on multiple types of hardware, including x86 and Sparc servers, and PCs. Apple's OS X, a replacement for Apple's earlier (non-Unix) Mac OS, is a hybrid kernel-based BSD variant derived from NeXTSTEP, Mach, and FreeBSD.

Unix interoperability was sought by establishing the POSIX standard. The POSIX standard can be applied to any operating system, although it was originally created for various Unix variants.

BSD and its Descendants

A subgroup of the Unix family is the Berkeley Software Distribution family, which includes FreeBSD, NetBSD, and OpenBSD. These operating systems are most commonly found on webservers, although they can also function as a personal computer OS. The Internet owes much of its existence to BSD, as many of the protocols now commonly used by computers to connect, send and receive data over a network were widely implemented and refined in BSD. The World Wide Web was also first demonstrated on a number of computers running an OS based on BSD called NeXTSTEP.

The first server for the World Wide Web ran on NeXTSTEP, based on BSD.

In 1974, University of California, Berkeley installed its first Unix system. Over time, students and staff in the computer science department there began adding new programs to make things easier, such as text editors. When Berkeley received new VAX computers in 1978 with Unix installed, the school's undergraduates modified Unix even more in order to take advantage of the computer's hardware possibilities. The Defense Advanced Research Projects Agency of the US Department of Defense took interest, and decided to fund the project. Many schools, corporations, and government organizations took notice and started to use Berkeley's version of Unix instead of the official one distributed by AT&T.

Steve Jobs, upon leaving Apple Inc. in 1985, formed NeXT Inc., a company that manufactured high-end computers running on a variation of BSD called NeXTSTEP. One of these computers was used by Tim Berners-Lee as the first webserver to create the World Wide Web.

Developers like Keith Bostic encouraged the project to replace any non-free code that originated with Bell Labs. Once this was done, however, AT&T sued. After two years of legal disputes, the BSD project spawned a number of free derivatives, such as NetBSD and FreeBSD (both in 1993), and OpenBSD (from NetBSD in 1995).

OS X

OS X (formerly "Mac OS X") is a line of open core graphical operating systems developed, marketed, and sold by Apple Inc., the latest of which is pre-loaded on all currently shipping Macintosh computers. OS X is the successor to the original classic Mac OS, which had been Apple's primary operating system since 1984. Unlike its predecessor, OS X is a UNIX operating system built on technology that had been developed at NeXT through the second half of the 1980s and up until Apple purchased the company in early 1997. The operating system was first released in 1999 as Mac OS X Server 1.0, with a desktop-oriented version (Mac OS X v10.0 "Cheetah") following in March 2001. Since then, six more distinct "client" and "server" editions of OS X have been released, until the two were merged in OS X 10.7 "Lion".

The standard user interface of OS X

Prior to its merging with OS X, the server edition – OS X Server – was architecturally identical to its desktop counterpart and usually ran on Apple's line of Macintosh server hardware. OS X Server included work group management and administration software tools that provide simplified access to key network services, including a mail transfer agent, a Samba server, an LDAP server, a domain name server, and others. With Mac OS X v10.7 Lion, all server aspects of Mac OS X Server have been integrated into the client version and the product re-branded as "OS X" (dropping "Mac" from the name). The server tools are now offered as an application.

Linux

Ubuntu, desktop Linux distribution

The Linux kernel originated in 1991, as a project of Linus Torvalds, while a university student in Finland. He posted information about his project on a newsgroup for computer students and programmers, and received support and assistance from volunteers who succeeded in creating a complete and functional kernel.

Linux is Unix-like, but was developed without any Unix code, unlike BSD and its variants. Because of its open license model, the Linux kernel code is available for study and modification, which resulted in its use on a wide range of computing machinery from supercomputers to smart-watches. Although estimates suggest that Linux is used on only 1.82% of all "desktop" (or laptop) PCs, it has been widely adopted for use in servers and embedded systems such as cell phones. Linux has superseded Unix on many platforms and is used on most supercomputers including the top 207. Many of the same computers are also on Green500 (but in different order), and Linux runs on the top 10. Linux is also commonly used on other small energy-efficient computers, such as smart-phones and smartwatches. The Linux kernel is used in some popular distributions, such as Red Hat, Debian, Ubuntu, Linux Mint and Google's Android.

Android, a popular mobile operating system based on a modified version of the Linux kernel

Google Chrome OS

Chrome OS is an operating system based on the Linux kernel and designed by Google. It is developed out in the open in the Chromium OS open source variant and Google makes a proprietary variant of it (similar to the split for the Chrome and Chromium browser). Since Chromium OS targets computer users who spend most of their time on the Internet, it is mainly a web browser with limited ability to run local applications, though it has a built-in file manager and media player (in later versions, (modified) Android apps have also been supported, since the browser has been made to support them). Instead, it relies on Internet applications (or Web apps) used in the web browser to accomplish tasks such as word processing. Chromium OS differs from Chrome OS in that Chromium is open-source and used primarily by developers whereas Chrome OS is the operating system shipped out in Chromebooks.

Microsoft Windows

Microsoft Windows is a family of proprietary operating systems designed by Microsoft Corporation and primarily targeted to Intel architecture based computers, with an estimated 88.9 percent total usage share on Web connected computers. The latest version is Windows 10.

In 2011, Windows 7 overtook Windows XP as most common version in use.

Microsoft Windows was first released in 1985, as an operating environment running on top of MS-DOS, which was the standard operating system shipped on most Intel architecture personal computers at the time. In 1995, Windows 95 was released which only used MS-DOS as a bootstrap. For backwards compatibility, Win9x could run real-mode MS-DOS and 16-bit Windows 3.x drivers. Windows ME, released in 2000, was the last version in the Win9x family. Later versions have all been based on the Windows NT kernel. Current client versions of Windows run on IA-32, x86-64 and 32-bit ARM microprocessors. In addition Itanium is still supported in older server version Windows Server 2008 R2. In the past, Windows NT supported additional architectures.

Server editions of Windows are widely used. In recent years, Microsoft has expended significant capital in an effort to promote the use of Windows as a server operating system. However, Windows' usage on servers is not as widespread as on personal computers as Windows competes against Linux and BSD for server market share.

ReactOS is a Windows-alternative operating system, which is being developed on the principles of Windows – without using any of Microsoft's code.

Other

There have been many operating systems that were significant in their day but are no longer so, such as AmigaOS; OS/2 from IBM and Microsoft; classic Mac OS, the non-Unix precursor to Apple's Mac OS X; BeOS; XTS-300; RISC OS; MorphOS; Haiku; BareMetal and FreeMint. Some are still used in niche markets and continue to be developed as minority platforms for enthusiast communities and specialist applications. OpenVMS, formerly from DEC, is still under active development by Hewlett-Packard. Yet other operating systems are used almost exclusively in academia, for operating systems education or to do research on operating system concepts. A typical example of a system that fulfills both roles is MINIX, while for example Singularity is used purely for research.

Other operating systems have failed to win significant market share, but have introduced innovations that have influenced mainstream operating systems, not least Bell Labs' Plan 9.

Components

The components of an operating system all exist in order to make the different parts of a computer work together. All user software needs to go through the operating system in order to use any of the hardware, whether it be as simple as a mouse or keyboard or as complex as an Internet component.

Kernel

With the aid of the firmware and device drivers, the kernel provides the most basic level of control over all of the computer's hardware devices. It manages memory access for programs in the RAM, it determines which programs get access to which hardware resources, it sets up or resets the CPU's operating states for optimal operation at all times, and it organizes the data for long-term non-volatile storage with file systems on such media as disks, tapes, flash memory, etc.

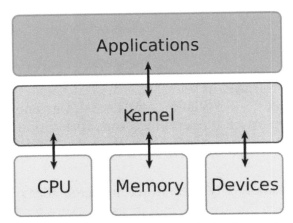

A kernel connects the application software to the hardware of a computer.

Program Execution

The operating system provides an interface between an application program and the computer hardware, so that an application program can interact with the hardware only by obeying rules and procedures programmed into the operating system. The operating system is also a set of services which simplify development and execution of application programs. Executing an application program involves the creation of a process by the operating system kernel which assigns memory space and other resources, establishes a priority for the process in multi-tasking systems, loads program binary code into memory, and initiates execution of the application program which then interacts with the user and with hardware devices.

Interrupts

Interrupts are central to operating systems, as they provide an efficient way for the operating system to interact with and react to its environment. The alternative – having the operating system "watch" the various sources of input for events (polling) that require action – can be found in older systems with very small stacks (50 or 60 bytes) but is unusual in modern systems with large stacks. Interrupt-based programming is directly supported by most modern CPUs. Interrupts provide a computer with a way of automatically saving local register contexts, and running specific code in response to events. Even very basic computers support hardware interrupts, and allow the programmer to specify code which may be run when that event takes place.

When an interrupt is received, the computer's hardware automatically suspends whatever program is currently running, saves its status, and runs computer code previously associated with the interrupt; this is analogous to placing a bookmark in a book in response to a phone call. In modern operating systems, interrupts are handled by the operating system's kernel. Interrupts may come from either the computer's hardware or the running program.

When a hardware device triggers an interrupt, the operating system's kernel decides how to deal with this event, generally by running some processing code. The amount of code being run depends on the priority of the interrupt (for example: a person usually responds to a smoke detector alarm before answering the phone). The processing of hardware interrupts is a task that is usually delegated to software called a device driver, which may be part of the operating system's kernel, part of another program, or both. Device drivers may then relay information to a running program by various means.

A program may also trigger an interrupt to the operating system. If a program wishes to access hardware, for example, it may interrupt the operating system's kernel, which causes control to be passed back to the kernel. The kernel then processes the request. If a program wishes additional resources (or wishes to shed resources) such as memory, it triggers an interrupt to get the kernel's attention.

Modes

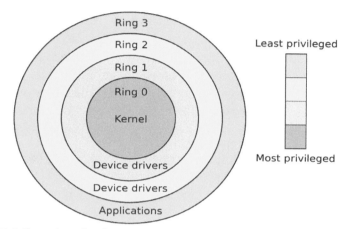

Privilege rings for the x86 available in protected mode. Operating systems determine which processes run in each mode.

Modern CPUs support multiple modes of operation. CPUs with this capability use at least two modes: protected mode and supervisor mode. The supervisor mode is used by the operating system's kernel for low level tasks that need unrestricted access to hardware, such as controlling how memory is written and erased, and communication with devices like graphics cards. Protected mode, in contrast, is used for almost everything else. Applications operate within protected mode, and can only use hardware by communicating with the kernel, which controls everything in supervisor mode. CPUs might have other modes similar to protected mode as well, such as the virtual modes in order to emulate older processor types, such as 16-bit processors on a 32-bit one, or 32-bit processors on a 64-bit one.

When a computer first starts up, it is automatically running in supervisor mode. The first few programs to run on the computer, being the BIOS or EFI, bootloader, and the operating system have unlimited access to hardware – and this is required because, by definition, initializing a protected environment can only be done outside of one. However, when the operating system passes control to another program, it can place the CPU into protected mode.

In protected mode, programs may have access to a more limited set of the CPU's instructions. A user program may leave protected mode only by triggering an interrupt, causing control to be passed back to the kernel. In this way the operating system can maintain exclusive control over things like access to hardware and memory.

The term "protected mode resource" generally refers to one or more CPU registers, which contain information that the running program isn't allowed to alter. Attempts to alter these resources generally causes a switch to supervisor mode, where the operating system can deal with the illegal operation the program was attempting (for example, by killing the program).

Memory Management

Among other things, a multiprogramming operating system kernel must be responsible for managing all system memory which is currently in use by programs. This ensures that a program does not interfere with memory already in use by another program. Since programs time share, each program must have independent access to memory.

Cooperative memory management, used by many early operating systems, assumes that all programs make voluntary use of the kernel's memory manager, and do not exceed their allocated memory. This system of memory management is almost never seen any more, since programs often contain bugs which can cause them to exceed their allocated memory. If a program fails, it may cause memory used by one or more other programs to be affected or overwritten. Malicious programs or viruses may purposefully alter another program's memory, or may affect the operation of the operating system itself. With cooperative memory management, it takes only one misbehaved program to crash the system.

Memory protection enables the kernel to limit a process' access to the computer's memory. Various methods of memory protection exist, including memory segmentation and paging. All methods require some level of hardware support (such as the 80286 MMU), which doesn't exist in all computers.

In both segmentation and paging, certain protected mode registers specify to the CPU what memory address it should allow a running program to access. Attempts to access other addresses trigger an interrupt which cause the CPU to re-enter supervisor mode, placing the kernel in charge. This is called a segmentation violation or Seg-V for short, and since it is both difficult to assign a meaningful result to such an operation, and because it is usually a sign of a misbehaving program, the kernel generally resorts to terminating the offending program, and reports the error.

Windows versions 3.1 through ME had some level of memory protection, but programs could easily circumvent the need to use it. A general protection fault would be produced, indicating a segmentation violation had occurred; however, the system would often crash anyway.

Virtual Memory

The use of virtual memory addressing (such as paging or segmentation) means that the kernel can choose what memory each program may use at any given time, allowing the operating system to use the same memory locations for multiple tasks.

If a program tries to access memory that isn't in its current range of accessible memory, but nonetheless has been allocated to it, the kernel is interrupted in the same way as it would if the program were to exceed its allocated memory. Under UNIX this kind of interrupt is referred to as a page fault.

When the kernel detects a page fault it generally adjusts the virtual memory range of the program which triggered it, granting it access to the memory requested. This gives the kernel discretionary power over where a particular application's memory is stored, or even whether or not it has actually been allocated yet.

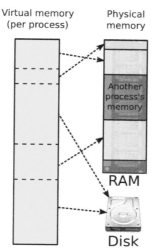

Virtual memory (per process)

Physical memory

Another process's memory

RAM

Disk

Many operating systems can "trick" programs into using memory scattered around the hard disk and RAM as if it is one continuous chunk of memory, called virtual memory.

In modern operating systems, memory which is accessed less frequently can be temporarily stored on disk or other media to make that space available for use by other programs. This is called swapping, as an area of memory can be used by multiple programs, and what that memory area contains can be swapped or exchanged on demand.

"Virtual memory" provides the programmer or the user with the perception that there is a much larger amount of RAM in the computer than is really there.

Multitasking

Multitasking refers to the running of multiple independent computer programs on the same computer; giving the appearance that it is performing the tasks at the same time. Since most computers can do at most one or two things at one time, this is generally done via time-sharing, which means that each program uses a share of the computer's time to execute.

An operating system kernel contains a scheduling program which determines how much time each process spends executing, and in which order execution control should be passed to programs. Control is passed to a process by the kernel, which allows the program access to the CPU and memory. Later, control is returned to the kernel through some mechanism, so that another program may be allowed to use the CPU. This so-called passing of control between the kernel and applications is called a context switch.

An early model which governed the allocation of time to programs was called cooperative multitasking. In this model, when control is passed to a program by the kernel, it may execute for as long as it wants before explicitly returning control to the kernel. This means that a malicious or malfunctioning program may not only prevent any other programs from using the CPU, but it can hang the entire system if it enters an infinite loop.

Modern operating systems extend the concepts of application preemption to device drivers and kernel code, so that the operating system has preemptive control over internal run-times as well.

The philosophy governing preemptive multitasking is that of ensuring that all programs are given regular time on the CPU. This implies that all programs must be limited in how much time they are allowed to spend on the CPU without being interrupted. To accomplish this, modern operating system kernels make use of a timed interrupt. A protected mode timer is set by the kernel which triggers a return to supervisor mode after the specified time has elapsed.

On many single user operating systems cooperative multitasking is perfectly adequate, as home computers generally run a small number of well tested programs. The AmigaOS is an exception, having preemptive multitasking from its very first version. Windows NT was the first version of Microsoft Windows which enforced preemptive multitasking, but it didn't reach the home user market until Windows XP (since Windows NT was targeted at professionals).

Disk Access and File Systems

File systems allow users and programs to organize and sort files
on a computer, often through the use of directories (or "folders").

Access to data stored on disks is a central feature of all operating systems. Computers store data on disks using files, which are structured in specific ways in order to allow for faster access, higher reliability, and to make better use of the drive's available space. The specific way in which files are stored on a disk is called a file system, and enables files to have names and attributes. It also allows them to be stored in a hierarchy of directories or folders arranged in a directory tree.

Early operating systems generally supported a single type of disk drive and only one kind of file system. Early file systems were limited in their capacity, speed, and in the kinds of file names and directory structures they could use. These limitations often reflected limitations in the operating systems they were designed for, making it very difficult for an operating system to support more than one file system.

While many simpler operating systems support a limited range of options for accessing storage systems, operating systems like UNIX and Linux support a technology known as a virtual file system or VFS. An operating system such as UNIX supports a wide array of storage devices, regardless of their design or file systems, allowing them to be accessed through a common application programming interface (API). This makes it unnecessary for programs to have any knowledge about the device they are accessing. A VFS allows the operating system to provide programs with access to an unlimited number of devices with an infinite variety of file systems installed on them, through the use of specific device drivers and file system drivers.

A connected storage device, such as a hard drive, is accessed through a device driver. The device driver understands the specific language of the drive and is able to translate that language into a standard language used by the operating system to access all disk drives. On UNIX, this is the language of block devices.

When the kernel has an appropriate device driver in place, it can then access the contents of the disk drive in raw format, which may contain one or more file systems. A file system driver is used to translate the commands used to access each specific file system into a standard set of commands that the operating system can use to talk to all file systems. Programs can then deal with these file systems on the basis of filenames, and directories/folders, contained within a hierarchical structure. They can create, delete, open, and close files, as well as gather various information about them, including access permissions, size, free space, and creation and modification dates.

Various differences between file systems make supporting all file systems difficult. Allowed characters in file names, case sensitivity, and the presence of various kinds of file attributes makes the implementation of a single interface for every file system a daunting task. Operating systems tend to recommend using (and so support natively) file systems specifically designed for them; for example, NTFS in Windows and ext3 and ReiserFS in Linux. However, in practice, third party drivers are usually available to give support for the most widely used file systems in most general-purpose operating systems (for example, NTFS is available in Linux through NTFS-3g, and ext2/3 and ReiserFS are available in Windows through third-party software).

Support for file systems is highly varied among modern operating systems, although there are several common file systems which almost all operating systems include support and drivers for. Operating systems vary on file system support and on the disk formats they may be installed on. Under Windows, each file system is usually limited in application to certain media; for example, CDs must use ISO 9660 or UDF, and as of Windows Vista, NTFS is the only file system which the operating system can be installed on. It is possible to install Linux onto many types of file systems. Unlike other operating systems, Linux and UNIX allow any file system to be used regardless of the media it is stored in, whether it is a hard drive, a disc (CD, DVD...), a USB flash drive, or even contained within a file located on another file system.

Device Drivers

A device driver is a specific type of computer software developed to allow interaction with hardware devices. Typically this constitutes an interface for communicating with the device, through the specific computer bus or communications subsystem that the hardware is connected to, providing commands to and/or receiving data from the device, and on the other end, the requisite interfaces to the operating system and software applications. It is a specialized hardware-dependent computer program which is also operating system specific that enables another program, typically an operating system or applications software package or computer program running under the operating system kernel, to interact transparently with a hardware device, and usually provides the requisite interrupt handling necessary for any necessary asynchronous time-dependent hardware interfacing needs.

The key design goal of device drivers is abstraction. Every model of hardware (even within the same class of device) is different. Newer models also are released by manufacturers that provide more reliable or better performance and these newer models are often controlled differently. Computers and their operating systems cannot be expected to know how to control every device, both now and in the future. To solve this problem, operating systems essentially dictate how every type of device should be controlled. The function of the device driver is then to translate these operating system mandated function calls into device specific calls. In theory a new device, which is controlled in a new manner, should function correctly if a suitable driver is available. This new driver ensures that the device appears to operate as usual from the operating system's point of view.

Under versions of Windows before Vista and versions of Linux before 2.6, all driver execution was co-operative, meaning that if a driver entered an infinite loop it would freeze the system. More recent revisions of these operating systems incorporate kernel preemption, where the kernel interrupts the driver to give it tasks, and then separates itself from the process until it receives a response from the device driver, or gives it more tasks to do.

Networking

Currently most operating systems support a variety of networking protocols, hardware, and applications for using them. This means that computers running dissimilar operating systems can participate in a common network for sharing resources such as computing, files, printers, and scanners using either wired or wireless connections. Networks can essentially allow a computer's operating system to access the resources of a remote computer to support the same functions as it could if those resources were connected directly to the local computer. This includes everything from simple communication, to using networked file systems or even sharing another computer's graphics or sound hardware. Some network services allow the resources of a computer to be accessed transparently, such as SSH which allows networked users direct access to a computer's command line interface.

Client/server networking allows a program on a computer, called a client, to connect via a network to another computer, called a server. Servers offer (or host) various services to other network computers and users. These services are usually provided through ports or numbered access points beyond the server's network address. Each port number is usually associated with a maximum of one running program, which is responsible for handling requests to that port. A daemon, being a user program, can in turn access the local hardware resources of that computer by passing requests to the operating system kernel.

Many operating systems support one or more vendor-specific or open networking protocols as well, for example, SNA on IBM systems, DECnet on systems from Digital Equipment Corporation, and Microsoft-specific protocols (SMB) on Windows. Specific protocols for specific tasks may also be supported such as NFS for file access. Protocols like ESound, or esd can be easily extended over the network to provide sound from local applications, on a remote system's sound hardware.

Security

A computer being secure depends on a number of technologies working properly. A modern operating system provides access to a number of resources, which are available to software running on the system, and to external devices like networks via the kernel.

The operating system must be capable of distinguishing between requests which should be allowed to be processed, and others which should not be processed. While some systems may simply distinguish between "privileged" and "non-privileged", systems commonly have a form of requester *identity*, such as a user name. To establish identity there may be a process of *authentication*. Often a username must be quoted, and each username may have a password. Other methods of authentication, such as magnetic cards or biometric data, might be used instead. In some cases, especially connections from the network, resources may be accessed with no authentication at all (such as reading files over a network share). Also covered by the concept of requester identity is *authorization*; the particular services and resources accessible by the requester once logged into a system are tied to either the requester's user account or to the variously configured groups of users to which the requester belongs.

In addition to the allow or disallow model of security, a system with a high level of security also offers auditing options. These would allow tracking of requests for access to resources (such as, "who has been reading this file?"). Internal security, or security from an already running program is only possible if all possibly harmful requests must be carried out through interrupts to the operating system kernel. If programs can directly access hardware and resources, they cannot be secured.

External security involves a request from outside the computer, such as a login at a connected console or some kind of network connection. External requests are often passed through device drivers to the operating system's kernel, where they can be passed onto applications, or carried out directly. Security of operating systems has long been a concern because of highly sensitive data held on computers, both of a commercial and military nature. The United States Government Department of Defense (DoD) created the *Trusted Computer System Evaluation Criteria* (TCSEC) which is a standard that sets basic requirements for assessing the effectiveness of security. This became of vital importance to operating system makers, because the TCSEC was used to evaluate, classify and select trusted operating systems being considered for the processing, storage and retrieval of sensitive or classified information.

Network services include offerings such as file sharing, print services, email, web sites, and file transfer protocols (FTP), most of which can have compromised security. At the front line of security are hardware devices known as firewalls or intrusion detection/prevention systems. At the operating system level, there are a number of software firewalls available, as well as intrusion detection/prevention systems. Most modern operating systems include a software firewall, which is enabled by default. A software firewall can be configured to allow or deny network traffic to or from a service or application running on the operating system. Therefore, one can install and be running an insecure service, such as Telnet or FTP, and not have to be threatened by a security breach because the firewall would deny all traffic trying to connect to the service on that port.

An alternative strategy, and the only sandbox strategy available in systems that do not meet the Popek and Goldberg virtualization requirements, is where the operating system is not running user programs as native code, but instead either emulates a processor or provides a host for a p-code based system such as Java.

Internal security is especially relevant for multi-user systems; it allows each user of the system to have private files that the other users cannot tamper with or read. Internal security is also vital if auditing is to be of any use, since a program can potentially bypass the operating system, inclusive of bypassing auditing.

User Interface

Every computer that is to be operated by an individual requires a user interface. The user interface is usually referred to as a shell and is essential if human interaction is to be supported. The user interface views the directory structure and requests services from the operating system that will acquire data from input hardware devices, such as a keyboard, mouse or credit card reader, and requests operating system services to display prompts, status messages and such on output hardware devices, such as a video monitor or printer. The two most common forms of a user interface have historically been the command-line interface, where computer commands are typed out line-by-line, and the graphical user interface, where a visual environment (most commonly a WIMP) is present.

A screenshot of the Bash command line. Each command is typed out after the 'prompt', and then its output appears below, working its way down the screen. The current command prompt is at the bottom.

Graphical User Interfaces

A screenshot of the KDE Plasma Desktop graphical user interface.
Programs take the form of images on the screen, and the files, folders (directories),
and applications take the form of icons and symbols. A mouse is used to navigate the computer.

Most of the modern computer systems support graphical user interfaces (GUI), and often include them. In some computer systems, such as the original implementation of the classic Mac OS, the GUI is integrated into the kernel.

While technically a graphical user interface is not an operating system service, incorporating support for one into the operating system kernel can allow the GUI to be more responsive by reducing the number of context switches required for the GUI to perform its output functions. Other operating systems are modular, separating the graphics subsystem from the kernel and the Operating System. In the 1980s UNIX, VMS and many others had operating systems that were built this way. Linux and Mac OS X are also built this way. Modern releases of Microsoft Windows such as Windows Vista implement a graphics subsystem that is mostly in user-space; however the graphics drawing routines of versions between Windows NT 4.0 and Windows Server 2003 exist mostly in kernel space. Windows 9x had very little distinction between the interface and the kernel.

Many computer operating systems allow the user to install or create any user interface they desire. The X Window System in conjunction with GNOME or KDE Plasma Desktop is a commonly found setup on most Unix and Unix-like (BSD, Linux, Solaris) systems. A number of Windows shell replacements have been released for Microsoft Windows, which offer alternatives to the included Windows shell, but the shell itself cannot be separated from Windows.

Numerous Unix-based GUIs have existed over time, most derived from X11. Competition among the various vendors of Unix (HP, IBM, Sun) led to much fragmentation, though an effort to standardize in the 1990s to COSE and CDE failed for various reasons, and were eventually eclipsed by the widespread adoption of GNOME and K Desktop Environment. Prior to free software-based toolkits and desktop environments, Motif was the prevalent toolkit/desktop combination (and was the basis upon which CDE was developed).

Graphical user interfaces evolve over time. For example, Windows has modified its user interface almost every time a new major version of Windows is released, and the Mac OS GUI changed dramatically with the introduction of Mac OS X in 1999.

Real-time Operating Systems

A real-time operating system (RTOS) is an operating system intended for applications with fixed deadlines (real-time computing). Such applications include some small embedded systems, automobile engine controllers, industrial robots, spacecraft, industrial control, and some large-scale computing systems.

An early example of a large-scale real-time operating system was Transaction Processing Facility developed by American Airlines and IBM for the Sabre Airline Reservations System.

Embedded systems that have fixed deadlines use a real-time operating system such as VxWorks, PikeOS, eCos, QNX, MontaVista Linux and RTLinux. Windows CE is a real-time operating system that shares similar APIs to desktop Windows but shares none of desktop Windows' codebase. Symbian OS also has an RTOS kernel (EKA2) starting with version 8.0b.

Some embedded systems use operating systems such as Palm OS, BSD, and Linux, although such operating systems do not support real-time computing.

Operating System Development as a Hobby

Operating system development is one of the most complicated activities in which a computing hobbyist may engage. A hobby operating system may be classified as one whose code has not been directly derived from an existing operating system, and has few users and active developers.

In some cases, hobby development is in support of a "homebrew" computing device, for example, a simple single-board computer powered by a 6502 microprocessor. Or, development may be for an architecture already in widespread use. Operating system development may come from entirely new concepts, or may commence by modeling an existing operating system. In either case, the hobbyist is his/her own developer, or may interact with a small and sometimes unstructured group of individuals who have like interests.

Examples of a hobby operating system include Syllable.

Diversity of Operating Systems and Portability

Application software is generally written for use on a specific operating system, and sometimes even for specific hardware. When porting the application to run on another OS, the functionality required by that application may be implemented differently by that OS (the names of functions, meaning of arguments, etc.) requiring the application to be adapted, changed, or otherwise maintained.

Unix was the first operating system not written in assembly language, making it very portable to systems different from its native PDP-11.

This cost in supporting operating systems diversity can be avoided by instead writing applications against software platforms like Java or Qt. These abstractions have already borne the cost of adaptation to specific operating systems and their system libraries.

Another approach is for operating system vendors to adopt standards. For example, POSIX and OS abstraction layers provide commonalities that reduce porting costs.

Market Share

2013 worldwide device shipments by operating system		
Operating system	**2012 (millions of units)**	**2013 (million of units)**
Android	504	878
Windows	346	328
iOS/Mac OS	214	267
BlackBerry	35	24
Others	1,117	803
Total	2,216	2,300

In 2014, Android was first (currently not replicated by others, in a single year) operating system ever to ship on a billion devices, becoming the most popular operating system by installed base.

References

- Lavington, Simon (1998). A History of Manchester Computers (2nd ed.). Swindon: The British Computer Society. pp. 50–52. ISBN 978-1-902505-01-5.

- Stallings, William (2008). Computer Organization & Architecture. New Delhi: Prentice-Hall of India Private Limited. p. 267. ISBN 978-81-203-2962-1.

- "Strategy Analytics: Android Captures Record 88 Percent Share of Global Smartphone Shipments in Q3 2016". November 2, 2016.

- "INFO: Windows 95 Multimedia Wave Device Drivers Must be 16 bit". Support.microsoft.com. Retrieved 2012-08-07.

Types of Operating Systems

Operating systems are best understood in confluence with the major types listed in the following section. Some of the types of operating systems elucidated in the chapter are mobile operating system, network operating system, embedded operating system, distributed operating system, Microsoft windows etc. Mobile operating system is the operating system used in mobile devices. The operating systems used in mobiles are android, iOS, colorOS, HTC Sense and cyanogenMod. This section strategically encompasses and incorporates the major types of operating systems, providing a complete understanding.

Mobile Operating System

A mobile operating system (or mobile OS) is an operating system for smartphones, tablets, personal digital assistants (PDAs), or other mobile devices. While computers such as typical laptops are mobile, the operating systems usually used on them are not considered mobile ones, as they were originally designed for desktop computers that historically did not have or need specific *mobile* features. This distinction is becoming blurred in some newer operating systems that are hybrids made for both uses. So-called mobile operating systems, or even only smartphones running them, now represent most (web) use (on weekends and averaged for whole weeks). Desktops, haven't been a majority on any day for a while. There is still regional variation, but most countries with desktop-majority have it only barely.

Mobile operating systems combine features of a personal computer operating system with other features useful for mobile or handheld use; usually including, and most of the following considered essential in modern mobile systems; a touchscreen, cellular, Bluetooth, Wi-Fi, Global Positioning System (GPS) mobile navigation, camera, video camera, speech recognition, voice recorder, music player, near field communication, and infrared blaster.

Mobile devices with mobile communications abilities (e.g., smartphones) contain two mobile operating systems – the main user-facing software platform is supplemented by a second low-level proprietary real-time operating system which operates the radio and other hardware. Research has shown that these low-level systems may contain a range of security vulnerabilities permitting malicious base stations to gain high levels of control over the mobile device.

Timeline

Mobile operating system milestones mirror the development of mobile phones and smartphones:

Pre-1993

- 1973–1993 – Mobile phones use embedded systems to control operation.

1993–1999

- 1994 – The first smartphone, the IBM Simon, has a touchscreen, email, and PDA features.

- 1996
  - Palm Pilot 1000 personal digital assistant is introduced with the Palm OS mobile operating system.
  - First Windows CE Handheld PC devices are introduced.

- 1999 – Nokia S40 OS is introduced officially along with the Nokia 7110.

2000s

- 2000 – Symbian becomes the first modern mobile OS on a smartphone with the launch of the Ericsson R380.

- 2001 – The Kyocera 6035 is the first smartphone with Palm OS.

- 2002
  - Microsoft's first Windows CE (Pocket PC) smartphones are introduced.
  - BlackBerry releases its first smartphone.

- 2005 – Nokia introduces Maemo OS on the first Internet tablet N770.

- 2007
  - Apple iPhone with iOS is introduced as an iPhone, "mobile phone" and "Internet communicator".
  - Open Handset Alliance (OHA) formed by Google, HTC, Sony, Dell, Intel, Motorola, Samsung, LG, etc.

- 2008 – OHA releases Android (based on Linux kernel) 1.0 with the HTC Dream (T-Mobile G1) as the first Android phone.

- 2009 –
  - Palm introduces webOS with the Palm Pre. By 2012, webOS devices were discontinued.
  - Samsung announces the Bada OS with the introduction of the Samsung S8500.

2010s

2010

- August – MIUI are release by Xiaomi Inc., which based on Google's Android Open Source Project (AOSP).

- November – Windows Phone OS phones are released but are not compatible with the prior Windows Mobile OS.

2011

- July – MeeGo the first mobile Linux, combining Maemo and Moblin, is introduced with the Nokia N9, a collaboration of Nokia, Intel, and Linux Foundation.

- September – Samsung, Intel, and the Linux Foundation announced that their efforts will shift from Bada, MeeGo to Tizen during 2011 and 2012.

- October – The Mer project was announced, based on an ultra-portable core for building products, composed of Linux, HTML5, QML, and JavaScript, which was derived from the MeeGo codebase.

2012

- July – Mozilla announced that the project formerly named *Boot to Gecko* (which was built atop an Android Linux kernel using Android drivers and services; however it used no Java-like code of Android) was now Firefox OS and had several handset OEMs on board.

- September – Apple releases iOS 6.

2013

- January – BlackBerry releases their new operating system for smartphones, BlackBerry 10.

- September – Apple releases iOS 7.

- October

  o Canonical announced Ubuntu Touch, a version of the Linux distribution expressly designed for smartphones. The OS is built on the Android Linux kernel, using Android drivers and services, but does not use any of the Java-like code of Android.

  o Google releases Android KitKat 4.4.

2014

- February – Microsoft releases Windows Phone 8.1

- August – Xiaomi releases MIUI v6

- September

  o Apple releases iOS 8

  o BlackBerry release BlackBerry 10.3 with integration with the Amazon Appstore

- November – Google releases Android 5.0 "Lollipop"

2015

- February – Google releases Android 5.1 *Lollipop*.

- September

    o   Apple releases iOS 9.

    o   Google releases Android 6.0 *Marshmallow*.

- November – Microsoft releases Windows 10 Mobile.

2016

- June – Apple announced iOS 10.

- August – Google released Android 7.0 "Nougat".

- September – Apple releases iOS 10.

- November - Tizen releases Tizen 3.0.

Current Software Platforms

These operating systems often run atop baseband or other real time operating systems that handle hardware aspects of the phone.

Android

Google Android Marshmallow OS

Android (based on the Linux kernel) is from Google Inc. Besides having the largest installed base worldwide on smartphones, it is also the most popular operating system for general purpose computers (a category that includes desktop computers and mobile devices), even though Android is not a popular operating system for regular (desktop) PCs. Although the Android operating system is free and open-source software, in actual devices, much of the software bundled with it (including Google apps and vendor-installed software) is proprietary and closed source.

Android's releases before 2.0 (1.0, 1.5, 1.6) were used exclusively on mobile phones. Android 2.x releases were mostly used for mobile phones but also some tablets. Android 3.0 was a tablet-oriented release and does not officially run on mobile phones. The current Android version is 7.1 Nougat.

Google Android 5.0, 6.0, 7.0

Android's releases are named after sweets or dessert items, except for the first and second releases:

- 1.0 – (API Level 1)

- 1.1 – Alpha: (API Level 2)

- 1.2 – Beta

- 1.5 – Cupcake: (API Level 3)

- 1.6 – Donut: (API Level 4)

- 2.0 – Eclair: (API Level 5)

- 2.0.1 – Eclair: (API Level 6)

- 2.1 – Eclair: (API Level 7)

- 2.2.x – Frozen Yogurt ("Froyo"): (API Level 8)

- 2.3 – Gingerbread (minor UI tweak): (API Level 9)

- 2.3.3 – Gingerbread: (API Level 10)

- 3.0 – Honeycomb (major UI revamp): (API Level 11)

- 3.1 – Honeycomb: (API Level 12)

- 3.2 – Honeycomb: (API Level 13)

- 4.0 – Ice Cream Sandwich (minor UI tweak): (API Level 14)

- 4.0.3 – Ice Cream Sandwich: (API Level 15)

- 4.1 – Jelly Bean: (API Level 16)

- 4.2 – Jelly Bean: (API Level 17)

- 4.3 – Jelly Bean: (API Level 18)

- 4.4.4 – KitKat: (API Level 19)

- 5.0, 5.0.1, 5.0.2 – Lollipop (major UI revamp): (API Level 21)

- 5.1, 5.1.1 – Lollipop: (API Level 22)

- 6.0 & 6.0.1 – Marshmallow: (API Level 23)

- 7.0 – Nougat (API Level 24)

AOKP

Android Open Kang Project (AOKP) is a custom ROM which is based on the Android Open Source Project (AOSP). Similar to CyanogenMod, AOKP allows Android users who can no longer obtain update support from their manufacturer to continue updating their OS version to the latest one based on official release from Google AOSP and heavy theme customization together with customizable system functions.

Current AOKP version list:

- AOKP – based on Android *Ice Cream Sandwich* 4.0.x

- AOKP – based on Android *Jelly Bean* 4.1.x – 4.3.x

- AOKP – based on Android *KitKat* 4.4.x

ColorOS

ColorOS is based on the open source Android Open Source Project (AOSP) and developed by OPPO Electronics Corp. As of 2016, OPPO officially releases ColorOS with every OPPO device, and released an official read-only memory (ROM) version for the OnePlus One smartphone.

Current ColorOS version list:

- ColorOS 1.0 (based on Android "Jelly Bean" 4.1.x – 4.3.x) (initial release)

- ColorOS 2.0 (based on Android "KitKat" 4.4.x) (minor UI upgrade)

- ColorOS 2.1 (based on Android "Lollipop" 5.0.x – 5.1.x) (minor UI upgrade)

CyanogenMod

CyanogenMod is based on the open source Android Open Source Project (AOSP). It is a custom ROM that was codeveloped by the CyanogenMod community. The OS does not include any proprietary apps unless the user installs them. Due to its open source nature, CyanogenMod allows Android users who can no longer obtain update support from their manufacturer to continue updating their OS version to the latest one based on official release from Google AOSP and heavy theme customization. The current version of the OS is CyanogenMod 13 which is based on Android Marshmallow.

Current CyanogenMod version list:

- CyanogenMod 3 (based on Android "Cupcake" 1.5.x, initial release)

- CyanogenMod 4 (based on Android "Cupcake" and "Donut" 1.5.x and 1.6.x)

- CyanogenMod 5 (based on Android "Eclair" 2.0/2.1)

- CyanogenMod 6 (based on Android "Froyo" 2.2.x)

- CyanogenMod 7 (based on Android "Gingerbread" 2.3.x)

- CyanogenMod 9 (based on Android "Ice Cream Sandwich" 4.0.x, major UI revamp)

- CyanogenMod 10 (based on Android "Jelly Bean" 4.1.x – 4.3.x)

- CyanogenMod 11 (based on Android "KitKat" 4.4.x)

- CyanogenMod 12 (based on Android "Lollipop" 5.0.x – 5.1.x, major UI revamp)

- CyanogenMod 13 (based on Android "Marshmallow" 6.0.x)

- CyanogenMod 14 (based on Android "Nougat" 7.x.x, still in progress and not officially launched yet)

Cyanogen OS

Cyanogen OS is based on CyanogenMod and maintained by Cyanogen Inc, however it includes proprietary apps and it is only available for commercial uses.

Current Cyanogen OS version list:

- Cyanogen OS 11s (based on Android "KitKat" 4.4.x, initial release)

- Cyanogen OS 12 (based on Android "Lollipop" 5.0.x, major UI revamp)

- Cyanogen OS 12.1 (based on android "Lollipop" 5.1.x)

- Cyanogen OS 13 (based on Android "Marshmallow" 6.0.x)

EMUI

Emotion User Interface (EMUI) is a ROM/OS that is developed by Huawei Technologies Co. Ltd.

and is based on Google's Android Open Source Project (AOSP). EMUI is preinstalled on most Huawei Smartphone devices and its subsidiaries the Honor series.

Current EMUI version list:

- EMUI 1.x (based on Android "Ice Cream Sandwich" and "Jelly Bean" 4.0.x and 4.1.x – 4.3.x) (initial release)

- EMUI 2.x (based on Android "Ice Cream Sandwich", "Jelly Bean" and "KitKat" 4.0.x, 4.1.x – 4.3.x and 4.4.x) (minor UI tweak)

- EMUI 3.x (based on Android "KitKat" and "Lollipop" 4.4.x and 5.0.x – 5.1.x) (minor UI tweak)

- EMUI 4.x (based on Android "Marshmallow" 6.x)

- EMUI 5.x (based on Android "Nougat" 7.x)

Flyme OS

Flyme OS is an operating system developed by Meizu Technology Co., Ltd., an open source OS based on Google Android Open Source Project (AOSP). Flyme OS is mainly installed on Meizu Smartphones such as the MX's series, however it also has official ROM support for a few Android devices.

Current Flyme OS version list:

- Flyme OS 1.x.x (based on Android "Ice Cream Sandwich" 4.0.3, initial release)

- Flyme OS 2.x.x (based on Android "Jelly Bean" 4.1.x – 4.2.x)

- Flyme OS 3.x.x (based on Android "Jelly Bean" 4.3.x)

- Flyme OS 4.x.x (based on Android "KitKat" 4.4.x)

- Flyme OS 5.x.x (based on Android "Lollipop" 5.0.x – 5.1.x)

HTC Sense

HTC Sense is a software suite developed by HTC, used primarily on the company's Android-based devices. Serving as a successor to HTC's TouchFLO 3D software for Windows Mobile, Sense modifies many aspects of the Android user experience, incorporating added features (such as an altered home screen and keyboard), widgets, HTC-developed applications, and redesigned applications. The first device with Sense, the HTC Hero, was released in 2009.

- HTC Sense 1.x (based on Android "Eclair" 2.0/2.1, initial release)

- HTC Sense 2.x (based on Android "Eclair", "Froyo" and "Gingerbread" 2.0/2.1, 2.2.x and 2.3.x, redesigned UI)

- HTC Sense 3.x (based on Android "Gingerbread" 2.3.x, redesigned UI)

- HTC Sense 4.x (based on Android "Ice Cream Sandwich" and "Jelly Bean" 4.0.x and 4.1.x, redesigned UI)

- HTC Sense 5.x (based on Android "Jelly Bean" 4.1.x – 4.3.x, redesigned UI)

- HTC Sense 6.x (based on Android "KitKat" 4.4.x, redesigned UI)

- HTC Sense 7.x (based on Android "Lollipop" 5.0.x, redesigned UI)

- HTC Sense 8.x (based on Android "Marshmallow" 6.0.x, redesigned UI)

MIUI

Mi User Interface (MIUI), developed by a Chinese electronic company Xiaomi Tech, is a mobile operating system which based on Google Android Open Source Project (AOSP). MIUI is found in Xiaomi smartphones such as the Mi and Redmi Series, however it also has official ROM support for a few Android devices. Although MIUI is based on AOSP, which is Open Source, it consists of closed source and proprietary software of its own.

Current MIUI version list:

- MIUI V1 – based on Android *Froyo* 2.2.x, initial release

- MIUI V2 – based on Android *Froyo* 2.2.x, redesigned UI

- MIUI V3 – based on Android *Gingerbread* 2.3.x, redesign UI

- MIUI V4 – based on Android *Ice Cream Sandwich* and *Jelly Bean* 4.0.x and 4.1.x, redesigned UI

- MIUI V5 – based on Android *Jelly Bean* and "KitKat" 4.1.x – 4.3.x and 4.4.x, redesigned UI

- MIUI V6 – based on Android *KitKat* and *Lollipop* 4.4.x and 5.0.x, redesigned UI

- MIUI V7 – based on Android *KitKat* and *Lollipop* and *Marshmallow* 4.4.x and 5.0.x and 6.0.x

- MIUI V8 – based on Android *Marshmallow* 6.0.x

LG UX

LG UX (formerly named Optimus UI) is a front-end touch interface developed by LG Electronics with partners, featuring a full touch user interface. It is sometimes incorrectly identified as an operating system. LG UX is used internally by LG for sophisticated feature phones and tablet computers, and is not available for licensing by external parties.

Optimus UI 2 which based on Android 4.1.2 has been released on the Optimus K II and the Optimus Neo 3. It features a more refined user interface compared to the prior version based on Android 4.1.1, would include together which new functionality such as voice shutter and quick memo.

Current LG UX version list:

- Optimus UI 1.x – based on Android *Gingerbread* 2.3.x, initial release

- Optimus UI 2.x – based on Android *Ice Cream Sandwich* and *Jelly Bean* 4.0.x and 4.1.x – 4.3.x, redesigned UI

- LG UX 3.x – based on Android *KitKat* and *Lollipop* 4.4.x and 5.0.x, redesigned UI

- LG UX 4.x – based on Android *Lollipop* 5.1.x and *Marshmallow* 5.1.x and 6.0.x, redesigned UI

OxygenOS

OxygenOS is based on the open source Android Open Source Project (AOSP) and is developed by OnePlus to replace Cyanogen OS on OnePlus devices such as the OnePlus One, and it is preinstalled on the OnePlus 2, OnePlus 3, and OnePlus X. As stated by Oneplus, OxygenOS is focused on stabilizing and maintaining of *stock* like those found on Nexus devices. It consists of mainly Google apps and minor UI customization to maintain the sleekness of *pure* Android.

Current OxygenOS version list:

- Oxygen OS 1.0.X (based on Android "Lollipop" 5.0.x) (initial release)

- Oxygen OS 2.0.X (based on Android "Lollipop" 5.1.x) (overall maintenance update)

- Oxygen OS 3.0.X (based on Android "Marshmallow" 6.0.0) (upgrade Android main version)

- Oxygen OS 3.1.X (based on Android "Marshmallow" 6.0.1) (maintenance update)

TouchWiz

TouchWiz is a front-end touch interface developed by Samsung Electronics with partners, featuring a full touch user interface. It is sometimes incorrectly identified as an independent operating system. TouchWiz is used internally by Samsung for smartphones, feature phones and tablet computers, and is not available for licensing by external parties. The Android version of TouchWiz also comes with Samsung-made apps preloaded (except starting with the Galaxy S6 which have removed all Samsung pre-loaded apps installed, leaving one with Galaxy Apps, to save storage space and initially due to the removal of MicroSD).

Current TouchWiz version list:

- TouchWiz 3.0 & 3.0 Lite – based on Android *Eclair* and *Froyo* 2.0/2.1 and 2.2.x, initial release

- TouchWiz 4.0 – based on Android *Gingerbread* and *Ice Cream Sandwich* 2.3.x and 4.0.x, redesigned UI

- TouchWiz Nature UX "1.0" and Lite – based on Android *Ice Cream Sandwich* and *Jelly Bean* 4.0.x and 4.1.x, redesigned UI

- TouchWiz Nature UX 2.x – based on Android *Jelly Bean* and *KitKat* 4.2.x – 4.3.x and 4.4.x, redesigned UI

- TouchWiz Nature UX 3.x – based on Android *KitKat* and *Lollipop* 4.4.x and 5.0.x, redesigned UI

- TouchWiz Nature UX 5.x – based on Android *Lollipop* 5.0.x – 5.1.x, redesigned UI

ZenUI

ZenUI is a front-end touch interface developed by ASUS with partners, featuring a full touch user interface. ZenUI is used by Asus for its Android phones and tablet computers, and is not available for licensing by external parties. ZenUI also comes preloaded with Asus-made apps like ZenLink (PC Link, Share Link, Party Link & Remote Link).

iOS

iOS (formerly named iPhone OS) is from Apple Inc. It has the second largest installed base worldwide on smartphones, but the largest profits, due to aggressive price competition between Android-based manufacturers. It is closed source and proprietary and built on open source Darwin core OS. The Apple iPhotne, iPod Touched h, iPad and second-generation Apple TV all use iOS, which is derived from macOS.

Native third party applications were not officially supported until the release of iPhone OS 2.0 on July 11, 2008. Before this, "jailbreaking" allowed third party applications to be installed, and this method is still available.

Currently all iOS devices are developed by Apple and manufactured by Foxconn or another of Apple's partners.

As of 2014, the global market share of iOS was 15.4%.

Current iOS version list:

- iPhone OS 1.x

- iPhone OS 2.x

- iPhone OS 3.x

- iOS 4.x

- iOS 5.x

- iOS 6.x

- iOS 7.x (major UI revamp)

- iOS 8.x

- iOS 9.x

- iOS 10.x

Windows 10 Mobile

Windows 10 Mobile (formerly called Windows Phone) is from Microsoft. It is closed source and proprietary. It has the third largest installed base on smartphones behind Android and iOS.

Unveiled on February 15, 2010, Windows Phone includes a user interface inspired by Microsoft's *Metro Design Language*. It is integrated with Microsoft services such as OneDrive and Office, Xbox Music, Xbox Video, Xbox Live games and Bing, but also integrates with many other non-Microsoft services such as Facebook and Google accounts. Windows Phone devices are made primarily by Microsoft Mobile/Nokia, and also by HTC and Samsung.

On 21 January 2015, Microsoft announced that the Windows Phone brand will be phased out and replaced with Windows 10 Mobile, bringing tighter integration and unification with its PC counterpart Windows 10, and provide a platform for smartphones and tablets with screen sizes under 8 inches.

As of 2016, Windows 10 Mobile global market share dropped below 0.6%.

Current Windows Phone version list:

- Windows Phone 7

- Windows Phone 7.5

- Windows Phone 7.8 – minor UI tweak

- Windows Phone 8 – GDR1, GDR2 & GDR3, & minor UI tweak

- Windows Phone 8.1 – GDR1 & GDR2, & minor UI tweak

- Windows 10 Mobile

BlackBerry 10

BlackBerry 10 (based on the QNX OS) is from BlackBerry. As a smart phone OS, it is closed source and proprietary, and only runs on phones and tablets manufactured by Blackberry.

Once one of the dominant platforms in the world, its global market share was reduced to 0.4% by the end of 2014.

Current BlackBerry 10 version list:

- BlackBerry 10.0

- BlackBerry 10.1

- BlackBerry 10.2

- BlackBerry 10.3 – major UI revamp

- BlackBerry 10.4 – developing, expected to release by 2016

Sailfish OS

Sailfish OS is from Jolla. It is partly open source and adopts GNU General Public License (GPL) (core and middleware), however the user interface is proprietary software (closed source).

After Nokia abandoned in 2011 the MeeGo project most of the MeeGo team left Nokia, and established Jolla as a company to use MeeGo and Mer business opportunities. Thanks to MER standard it can be launched on any hardware with kernel compatible with MER. In 2012 Linux Sailfish OS based on MeeGo and using middleware of MER core stack distribution has been launched for public use. The first device, the Jolla smartphone, was unveiled on 20 May 2013. In 2015 has been launched Jolla Tablet and the BRICS countries has declared it officially supported OS there. Jolla started licensing Sailfish OS 2.0 for 3rd parties. Sold already devices are updateable to Sailfish 2.0 without limitations.

Each Sailfish OS version releases are named after Finnish lakes:

- 1.0.0.5 – Update – (Kaajanlampi)
- 1.0.1.1x – Update 1 (Laadunjärvi)
- 1.0.2.5 – Update 2 (Maadajävri)
- 1.0.3.8 – Update 3 (Naamankajärvi)
- 1.0.4.20 – Update 4 (Ohijärvi)
- 1.0.5.1x – Update 5 (Paarlamp)
- 1.0.7.16 – Update 7 (Saapunki)
- 1.0.8.19 – Update 8 (Tahkalampi)
- 1.1.0.3x – Update 9 (Uitukka)
- 1.1.1.2x – Update 10 (Vaarainjärvi)
- 1.1.2.1x – Update 11 (Yliaavanlampi)
- 1.1.4.28 – Update 13 (Äijänpäivänjärvi)
- 1.1.6.27 – Update 15 (Aaslakkajärvi)
- 1.1.7.24 – Update 16 (Björnträsket)
- 1.1.9.28 – Update 17 pre-transition to Sailfish OS 2.0 (Eineheminlampi) (major UI revamp)
- 2.0.0.10 – Update 18 complete-transition to Sailfish 2.0 (Saimaa) (minor UI and functionality improvement)

Tizen

Tizen is hosted by the Linux Foundation and support from the Tizen Association, guided by a Technical Steering Group composed of Intel and Samsung.

Tizen is an operating system for devices including smartphones, tablets, in-vehicle infotainment (IVI) devices, and smart TVs. It is an open source system (however the SDK was closed source and proprietary) that aims to offer a consistent user experience across devices. Tizen's main components are the Linux kernel and the WebKit runtime. According to Intel, Tizen "combines the best of LiMo and MeeGo." HTML5 apps are emphasized, with MeeGo encouraging its members to transition to Tizen, stating that the "future belongs to HTML5-based applications, outside of a relatively small percentage of apps, and we are firmly convinced that our investment needs to shift toward HTML5." Tizen will be targeted at a variety of platforms such as handsets, touch pc, smart TVs and in-vehicle entertainment. On May 17, 2013, Tizen released version 2.1, code-named Nectarine.

Currently Tizen are the fourth largest Mobile OS in term of market share. Tizen has the second-largest market share in the budget segment of smartphones in India as of Q4 2015.

Current Tizen version list:

- 1.0 (Larkspur)

- 2.0 (Magnolia)

- 2.1 (Nectarine)

- 2.2.x

- 2.3.x

- 2.4.x (minor UI tweaks)

- 3.0 (under development)

Ubuntu Touch OS

Ubuntu Touch OS is from Canonical Ltd.. It is open source and uses the GPL license. The OS is built on the Android Linux kernel, using Android drivers and services via an LXC container, but does not use any of the Java-like code of Android.

Current Ubuntu Touch version list:

- Preview Version (initial release)

- OTA 2.x

- OTA 3.x

- OTA 4.x

- OTA 5.x

- OTA 6.x

- OTA 7.x

- OTA 8.x

- OTA 9.x

- OTA 10.x

- OTA 11.x

- OTA 12.x

- OTA 13.x

H5OS

H5OS is from Acadine Technologies. The OS is based on Firefox OS.

Current H5OS version list:

- v1.0 (initial release)

Discontinued Software Platforms

Firefox OS

Firefox OS is from Mozilla. It was an open source mobile operating system released under the Mozilla Public License built on the Android Linux kernel and used Android drivers, but did not use any Java-like code of Android.

According to Ars Technica, "Mozilla says that B2G is motivated by a desire to demonstrate that the standards-based open Web has the potential to be a competitive alternative to the existing single-vendor application development stacks offered by the dominant mobile operating systems." In September 2016, Mozilla announced that work on Firefox OS has ceased, and all B2G-related code would be removed from mozilla-central.

Bada

Bada platform (stylized as bada; Korean: 바다) was an operating system for mobile devices such as smartphones and tablet computers. It was developed by Samsung Electronics. Its name is derived from "바다 (bada)", meaning "ocean" or "sea" in Korean. It ranges from mid- to high-end smartphones. To foster adoption of Bada OS, since 2011 Samsung reportedly has considered releasing the source code under an open-source license, and expanding device support to include Smart TVs. Samsung announced in June 2012 intentions to merge Bada into the Tizen project, but would meanwhile use its own Bada operating system, in parallel with Google Android OS and Microsoft Windows Phone, for its smartphones. All Bada-powered devices are branded under the Wave name, but not all of Samsung's Android-powered devices are branded under the name Galaxy. On 25 February 2013, Samsung announced that it will stop developing Bada, moving development to Tizen instead.Bug reporting was finally terminated in April 2014.

Symbian

The Symbian platform was developed by Nokia for some models of smartphones. It is proprietary software. The operating system was discontinued in 2012, although a slimmed-down version for basic phones was still developed until July 2014. Microsoft officially shelved the platform in favor of Windows Phone after its acquisition of Nokia.

Nokia X Platform

The Nokia X platform was developed by Nokia Corporation and later on maintained by Microsoft Mobile. It was a project which is based on the open source Android Open Source Project (AOSP), but replaced all the Google Services and Apps with Nokia and Microsoft apps. Its overall UI mimics the Windows Phone UI.

Windows Mobile

Windows Mobile is a discontinued operating system from Microsoft that it replaced with Windows Phone. It is closed source and proprietary.

The Windows CE operating system and Windows Mobile middleware was widely spread in Asia (which mostly uses Android now). The two improved variants of this operating system, Windows Mobile 6 Professional (for touch screen devices) and Windows Mobile 6 Standard, were unveiled in February 2007. It was criticized for having a user interface which is not optimized for touch input by fingers; instead, it is more usable with a stylus. Like iOS, and most other Mobile OS, it supports both touch screen, physical and Bluetooth keyboard configurations.

Windows Mobile's market share sharply declined to only 5% in Q2 of 2010. Microsoft phased out the Windows Mobile OS to focus on Windows Phone.

Palm OS

Palm OS/Garnet OS was from Access Co. It is closed source and proprietary. webOS was introduced by Palm in January 2009 as the successor to Palm OS with Web 2.0 technologies, open architecture and multitasking abilities.

webOS

webOS was developed by Palm, although some parts are open source. webOS is a proprietary mobile operating system running on the Linux kernel, initially developed by Palm, which launched with the Palm Pre. After being acquired by HP, two phones (the Veer and the Pre 3) and a tablet (the Touch-Pad) running webOS were introduced in 2011. On August 18, 2011, HP announced that webOS hardware would be discontinued, but would continue to support and update webOS software and develop the webOS ecosystem. HP released webOS as open source under the name Open webOS, and plans to update it with additional features. On February 25, 2013 HP announced the sale of WebOS to LG Electronics, who used the operating system for its "smart" or Internet-connected TVs. However, HP retained patents underlying WebOS and cloud-based services such as the App Catalog.

Maemo

Maemo was a platform developed by Nokia for smartphones and Internet tablets. It is open source and GPL, based on Debian GNU/Linux and draws much of its graphical user interface (GUI), frameworks, and libraries from the GNOME project. It uses the Matchbox window manager and the GTK-based Hildon as its GUI and application framework.

MeeGo

MeeGo was from non-profit organization The Linux Foundation. It is open source and GPL. At the 2010 Mobile World Congress in Barcelona, Nokia and Intel both unveiled *MeeGo*, a mobile operating system that combined Moblin and Maemo to create an open-sourced experience for users across all devices. In 2011 Nokia announced that it would no longer pursue MeeGo in favor of Windows Phone. Nokia announced the Nokia N9 on June 21, 2011 at the Nokia Connection event in Singapore. LG announced its support for the platform.

LiMo

LiMo was from the LiMo Foundation. They launched LiMo 4 on February 14, 2011. It delivers middleware and application functionality, including a flexible user interface, extended widget libraries, 3D window effects, advanced multimedia, social networking, and location-based service frameworks, sensor frameworks, multi-tasking and multitouch abilities. Also, support for scalable screen resolution and consistent APIs means that the platform can deliver a consistent user experience across multiple device types and form factors.

Market Share

In 2006, Android, iOS, and Windows Phone did not exist and only 64 million smartphones were sold. In 2015 Q1, global market share was 80.7% for Android, 15.4% for iOS, 2.8% for Windows Phone, 0.6% for Blackberry and remaining 0.5% for all other platforms. In 2016 Q1, more than a billion smartphones were sold and global market share was 84.1% for Android, 14.8% for iOS, 0.7% for Windows Phone, 0.2% for Blackberry and remaining 0.2% for all other platforms.

Crossover to Mobile More Popular

According to StatCounter web use statistics (a proxy for all use), in the week from 7–13 November 2016, "mobile" (meaning smartphones) alone (without tablets) overtook desktop, for the first time, with them highest ranked at 48.13%. Mobile-majority applies to countries such as Paraguay in South America, Poland in Europe and Turkey; and most of Asia and Africa. The rest of the world is still desktop-majority, with it e.g. in the United States at 54.89%. On 22 October 2016 (and subsequent weekends), mobile has shown majority, Since 27 October, the desktop hasn't shown majority, not even on weekdays.

Formerly, according to StatCounter press release, the world has turned desktop-minority; as of October 2016, at about 49% desktop use for that month, but mobile wasn't ranked higher, tablet share had to be added to it to exceed desktop share.

World-wide Share or Shipments

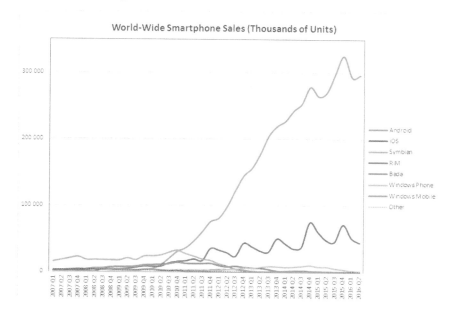

Quarter	Windows Mobile	BlackBerry OS	Symbian	iOS	Android	Bada	Windows Phone	Other	Total smartphones	Total phones
2016 Q2	-	400	-	44,395	296.912	-	1,971	680.6	344,359	n/a
2016 Q1	-	660	-	51,630	293,771	-	2,400	791	349,251	n/a
2015 Q4	-	906.9	-	71,526	**325,394**	-	4,395	887.3	**403,109**	n/a
2015 Q3	-	977	-	46,062	298,797	-	5,874	1,133	352,844	477,898
2015 Q2	-	1,153	-	48,086	271,010	-	8,198	1,229	329,676	445,758
2015 Q1	-	1,325	-	60,177	265,012	-	8,271	1,268	336,054	460,261
2014 Q4	-	1,734	-	**74,832**	279,058	-	**10,425**	1,286	367,334	n/a

Gartner: Worldwide smartphone sales (thousands of units)

2014 Q3	-	2,420	-	38,187	254,354	-	9,033	1,310	305,384	461,064
2014 Q2	-	2,044	-	35,345	243,484	-	8,095	2,044	290,384	444,190
2014 Q1	-	1,714	-	43,062	227,549	-	7,580	1,371	281,637	448,966
2013 Q4	-	1,807	-	50,224	219,613	-	8,534	1,994	282,171	**490,342**
2013 Q3	-	4,401	458	30,330	205,023	633	8,912	475	250,232	455,642
2013 Q2	-	6,180	631	31,900	177,898	838	7,408	472	225,326	435,158
2013 Q1	-	6,219	1,349	38,332	156,186	1,371	5,989	600	210,046	425,822
2012 Q4	-	7,333	2,569	43,457	144,720	2,684	6,186	713	207,662	472,076
2012 Q3	-	8,947	4,405	23,550	122,480	**5,055**	4,058	684	169,179	427,730
2012 Q2	-	7,991	9,072	28,935	98,529	4,209	4,087	863	153,686	419,008
2012 Q1	-	9,939	12,467	33,121	81,067	3,842	2,713	1,243	144,392	419,108
2011 Q4	-	13,185	17,458	35,456	75,906	3,111	2,759	1,167	149,042	476,555
2011 Q3	-	12,701	19,500	17,295	60,490	2,479	1,702	1,018	115,185	440,502
2011 Q2	-	12,652	23,853	19,629	46,776	2,056	1,724	1,051	107,740	428,661
2011 Q1	982	13,004	27,599	16,883	36,350	1,862	1,600	1,495	99,775	427,846
2010 Q4	3,419	**14,762**	**32,642**	16,011	30,801	2,027	0	1,488	101,150	452,037
2010 Q3	2,204	12,508	29,480	13,484	20,544	921	-	1,991	81,133	417,086
2010 Q2	3,059	11,629	25,387	8,743	10,653	577	-	2,011	62,058	367,987
2010 Q1	3,696	10,753	24,068	8,360	5,227	-	-	2,403	54,506	359,605
2009 Q4	4,203	10,508	23,857	8,676	4,043	-	-	2,517	53,804	347,103
2009 Q3	3,260	8,523	18,315	7,040	1,425	-	-	2,531	41,093	308,895
2009 Q2	3,830	7,782	20,881	5,325	756	-	-	2,398	40,972	286,122
2009 Q1	3,739	7,534	17,825	3,848	575	-	-	2,986	36,507	269,120
2008 Q4	**4,714**	7,443	17,949	4,079	639	-	-	3,319	38,143	314,708
2008 Q3	4,053	5,800	18,179	4,720	0	-	-	3,763	36,515	308,532
2008 Q2	3,874	5,594	18,405	893	-	-	-	3,456	32,221	304,722
2008 Q1	3,858	4,312	18,400	1,726	-	-	-	**4,113**	32,408	294,283
2007 Q4	4,374	4,025	22,903	1,928	-	-	-	3,536	36,766	330,055
2007 Q3	4,180	3,192	20,664	1,104	-	-	-	3,612	32,752	291,142
2007 Q2	3,212	2,471	18,273	270	-	-	-	3,628	27,855	272,604
2007 Q1	2,931	2,080	15,844	-	-	-	-	4,087	24,943	259,039

Gartner: Worldwide smartphone sales (% of smartphones / % of all phones)

Year	Windows Mobile	RIM	Symbian	iOS	Android	Bada	Windows Phone	Other smart-phones	Total smart-phones
2015 H1	-	0.37%/0.27%	-	16.26%/11.95%	80.52%/59.16%	-	2.47%/1.82%	0.38%/0.28%	100.0% / 73.48%
2014	-	0.6%/0.4%	-	15.4%/10.2%	80.7%/53.4%	-	2.8%/1.9%	0.5%/0.3%	100.0% / 66.2%
2013	-	1.9%/1.0%	-	15.6%/8.3%	78.4%/42.0%	-	3.2%/1.7%	0.9%/0.5%	100.0% / 57.6%
2012	-	5.0%/2.0%	-	19.1%/7.4%	66.4%/25.9%	-	2.5%/1.0%	6.9%/2.7%	100.0% / 38.9%
2011					N/A				
2010	-	16.0%/3.0%	37.6%/7.0%	15.7%/2.9%	22.7%/4.2%	-	4.2%/0.8%	3.8%/0.7%	100.0% / 18.6%
2009	8.7%/1.2%	19.9%/2.8%	46.9%/6.7%	14.4%/2.1%	3.9%/0.6%	-	-	6.1%/0.9%	100.0% / 14.2%
2008	11.8%/1.3%	16.6%/1.9%	52.4%/6.0%	8.2%/0.9%	0.5%/0.1%	-	-	10.5%/1.2%	100.0% / 11.4%
2007	12.0%/1.3%	9.6%/1.0%	63.5%/6.7%	2.7%/0.3%	-	-	-	12.1%/1.3%	100.0% / 10.6%

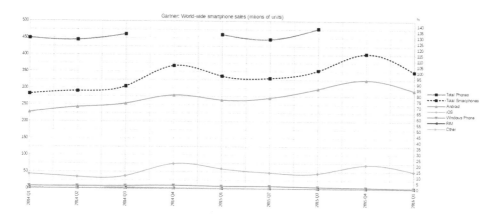

Gartner: Worldwide smartphone sales (millions of units ; % of smartphones)

Quarter	Android		iOS		Windows 10/ Phone		BlackBerry OS		Other		Total smartphones
2016 Q1	293.771	84.11%	51.630	14.78%	2.400	0.69%	0.660	0.19%	0.791	0.23%	349.251
2015 Q4	325.394	80.72%	71.526	17.74%	4.395	1.09%	0.907	0.22%	0.887	0.22%	403.109
2015 Q3	298.797	84.68%	46.062	13.05%	5.874	1.66%	0.977	0.28%	1.134	0.32%	352.844
2015 Q2	271.010	82.20%	48.086	14.59%	8.198	2.49%	1.153	0.35%	1.229	0.37%	329.676
2015 Q1	265.012	78.86%	60.177	17.91%	8.271	2.46%	1.325	0.39%	1.268	0.38%	336.054
2014 Q4	279.058	75.97%	74.832	20.37%	10.425	2.84%	1.734	0.47%	1.287	0.35%	367.334
2014 Q3	254.354	83.29%	38.187	12.50%	9.033	2.96%	2.420	0.79%	1.310	0.43%	305.384
2014 Q2	243.484	83.85%	35.345	12.17%	8.095	2.79%	2.044	0.70%	2.044	0.70%	290.384
2014 Q1	227.549	80.80%	43.062	15.29%	7.580	2.69%	1.714	0.61%	1.371	0.49%	281.637
Quarter	Android		iOS		Windows 10/ Phone		BlackBerry OS		Other		Total smartphones

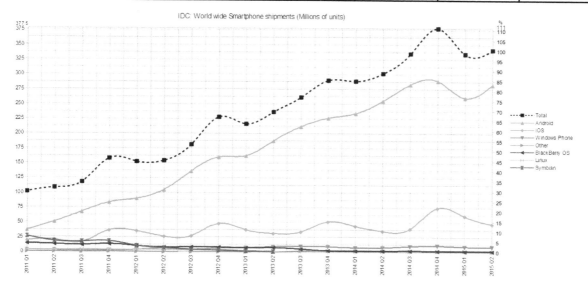

IDC: Worldwide smartphone shipments (millions of units; % of smartphones)

Quarter	Android	Android	iOS	iOS	Symbian	Symbian	BlackBerry OS	BlackBerry	Linux	Linux	Windows Phone	Windows Phone	Other	Other	Total
2015 Q2	282.76	82.80%	47.3	13.9%	-	0.00%	1.02	0.30%	-	0.00%	8.8	2.60%	1.37	0.40%	341.5
2015 Q1	260.8	78.00%	61.2	18.30%	-	0.00%	1.00	0.30%	-	0.00%	9.03	2.70%	2.34	0.70%	334.4
2014 Q4	289.1	76.58%	74.5	19.74%	-	0.00%	1.40	0.37%	-	0.00%	10.70	2.83%	1.80	0.48%	377.5
2014 Q3	283.0	84.48%	39.2	11.70%	-	0.00%	1.68	0.50%	-	0.00%	9.72	2.90%	2.00	0.60%	335.0
2014 Q2	255.3	84.73%	35.2	11.68%	-	0.00%	1.5	0.50%	-	0.00%	7.4	2.46%	1.9	0.63%	301.3
2014 Q1	234.1	81.20%	43.8	15.20%	-	0.00%	1.4	0.50%	-	0.00%	7.2	2.50%	2.0	0.70%	288.3
2013 Q4	226.1	78.07%	51.0	17.61%	-	0.00%	1.7	0.59%	-	0.00%	8.8	3.04%	2.0	0.69%	289.6
2013 Q3	211.6	81.04%	33.8	12.95%	-	0.00%	4.5	1.72%	-	0.00%	9.5	3.64%	1.7	0.65%	261.1
2013 Q2	187.4	79.27%	31.2	13.20%	0.5	0.21%	6.8	2.88%	1.8	0.76%	8.7	3.68%	0.0	0.00%	236.4
2013 Q1	162.1	74.98%	37.4	17.30%	1.2	0.56%	6.3	2.91%	2.1	0.97%	7.0	3.24%	0.1	0.05%	216.2
2012 Q4	159.8	70.15%	47.8	20.98%	2.7	1.19%	7.4	3.25%	3.8	1.67%	6.0	2.63%	0.3	0.13%	227.8
2012 Q3	136.0	75.10%	26.9	14.85%	4.1	2.26%	7.7	4.25%	2.8	1.55%	3.6	1.99%	0.0	0.00%	181.1
2012 Q2	104.8	68.05%	26.0	16.88%	6.8	4.42%	7.4	4.81%	3.5	2.27%	5.4	3.51%	0.1	0.06%	154.0
2012 Q1	89.9	59.03%	35.1	23.05%	10.4	6.83%	9.7	6.37%	3.5	2.30%	3.3	2.17%	0.4	0.26%	152.3
2011 Q4	83.4	52.85%	36.3	23.00%	18.3	11.60%	12.8	8.11%	3.8	2.41%	2.4	1.52%	0.8	0.51%	157.8
2011 Q3	67.7	57.32%	16.3	13.80%	17.3	14.65%	11.3	9.57%	3.9	3.30%	1.4	1.19%	0.1	0.08%	118.1
2011 Q2	50.8	46.86%	20.4	18.82%	18.3	16.88%	12.5	11.53%	3.3	3.04%	2.5	2.31%	0.6	0.55%	108.4
2011 Q1	36.7	36.12%	18.6	18.31%	26.4	25.98%	13.8	13.58%	3.2	3.15%	2.6	2.56%	0.3	0.30%	101.6

Market Share by Country or Region

Kantar Worldpanel: ComTech smartphone OS market share (% of smartphones)

Region	USA			EU5			China			Australia			Russia			Brazil		
Quarter	iOS	Android	Windows	iOS	Android	Windows	iOS	Android	Windows	iOS	Android	Windows	iOS	Android	Windows	iOS	Android	Windows
2015 Q3	29.2%	65.9%	3.9%	14.4%	74.0%	10.6%	19.1%	77.4%	3.0%	36.8%	54.5%	7.4%	10.5%	75.9%	11.5%	4.0%	91.4%	4.7%
2015 Q2	30.5%	66.1%	3.0%	17.5%	71.3%	10.0%	20.1%	79.0%	0.5%	34.6%	57.6%	6.4%	11.4%	75.8%	10.9%	3.8%	89.0%	5.5%
2015 Q1	36.5%	58.1%	4.3%	20.3%	68.4%	9.9%	26.1%	72.0%	1.2%	38.4%	52.3%	7.3%	13.4%	73.2%	11.2%	3.3%	89.6%	6.3%
2014 Q4	47.7%	47.6%	3.8%	24.1%	66.1%	8.9%	21.5%	77.0%	0.7%	45.1%	43.7%	9.2%	14.8%	71.2%	10.6%	5.5%	89.0%	4.0%
2014 Q3	32.6%	61.8%	4.3%	15.4%	73.9%	9.2%	15.2%	83.4%	0.4%	34.7%	58.1%	6.2%	-	-	-	6.1%	88.2%	3.6%
2014 Q2	31.5%	62.0%	3.8%	15.3%	74.0%	8.8%	12.8%	84.3%	0.9%	25.5%	68.0%	5.3%	-	-	-	3.9%	89.0%	4.5%
2014 Q1	35.9%	57.6%	5.3%	19.2%	70.7%	8.1%	17.9%	80.0%	1.0%	33.1%	57.3%	6.9%	-	-	-	3.0%	87.6%	5.5%
2013 Q4	43.9%	50.6%	4.3%	18.5%	68.6%	10.3%	19.0%	78.6%	1.1%	35.2%	57.2%	5.2%	-	-	-	4.2%	86.7%	4.0%
2013 Q3	35.9%	57.3%	4.6%	14.6%	71.9%	9.8%	13.8%	81.1%	2.5%	32.9%	55.3%	9.3%	-	-	-	4.3%	83.8%	3.4%
2013 Q2	42.5%	51.5%	4%	18.5%	69.8%	6.9%	24.7%	67.8%	4.9%	27.6%	64.6%	5.3%	-	-	-	3.5%	79.8%	6.2%
2013 Q1	43.7%	49.3%	5.6%	19.4%	68.8%	6.5%	24.6%	69.4%	2%	31%	61.7%	4.1%	-	-	-	5.8%	76.7%	4.7%
2012 Q4	51.2%	44.2%	2.6%	25.6%	61.1%	5.4%	21.9%	72.5%	0.9%	38.4%	55.8%	2.8%	-	-	-	4.2%	68.2%	8.0%
2012 Q4	35.7%	57.5%	2.9%	16.5%	67.1%	4.9%	18.6%	65.2%	5.7%	23.2%	67.1%	4.9%	-	-	-	5.4%	58.1%	8.0%
2012 Q2	39.2%	52.6%	2.9%	16.2%	64.5%	4.7%	26.7%	60.7%	6.2%	27.5%	60.8%	5.2%	-	-	-	2.9%	49.0%	5.4%
2012 Q1	44.6%	47.9%	3.7%	20.4%	58.1%	4.1%	-	-	-	33.8%	52.9%	3.3%	-	-	-	5.3%	48.3%	3.8%

Mobile Internet Traffic Share

As of November 2013, mobile data use showed 55.17% of mobile data traffic to be from iOS, 33.89% from Android, 4.49% from Java ME (Nokia S40), 4.12% from Symbian, 1.65% from Windows Phone and 1% from BlackBerry. Many mobile browsers such as Internet Explorer Mobile, Firefox for Mobile, and Google Chrome can be switched to *Desktop view* by users, which identifies devices with the analogous desktop versions of those browsers. In these cases, the mobile use would be excluded from these statistics.

Android (Operating System)

Android is a mobile operating system developed by Google, based on the Linux kernel and designed primarily for touchscreen mobile devices such as smartphones and tablets. Android's user interface is mainly based on direct manipulation, using touch gestures that loosely correspond to real-world actions, such as swiping, tapping and pinching, to manipulate on-screen objects, along with a virtual keyboard for text input. In addition to touchscreen devices, Google has further developed Android TV for televisions, Android Auto for cars, and Android Wear for wrist watches, each with a specialized user interface. Variants of Android are also used on notebooks, game consoles, digital cameras, and other electronics.

Android has the largest installed base of all operating systems (OS) of any kind.[b] Android has been the best selling OS on tablets since 2013, and on smartphones it is dominant by any metric.

Initially developed by Android, Inc., which Google bought in 2005, Android was unveiled in 2007 along with the founding of the Open Handset Alliance – a consortium of hardware, software, and telecommunication companies devoted to advancing open standards for mobile devices. As of July 2013, the Google Play store has had over one million Android applications ("apps") published – including many "business-class apps" that rival competing mobile platforms – and over 50 billion applications downloaded. An April–May 2013 survey of mobile application developers found that 71% of developers create applications for Android, and a 2015 survey found that 40% of full-time professional developers see Android as their priority target platform, which is comparable to Apple's iOS on 37% with both platforms far above others. In September 2015, Android had 1.4 billion monthly active devices.

Android's source code is released by Google under open source licenses, although most Android devices ultimately ship with a combination of open source and proprietary software, including proprietary software required for accessing Google services. Android is popular with technology companies that require a ready-made, low-cost and customizable operating system for high-tech devices. Its open nature has encouraged a large community of developers and enthusiasts to use the open-source code as a foundation for community-driven projects, which deliver updates to older devices, add new features for advanced users or bring Android to devices originally shipped with other operating systems. The success of Android has made it a target for patent (and copyright) litigation as part of the so-called "smartphone wars" between technology companies.

History

Android, Inc. was founded in Palo Alto, California in October 2003 by Andy Rubin (co-founder of Danger), Rich Miner (co-founder of Wildfire Communications, Inc.), Nick Sears (once VP at

T-Mobile), and Chris White (headed design and interface development at WebTV) to develop, in Rubin's words, "smarter mobile devices that are more aware of its owner's location and preferences". The early intentions of the company were to develop an advanced operating system for digital cameras. Though, when it was realized that the market for the devices was not large enough, the company diverted its efforts toward producing a smartphone operating system that would rival Symbian and Microsoft Windows Mobile. Despite the past accomplishments of the founders and early employees, Android Inc. operated secretly, revealing only that it was working on software for mobile phones. That same year, Rubin ran out of money. Steve Perlman, a close friend of Rubin, brought him $10,000 in cash in an envelope and refused a stake in the company.

Former Android logo wordmark (2007-2014)

In July 2005, Google acquired Android Inc. for at least $50 million, whose key employees, including Rubin, Miner and White, stayed at the company after the acquisition. Not much was known about Android Inc. at the time, but many assumed that Google was planning to enter the mobile phone market with this move. At Google, the team led by Rubin developed a mobile device platform powered by the Linux kernel. Google marketed the platform to handset makers and carriers on the promise of providing a flexible, upgradeable system. Google had lined up a series of hardware component and software partners and signaled to carriers that it was open to various degrees of cooperation on their part.

Speculation about Google's intention to enter the mobile communications market continued to build through December 2006. An earlier prototype codenamed "Sooner" had a closer resemblance to a BlackBerry phone, with no touchscreen, and a physical, QWERTY keyboard, but was later re-engineered to support a touchscreen, to compete with other announced devices such as the 2006 LG Prada and 2007 Apple iPhone. In September 2007, *InformationWeek* covered an Evalueserve study reporting that Google had filed several patent applications in the area of mobile telephony.

Eric Schmidt, Andy Rubin and Hugo Barra at a 2012 press conference announcing Google's Nexus 7 tablet

On November 5, 2007, the Open Handset Alliance, a consortium of technology companies including Google, device manufacturers such as HTC, Sony and Samsung, wireless carriers such as Sprint Nextel and T-Mobile, and chipset makers such as Qualcomm and Texas Instruments, unveiled itself, with a goal to develop open standards for mobile devices. That day, Android was unveiled as its first product, a mobile device platform built on the Linux kernel. The first commercially available smartphone running Android was the HTC Dream, released on October 22, 2008.

Since 2008, Android has seen numerous updates which have incrementally improved the operating system, adding new features and fixing bugs in previous releases. Each major release is named in alphabetical order after a dessert or sugary treat; for example, version 1.5 "Cupcake" was followed by 1.6 "Donut". In 2010, Google launched its Nexus series of devices – a line of smartphones and tablets running the Android operating system, and built by manufacturing partners. HTC collaborated with Google to release the first Nexus smartphone, the Nexus One. Google has since updated the series with newer devices, such as the Nexus 5 phone (made by LG) and the Nexus 7 tablet (made by Asus). Google releases the Nexus phones and tablets to act as their flagship Android devices, demonstrating Android's latest software and hardware features. From 2013 until 2015, Google offered several Google Play Edition devices over Google Play. While not carrying the Google Nexus branding, these were Google-customized Android phones and tablets that also ran the latest version of Android, free from manufacturer or carrier modifications.

From 2010 to 2013, Hugo Barra served as product spokesperson, representing Android at press conferences and Google I/O, Google's annual developer-focused conference. Barra's product involvement included the entire Android ecosystem of software and hardware, including Honeycomb, Ice Cream Sandwich, Jelly Bean and KitKat operating system launches, the Nexus 4 and Nexus 5 smartphones, the Nexus 7 and Nexus 10 tablets, and other related products such as Google Now and Google Voice Search, Google's speech recognition product comparable to Apple's Siri. In 2013, Barra left the Android team for Chinese smartphone maker Xiaomi. The same year, Larry Page announced in a blog post that Andy Rubin had moved from the Android division to take on new projects at Google. He was replaced by Sundar Pichai who became the new head of Android and Chrome OS, and, later, by Hiroshi Lockheimer when Pichai became CEO of Google.

In 2014, Google launched Android One, a line of smartphones mainly targeting customers in the developing world. In May 2015, Google announced Project Brillo as a cut-down version of Android that uses its lower levels (excluding the user interface), intended for the "Internet of Things" (IoT) embedded systems.

University of Cambridge research in 2015, concluded that almost 90% of Android phones in use had known but unpatched security vulnerabilities due to lack of updates and support. In a year since (mid-2015) that report, well over a billion Android smartphones have been sold (more than the just over billion sold in 2014); and Android 5.0 (with better security) and later, went from 5.4% market share to currently over half, which means that the 90% number must be very outdated; those phones now very likely represent less than half of all Android phones. Recent devices do get security updates; Android 5.0 introduced an improved centralized update system.

Features

Interface

Android's default user interface is mainly based on direct manipulation, using touch inputs that loosely correspond to real-world actions, like swiping, tapping, pinching, and reverse pinching to manipulate on-screen objects, along with a virtual keyboard. Game controllers and full-size physical keyboards are supported via Bluetooth or USB. The response to user input is designed to be immediate and provides a fluid touch interface, often using the vibration capabilities of the device to provide haptic feedback to the user. Internal hardware, such as accelerometers, gyroscopes and proximity sensors are used by some applications to respond to additional user actions, for example adjusting the screen from portrait to landscape depending on how the device is oriented, or allowing the user to steer a vehicle in a racing game by rotating the device, simulating control of a steering wheel.

Android devices boot to the homescreen, the primary navigation and information "hub" on Android devices that is analogous to the desktop found on personal computers. (Android also runs on regular personal computers, as described below). Android homescreens are typically made up of app icons and widgets; app icons launch the associated app, whereas widgets display live, auto-updating content, such as the weather forecast, the user's email inbox, or a news ticker directly on the homescreen. A homescreen may be made up of several pages, between which the user can swipe back and forth, though Android's homescreen interface is heavily customisable, allowing users to adjust the look and feel of the devices to their tastes. Third-party apps available on Google Play and other app stores can extensively re-theme the homescreen, and even mimic the look of other operating systems, such as Windows Phone. Most manufacturers, and some wireless carriers, customise the look and feel of their Android devices to differentiate themselves from their competitors. Applications that handle interactions with the homescreen are called "launchers" because they, among other purposes, launch the applications installed on a device.

Along the top of the screen is a status bar, showing information about the device and its connectivity. This status bar can be "pulled" down to reveal a notification screen where apps display important information or updates, such as a newly received email or SMS text, in a way that does not immediately interrupt or inconvenience the user. Notifications are persistent until read by tapping it, which opens the relevant app, or dismissed by sliding it off the screen. Beginning on Android 4.1, "expanded notifications" can display expanded details or additional functionality; for instance, a music player can display playback controls, and a "missed call" notification provides buttons for calling back or sending the caller an SMS message.

Android provides the ability to run applications that change the default launcher, and hence the appearance and externally visible behaviour of Android. These appearance changes include a multi-page dock or no dock, and many more changes to fundamental features of the user interface.

Applications

Applications ("apps"), which extend the functionality of devices, are written using the Android software development kit (SDK) and, often, the Java programming language that has complete access to the Android APIs. Java may be combined with C/C++, together with a choice of non-default runtimes that allow better C++ support; the Go programming language is also supported since its version 1.4, which can also be used exclusively although with a restricted set of Android APIs. The SDK includes a comprehensive set of development tools, including a debugger, software libraries, a handset emulator based on QEMU, documentation, sample code, and tutorials. Initially, Google's supported integrated development environment (IDE) was Eclipse using the Android Development Tools (ADT) plugin; in December 2014, Google released Android Studio, based on IntelliJ IDEA, as its primary IDE for Android application development. Other development tools are available, including a native development kit (NDK) for applications or extensions in C or C++, Google App Inventor, a visual environment for novice programmers, and various cross platform mobile web applications frameworks. In January 2014, Google unveiled an framework based on Apache Cordova for porting Chrome HTML 5 web applications to Android, wrapped in a native application shell.

Android has a growing selection of third-party applications, which can be acquired by users by downloading and installing the application's APK (Android application package) file, or by downloading them using an application store program that allows users to install, update, and remove applications from their devices. Google Play Store is the primary application store installed on Android devices that comply with Google's compatibility requirements and license the Google Mobile Services software. Google Play Store allows users to browse, download and update applications published by Google and third-party developers; as of July 2013, there are more than one million applications available for Android in Play Store. As of July 2013, 50 billion applications have been installed. Some carriers offer direct carrier billing for Google Play application purchases, where the cost of the application is added to the user's monthly bill.

Due to the open nature of Android, a number of third-party application marketplaces also exist for Android, either to provide a substitute for devices that are not allowed to ship with Google Play Store, provide applications that cannot be offered on Google Play Store due to policy violations, or for other reasons. Examples of these third-party stores have included the Amazon Appstore, GetJar, and SlideMe. F-Droid, another alternative marketplace, seeks to only provide applications that are distributed under free and open source licenses.

Memory Management

Since Android devices are usually battery-powered, Android is designed to manage processes to keep power consumption at a minimum. When an application is not in use the system suspends its operation so that, while available for immediate use rather than closed, it does not use battery power or CPU resources.

Android manages the applications stored in memory automatically: when memory is low, the system will begin invisibly and automatically closing inactive processes, starting with those that have been inactive for longest. Lifehacker reported in 2011 that third-party task killers were doing more harm than good.

Virtual Reality

At Google I/O on May 2016, Google announced Daydream, a virtual reality platform that relies on a smartphone and provides VR capabilities through a virtual reality headset and controller designed by Google itself. The platform is built into Android starting with Android Nougat, differentiating from standalone support for VR capabilities. The software is available for developers, and was released in 2016.

Hardware

HTC Dream or T-Mobile G1, the first commercially released device running Android (2008).

The main hardware platform for Android is the ARM (ARMv7 and ARMv8-A architectures), with x86 and MIPS architectures also officially supported in later versions of Android. Since Android 5.0 "Lollipop", 64-bit variants of all platforms are supported in addition to the 32-bit variants. The unofficial Android-x86 project provided support for the x86 architectures ahead of the official support. MIPS architecture was also supported before Google did. Since 2012, Android devices with Intel processors began to appear, including phones and tablets. While gaining support for 64-bit platforms, Android was first made to run on 64-bit x86 and then on ARM64.

Requirements for the minimum amount of RAM for devices running Android 5.1 range from 512 MB of RAM for normal-density screens, to about 1.8 GB for high-density screens. The recommendation for Android 4.4 is to have at least 512 MB of RAM, while for "low RAM" devices 340 MB is the required minimum amount that does not include memory dedicated to various hardware components such as the baseband processor. Android 4.4 requires a 32-bit ARMv7, MIPS or x86 architecture processor (latter two through unofficial ports), together with an OpenGL ES 2.0 compatible graphics processing unit (GPU). Android supports OpenGL ES 1.1, 2.0, 3.0, 3.1 and as of latest major version, 3.2 and Vulkan. Some applications may explicitly require a certain version of the OpenGL ES, and suitable GPU hardware is required to run such applications.

Android devices incorporate many optional hardware components, including still or video cameras, GPS, orientation sensors, dedicated gaming controls, accelerometers, gyroscopes, barometers, magnetometers, proximity sensors, pressure sensors, thermometers, and touchscreens. Some hardware components are not required, but became standard in certain classes of devices, such as smartphones, and additional requirements apply if they are present. Some other hardware was initially required, but those requirements have been relaxed or eliminated altogether. For example, as Android was developed initially as a phone OS, hardware such as microphones were required, while over time the phone function became optional. Android used to require an autofocus camera, which was relaxed to a fixed-focus camera if present at all, since the camera was dropped as a requirement entirely when Android started to be used on set-top boxes.

In addition to running on smartphones and tablets, several vendors run Android natively on regular PC hardware with a keyboard and mouse. In addition to their availability on commercially available hardware, similar PC hardware-friendly versions of Android are freely available from the Android-x86 project, including customized Android 4.4. Using the Android emulator that is part of the Android SDK, or by using BlueStacks or Andy, Android can also run non-natively on x86. Chinese companies are building a PC and mobile operating system, based on Android, to "compete directly with Microsoft Windows and Google Android". The Chinese Academy of Engineering noted that "more than a dozen" companies were customising Android following a Chinese ban on the use of Windows 8 on government PCs.

Development

Android is developed in private by Google until the latest changes and updates are ready to be released, at which point the source code is made available publicly. This source code will only run without modification on select devices, usually the Nexus series of devices. The source code is, in turn, adapted by original equipment manufacturers (OEMs) to run on their hardware. Android's source code does not contain the often proprietary device drivers that are needed for certain hardware components.

Android green figure, next to its original packaging

In 2007, the green Android logo was designed for Google by graphic designer Irina Blok. The design team was tasked with a project to create a universally identifiable icon with the specific inclusion of a robot in the final design. After numerous design developments based on science-fiction and space movies, the team eventually sought inspiration from the human symbol on restroom doors and modified the figure into a robot shape. As Android is open-sourced, it was agreed that the logo should be likewise, and since its launch the green logo has been reinterpreted into countless variations on the original design.

Update Schedule

Google provides major incremental upgrades to Android every six to nine months, with confectionery-themed names, which most devices are capable of receiving over the air. The latest major release is Android 7.0 "Nougat".

Compared to its primary rival mobile operating system, iOS, Android updates typically reach various devices with significant delays. Except for devices with the Google Nexus brand, updates often arrive months after the release of the new version, or not at all. This is partly due to the extensive variation in hardware of Android devices, to which each upgrade must be specifically tailored, as the official Google source code only runs on their own Nexus devices. Porting Android to specific hardware is a time- and resource-consuming process for device manufacturers, who prioritize their newest devices and often leave older ones behind. Hence, older smartphones are frequently not updated if the manufacturer decides it is not worth the investment of resources, although the device may be compatible. This problem is compounded when manufacturers customize Android with their own interface and apps, which must be reapplied to each new release. Additional delays can be introduced by wireless carriers who, after receiving updates from manufacturers, further customize and brand Android to their needs and conduct extensive testing on their networks before sending the upgrade out to users.

The lack of after-sale support from manufacturers and carriers has been widely criticized by consumer groups and the technology media. Some commentators have noted that the industry has a financial incentive not to upgrade their devices, as the lack of updates for existing devices fuels the purchase of newer ones, an attitude described as "insulting". *The Guardian* complained that the method of distribution for updates is complicated only because manufacturers and carriers have designed it that way. In 2011, Google partnered with a number of industry players to announce an "Android Update Alliance", pledging to deliver timely updates for every device for 18 months after its release; however, there has not been another official word about that alliance since its announcement.

In 2012, Google began decoupling certain aspects of the operating system (particularly core applications) so they could be updated through Google Play Store independently of the operating system. One of these components, Google Play Services, is a closed-source system-level process providing APIs for Google services, installed automatically on nearly all devices running Android version 2.2 and higher. With these changes, Google can add new operating system functionality through Play Services and application updates without having to distribute an upgrade to the operating system itself. As a result, Android 4.2 and 4.3 contained relatively fewer user-facing changes, focusing more on minor changes and platform improvements.

In May 2016, it was announced that Google is considering "shaming" smartphone makers who fail to release updated versions of Android to their devices.

Linux kernel

Android's kernel is based on one of the Linux kernel's long-term support (LTS) branches. Since April 2014, Android devices mainly use versions 3.4, 3.10 or 3.18 of the Linux kernel. The specific kernel version depends on the actual Android device and its hardware platform; Android has used various kernel versions since the version 2.6.25 that was used in Android 1.0.

Android's variant of the Linux kernel has further architectural changes that are implemented by Google outside the typical Linux kernel development cycle, such as the inclusion of components like Binder, ashmem, pmem, logger, wakelocks, and different out-of-memory (OOM) handling. Certain features that Google contributed back to the Linux kernel, notably a power management feature called "wakelocks", were rejected by mainline kernel developers partly because they felt that Google did not show any intent to maintain its own code. Google announced in April 2010 that they would hire two employees to work with the Linux kernel community, but Greg Kroah-Hartman, the current Linux kernel maintainer for the stable branch, said in December 2010 that he was concerned that Google was no longer trying to get their code changes included in mainstream Linux. Some Google Android developers hinted that "the Android team was getting fed up with the process," because they were a small team and had more urgent work to do on Android.

In August 2011, Linus Torvalds said that "eventually Android and Linux would come back to a common kernel, but it will probably not be for four to five years". In December 2011, Greg Kroah-Hartman announced the start of Android Mainlining Project, which aims to put some Android drivers, patches and features back into the Linux kernel, starting in Linux 3.3. Linux included the autosleep and wakelocks capabilities in the 3.5 kernel, after many previous attempts at merger. The interfaces are the same but the upstream Linux implementation allows for two different suspend modes: to memory (the traditional suspend that Android uses), and to disk (hibernate, as it is known on the desktop). Google maintains a public code repository that contains their experimental work to re-base Android off the latest stable Linux versions.

The flash storage on Android devices is split into several partitions, such as /system for the operating system itself, and /data for user data and application installations. In contrast to desktop

Linux distributions, Android device owners are not given root access to the operating system and sensitive partitions such as /system are read-only. However, root access can be obtained by exploiting security flaws in Android, which is used frequently by the open-source community to enhance the capabilities of their devices, but also by malicious parties to install viruses and malware.

Android is a Linux distribution according to the Linux Foundation, Google's open-source chief Chris DiBona, and several journalists. Others, such as Google engineer Patrick Brady, say that Android is not Linux in the traditional Unix-like Linux distribution sense; Android does not include the GNU C Library (it uses Bionic as an alternative C library) and some of other components typically found in Linux distributions.

Software Stack

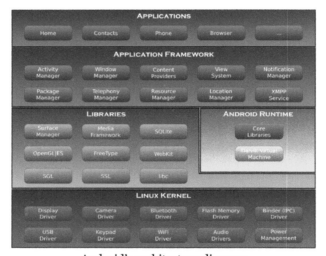

Android's architecture diagram

On top of the Linux kernel, there are the middleware, libraries and APIs written in C, and application software running on an application framework which includes Java-compatible libraries. Development of the Linux kernel continues independently of other Android's source code bases.

Until version 5.0, Android used Dalvik as a process virtual machine with trace-based just-in-time (JIT) compilation to run Dalvik "dex-code" (Dalvik Executable), which is usually translated from the Java bytecode. Following the trace-based JIT principle, in addition to interpreting the majority of application code, Dalvik performs the compilation and native execution of select frequently executed code segments ("traces") each time an application is launched. Android 4.4 introduced Android Runtime (ART) as a new runtime environment, which uses ahead-of-time (AOT) compilation to entirely compile the application bytecode into machine code upon the installation of an application. In Android 4.4, ART was an experimental feature and not enabled by default; it became the only runtime option in the next major version of Android, 5.0.

For its Java library, the Android platform uses a subset of the now discontinued Apache Harmony project. In December 2015, Google announced that the next version of Android would switch to a Java implementation based on OpenJDK.

Android's standard C library, Bionic, was developed by Google specifically for Android, as a derivation of the BSD's standard C library code. Bionic itself has been designed with several major features specific to the Linux kernel. The main benefits of using Bionic instead of the GNU C Library (glibc) or uClibc are its smaller runtime footprint, and optimization for low-frequency CPUs. At the same time, Bionic is licensed under the terms of the BSD licence, which Google finds more suitable for the Android's overall licensing model.

Aiming for a different licensing model, toward the end of 2012, Google switched the Bluetooth stack in Android from the GPL-licensed BlueZ to the Apache-licensed BlueDroid.

Android does not have a native X Window System by default, nor does it support the full set of standard GNU libraries. This made it difficult to port existing Linux applications or libraries to Android, until version r5 of the Android Native Development Kit brought support for applications written completely in C or C++. Libraries written in C may also be used in applications by injection of a small shim and usage of the JNI.

Since Marshmallow, "Toybox", a collection of command line utilities (mostly for use by apps, as Android doesn't provide a command line interface by default), replaced similar "Toolbox" collection.

Android has another operating system, Trusty OS, within it, as a part of "Trusty" "software components supporting a Trusted Execution Environment (TEE) on mobile devices." "Trusty and the Trusty API are subject to change. [..] Applications for the Trusty OS can be written in C/C++ (C++ support is limited), and they have access to a small C library. [..] All Trusty applications are single-threaded; multithreading in Trusty userspace currently is unsupported. [..] Third-party application development is not supported in" the current version, and software running on the OS and processor for it, run the "DRM framework for protected content. [..] There are many other uses for a TEE such as mobile payments, secure banking, full-disk encryption, multi-factor authentication, device reset protection, replay-protected persistent storage, wireless display ("cast") of protected content, secure PIN and fingerprint processing, and even malware detection."

Open-source Community

Android has an active community of developers and enthusiasts who use the *Android Open Source Project* (AOSP) source code to develop and distribute their own modified versions of the operating system. These community-developed releases often bring new features and updates to devices faster than through the official manufacturer/carrier channels, with a comparable level of quality; provide continued support for older devices that no longer receive official updates; or bring Android to devices that were officially released running other operating systems, such as the HP TouchPad. Community releases often come pre-rooted and contain modifications not provided by the original vendor, such as the ability to overclock or over/undervolt the device's processor. CyanogenMod is the most widely used community firmware, and acts as a foundation for numerous others. Android-x86 is a version of Android for IBM PC compatibles. There have also been attempts with varying degrees of success to port Android to iPhones, notably the iDroid Project.

Historically, device manufacturers and mobile carriers have typically been unsupportive of third-party firmware development. Manufacturers express concern about improper functioning of devices running unofficial software and the support costs resulting from this. Moreover, modified firmwares such as CyanogenMod sometimes offer features, such as tethering, for which carriers would otherwise charge a premium. As a result, technical obstacles including locked bootloaders and restricted access to root permissions are common in many devices. However, as community-developed software has grown more popular, and following a statement by the Librarian of Congress in the United States that permits the "jailbreaking" of mobile devices, manufacturers and carriers have softened their position regarding third party development, with some, including HTC, Motorola, Samsung and Sony, providing support and encouraging development. As a result of this, over time the need to circumvent hardware restrictions to install unofficial firmware has lessened as an increasing number of devices are shipped with unlocked or unlockable bootloaders, similar to Nexus series of phones, although usually requiring that users waive their devices' warranties to do so. However, despite manufacturer acceptance, some carriers in the US still require that phones are locked down, frustrating developers and customers.

Security and Privacy

Scope of Surveillance by Public Institutions

As part of the broader 2013 mass surveillance disclosures it was revealed in September 2013 that the American and British intelligence agencies, the National Security Agency (NSA) and Government Communications Headquarters (GCHQ), respectively, have access to the user data on iPhone, BlackBerry, and Android devices. They are reportedly able to read almost all smartphone information, including SMS, location, emails, and notes. In January 2014, further reports revealed the intelligence agencies' capabilities to intercept the personal information transmitted across the Internet by social networks and other popular applications such as Angry Birds, which collect personal information of their users for advertising and other commercial reasons. GCHQ has, according to *The Guardian*, a wiki-style guide of different apps and advertising networks, and the different data that can be siphoned from each. Later that week, the Finnish Angry Birds developer Rovio announced that it was reconsidering its relationships with its advertising platforms in the light of these revelations, and called upon the wider industry to do the same.

The documents revealed a further effort by the intelligence agencies to intercept Google Maps searches and queries submitted from Android and other smartphones to collect location information in bulk. The NSA and GCHQ insist their activities are in compliance with all relevant domestic and international laws, although the Guardian stated "the latest disclosures could also add to mounting public concern about how the technology sector collects and uses information, especially for those outside the US, who enjoy fewer privacy protections than Americans."

Common Security Threats

Research from security company Trend Micro lists premium service abuse as the most common type of Android malware, where text messages are sent from infected phones to premium-rate telephone numbers without the consent or even knowledge of the user. Other malware displays unwanted and intrusive advertisements on the device, or sends personal information to unauthorised third parties. Security threats on Android are reportedly growing exponentially; however, Google engineers have argued that the malware and virus threat on Android is being exaggerated by security companies for commercial reasons, and have accused the security industry of playing on fears to sell virus protection software to users. Google maintains that dangerous malware is actually extremely rare, and a survey conducted by F-Secure showed that only 0.5% of Android malware reported had come from the Google Play store.

Android's fragmentation is a problem for security, since patches to bugs found in the core operating system often do not reach users of older and lower-price devices. One set of researchers say that the failure of vendors to support older devices with patches and updates leaves more than 87% of active devices vulnerable. However, the open-source nature of Android allows security contractors to take existing devices and adapt them for highly secure uses. For example, Samsung has worked with General Dynamics through their Open Kernel Labs acquisition to rebuild *Jelly Bean* on top of their hardened microvisor for the "Knox" project.

Android smartphones have the ability to report the location of Wi-Fi access points, encountered as phone users move around, to build databases containing the physical locations of hundreds of millions of such access points. These databases form electronic maps to locate smartphones, allowing them to run apps like Foursquare, Google Latitude, Facebook Places, and to deliver location-based ads. Third party monitoring software such as TaintDroid, an academic research-funded project, can, in some cases, detect when personal information is being sent from applications to remote servers.

Technical Security Features

Android applications run in a sandbox, an isolated area of the system that does not have access to the rest of the system's resources, unless access permissions are explicitly granted by the user when the application is installed. Before installing an application, Play Store displays all required permissions: a game may need to enable vibration or save data to an SD card, for example, but should not need to read SMS messages or access the phonebook. After reviewing these permissions, the user can choose to accept or refuse them, installing the application only if they accept. The sandboxing and permissions system lessens the impact of vulnerabilities and bugs in applications, but developer confusion and limited documentation has resulted in applications routinely requesting unnecessary permissions, reducing its effectiveness. Google has now pushed an update to Android Verify Apps feature, which will now run in background to detect malicious processes and crack them down.

In Android 6.0 *Marshmallow*, the permissions system was changed to allow the user to control an application's permissions individually, to block applications if desired from having access to the device's contacts, calendar, phone, sensors, SMS, location, microphone and camera. Full permission control is only possible with root access to the device.

Google uses Google Bouncer malware scanner to watch over and scan applications available in the Google Play Store. It is intended to flag suspicious apps and warn users of any potential threat with an application before they download it. Android version 4.2 *Jelly Bean* was released in 2012, with enhanced security features, including a malware scanner built into the system, which works in combination with Google Play but can scan apps installed from third party sources as well, and an alert system which notifies the user when an app tries to send a premium-rate text message, blocking the message unless the user explicitly authorises it. Several security firms, such as Lookout Mobile Security, AVG Technologies, and McAfee, have released antivirus software for Android devices. This software is ineffective as sandboxing also applies to such applications, limiting their ability to scan the deeper system for threats.

In August 2013, Google released Android Device Manager (ADM), a component that allows users to remotely track, locate, and wipe their Android device through a web interface. In December 2013, Google released ADM as an Android application on the Google Play store, where it is available to devices running Android version 2.2 and higher.

Licensing

The source code for Android is open-source: it is developed in private by Google, with the source code released publicly when a new version of Android is released. Google publishes most of the code (including network and telephony stacks) under the non-copyleft Apache License version 2.0. which allows modification and redistribution. The license does not grant rights to the "Android" trademark, so device manufacturers and wireless carriers have to license it from Google under individual contracts. Associated Linux kernel changes are released under the copyleft GNU General Public License version 2, developed by the Open Handset Alliance, with the source code publicly available at all times. Typically, Google collaborates with a hardware manufacturer to produce a flagship device (part of the Nexus series) featuring the new version of Android, then makes the source code available after that device has been released. The only Android release which was not immediately made available as source code was the tablet-only 3.0 *Honeycomb* release. The reason, according to Andy Rubin in an official Android blog post, was because *Honeycomb* was rushed for production of the Motorola Xoom, and they did not want third parties creating a "really bad user experience" by attempting to put onto smartphones a version of Android intended for tablets.

Only the base Android operating system (including some applications) is open-source software, whereas most Android devices ship with a substantial amount of proprietary software, such as Google Mobile Services, which includes applications such as Google Play Store, Google Search, and Google Play Services – a software layer that provides APIs for the integration with Google-provided services, among others. These applications must be licensed from Google by device makers, and can only be shipped on devices which meet its compatibility guidelines and other requirements. Custom, certified distributions of Android produced by manufacturers (such as TouchWiz and HTC Sense) may also replace certain stock Android apps with their own proprietary variants and add additional software not included in the stock Android operating system. There may also be "binary blob" drivers required for certain hardware components in the device.

Some stock applications in AOSP code that were formerly used by earlier versions of Android, such as Search, Music, and Calendar, have been abandoned by Google in favor of non-free replacements distributed through Play Store (Google Search, Google Play Music, and Google Calendar) that are no longer open-source. Moreover, open-source variants of some applications also exclude functions that are present in their non-free versions, such as Photosphere panoramas in Camera, and a Google Now page on the default home screen (exclusive to the proprietary version "Google Now Launcher", whose code is embedded within that of the main Google application).

Richard Stallman and the Free Software Foundation have been critical of Android and have recommended the usage of alternatives such as Replicant, because drivers and firmware vital for the proper functioning of Android devices are usually proprietary, and because the Google Play Store application can forcibly install or deinstall applications and, as a result, invite non-free software.

Leverage Over Manufacturers

Google licenses their Google Mobile Services software, along with Android trademarks, only to hardware manufacturers for devices that meet Google's compatibility standards specified in the Android Compatibility Program document. Thus, forks of Android that make major changes to the operating system itself do not include any of Google's non-free components, stay incompatible with applications that require them, and must ship with an alternative software marketplace in lieu of Google Play Store. Examples of such Android forks are Amazon's Fire OS (which is used on the Kindle Fire line of tablets, and oriented toward Amazon services), the Nokia X Software Platform (a fork used by the Nokia X family, oriented primarily toward Nokia and Microsoft services), and other forks that exclude Google apps due to the general unavailability of Google services in certain regions (such as China). In 2014, Google also began to require that all Android devices which license the Google Mobile Services software display a prominent "Powered by Android" logo on their boot screens.

Members of the Open Handset Alliance, which include the majority of Android OEMs, are also contractually forbidden from producing Android devices based on forks of the OS; in 2012, Acer Inc. was forced by Google to halt production on a device powered by Alibaba Group's Aliyun OS with threats of removal from the OHA, as Google deemed the platform to be an incompatible version of Android. Alibaba Group defended the allegations, arguing that the OS was a distinct platform from Android (primarily using HTML5 apps), but incorporated portions of Android's platform to allow backwards compatibility with third-party Android software. Indeed, the devices did ship with an application store which offered Android apps; however, the majority of them were pirated.

Reception

Android-x86 running on an ASUS EeePC netbook; Android
has been unofficially ported to traditional PCs for use as a desktop operating system.

Android received a lukewarm reaction when it was unveiled in 2007. Although analysts were impressed with the respected technology companies that had partnered with Google to form the Open Handset Alliance, it was unclear whether mobile phone manufacturers would be willing to replace their existing operating systems with Android. The idea of an open-source, Linux-based development platform sparked interest, but there were additional worries about Android facing strong competition from established players in the smartphone market, such as Nokia and Microsoft, and rival Linux mobile operating systems that were in development. These established players were skeptical: Nokia was quoted as saying "we don't see this as a threat," and a member of Microsoft's Windows Mobile team stated "I don't understand the impact that they are going to have."

Since then Android has grown to become the most widely used smartphone operating system and "one of the fastest mobile experiences available." Reviewers have highlighted the open-source nature of the operating system as one of its defining strengths, allowing companies such as Nokia (Nokia X family), Amazon (Kindle Fire), Barnes & Noble (Nook), Ouya, Baidu and others to fork the software and release hardware running their own customised version of Android. As a result, it has been described by technology website Ars Technica as "practically the default operating system for launching new hardware" for companies without their own mobile platforms. This openness and flexibility is also present at the level of the end user: Android allows extensive customisation of devices by their owners and apps are freely available from non-Google app stores and third party websites. These have been cited as among the main advantages of Android phones over others.

Despite Android's popularity, including an activation rate three times that of iOS, there have been reports that Google has not been able to leverage their other products and web services successfully to turn Android into the money maker that analysts had expected. The Verge suggested that Google is losing control of Android due to the extensive customization and proliferation of non-Google apps and services – Amazon's Kindle Fire line uses Fire OS, a heavily modified fork of Android which does not include or support any of Google's proprietary components, and requires that users obtain software from its competing Amazon Appstore instead of Play Store. In 2014, in an effort to improve prominence of the Android brand, Google began to require that devices featuring its proprietary components display an Android logo on the boot screen.

Android has suffered from "fragmentation", a situation where the variety of Android devices, in terms of both hardware variations and differences in the software running on them, makes the task of developing applications that work consistently across the ecosystem harder than rival platforms such as iOS where hardware and software varies less. For example, according to data from OpenSignal in July 2013, there were 11,868 models of Android device, numerous different screen sizes and eight Android OS versions simultaneously in use, while the large majority of iOS users have upgraded to the latest iteration of that OS. Critics such as Apple Insider have asserted that fragmentation via hardware and software pushed Android's growth through large volumes of low end, budget-priced devices running older versions of Android. They maintain this forces Android developers to write for the "lowest common denominator" to reach as many users as possible, who have too little incentive to make use of the latest hardware or software features only available on a smaller percentage of devices. However, OpenSignal, who develops both Android and iOS apps, concluded that although fragmentation can make development trickier, Android's wider global reach also increases the potential reward.

Market Share

Research company Canalys estimated in the second quarter of 2009, that Android had a 2.8% share of worldwide smartphone shipments. By the fourth quarter of 2010, this had grown to 33% of the market becoming the top-selling smartphone platform, overtaking Symbian. By the third quarter of 2011, Gartner estimated that more than half (52.5%) of the smartphone sales belonged to Android. By the third quarter of 2012 Android had a 75% share of the global smartphone market according to the research firm IDC.

In July 2011, Google said that 550,000 Android devices were being activated every day, up from 400,000 per day in May, and more than 100 million devices had been activated with 4.4% growth per week. In September 2012, 500 million devices had been activated with 1.3 million activations per day. In May 2013, at Google I/O, Sundar Pichai announced that 900 million Android devices had been activated.

Android market share varies by location. In July 2012, "mobile subscribers aged 13+" in the United States using Android were up to 52%, and rose to 90% in China. During the third quarter of 2012, Android's worldwide smartphone shipment market share was 75%, with 750 million devices activated in total. In April 2013 Android had 1.5 million activations per day. As of May 2013, 48 billion applications ("apps") have been installed from the Google Play store, and by September 2013, one billion Android devices have been activated.

As of July 2013, the Google Play store has had over one million Android applications published, and over 50 billion applications downloaded. A developer survey conducted in April–May 2013 found that Android is used by 71% of mobile developers. The operating system's success has made it a target for patent litigation as part of the so-called "smartphone wars" between technology companies.

Android devices account for more than half of smartphone sales in most markets, including the US, while "only in Japan was Apple on top" (September–November 2013 numbers). At the end of 2013, over 1.5 billion Android smartphones have been sold in the four years since 2010, making Android the most sold phone and tablet OS. Three billion Android smartphones are estimated to be sold by the end of 2014 (including previous years). According to Gartner research company, Android-based devices outsold all contenders, every year since 2012. In 2013, it outsold Windows 2.8:1 or by 573 million. As of 2015, Android has the largest installed base of all operating systems; Since 2013, devices running it also sell more than Windows, iOS and Mac OS X devices combined.

According to StatCounter, which tracks only the use for browsing the web, Android is the most popular mobile operating system since August 2013. Android is the most popular operating system for web browsing in India and several other countries (e.g. virtually all of Asia, with Japan and North Korea exceptions). According to StatCounter, Android is most used on mobile in all African countries, and it stated "mobile usage has already overtaken desktop in several countries including India, South Africa and Saudi Arabia", with virtually all countries in Africa having done so already (except for seven countries, including Egypt), such as Ethiopia and Kenya in which mobile (including tablets) usage is at 90.46% (Android only, accounts for 75.81% of all use there).

While Android phones in the Western world commonly include Google's proprietary add-ons (such as Google Play) to the otherwise open-source operating system, this is increasingly not the case in emerging markets; "ABI Research claims that 65 million devices shipped globally with open-source Android in the second quarter of , up from 54 million in the first quarter"; depending on country, percent of phones estimated to be based only on Android's source code (AOSP), forgoing the Android trademark: Thailand (44%), Philippines (38%), Indonesia (31%), India (21%), Malaysia (24%), Mexico (18%), Brazil (9%).

According to a January 2015 Gartner report, "Android surpassed a billion shipments of devices in 2014, and will continue to grow at a double-digit pace in 2015, with a 26 percent increase year over year." This made it the first time that any general-purpose operating system has reached more than one billion end users within a year: by reaching close to 1.16 billion end users in 2014, Android shipped over four times more than iOS and OS X combined, and over three times more than Microsoft Windows. Gartner expected the whole mobile phone market to "reach two billion units in 2016", including Android.

According to a Statistica's estimate, Android smartphones had an installed base of 1.8 billion units in 2015, which was 76% of the estimated total number of smartphones worldwide.[c] Android has the largest installed base of any mobile operating system and, since 2013, the highest-selling operating system overall with sales in 2012, 2013 and 2014 close to the installed base of all PCs. In the third quarter of 2015, Android's share of the global smartphone shipment market was 84.7%, the highest ever. As of September 28, 2016, with 52.5% market share, Samsung remains the leading OEM for shipping Android running smartphoens and tablets, followed by followed by LG, Huawei, Motorola, Lenovo, Sony, HTC, Asus, Alcatel and Xiaomi.

By August 2016, the two biggest continents have gone mobile-majority, judged by web use ("desktop" has 46.92%–55.16% use worldwide, depending on day of the week, making some weeks desktop-minority; lowest full month was at 50.05%); because of Android, that has majority use on smartphones in virtually all countries (all continents have gone Android-majority, including North America except for Oceania, because of Australia), with few exceptions (all of which have iOS-majority); in the US, Android is close to iOS, having exchanged majority position a few times, Canada and the following are also exceptions: Japan, Philippines, Australia and the only exceptions in Europe are the UK, Switzerland, Belgium and the Nordic countries Denmark, Iceland, Sweden and Norway.

By 2016, Android was on the majority of smartphones in virtually all countries in the world, excluding United States and Canada (while including North America continent as a whole), Australia and Japan. A few countries, such as the UK, lose Android-majority if tablets are included.

Adoption on Tablets

Despite its success on smartphones, initially Android tablet adoption was slow. One of the main causes was the chicken or the egg situation where consumers were hesitant to buy an Android tablet due to a lack of high quality tablet applications, but developers were hesitant to spend time and resources developing tablet applications until there was a significant market for them. The content and app "ecosystem" proved more important than hardware specs as the selling point for tablets. Due to the lack of Android tablet-specific applications in 2011, early Android tablets had to make do with existing smartphone applications that were ill-suited to larger screen sizes, whereas the dominance of Apple's iPad was reinforced by the large number of tablet-specific iOS applications.

Despite app support in its infancy, a considerable number of Android tablets (alongside those using other operating systems, such as the HP TouchPad and BlackBerry PlayBook) were rushed out to market in an attempt to capitalize on the success of the iPad. *InfoWorld* has suggested that some Android manufacturers initially treated their first tablets as a "Frankenphone business", a short-term low-investment opportunity by placing a smartphone-optimized Android OS (before

Android 3.0 *Honeycomb* for tablets was available) on a device while neglecting user interface. This approach, such as with the Dell Streak, failed to gain market traction with consumers as well as damaging the early reputation of Android tablets. Furthermore, several Android tablets such as the Motorola Xoom were priced the same or higher than the iPad, which hurt sales. An exception was the Amazon Kindle Fire, which relied upon lower pricing as well as access to Amazon's ecosystem of applications and content.

The first-generation Nexus 7 tablet, running Android 4.1 Jelly Bean

This began to change in 2012, with the release of the affordable Nexus 7 and a push by Google for developers to write better tablet applications. According to International Data Corporation, shipments of Android-powered tablets surpassed iPads in Q3 2012.

As of the end of 2013, over 191.6 million Android tablets had sold in three years since 2011. This made Android tablets the most-sold type of tablet in 2013, surpassing iPads in the second quarter of 2013.

According to the StatCounter's June 2015 web use statistics, Android tablets represent the majority of tablet devices used on the South American (then lost majority) and African continents (60.23%), while they have equaled with the iPad's market share in major countries on all continents (with the North America as an exception, though in El Salvador Android has the majority), and getting close to representing the majority on the whole Asian continent having done so already in India (65.9%), Indonesia (62.22%), and most Middle-Eastern countries. In about half of the European countries, Android tablets have a majority market share. China is an exception for the major developing countries, in which Android phablets (classified as smartphones while similar in size to tablets) are more popular than Android tablets or iPads.

By March 2016, Infoworld stated that Android tablets and smartphones can be a "real part of your business [..] there's no longer a reason to keep Android at arm's length. It can now be as integral to your mobile portfolio as Apple's iOS devices are" as they have "business-class apps", no longer just "OK for email". In 2015, they stated that "Microsoft's Office UI is better on iOS and Android" than in Microsoft's own mobile app for Windows.

Platform Usage

Charts in this section provide breakdowns of Android versions, based on devices accessing the Google Play Store in a seven-day period ending on November 7, 2016. Therefore, these statistics exclude devices running various Android forks that do not access the Google Play Store, such as Amazon's Fire tablets.

Version	Code name	Release date	API level	DVM/ART	Distribution	First devices to run version
7.1	Nougat	October 4, 2016	25	ART	less than 0.1%	
7.0	Nougat	August 22, 2016	24	ART	0.3%	Nexus 5X, Nexus 6P
6.0	Marshmallow	October 5, 2015	23	ART	24.0%	Nexus 5X, Nexus 6P
5.1	Lollipop	March 9, 2015	22	ART	22.8%	Android One
5.0		November 3, 2014	21	ART 2.1.0	11.3%	Nexus 6
4.4	KitKat	October 31, 2013	19	DVM (and ART 1.6.0)	25.2%	Nexus 5
4.3	Jelly Bean	July 24, 2013	18	DVM	2.0%	Nexus 7 2013
4.2		November 13, 2012	17	DVM	6.8%	Nexus 4, Nexus 10
4.1		July 9, 2012	16	DVM	4.9%	Nexus 7
4.0	Ice Cream Sandwich	December 16, 2011	15	DVM	1.3%	Galaxy Nexus
2.3.3+	Gingerbread	February 9, 2011	10	DVM 1.4.0	1.3%	Nexus S
2.2	Froyo	May 20, 2010	8	DVM	0.1%	Droid 2

Since May 2016, more than half of devices have OpenGL ES 3.0 or higher.

Application Piracy

In general, paid Android applications can easily be pirated. In a May 2012 interview with Eurogamer, the developers of Football Manager stated that the ratio of pirated players vs legitimate players was 9:1 for their game Football Manager Handheld. However, not every developer agreed that piracy rates were an issue; for example, in July 2012 the developers of the game Wind-up Knight said that piracy levels of their game were only 12%, and most of the piracy came from China, where people cannot purchase apps from Google Play.

In 2010, Google released a tool for validating authorized purchases for use within apps, but developers complained that this was insufficient and trivial to crack. Google responded that the tool, especially its initial release, was intended as a sample framework for developers to modify and build upon depending on their needs, not as a finished piracy solution. Android "Jelly Bean" introduced the ability for paid applications to be encrypted, so that they may work only on the device for which they were purchased.

Legal Issues

Both Android and Android phone manufacturers have been involved in numerous patent lawsuits. On August 12, 2010, Oracle sued Google over claimed infringement of copyrights and patents related to the Java programming language. Oracle originally sought damages up to $6.1 billion, but this valuation was rejected by a United States federal judge who asked Oracle to revise the estimate. In response, Google submitted multiple lines of defense, counterclaiming that Android did not infringe on Oracle's patents or copyright, that Oracle's patents were invalid, and several other defenses. They said that Android's Java runtime environment is based on Apache Harmony, a clean room implementation of the Java class libraries, and an independently developed virtual machine called Dalvik. In May 2012, the jury in this case found that Google did not infringe on Oracle's patents, and the trial judge ruled that the structure of the Java APIs used by Google was not copyrightable. The parties agreed to zero dollars in statutory damages for a small amount of copied code. On May 9, 2014, the Federal Circuit partially reversed the district court ruling, ruling in Oracle's favor on the copyrightability issue, and remanding the issue of fair use to the district court.

In December 2015, Google announced that the next major release of Android (Android Nougat) would switch to OpenJDK, which is the official open-source implementation of the Java platform, instead of using the now-discontinued Apache Harmony project as its runtime. Code reflecting this change was also posted to the AOSP source repository. In its announcement, Google claimed this was part of an effort to create a "common code base" between Java on Android and other platforms. Google later admitted in a court filing that this was part of an effort to address the disputes with Oracle, as its use of OpenJDK code is governed under the GNU General Public License (GPL) with a linking exception, and that "any damages claim associated with the new versions expressly licensed by Oracle under OpenJDK would require a separate analysis of damages from earlier releases". In June 2016, a United States federal court ruled in favor of Google, stating that its use of the APIs was fair use.

In addition to lawsuits against Google directly, various proxy wars have been waged against Android indirectly by targeting manufacturers of Android devices, with the effect of discouraging manufacturers from adopting the platform by increasing the costs of bringing an Android device to market. Both Apple and Microsoft have sued several manufacturers for patent infringement, with Apple's ongoing legal action against Samsung being a particularly high-profile case. In October 2011, Microsoft said they had signed patent license agreements with ten Android device manufacturers, whose products account for *"70% in the U.S.".* and 55% of the worldwide revenue for Android devices. These include Samsung and HTC. Samsung's patent settlement with Microsoft included an agreement to allocate more resources to developing and marketing phones running Microsoft's Windows Phone operating system. Microsoft has also tied its own Android software to patent licenses, requiring the bundling of Microsoft Office Mobile and Skype applications on Android devices to subsidize the licensing fees, while at the same time helping to promote its software lines.

Google has publicly expressed its frustration for the current patent landscape in the United States, accusing Apple, Oracle and Microsoft of trying to take down Android through patent litigation, rather than innovating and competing with better products and services. In September 2011, Google purchased Motorola Mobility for US$12.5 billion, which was viewed in part as a defensive measure to protect Android, since Motorola Mobility held more than 17,000 patents. In December 2011, Google bought over a thousand patents from IBM.

In 2013, FairSearch, a lobbying organization supported by Microsoft, Oracle and others, filed a complaint regarding Android with the European Commission, alleging that its free-of-charge distribution model constituted anti-competitive predatory pricing. The Free Software Foundation Europe, whose donors include Google, disputed the Fairsearch allegations. On April 20, 2016, the EU filed a formal antitrust complaint against Google based upon the FairSearch allegations, arguing that its leverage over Android vendors, including the mandatory bundling of the entire suite of proprietary Google software, hindering the ability for competing search providers to be integrated into Android, and barring vendors from producing devices running forks of Android, constituted anti-competitive practices.

Other Uses

Ouya, a video game console which runs Android

The open and customizable nature of Android allows it to be used on other electronics aside from smartphones and tablets, including laptops and netbooks, smartbooks, smart TVs (Android TV, Google TV) and cameras (E.g. Galaxy Camera). In addition, the Android operating system has seen applications on smart glasses (Google Glass), smartwatches, headphones, car CD and DVD players, mirrors, portable media players, landline and Voice over IP phones. Ouya, a video game console running Android, became one of the most successful Kickstarter campaigns, crowdfunding US$8.5m for its development, and was later followed by other Android-based consoles, such as Nvidia's Shield Portable – an Android device in a video game controller form factor.

In 2011, Google demonstrated "Android@Home", a home automation technology which uses Android to control a range of household devices including light switches, power sockets and thermostats. Prototype light bulbs were announced that could be controlled from an Android phone or tablet, but Android head Andy Rubin was cautious to note that "turning a lightbulb on and off is nothing new", pointing to numerous failed home automation services. Google, he said, was thinking more ambitiously and the intention was to use their position as a cloud services provider to bring Google products into customers' homes.

Parrot unveiled an Android-based car stereo system known as Asteroid in 2011, followed by a successor, the touchscreen-based Asteroid Smart, in 2012. In 2013, Clarion released its own Android-based car stereo, the AX1. In January 2014, at the Consumer Electronics Show (CES), Google announced the formation of the Open Automotive Alliance, a group including several major automobile makers (Audi, General Motors, Hyundai, and Honda) and Nvidia, which aims to produce Android-based in car entertainment systems for automobiles, "[bringing] the best of Android into the automobile in a safe and seamless way."

On March 18, 2014, Google announced Android Wear, an Android-based platform specifically intended for smartwatches and other wearable devices; only a developer preview was made publicly available. This was followed by the unveiling of two Android-Wear-based devices, the LG G Watch and Moto 360.

On June 25, 2014, at Google I/O, it was announced that Android TV, a Smart TV platform, is replacing the previously released Google TV. Google also announced Android Auto for use in cars.

Android comes preinstalled on a few laptops (a similar functionality of running Android applications is also available in Google's Chrome OS) and can also be installed on personal computers by end users. On those platforms Android provides additional functionality for physical keyboards and mice, together with the "Alt-Tab" key combination for switching applications quickly with a keyboard. In December 2014, one reviewer commented that Android's notification system is "vastly more complete and robust than in most environments" and that Android is "absolutely usable" as one's primary desktop operating system.

In October 2015, *The Wall Street Journal* reported that Android will serve as Google's future main laptop operating system, with the plan to fold Chrome OS into it by 2017. Google's Sundar Pichai, who led the development of Android, explained that "mobile as a computing paradigm is eventually going to blend with what we think of as desktop today." and back in 2009, Google co-founder Sergey Brin himself said that Chrome OS and Android would "likely converge over time." Lockheimer, who replaced Pichai as head of Android and Chrome OS, responded to this claim with an official Google blog post stating that "While we've been working on ways to bring together the best of both operating systems, there's no plan to phase out Chrome OS [which has] guaranteed auto-updates for five years". That is unlike Android where support is shorter with "EOL dates [being..] at least 3 years [into the future] for Android tablets for education".

IOS

iOS (formerly iPhone OS) is a mobile operating system created and developed by Apple Inc. exclusively for its hardware. It is the operating system that presently powers many of the company's mobile devices, including the iPhone, iPad, and iPod touch. It is the second most popular mobile operating system globally after Android by sales. iPad tablets are also the second most popular, by sales, against Android since 2013, when Android tablet sales increased by 127%.

Originally unveiled in 2007 for the iPhone, it has been extended to support other Apple devices such as the iPod Touch (September 2007) and the iPad (January 2010). As of June 2016, Apple's App Store contained more than 2 million iOS applications, 725,000 of which are native for iPads. These mobile apps have collectively been downloaded more than 130 billion times.

The iOS user interface is based upon direct manipulation, using multi-touch gestures. Interface control elements consist of sliders, switches, and buttons. Interaction with the OS includes gestures such as *swipe, tap, pinch*, and *reverse pinch*, all of which have specific definitions within the context of the iOS operating system and its multi-touch interface. Internal accelerometers are used by some applications to respond to shaking the device (one common result is the undo command) or rotating it in three dimensions (one common result is switching between portrait and landscape mode).

Major versions of iOS are released annually. The current version, iOS 10, was released on September 13, 2016. It runs on the iPhone 5 and later, iPad (4th generation) and later, iPad Pro, iPad Mini 2 and later, and the 6th-generation iPod Touch. In iOS, there are four abstraction layers: the Core

OS, Core Services, Media, and Cocoa Touch layers. iOS 10 dedicates around 1.8GB of the device's flash memory for itself.

History

Original iOS logo, used until 2013 (left) and new logo from 2013 onwards (right)

In 2005, when Steve Jobs began planning the iPhone, he had a choice to either "shrink the Mac, which would be an epic feat of engineering, or enlarge the iPod". Jobs favored the former approach but pitted the Macintosh and iPod teams, led by Scott Forstall and Tony Fadell, respectively, against each other in an internal competition, with Forstall winning by creating the iPhone OS. The decision enabled the success of the iPhone as a platform for third-party developers: using a well-known desktop operating system as its basis allowed the many third-party Mac developers to write software for the iPhone with minimal retraining. Forstall also was responsible for creating a software developer's kit for programmers to build iPhone apps, as well as an App Store within iTunes.

The operating system was unveiled with the iPhone at the Macworld Conference & Expo, January 9, 2007, and released in June of that year. At first, Apple marketing literature did not specify a separate name for the operating system, stating simply what Steve Jobs claimed: "iPhone runs OS X" and runs "desktop applications" when in fact it runs a variant of [Mac] OS X, that doesn't run OS X software unless it has been ported to the incompatible operating system. Initially, third-party applications were not supported. Steve Jobs' reasoning was that developers could build web applications that "would behave like native apps on the iPhone". On October 17, 2007, Apple announced that a native Software Development Kit (SDK) was under development and that they planned to put it "in developers' hands in February". On March 6, 2008, Apple released the first beta, along with a new name for the operating system: "iPhone OS".

On September 5, 2007, Apple released the iPod Touch, which had most of the non-phone capabilities of the iPhone. Apple also sold more than one million iPhones during the 2007 holiday season. On January 27, 2010, Apple announced the iPad, featuring a larger screen than the iPhone and iPod Touch, and designed for web browsing, media consumption, and reading iBooks.

In June 2010, Apple rebranded iPhone OS as "iOS". The trademark "IOS" had been used by Cisco for over a decade for its operating system, IOS, used on its routers. To avoid any potential lawsuit, Apple licensed the "IOS" trademark from Cisco.

By late 2011, iOS accounted for 60% of the market share for smartphones and tablets. By the end of 2014, iOS accounted for 14.8% of the smartphone market and 27.6% of the tablet and two-in-one market. As of February 2015, StatCounter reported iOS was used on 23.18% of smartphones and 66.25% of tablets worldwide.

Software Updates

Apple provides major updates to the iOS operating system annually via iTunes and also, for iOS 5 and later, over the air. The latest version is iOS 10, which is available for the iPhone 5, iPhone 5C, iPhone 5S, iPhone 6 and 6 Plus, iPhone 6S and 6S Plus, iPhone SE, iPhone 7 and 7 Plus, the fourth generation iPad, the first and second generation iPad Air, the iPad Pro, the second, third and fourth generation iPad Mini, and the sixth generation iPod Touch. The OS update was released on September 13, 2016.

Before the iOS 4 release in 2010, iPod Touch users had to pay for system software updates. Apple claimed that this was the case because the iPod Touch was not a 'subscription device' like the iPhone (i.e., it was a one-off purchase). Apple said it had 'found a way' to deliver software updates for free to iPod Touch users at WWDC 2010 when iOS 4 was unveiled.

Platform Usage

Charts in this section provide breakdowns of iOS versions, based on devices accessing the App Store as of October 25, 2016.

Version	Release date	Distribution (as of Oct. 2016)	Devices shipped with version
iOS 10	September 13, 2016	60%	iPhone 7, iPhone 7 Plus
iOS 9	September 16, 2015	32%	iPhone 6S, iPhone 6S Plus, iPhone SE, iPad Pro, iPad Mini 4
iOS 8 and earlier	N/A	8%	N/A

Features

Home Screen

iOS 10 running on an iPhone (left) and on an iPad Pro (right)

The home screen, rendered by SpringBoard, displays application icons and a dock at the bottom where users can pin their most frequently used apps. The home screen appears whenever the user unlocks the device or presses the physical "Home" button whilst in another app. Before iOS 4 on the iPhone 3GS+, the screen's background could be customized through jailbreaking, but can now be changed out-of-the-box. The screen has a status bar across the top to display data, such as time, battery level, and signal strength. The rest of the screen is devoted to the current application. When a passcode is set and a user switches on the device, the passcode must be entered at the Lock Screen before access to the Home screen is granted.

In iPhone OS 3, Spotlight was introduced, allowing users to search media, apps, emails, contacts, messages, reminders, calendar events, and similar content. In iOS 7 and later, Spotlight is accessed by pulling down anywhere on the home screen (except for the top and bottom edges that open Notification Center and Control Center). In iOS 9, there are two ways to access Spotlight. As with iOS 7 and 8, pulling down on any homescreen will show Spotlight. However, it can also be accessed as it was in iOS 3 – 6. This gives a Spotlight endowed with Siri suggestions, which include app suggestions, contact suggestions and news. In iOS 10, Spotlight is at the top of the now-dedicated "Today" panel.

Since iOS 3.2, users are able to set a background image for the Home screen. This feature is only available on third-generation devices or newer – iPhone 3GS+, iPod Touch 3rd generation+ (iOS 4.0+), and all iPad models (iOS 3.2+).

Researchers found that users organize icons on their homescreens based on usage-frequency and relatedness of the applications, as well as for reasons of usability and aesthetics.

System font

iOS originally used Helvetica as the system font. With the release of the iPhone 4 and iOS 4, iOS switched to Helvetica Neue with Retina Displays, but retained Helvetica as the system font for older devices. iOS 7 provided the ability to scale text or switch to Neue Bold as the default system font, as accessibility options. iOS 9 changed the font to San Francisco, a Apple-designed font for maximum legibility on computer and mobile displays, originally introduced as the system font for the Apple Watch.

Folders

iOS 4 introduced folders, which were created when two applications are in "jiggle mode"(with the exception of Newsstand in iOS 5-6) are dragged together to create it, and from then on, more can be added using the same procedure. It can be up to 12 on iPhone 4S and earlier and iPod Touch, 16 on iPhone 5, and 20 on iPad. A title for the folder is automatically selected by the category of applications inside, but the name can also be edited by the user. When apps inside folders receive badges, the numbers shown by the badges is added up and shown on the folder. Folders cannot be put into other folders, though an unofficial workaround exists that enables folders to be nested within folders. iOS 7 updated the folders with pages like on the SpringBoard. Each page can hold nine apps, and the Newsstand app is now able to be placed into a folder.

Notification Center

Before iOS 5, notifications were delivered in a modal window and couldn't be viewed after being dismissed. In iOS 5, Apple introduced Notification Center, which allows users to view a history of notifications. The user can tap a notification to open its corresponding app, or clear it. Notifications are now delivered in banners that appear briefly at the top of the screen. If a user taps a received notification, the application that sent the notification will be opened. Users can also choose to view notifications in modal alert windows by adjusting the application's notification settings. Introduced with iOS 8, widgets are now accessible through the Notification Center, defined by 3rd parties.

When an app sends a notification while closed, a red badge appears on its icon. This badge tells the user, at a glance, how many notifications that app has sent. Opening the app clears the badge.

Accessibility

Located in Settings > General > Accessibility. This allows the user to customize various aspects of iOS to assist the user if assistance is needed in the area of seeing or hearing, and allows the addition of accessibility shortcuts.

Multitasking

Multitasking for iOS was first released in June 2010 along with the release of iOS 4. Only certain devices—iPhone 4, iPhone 3GS, and iPod Touch 3rd generation—were able to multitask. The iPad did not get multitasking until iOS 4.2.1 in November. Currently, multitasking is supported on iPhone 3GS+, iPod Touch 3rd generation+, and all iPad models.

Implementation of multitasking in iOS has been criticized for its approach, which limits the work that applications in the background can perform to a limited function set and requires application developers to add explicit support for it.

Before iOS 4, multitasking was limited to a selection of the applications Apple included on the device. Users could, however "jailbreak" their device in order to unofficially multitask. Starting with iOS 4, on third-generation and newer iOS devices, multitasking is supported through seven background APIs:

1. Background audio – application continues to run in the background as long as it is playing audio or video content

2. Voice over IP – application is suspended when a phone call is not in progress

3. Background location – application is notified of location changes

4. Push notifications

5. Local notifications – application schedules local notifications to be delivered at a predetermined time

6. Task completion – application asks the system for extra time to complete a given task

7. Fast app switching – application does not execute any code and may be removed from memory at any time

In iOS 5, three new background APIs were introduced:

1. Newsstand – application can download content in the background to be ready for the user

2. External Accessory – application communicates with an external accessory and shares data at regular intervals

3. Bluetooth Accessory – application communicates with a bluetooth accessory and shares data at regular intervals

In iOS 7, Apple introduced a new multitasking feature, providing all apps with the ability to perform background updates. This feature prefers to update the user's most frequently used apps and prefers to use WiFi networks over a cellular network, without markedly reducing the device's battery life.

Switching Applications

In iOS 4.0 to iOS 6.x, double-clicking the home button activates the application switcher. A scrollable dock-like interface appears from the bottom, moving the contents of the screen up. Choosing an icon switches to an application. To the far left are icons which function as music controls, a rotation lock, and on iOS 4.2 and above, a volume controller.

With the introduction of iOS 7, double clicking the home button also activates the application switcher. However, unlike previous versions it displays screenshots of open applications on top of the icon and horizontal scrolling allows for browsing through previous apps, and it is possible to close applications by dragging them up, similar to how WebOS handled multiple cards.

With the introduction of iOS 9, the application switcher received a significant visual change; whilst still retaining the card metaphor introduced in iOS 7, the application icon is smaller, and appears above the screenshot (which is now larger, due to the removal of "Recent and Favorite Contacts"), and each application "card" overlaps the other, forming a rolodex effect as the user scrolls. Now, instead of the home screen appearing at the leftmost of the application switcher, it appears rightmost.

Ending Tasks

In iOS 4.0 to iOS 6.x, briefly holding the icons in the application switcher makes them "jiggle" (similarly to the homescreen) and allows the user to *force* quit the applications by tapping the red minus circle that appears at the corner of the app's icon. Clearing applications from multitasking stayed the same from iOS 4.0 through 6.1.6, the last version of iOS 6.

As of iOS 7, the process has become faster and easier. In iOS 7, instead of holding the icons to close them, they are closed by simply swiping them upwards off the screen. Up to three apps can be cleared at a time compared to one in versions up to iOS 6.1.6.

Task Completion

Task completion allows apps to continue a certain task after the app has been suspended. As of iOS 4.0, apps can request up to ten minutes to complete a task in the background. This doesn't extend to background up- and downloads though (e.g. if you start a download in one application, it won't finish if you switch away from the application).

Siri

Siri is a personal assistant and knowledge navigator which works as an application on supported devices. The service, directed by the user's spoken commands, can do a variety of different tasks, such as call or text someone, open an app, search the web, lookup sports information, find directions or locations, and answer general knowledge questions (e.g. "How many cups are in a gallon?"). Siri was updated in iOS 7 with a new interface, faster answers, Wikipedia, Twitter, and Bing support and the voice was changed to sound more human. Siri is currently only available on the iPhone 4S and later iPhones, the fifth and sixth generation iPod Touch, all of the models of the iPad Mini, and the third-generation and later iPads.

Game Center

Game Center is an online multiplayer "social gaming network" released by Apple. It allows users to "invite friends to play a game, start a multiplayer game through matchmaking, track their achievements, and compare their high scores on a leaderboard." iOS 5 and above adds support for profile photos.

Game Center was announced during an iOS 4 preview event hosted by Apple on April 8, 2010. A preview was released to registered Apple developers in August. It was released on September 8, 2010 with iOS 4.1 on iPhone 4, iPhone 3GS, and iPod Touch 2nd generation through 4th generation. Game Center made its public debut on the iPad with iOS 4.2.1. There is no support for the iPhone 3G, original iPhone and the first-generation iPod Touch (the latter two devices did not have Game Center because they did not get iOS 4). However, Game Center is unofficially available on the iPhone 3G via a hack.

Development

Authorized third-party native applications are available through Apple's App Store for devices running iPhone OS 2.0 and higher. Native apps must be written in Swift or Objective-C (with some elements optionally in C or C++) and compiled specifically for iOS and the 64-bit ARM architecture or previous 32-bit one (typically using Xcode). Third-party attempts have been made to allow apps written with Java, .NET, and Adobe Flash to run on iOS devices, but due to Apple restrictions these are generally not available in the iOS App Store.

The Safari web browser supports web applications as with other web browsers. Hybrid apps embed a mobile web site inside a native app, possibly using a hybrid framework like Apache Cordova or React Native.

iOS shares some frameworks with Apple's desktop operating system macOS, such as Core Foundation and Foundation Kit; however, its UI toolkit is Cocoa Touch rather than macOS' Cocoa, providing the UIKit rather than the AppKit framework, preventing source compatibility with desktop applications. Also, Unix-like shell access is strictly apps-only, preventing it from being fully Unix despite its Darwin foundation from macOS itself.

SDK

On October 17, 2007, in an open letter posted to Apple's "Hot News" weblog, Steve Jobs announced that a software development kit (SDK) would be made available to third-party developers in February 2008. The SDK was released on March 6, 2008, and allows developers to make applications for the iPhone and iPod Touch, as well as test them in an "iPhone simulator". However, loading an application onto the devices is only possible after paying an iPhone Developer Program fee.

iOS SDK 9.1 included in Xcode 7.1

The fees to join the respective developer programs for iOS and macOS were each set at US$99.00 per year. As of July 20, 2011, Apple released Xcode on its Mac App Store free to download for all Mac OS X Lion users, instead of as a standalone download. Users can create and develop iOS and macOS applications using a free copy of Xcode; however, they cannot test their applications on a physical iOS device, or publish them to the App store, without first paying the yearly $99.00 iPhone Developer or Mac Developer Program fee.

Since the release of Xcode 3.1, Xcode is the development environment for the iOS SDK.

Developers are able to set any price above a set minimum for their applications to be distributed through the App Store, keeping 70% for the developer, and leaving 30% for Apple. Alternatively, they may opt to release the application for free and need not pay any costs to release or distribute the application except for the membership fee.

Market Share

iOS is the second most popular mobile operating system in the world, after Android. Sales of iPads in recent years are also behind Android, while, by web use (a proxy for all use), iPads (using iOS) are still most popular.

By the middle of 2012, there were 410 million devices activated. At WWDC 2014, Tim Cook said 800 million devices had been sold by June 2014.

During Apple's quarterly earnings call in January 27, 2015, Apple announced that they have now sold one billion iOS devices since 2007 (a little less than Android sold in 2014 only).

Jailbreaking

Since its initial release, iOS has been subject to a variety of different hacks centered around adding functionality not allowed by Apple. Prior to the 2008 debut of Apple's native iOS App Store, the primary motive for jailbreaking was to bypass Apple's purchase mechanism for installing the App

Store's native applications. Apple claimed that it will not release iOS software updates designed specifically to break these tools (other than applications that perform SIM unlocking); however, with each subsequent iOS update, previously un-patched jailbreak exploits are usually patched.

Since the arrival of Apple's native iOS App Store, and—along with it—third-party applications, the general motives for jailbreaking have changed. People jailbreak for many different reasons, including gaining filesystem access, installing custom device themes, and modifying SpringBoard. An additional motivation is that it may enable the installation of pirated apps. On some devices, jailbreaking also makes it possible to install alternative operating systems, such as Android and the Linux kernel. Primarily, users jailbreak their devices because of the limitations of iOS. Depending on the method used, the effects of jailbreaking may be permanent or temporary.

In 2010, the Electronic Frontier Foundation (EFF) successfully convinced the U.S. Copyright Office to allow an exemption to the general prohibition on circumvention of copyright protection systems under the Digital Millennium Copyright Act (DMCA). The exemption allows jailbreaking of iPhones for the sole purpose of allowing legally obtained applications to be added to the iPhone. The exemption does not affect the contractual relations between Apple and an iPhone owner, for example, jailbreaking voiding the iPhone warranty; however, it is solely based on Apple's discretion on whether they will fix jailbroken devices in the event that they need to be repaired. At the same time, the Copyright Office exempted unlocking an iPhone from DMCA's anticircumvention prohibitions. Unlocking an iPhone allows the iPhone to be used with any wireless carrier using the same GSM or CDMA technology for which the particular phone model was designed to operate.

Unlocking

Initially most wireless carriers in the US did not allow iPhone owners to unlock it for use with other carriers. However AT&T allowed iPhone owners who have satisfied contract requirements to unlock their iPhone. Instructions to unlock the device are available from Apple, but it is ultimately the sole discretion of the carrier to authorize the device to be unlocked. This allows the use of a carrier-sourced iPhone on other networks. However, because T-Mobile primarily uses a different band than AT&T for its 3G, the iPhone will only work at 3G speeds on the T-Mobile 1900MHz network. There are programs to break these restrictions, but are not supported by Apple and most often not a permanent unlock - a soft-unlock.

Digital Rights Management

The closed and proprietary nature of iOS has garnered criticism, particularly by digital rights advocates such as the Electronic Frontier Foundation, computer engineer and activist Brewster Kahle, Internet-law specialist Jonathan Zittrain, and the Free Software Foundation who protested the iPad's introductory event and have targeted the iPad with their "Defective by Design" campaign. Competitor Microsoft, via a PR spokesman, criticized Apple's control over its platform.

At issue are restrictions imposed by the design of iOS, namely digital rights management (DRM) intended to lock purchased media to Apple's platform, the development model (requiring a yearly subscription to distribute apps developed for the iOS), the centralized approval process for apps, as well as Apple's general control and lockdown of the platform itself. Particularly at issue is the ability for Apple to remotely disable or delete apps at will.

Some in the tech community have expressed concern that the locked-down iOS represents a growing trend in Apple's approach to computing, particularly Apple's shift away from machines that hobbyists can "tinker with" and note the potential for such restrictions to stifle software innovation. Former Facebook developer Joe Hewitt protested against Apple's control over its hardware as a "horrible precedent" but praised iOS's sandboxing of apps.

Kernel

The iOS kernel is the XNU kernel of Darwin. The original iPhone OS (1.0) up to iPhone OS 3.1.3 used Darwin 9.0.0d1. iOS 4 was based on Darwin 10. iOS 5 was based on Darwin 11. iOS 6 was based on Darwin 13. iOS 7 and iOS 8 are based on Darwin 14. iOS 9 is based on Darwin 15. iOS 10 is based on Darwin 16.

Devices

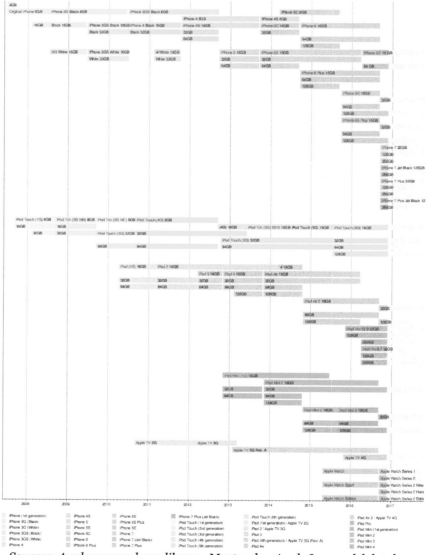

Sources: Apple press release library, Mactracker Apple Inc. model database

ColorOS

ColorOS is computer software, an operating system created by OPPO Electronics (OPPO) of Guangdong, China. It is a fork of Google's operating system Android. The major difference between Google Android and OPPO ColorOS is that the later includes some features unavailable in the former. Such features include: gestures for screen off, screen on, communication, a security centre, lock screen magazines, options for long screen shot, eye protection, and others. ColorOS, in some respects, looks similar to iOS made by Apple, and some users have said that they dislike its design. ColorOS was available for OnePlus smartphones from their forums page.

HTC Sense

HTC Sense is a software suite developed by HTC, used primarily on the company's Android-based devices. Serving as a successor to HTC's TouchFLO 3D software for Windows Mobile, Sense modifies many aspects of the Android user experience, incorporating additional features (such as an altered home screen and keyboard), additional widgets, re-designed applications, and additional HTC-developed applications. The first device with Sense, the HTC Hero, was released in 2009. The HD2 running Windows Mobile 6.5, released later the same year, included Sense. Following the release of the Hero, all future Android devices by HTC were shipped with Sense, except for the Nexus One, the T-Mobile G2, the HTC First, and the Nexus 9 which used a stock version of Android. Also some HTC smartphones that are using MediaTek processors come without HTC Sense.

At the Mobile World Congress 2010, HTC debuted their new updated HTC Sense UI on the HTC Desire and HTC Legend, with an upgrade available for the Hero and Magic. The new version was based upon Android 2.1 and featured interface features such as the Friend Stream widget, which aggregated Twitter, Facebook and Flickr information and Leap, which allows access to all home screens at once.

When the HTC Sensation was released, it featured HTC Sense 3.0, which added interface elements, including an updated lock screen that allows applications to be pinned directly to it for easier access. The HTC EVO 3D also features Sense 3.0.

Two versions of Sense were developed for Android 4.0. Sense 4.0, included on HTC's new devices beginning in 2012 (such as the HTC One X), was designed to provide a refreshed and more minimalist look closer to stock Android than previous versions, while integrating features provided by Android 4.0. Sense 3.6, which was distributed through updates to older HTC phones, was designed to maintain a closer resemblance to previous versions of Sense on Android 2.3.

Versions

HTC Sense (2009)

The original version of Sense was first introduced by the HTC Hero.

Espresso (2010)

Espresso was the codename for the version of Sense running atop T-Mobile myTouch devices. It debuted on the T-Mobile myTouch 3G (HTC Espresso) and the T-Mobile myTouch 4G (HTC

Glacier). It features all of the widgets and apps of regular Sense, but the color of apps and certain interface elements are blue instead of green. "Pushed in" apps appear on the home screen.

Sense 2.0 (2010)

Sense 2.0 debuted on the HTC Desire and HTC Legend and provided upgrades for the HTC Hero and HTC Magic. It introduced FriendStream and the Leap feature similar to Macintosh OS X's Mission Control.

Sense 3.0 (2011)

Sense 3.0 debuted on the HTC Sensation. This version introduced HTC Watch, a movie streaming service, and updated the lockscreen with app shortcuts for easier access. Additional lockscreen styles included widgets that display content such as weather and photos. It also features 3D home-screen transition effects when swiping among homescreens.

Sense 3.6 (2012)

Legacy HTC devices that received updates to Android 4.0 use Sense 3.6; an update integrating select features from Sense 4 (such as the updated home screen), but retaining elements of Sense 3.5, such as its glossy design and certain interface behaviors.

Sense 4.0 (2012)

Sense 4.0 was first introduced by the HTC One series of devices with Android 4.0 unveiled in 2012; the One X, One S, and One V. Many aspects of the Sense interface were modified to closer resemble the standard Android interface (such as its home screen, which now uses a dock of shortcuts instead of the fixed "All Apps", "Phone", and "Personalize" buttons of previous versions), a new application switcher using cards, updated stock apps, and Beats Audio support.

Sense 4.1 (2012)

Sense 4.1 was a minor update to the original Sense 4.0. It ran on top of Android 4.0.4 as opposed to Android 4.0.3, and included many bug fixes and optimizations. The only device of the original HTC One series not to receive this update was the HTC One V.

Sense 4.5 or 4+ (2012)

Announced in 2012 for the HTC One X+, updates with Sense 4+ was also released with Android 4.1.2 updates for the One X, One S, Evo 4G LTE, One SV LTE / 3G and Desire X..

Sense 5 (2013)

Announced in April 2013 for the 2013 HTC One; it features a more minimalistic design and a new scrolling news aggregator on the home screen known as "BlinkFeed", which displays a scrolling grid of news headlines and social network content. By default, Sense 5 uses three home screen pages: two with the traditional grid for apps and widgets (as with previous devices, but using a grid with fewer spaces for apps by default), and the default screen with a redesigned clock and BlinkFeed, although more pages can still be added. Sense 5.0 was not only going to be exclusive to the HTC One; on February 28, 2013, HTC announced that it would provide updates for the Butterfly, One S (later discontinued), and the One X/X+ to Sense 5.0 in the coming months.

Sense 5.5 (2013)

Announced in September 2013 for the HTC One Max; it adds RSS and Google+ support to Blink-Feed, allows users to disable BlinkFeed entirely, adds a tool for making animated GIFs, and additional Highlights themes.

Sense 6.0 (2014)

Sense 6.0, nicknamed "Sixth Sense", was announced alongside the 2014 HTC One (M8) on March 25, 2014. Based on Android 4.4 "KitKat", it is similar to Sense 5, but offers new customization options (such as color themes and new font choices), increased use of transparency effects (particularly on the home screen, and on Sense 6.0 devices which use on-screen buttons), and updates to some of its included apps. BlinkFeed, Gallery, TV, and Zoe are now updated independently of Sense through Google Play Store.

The HTC One (2013), One Mini and One Max are updated to 6.0 via a software update.

Sense 7.0 (2015)

Sense 7.0 was announced at the Mobile World Congress on March 1, 2015 alongside the HTC One M9. It is based on Android 5.0 "Lollipop", and is largely the same as Sense 6.0 as far as the default user interface is concerned, save for a few tweaked icons and a new weather clock widget. Perhaps the most notable new feature is the new user interface theming app (simply called "Themes"), which allows users to alter the color schemes, icons, sounds, and fonts throughout the operating system. Users can either create their own themes from scratch or download pre-made ones created by HTC or fellow users. Another major new feature is the ability to customize the navigation buttons across the bottom of the display; users can now change their order and add a fourth button, such as a power button or one that hides the navigation bar altogether.

Advertisements in Blinkfeed

HTC confirmed that advertisements will be displayed in the Blinkfeed. However, HTC has given the option for the user to opt-out from receiving these advertisements. In August 2015, owners of HTC M8 and M9 in the United States reported in reddit that they have received a push-notification promoting the upcoming Fantastic Four movie theme.

List of Devices with HTC Sense

Sense 8.0

- HTC 10

Sense 7.0

- HTC One A9
- HTC Desire 626
- HTC Desire 828
- HTC One M9
- HTC One E9s
- HTC One E9+
- HTC One M8 (via software update)
- HTC One ME
- HTC Desire 728
- HTC Desire Eye (via software update)

Sense 6.1

- HTC Desire 510

Sense 6.0

- HTC One (M8)
- HTC One (via software update)
- HTC One Max (via software update)
- HTC One Mini 2
- HTC One Mini (via software update)
- HTC One E8
- HTC One (M8 EYE)
- HTC Butterfly S (via Android 4.4.2 update)
- HTC Butterfly 2
- HTC Desire 816G
- HTC Desire 816
- HTC Desire 610
- HTC Desire 620
- HTC Desire 820

- HTC Desire 820Q

- HTC Desire 826

- HTC Desire Eye

- HTC Droid DNA (via Flashing a ROM)

Sense 5.5

- HTC Butterfly/Droid DNA (via Android 4.4 update)

- HTC Desire 601 (via Android 4.4 update)

- HTC One (via software update)

- HTC One Max

- HTC One Mini (via software update)

Sense 5.0

- HTC Desire 700 dual sim

- HTC Desire 616

- HTC Desire 601

- HTC Desire 300

- HTC Desire 600

- HTC Desire 500

- HTC Desire 310

- HTC Butterfly S

- HTC One Mini

- HTC One

- HTC One X+ (via Android 4.2 update)

- HTC Evo 4G LTE (via Android 4.3 update)

- HTC One X (via Android 4.2 update, international version only)

- HTC One XL (via Android 4.2 update, international version only)

- HTC Butterfly/Droid DNA (via Android 4.2 update)

- HTC One SV (via Android 4.2 update)

Sense 4+

- HTC Desire 501
- HTC One X+
- HTC One X (via Android 4.1 update)
- HTC One S (via Android 4.1 update)
- HTC Evo 4G LTE (via Android 4.1 update)
- HTC J
- HTC Butterfly/Droid DNA
- HTC One SV (via Android 4.1 update)
- HTC Desire X (via Android 4.1 update)

Sense 4.1

- HTC One S (via software update)
- HTC Desire X
- HTC One SV
- HTC One X (via software update)
- HTC One VX

Sense 4.0

- HTC Desire 200
- HTC One V
- HTC One X
- HTC One S
- HTC Desire C
- HTC Desire V
- HTC Desire VC
- HTC Droid Incredible 4G LTE

Sense 3.6

Sense 3.6 is exclusively obtained through Android 4.0 updates for existing devices.

- HTC Sensation XL
- HTC Sensation XE
- HTC Sensation
- HTC Evo 3D (pre-loaded on Virgin Mobile version)
- HTC Evo Design 4G (pre-loaded on Boost Mobile version)
- HTC Incredible S (all variants)
- HTC Rezound
- HTC Desire S
- HTC Sensation 4G

Sense 3.5

- HTC Desire S
- HTC Desire HD/HTC Inspire 4G
- HTC Explorer
- HTC Rhyme

Sense 2.0 / 2.1

- HTC ChaCha (Sense 2.1 for Messenger)
- HTC Salsa (Sense 2.1 for Messenger)
- HTC Desire Z
- HTC Desire
- HTC Flyer (Sense 2.1 for Tablet)
- HTC Jetstream (Sense 2.1 for Tablet)
- HTC Wildfire S

Sense 1.0

- HTC Evo Shift 4G
- HTC EVO 4G
- HTC Droid Incredible
- HTC Aria / Gratia
- HTC Legend
- HTC Wildfire

- HTC Merge

Original Sense

- HTC Droid Eris

- HTC Hero / HTC Hero CDMA (Sprint)

- HTC Tattoo

Espresso Sense

- T-Mobile myTouch 3G Slide: Espresso Sense 1.0

- T-Mobile myTouch 4G: Espresso Sense 2.0

- T-Mobile myTouch 4G Slide: Espresso Sense 3.0

HTC Devices Without Sense

Most HTC devices released since the introduction of Sense incorporate it, but several do not, including the Nexus One (released as the first device in the Nexus series), the T-Mobile G2 (a variation of the HTC Desire Z with stock Android), the HTC First (after Facebook Home is disabled), and a special edition HTC One released on Google Play in June 2013. In March 2014 HTC announced the Desire 310 running Android 4.2.2 with the addition of Blinkfeed and Video Highlights. Like predecessor the HTC One (M8) also got a Google Play Edition, running Android 4.4.2. The Nexus 9 Tablet was unveiled by Google on October 15, 2014 running Android 5.0.

CyanogenMod

CyanogenMod, usually abbreviated to CM, is an open-source operating system for smartphones and tablet computers, based on the Android mobile platform. It is developed as free and open source software based on the official releases of Android by Google, with added original and third-party code. It is based on a rolling release development model.

CyanogenMod offers features and options not found in the official firmware distributed by mobile device vendors. Features supported by CyanogenMod include native theming support, FLAC audio codec support, a large Access Point Name list, *Privacy Guard* (per-application permission management application), support for tethering over common interfaces, CPU overclocking and other performance enhancements, unlockable bootloader and root access, soft buttons and other "tablet tweaks", toggles in the notification pull-down (such as Wi-Fi, Bluetooth and GPS), and other interface enhancements. CyanogenMod does not contain spyware or bloatware, according to its developers. CyanogenMod is also said to increase performance and reliability compared with official firmware releases.

Although only a subset of total CyanogenMod users elect to report their use of the firmware, as of March 23, 2015, some reports indicate that over 50 million people run CyanogenMod on their phones.

In 2013, project founder Steve Kondik announced that venture funding had been obtained to establish Cyanogen Inc. as a commercial enterprise to develop and market the firmware more widely. This announcement has led to controversy within the community, with some developers asserting that rights and licensing issues, acknowledging/compensating past developers and honoring the original ethos of the community project, are not being adequately addressed. These claims were rejected by Kondik, who affirmed support for the community and stated that most CyanogenMod code, as with Android generally, is bound by a non-restrictive Apache license.

History and Development

Soon after the introduction of HTC Dream (named the "T-Mobile G1" in the United States) mobile phone in September 2008, a method was discovered to attain privileged control (termed "root access") within Android's Linux-based subsystem. Having root access, combined with the open source nature of the Android operating system, allowed the phone's stock firmware to be modified and re-installed onto the phone.

In the following year, modified firmwares for the Dream were developed and distributed by Android enthusiasts. One, maintained by a developer named *JesusFreke*, became popular among Dream owners. In August 2009, JesusFreke stopped work on his firmware, and suggested users switch to a version of his ROM that had been further enhanced by developer *Cyanogen* (Steve Kondik) called "CyanogenMod".

CyanogenMod grew in popularity, and a community of developers, called the CyanogenMod Team (and informally "Team Douche") made contributions. Within a few months, the number of devices and features supported by CyanogenMod blossomed, and CyanogenMod became one of the popular Android firmware distributions.

Similar to many open source projects, CyanogenMod is developed using a distributed revision control system with the official repositories being hosted on GitHub. Contributors submit new features or bugfix changes using Gerrit. Contributions may be tested by anyone, voted up or down by registered users, and ultimately accepted into the code by one of a handful of CyanogenMod developers.

A version of ADW.Launcher, an alternative launcher (home screen) for the Android operating system, became the default launcher on CyanogenMod 5.0.8. The launcher provides additional features not provided by the default Android launcher, including more customization abilities (including icon themes, effects, and behavior), the ability to backup and restore configuration settings, and other features. As of version 9, CyanogenMod's own launcher, Trebuchet, is included with the firmware.

Initially, CyanogenMod releases were provided on a nightly, milestone, and "stable version" schedule; as of CyanogenMod 11 M6, the "stable" label will no longer be used, having been supplanted by "milestone" *M-builds* that are part of the CyanogenMod's rolling release development model.

Some unofficial builds for supported devices are listed in CyanogenMod.

Current CyanogenMod version list:

- CyanogenMod 3 (based on Android "Cupcake" 1.5.x, initial release)
- CyanogenMod 4 (based on Android "Cupcake" and "Donut" 1.5.x and 1.6.x)

- CyanogenMod 5 (based on Android "Eclair" 2.0/2.1)

- CyanogenMod 6 (based on Android "Froyo" 2.2.x)

- CyanogenMod 7 (based on Android "Gingerbread" 2.3.x)

- CyanogenMod 9 (based on Android "Ice Cream Sandwich" 4.0.x, major UI revamp)

- CyanogenMod 10 (based on Android "Jelly Bean" 4.1.x – 4.3.x)

- CyanogenMod 11 (based on Android "KitKat" 4.4.x)

- CyanogenMod 12 (based on Android "Lollipop" 5.0.x – 5.1.x, major UI revamp)

- CyanogenMod 13 (based on Android "Marshmallow" 6.0.x)

- CyanogenMod 14 (based on Android "Nougat" 7.0.x)

CyanogenMod 7

CyanogenMod 7 firmware is based on Android 2.3 Gingerbread with additional custom code contributed by the CyanogenMod Team. The custom portions of CyanogenMod are primarily written by Cyanogen (Steve Kondik) but include contributions from the xda-developers community (such as an improved launcher tray, dialer, and browser) and code from established open source projects (such as BusyBox in the shell).

CyanogenMod 7 development began when Google released Android 2.3's source code. On 15 February 2011, the first release candidates of CyanogenMod 7 were rolled out on several of the supported devices. The fourth release candidate was released on 30 March 2011 and brought increased support for the Nook Color and similar devices as well as many bug fixes. On 11 April 2011, the public version of CyanogenMod 7.0 was released, based on Android 2.3.3. CyanogenMod 7.1 was released on 10 October 2011, based on Android 2.3.4. The latest stable version, CyanogenMod 7.2 was released on 16 June 2012, based on Android 2.3.7, bringing a predictive phone dialer, lockscreen updates, ICS animation backports and many bug fixes.

A Motorola Flipout displaying the CyanogenMod 7.2 (Android 2.3) boot animation.

CyanogenMod 8

CyanogenMod version 8 was planned to be based on Android 3.x Honeycomb. However, as the source code for Honeycomb wasn't provided by Google until it appeared in the source tree history of its successor, Android 4.0 Ice Cream Sandwich, the release schedule advanced from Cyanogen-Mod 7 (Gingerbread) directly to CyanogenMod 9 (Ice Cream Sandwich).

CyanogenMod 9

CyanogenMod 9 is based on Google's Android 4.0 Ice Cream Sandwich and the first version of CyanogenMod to use the Trebuchet launcher. Steve Kondik and his team have announced that they had begun work on the new release after Google released the source code of Android 4.0.1. Development on this release took longer than with previous releases due to the significance of the changes between Android 2.3 "Gingerbread" and 4.0 "Ice Cream Sandwich", and the team took this opportunity to clarify their vision for the ROM and rethink any modifications which were no longer necessary due to improvements within Android.

By the last days of November 2011, some alpha versions had been distributed, in particular for the Samsung mobile phones Nexus S and Galaxy S. On 9 August 2012, after various betas and release candidates, CyanogenMod released the finished version of CyanogenMod 9. Given that the next version of Android, 4.1 "Jelly Bean", had already been released by that point, development moved swiftly on to CyanogenMod 10. On 29 August 2012, CyanogenMod released a minor update, version 9.1.0, bringing bugfixes and an app called SimplyTapp for NFC payments.

On 4 April 2012, during development, CyanogenMod unveiled "Cid", the new CyanogenMod mascot, which replaced the previous mascot, Andy the skateboarding "bugdroid". Designed by user *Ciao*, Cid (C.I.D.) is an abbreviation of "Cyanogenmod ID".

CyanogenMod 10

CyanogenMod 10.0

> In early July 2012, the CyanogenMod team announced, via its Google+ account, that Cy-anogenMod 10 would be based on Android 4.1 Jelly Bean. Nightly builds of CyanogenMod 10 were made available for many devices supported by CyanogenMod 9. Starting with the September 2012 M1 build, the CyanogenMod team began monthly "M-series" releases. At the beginning of each month, a soft freeze of the CyanogenMod codebase is put into effect; once the team deems a build stable enough for daily use, it is released under the milestone or "M" series.

> On 13 November 2012, final stable builds were released for several devices.

CyanogenMod 10.1

> CyanogenMod 10.1 is based on Android 4.2 Jelly Bean. Nightly versions are currently being released for an array of devices, along with M Snapshots (Monthly Snapshots) which are being released for select devices.

> On 24 June 2013, the CyanogenMod 10.1.0 codebase (based on Android version 4.2.2) was

moved to "stable" status, with a majority of currently-supported devices receiving stable builds on the same day. CyanogenMod's developers have indicated that they will continue the Monthly Snapshot schedule to incorporate new features until the next Cyanogenmod release. Unfortunately, many devices utilizing Samsung Exynos and Nvidia Tegra 2 SoC's were not part of the initial release.

CyanogenMod 10.2

The first nightly release of CyanogenMod 10.2, which is based on Android 4.3 Jelly Bean, began rolling out for a selected number of devices on 14 August 2013. It brings in some new enhancements to the system, such as Bluetooth Low Energy and OpenGL ES 3.0 support, a renewed Phone app, 4K resolution support as well as many security and stability improvements.

CyanogenMod 11

CyanogenMod 11

On 6 November 2013 the CyanogenMod team started pushing the code of CyanogenMod 11, based on Android 4.4 KitKat, to GitHub. The first nightly release of CyanogenMod 11.0 began rolling out for a selected number of devices on 5 December 2013. Since then, M-builds have been released every month for supported devices, offering a more stable experience than nightlies. With build M6 it was clarified that CyanogenMod would no longer be releasing final builds specially tagged "stable", but instead would utilize the rolling release model with M-builds representing a stable channel.

The global OnePlus One is shipped with a variant of CyanogenMod 11 M9 known as "Cyanogen-Mod 11S". The latest version of CyanogenMod 11S for the One is 11.0-XNPH05Q, based on Cyano-genMod 11 M11 and Android 4.4.4 "KitKat", and was released as an over-the-air (OTA) update in February 2015.

CyanogenMod 12

The first nightly release of CyanogenMod 12, based on Android 5.0 Lollipop, began rolling out for a selected number of devices on 6 January 2015. A stable snapshot was released on 25 June 2015 and a security patch snapshot was released on 1 September 2015.

Cyanogen OS 12, a variant of CyanogenMod 12 for the OnePlus One and Yu Yureka was released in April 2015. Yu Yuphoria got Cyanogen OS 12 out-of-the-box when it was launched in May 2015.

CyanogenMod 12.1

The first nightly release of CyanogenMod 12.1, based on Android 5.1, was announced on 16 April 2015. A stable snapshot build was released on 1 September 2015 but nightly builds continue to roll out every day.

Lenovo ZUK Z1, Wileyfox Swift and Storm got Cyanogen OS 12.1 out-of-the-box when it was launched in September 2015. YU's Yureka, Yureka Plus, and Yuphoria got a Cyanogen OS 12.1 OTA update.

CyanogenMod 13

The first nightly release of CyanogenMod 13.0, based on Android 6.0, was released on 23 November 2015 for a small number of devices, but was gradually developed for other devices. A few weeks after the first nightly release of CyanogenMod 13.0 for Android 6.0, CyanogenMod was given a minor update, and was based on Android 6.0.1. First stable builds were released on 2016-03-15.

CyanogenMod 14.0

Although no official statement has been made, it is presumed CyanogenMod are not writing code for CyanogenMod 14. They have skipped to producing nightly builds for CyanogenMod 14.1 instead. Code initially written for CyanogenMod 14 is now being cherry-picked into the cm-14.1 branch.

CyanogenMod 14.1

The first experimental build of Cyanogenmod 14.1 based on Android 7.1 was released for Oneplus 3 device. on 4 November 2016. On 8 November 2016, official nightlies began for angler (Huawei Nexus 6P), bullhead (LG Nexus 5X), cancro (Xiaomi Mi3w/Mi4), d855 (LG G3), falcon/peregrine/thea/titan (Moto G variants), h811/h815 (LG G4), klte/kltedv/kltespr/klteusc/kltevzw (Samsung Galaxy S5), oneplus3 (OnePlus 3), Z00L/Z00T (Zenphone 2). It is missing some of the signature features of CyanogenMod however, and is considered a "work in progress". This version will add multi-window support.

Cyanogen Inc.

Cyanogen Inc. is a venture funded company with offices in Seattle and Palo Alto, California, announced officially in September 2013, which aims to commercialize CyanogenMod.

Cyanogen logo from March 2015

Cyanogen logo from April 2014

The funding was led by Mitch Lasky of Benchmark and raised $7 million.

Commercialization Controversy

Rumors of plans to commercialize CyanogenMod as well as the subsequent announcement of Cyanogen Inc. has led to a certain level of discord within the CyanogenMod community. Several CyanogenMod developers have raised concerns that developers who had provided their work in the past were not being appropriately acknowledged or compensated for their free work on what was now a commercial project, further that the original ethos of the community project was being undermined and that these concerns were not being adequately addressed by Cyanogen Inc. Examples include the "Focal" camera app developer Guillaume Lesniak ("'xplodwild') whose app was withdrawn from CyanogenMod allegedly following demands by the new company to adopt closed-source modifications and licensing.

In response, Steve Kondik affirmed commitment to the community, stating that the majority of CyanogenMod historically did not use GPL but the Apache licence (the same license used by Google for Android), and dual licensing was being proposed in order to offer "a stronger degree of protection for contributors... while still offering CM some of the freedoms that the Apache license offers":

 Google has gone to great lengths to avoid the GPL by building their own low level components such as Dalvik and Bionic. In CM, the only GPL component that currently comes to mind that we've added is our Torch app (originally called Nexus One Torch) [...] The Apache license specifically ALLOWS precisely what you suggest it doesn't. A dual-license would do the same, but also protect contributors by forcing unaffiliated entities to contribute back if they use the software in a commercial context. It's not so that CM can close the source and still ship it to our users. Again, we don't have any plans to change licenses.

Focal is a special case– it has to be GPL because [...] Focal uses a number of GPL components under the hood [...] I proposed the dual-license extension as a way to work around some of the inherent problems with the GPL and give a greater degree of freedom to both him and CM as an organization. This is a very common licensing model in the open-source world.

But none of this matters. We're not closing the source or changing the license of any code that has been contributed to the project.

Developer *Entropy512* also observed that CyanogenMod was legally bound by its position to make some of the firmware changes, because of the Android license and marketing conditions ("CTS terms") which specify what apps may and may not do, and these were raised in part by Android developers at Google informally speculatively as a result of perceptions of CyanogenMod's high profile in the market.

In his 2013 blog post on Cyanogen's funding, venture funder Mitch Lasky stated:

> Benchmark has a long history of supporting open source projects intent on becoming successful enterprises. Our open source history includes Red Hat, MySQL, SpringSource, JBoss, Eucalyptus, Zimbra, Elasticsearch, HortonWorks, and now Cyanogen. We've been behind many of the most successful open source software companies in the world. We have a deep respect for the special needs of these businesses, and how to build companies while preserving the transparency and vigor of the open source communities.

In January 2015, it was reported that Microsoft had invested in Cyanogen, and that this might be part of a strategy to create an Android version that worked well with Microsoft platforms. In April 2015, Cyanogen announced a strategic partnership with Microsoft, to integrate Microsoft apps and services into Cyanogen OS. In January 2016, Cyanogen rolled out an update that started advertising Microsoft applications when a user attempts to open certain file types on Cyanogen OS phones.

Industry Reaction

Early responses of tablet and smartphone manufacturers and mobile carriers were typically unsupportive of third-party firmware development such as CyanogenMod. Manufacturers expressed concern about improper functioning of devices running unofficial software and the related support costs. Moreover, modified firmwares such as CyanogenMod sometimes offer features for which carriers would otherwise charge a premium (e.g., tethering). As a result, technical obstacles including locked bootloaders and restricted access to root permissions were common in many devices.

However, as community-developed software has grown more popular and following a statement by the U.S. Library of Congress that permits "jailbreaking" mobile devices, manufacturers and carriers have softened their position regarding CyanogenMod and other unofficial firmware distributions, with some, including HTC, Motorola, Samsung and Sony Ericsson, providing support and encouraging development. As a result of this, in 2011 the need to circumvent hardware restrictions to install unofficial firmware lessened as an increasing number of devices shipped with unlocked or unlockable bootloaders, similar to the Nexus series of phones. Device manufacturers HTC and Motorola announced that they would support aftermarket software developers by making the bootloaders of all new devices unlockable, although this still violates a device's warranty. Samsung sent several Galaxy S II phones to the CyanogenMod team with the express purpose of bringing CyanogenMod to the device, and mobile carrier T-Mobile USA voiced its support for the CyanogenMod project, tweeting "CM7 is great!".

Phone manufacturers have also taken to releasing "developer editions" of phones that are unlocked.

Licensing

Until version 4.1.11.1, CyanogenMod included proprietary software applications provided by Google, such as Gmail, Maps, Android Market (now known as Play Store), Talk (now Hangouts), and YouTube, as well as proprietary hardware drivers. These packages were included with the vendor distributions of Android, but not licensed for free distribution. After Google sent a cease and desist letter to CyanogenMod's chief developer, Steve Kondik, in late September 2009 demanding he stop distributing the aforementioned applications, development ceased for a few days. The reaction from many CyanogenMod users towards Google was hostile, with some claiming that Google's legal threats hurt their own interests, violated their informal corporate motto "Don't be evil" and was a challenge to the open-source community Google claimed to embrace.

Following a statement from Google clarifying its position and a subsequent negotiation between Google and Cyanogen, it was resolved that the CyanogenMod project would continue, in a form that did not directly bundle in the proprietary "Google Experience" components. It was determined that the proprietary Google apps may be backed-up from the Google-supplied firmware on the phone and then re-installed onto CyanogenMod releases without infringing copyright.

On 28 September 2009, Cyanogen warned that while issues no longer remain with Google, there were still potential licensing problems regarding proprietary, closed-source device drivers. On 30 September 2009, Cyanogen posted an update on the matter. Kondik wrote he was rebuilding the source tree, and that he believed the licensing issues with drivers could be worked out. He added that he was also receiving assistance from Google employees. On 16 June 2012, the CyanogenMod 7.2 release announcement stated, "CyanogenMod does still include various hardware-specific code, which is also slowly being open-sourced anyway."

Replicant is a CyanogenMod fork that removes all proprietary software and drivers and thus avoids all aforementioned legal issues. However, Replicant does not support devices which depend on proprietary drivers, which is most phones as of 2016.

Version history

CyanogenMod main version	Android version	Last or major release	Recommended build release date	Notable changes
3	Android 1.5 (Cupcake)	3.6.8.1	1 July 2009	3.6.8 onwards based on Android 1.5r3
		3.9.3	22 July 2009	3.9.3 onwards has FLAC support
4	Android 1.5/1.6 (Cupcake/ Donut)	4.1.4	30 August 2009	4.1.4 onwards based on Android 1.6 (Donut); QuickOffice removed from 4.1.4 onwards; Google proprietary software separated due to cease and desist from 4.1.99 onwards
		4.2.15.1	24 October 2009	4.2.3 onwards has USB tethering support; 4.2.6 onwards based on Android 1.6r2; 4.2.11 onwards added pinch zoom for Browser, pinch zoom and swipe for Gallery.
5	Android 2.0/2.1 (Eclair)	5.0.8	19 July 2010	Introduced ADW.Launcher as the default launcher.

CyanogenMod main version	Android version	Last or major release	Recommended build release date	Notable changes
6	Android 2.2 (Froyo)	6.0.0	28 August 2010	Introduced dual camera and ad hoc Wi-Fi support, Just-in-time (JIT) compiler for more performance
		6.1.3	6 December 2010	6.1.0 onwards based on Android 2.2.1.
7	Android 2.3 (Gingerbread)	7.0.3	10 April 2011	7.0.0 onwards based on Android 2.3.3
		7.1.0	10 October 2011	Based on Android 2.3.7
		7.2.0	16 June 2012	New devices, updated translations, predictive phone dialer, ability to control haptic feedback in quiet hours, lockscreen updates, ICS animation backports, ability to configure the battery status bar icon, many bug fixes
8	Android 3.x (Honeycomb)	N/A	N/A	CyanogenMod 8 was never released due to Google not releasing the source code for Android 3.0 Honeycomb.
9	Android 4.0 (Ice Cream Sandwich)	9.1	29 August 2012	Advanced security: deactivated root usage by default. Added support for SimplyTapp. Introduced Cyanogen's own launcher, Trebuchet.
10	Android 4.1 (Jelly Bean)	10.0.0	13 November 2012	Expandable desktop mode. Built-in, root-enabled file manager.
	Android 4.2 (Jelly Bean)	10.1.3	24 June 2013	
	Android 4.3 (Jelly Bean)	10.2.1	31 January 2014	Phone: *Blacklist*-Feature added.
11	Android 4.4 (KitKat)	11.0 XNG3C	31 August 2015	*WhisperPush*: Integration of TextSecure's (now Signal's) end-to-end encryption protocol as an opt-in feature. Enabled sending encrypted instant messages to other users of CM and Signal. This feature was discontinued in February 2016. *CyanogenMod ThemeEngine*: new powerful theme engine that let user apply and mix custom themes that can edit resources file
12	Android 5.0 (Lollipop)	12.0 YNG4N	1 September 2015	*LiveDisplay*: advanced display management tool, with features such as color, gamma, saturation and temperature calibration *Updates to theme engine*: allows now separate theming for packages (used on CyanogenMod for NavigationBar and StatusBar, on CyanogenOS for AppThemer, which allows you to apply a different theme for each app) *UI Revamp*: all applications have been updated to the material theme *AudioFX and Eleven*: two new audio-related apps (AudioFX replacing DSPManager and Eleven replacing Music)
	Android 5.1 (Lollipop)	12.1 YOG7DAO	27 January 2016	*CyanogenPlatform SDK*: allows third-party developers to add custom APIs to integrate their app with CyanogenMod

CyanogenMod main version	Android version	Last or major release	Recommended build release date	Notable changes
13	Android 6.0 (Marshmallow)	13.0 ZNH5Y	15 August 2016	Wi-Fi Tethering, profiles, Do Not Disturb/ Priority Mode, Privacy Guard/App data usage, Bluetooth Devices battery support, reintroduction of Lockscreen Wallpaper picker, Lockscreen Weather and new Weather plug-in support, Lockscreen Blur support and the ability to disable the effect, Live Lockscreen support, new LiveDisplay hardware enhancements and API, Snap Camera, Gello Browser, improved translations, Cyanogen Apps support, additional CM SDK APIs, security fixes
14	Android 7.0 (Nougat)	N/A		Skipped, since Google soon released 7.1 before the development of CM 14.0 is completed.
	Android 7.1 (Nougat)	14.1	9 November 2016	CM14.1 is considered a "work in progress" and missing some of the signature features of CyanogenMod. Changelog is unknown.

Legend:

   Old version   Older version, still supported   Latest version   Latest preview version   Future release

Cyanogen OS

Cyanogen commercially develops operating systems pre-installed on some devices (OnePlus One, YU Yureka, YU Yuphoria, Andromax Q, BQ Aquaris X5, Lenovo ZUK Z1, Wileyfox Swift, Wileyfox Storm) based upon the CyanogenMod source code.

Cyanogen OS is often distributed with additional bundled proprietary apps such as the Google Play ecosystem, and a suite of software unique to Cyanogen OS known as C-Apps. CyanogenMod does not include either by default, but users can obtain them separately if they wish.

Initially distinguished with the suffix -S *(CyanogenMod 11S)*, with version 12 Cyanogen rebranded the custom offering as Cyanogen OS. Cyanogen started pushing Cyanogen OS 13 based on Android 6.0.1 to OnePlus One phones OTA on April 9, 2016 phase wise by the code name ZNH0EAS26M. CyanogenMod can be installed on Cyanogen OS devices.

Differences between Cyanogenmod and Cyanogen OS

Name	Stock or replacement firmware?	Based on:	Pre-installed or manual installation required?	Root access (Superuser)?	Developers:
Cyanogen OS	Stock firmware pre-installed on some smartphones.	Android Open Source Project.	Comes pre-installed on some devices.	No	Cyanogen
CyanogenMod	Replacement firmware for devices with Android pre-installed.		Manual installation required	Yes	Cyanogen and The CyanogenMod community

Supported Devices

CyanogenMod officially supports a large number of devices, including most Nexus and Google Play Edition devices. It provides SNAPSHOT (stable) and NIGHTLY builds for more than 150 devices (on the current development branch).

Network Operating System

The term network operating system is used to refer to two rather different concepts:

- A specialised operating system for a network device such as a router, switch or firewall.

- An operating system oriented to computer networking, to allow shared file and printer access among multiple computers in a network, to enable the sharing of data, users, groups, security, applications, and other networking functions. Typically over a local area network (LAN), or private network. This sense is now largely historical, as common operating systems generally now have such features included.

Network Device Operating Systems

Network operating systems can be embedded in a router or hardware firewall that operates the functions in the network layer (layer 3).

- Examples:

    o JUNOS, used in routers and switches from Juniper Networks

    o Cisco Internetwork Operating System (IOS)

    o TiMOS, used in routers from Alcatel-Lucent

    o Versatile Routing Platform (VRP), used in routers from Huawei

    o RouterOS, software which turns a PC or MikroTik hardware into a dedicated router

    o ZyNOS, used in network devices made by ZyXEL.

    o Extensible Operating System used in switches from Arista

    o ExtremeXOS (EXOS), used in network devices made by Extreme Networks

    o Embedded Linux, in distributions like Openwrt and DD-WRT which run on low-cost platforms such as the Linksys WRT54G

- Open source network operating system examples:

    o Cumulus Linux distribution, which uses the full TCP/IP stack of Linux.

    o Dell Networking Operating System (DNOS) is the new name for the operating system running on switches from Dell Networking; it will run atop NetBSD o   Open Network Operating System (ONOS)

o   PicOS, Linux-based OpenFlow-supporting switching operating system from made by Pica8

o   VyOS, an open source fork of the Vyatta routing package

o   OpenSwitch Linux Network Operating System from Hewlett-Packard.

Historic Network Operating Systems

Early microcomputer operating systems such as CP/M, DOS and classic Mac OS were designed for one user on one computer. As local area network technology became available, two general approaches to handle sharing arose.

Peer-to-peer

In a peer-to-peer network operating system users are allowed to share resources and files located on their computers and access shared resources from others. This system is not based with having a file server or centralized management source. A peer-to-peer network sets all connected computers equal; they all share the same abilities to use resources available on the network.

- Examples:

  o   AppleShare used for networking connecting Apple products.

  o   LANtastic supporting DOS, Microsoft Windows, and OS/2 computers

  o   Windows for Workgroups used for networking peer-to-peer Windows computers.

The advantages include:

- Ease of setup

- Less hardware needed, no server need be acquired

The disadvantages include:

- No central location for storage

- Less security than the client–server model

Client-server

Network operating systems can be based on a client–server model (architecture) in which a server enables multiple clients to share resources. Client-server network operating systems allow networks to centralize functions and applications in one or more dedicated file servers. The server is the center of the system, allowing access to resources and instituting security. The network operating system provides the mechanism to integrate all the components on a network to allow multiple users to simultaneously share the same resources regardless of physical location.

- Examples:
  - Novell NetWare
  - Windows Server
  - Banyan VINES

The advantages include:

- Centralized servers are more stable.

- Security is provided through the server.

- New technology and hardware can be easily integrated into the system.

- Hardware and the operating system can be specialized, with a focus on performance.

- Servers are able to be accessed remotely from different locations and types of systems.

The disadvantages include:

- Buying and running a server raises costs.

- Dependence on a central location for operation.

- Requires regular maintenance and updates.

Junos OS

Junos OS (more formally Juniper Network Operating System) is the FreeBSD-based operating system used in Juniper Networks hardware routers. It is an operating system that is used in Juniper's routing, switching and security devices. Juniper offers a Software Development Kit (SDK) to partners and customers to allow additional customization. The biggest competitor of Junos is Cisco Systems' IOS.

Junos OS was formerly branded as Juniper Junos, and is commonly referred to as simply Junos, though this is a general brand name of Juniper Networks, including other product lines such as Junos Fusion.

Versioning

Junos provides a single code base across most of Juniper's platforms. Juniper has issued a new release of Junos every 90 days since 1998.

Features

Junos supports a variety of routing protocols. With the introduction of the SRX and J-series (past version 9.3) platforms, it also supports "flow mode", which includes stateful firewalling, NAT, and IPSec. Its a flexible routing policy language that is used for controlling route advertisements and path selection.

Junos generally adheres to industry standards for routing and MPLS.

The operating system supports high availability mechanisms that are not standard to Unix, such as Graceful Restart.

Architecture

Junos operating system is primarily based on FreeBSD. Because FreeBSD offers a Unix-like environment, customers can access a Unix shell and execute normal Unix commands. Junos runs on most or all Juniper hardware systems. After Juniper acquired NetScreen, it integrated ScreenOS security functions into its own Junos network operating system.

Junos Command Line Interface (CLI)

The Junos CLI is a text-based command interface for configuring, troubleshooting, and monitoring the Juniper device and network traffic associated with it. It supports two types of command modes.

- Operational Mode

- Configuration Mode

The functions of *Operational Mode* include control of the CLI environment, monitoring of hardware status, and display of information about network data that passes though or into the hardware. The *Configuration mode* is used for configuring the Juniper router, switch, or security device, by adding, deleting, or modifying statements in the configuration hierarchy.

Junos SDK

Through the Juniper Developer Network (JDN) Juniper Networks provides the Junos SDK to its customers and 3rd-party developers who want to develop applications for Junos-powered devices such as Juniper Networks routers, switches, and service gateway systems. It provides a set of tools and application programming interfaces (APIs), including interfaces to Junos routing, firewall filter, UI and traffic services functions. Juniper Networks also employs the Junos SDK internally to develop parts of Junos and many Junos applications such as OpenFlow for Junos, and other traffic services.

Market Share

Juniper as of June 13, 2008 had 5 percent of the $4.2 billion enterprise-router market, 18 percent of the $4.7 billion service-provider edge-router market and 30 percent of the $2.7 billion service-provider core-router market, according to the Dell'Oro Group.

ZyNOS

ZyNOS is the proprietary operating system used on network devices made by the ZyXEL Communications Corporation. The name is a contraction of ZyXEL and Network Operating System (NOS).

History

The ZyXEL Communications Corporation first introduced ZyNOS in 1998.

Versions

ZyXEL released ZyNOS version 4.0 for their GS2200 series 24 and 48 port ethernet switches in April, 2012. It appears that versions differ between ZyXEL products.

Access Methods

Web and/or command line interface (CLI) depending on the device. Web access is accomplished by connecting an ethernet cable between a PC and an open port on the device and entering the IP address of the device into the Web browser. An RS-232 serial console port is provided on some devices for CLI access, which is accomplished by using SSH or telnet.

CLI Command Types

Listed below are the categories that the CLI commands are grouped by.

- system-related commands
- exit command
- Ethernet-related commands
- WAN-related commands
- WLAN-related commands
- IP-related commands
- PPP-related commands
- bridge-related commands
- RADIUS-related commands
- 802.1x-related commands
- firewall-related commands
- configuration-related commands
- SMT-related commands.

Web Configurator

The Web Configurator is divided into the following categories:

- basic settings
- advanced application
- IP application
- management

Security Advisories

As of March 2014, Danish computer security company Secunia reports no unpatched advisories or vulnerabilities on ZyNOS version 4.x.

As of March 2014, Secunia reports seven advisories and six vulnerabilities on ZyNOS version 3.x. Five advisories are unpatched; Secunia rates the most severe unpatched advisory as less critical.

As of January 2015, a DNS vulnerability has been found in certain ZyNOS firmware versions. The versions that are affected have not been narrowed down. The attack can be done from a remote location regardless if the user interface is accessible from the outside of a LAN.

Cisco Systems

Cisco Systems, Inc. (known as Cisco) is an American multinational technology conglomerate head-quartered in San José, California, that develops, manufactures, and sells networking hardware, telecommunications equipment, and other high-technology services and products. Through its numerous acquired subsidiaries, such as OpenDNS, Cisco Meraki, and Cisco Jasper, Cisco specializes into specific tech markets, such as Internet of Things (IoT), domain security, and energy management.

Cisco is the largest networking company in the world. The stock was added to the Dow Jones Industrial Average on June 8, 2009, and is also included in the S&P 500 Index, the Russell 1000 Index, NASDAQ-100 Index and the Russell 1000 Growth Stock Index.

Cisco Systems was founded in December 1984 by Leonard Bosack and Sandy Lerner, two Stanford University computer scientists, who pioneered the concept of a local area network (LAN) being used to connect geographically disparate computers over a multiprotocol router system, which was unheard of technology at the time. By the time the company went public in 1990, when it was listed on the NASDAQ, Cisco had a market capitalization of $224 million. Cisco was the most valuable company in the world by 2000, with a more than $500 billion market capitalization.

History

1984–1995: Origins and Initial Growth

Leonard Bosack (pictured) and Sandy Lerner, two Stanford University computer scientists, founded Cisco in 1984.

Cisco Systems was founded in December 1984 by Leonard Bosack, who was in charge of the Stanford University computer science department's computers, and his wife Sandy Lerner, who managed the Graduate School of Business' computers.

Despite founding Cisco in 1984, Bosack, along with Kirk Lougheed, continued to work at Stanford on Cisco's first product. It consisted of exact replicas of Stanford's "Blue Box" router and a stolen copy of the University's multiple-protocol router software. The software was originally written some years earlier at Stanford medical school by research engineer William Yeager. Bosack and Lougheed adapted it into what became the foundation for Cisco IOS. On July 11, 1986, Bosack and Lougheed were forced to resign from Stanford and the university contemplated filing criminal complaints against Cisco and its founders for the theft of its software, hardware designs and other intellectual properties. In 1987, Stanford licensed the router software and two computer boards to Cisco.

In addition to Bosack, Lerner and Lougheed, Greg Satz, a programmer, and Richard Troiano, who handled sales, completed the early Cisco team. The company's first CEO was Bill Graves, who held the position from 1987 to 1988. In 1988, John Morgridge was appointed CEO.

The name "Cisco" was derived from the city name *San Francisco*, which is why the company's engineers insisted on using the lower case "cisco" in its early years. The logo is intended to depict the two towers of the Golden Gate Bridge.

On February 16, 1990, Cisco Systems went public (with a market capitalization of $224 million) and was listed on the NASDAQ stock exchange. On August 28, 1990, Lerner was fired. Upon hearing the news, her husband Bosack resigned in protest. The couple walked away from Cisco with $170 million, 70% of which was committed to their own charity.

Although Cisco was not the first company to develop and sell dedicated network nodes, it was one of the first to sell commercially successful routers supporting multiple network protocols. Classical, CPU-based architecture of early Cisco devices coupled with flexibility of operating system IOS allowed for keeping up with evolving technology needs by means of frequent software upgrades. Some popular models of that time (such as Cisco 2500) managed to stay in production for almost a decade virtually unchanged—a rarity in high-tech industry. Although Cisco was strongly rooted in the enterprise environment, the company was quick to capture the emerging service provider environment, entering the SP market with new, high-capacity product lines such as Cisco 7000 and Cisco 8500.

Between 1992 and 1994, Cisco acquired several companies in Ethernet switching, such as Kalpana, Grand Junction, and most notably, Mario Mazzola's Crescendo Communications which together formed the Catalyst business unit. At the time, the company envisioned layer 3 routing and layer 2 (Ethernet, Token Ring) switching as complementary functions of different intelligence and architecture—the former was slow and complex, the latter was fast but simple. This philosophy dominated the company's product lines throughout the 1990s.

In 1995, John Morgridge was succeeded by John Chambers.

1996–2005: Internet and Silicon Intelligence

The phenomenal growth of the Internet in mid-to-late 1990s quickly changed the telecom landscape. As the Internet Protocol (IP) became widely adopted, the importance of multi-protocol routing declined. Nevertheless, Cisco managed to catch the Internet wave, with products ranging from modem access shelves (AS5200) to core GSR routers that quickly became vital to Internet service providers and by 1998 gave Cisco de facto monopoly in this critical segment.

John T. Chambers led Cisco as its CEO between 1995 and 2015.
(Pictured at 2010 World Economic Forum, in Davos, Switzerland).

In late March 2000, at the height of the dot-com bubble, Cisco became the most valuable company in the world, with a market capitalization of more than US$500 billion. In July 2014, with a market cap of about US$129 billion, it is still one of the most valuable companies.

Meanwhile, the growth of Internet bandwidth requirements kept challenging traditional, software-based packet processing architectures.

The perceived complexity of programming routing functions in silicon, led to formation of several startups determined to find new ways to process IP and MPLS packets entirely in hardware and blur boundaries between routing and switching. One of them, Juniper Networks, shipped their first product in 1999 and by 2000 chipped away about 30% from Cisco SP Market share. Cisco answered the challenge with homegrown ASICs and fast processing cards for GSR routers and Catalyst 6500 switches. In 2004, Cisco also started migration to new high-end hardware CRS-1 and software architecture IOS-XR.

2006–2012: The Human Network

Russian President Dmitry Medvedev and California Governor Arnold Schwarzenegger at Cisco, 2010.

As part of a massive rebranding campaign in 2006, Cisco Systems adopted the shortened name "Cisco" and created "The Human Network" advertising campaign. These efforts were meant to make Cisco a "household" brand—a strategy designed to support the low-end Linksys products and future consumer products (such as Flip Video camera acquired by Cisco in 2009).

On the more traditional business side, Cisco continued to develop its extensive enterprise-focused routing, switching and security portfolio. The quickly growing importance of Ethernet also influenced the company's product lines, prompting the company to morph the successful Catalyst 6500 Ethernet switch into all-purpose Cisco 7600 routing platform. However, limits of IOS and aging Crescendo architecture also forced Cisco to look at merchant silicon in the carrier Ethernet segment. This resulted in a new ASR9000 product family intended to consolidate company's carrier ethernet and subscriber management business around EZChip-based hardware and IOS-XR. Cisco also expanded into new markets by acquisition—one example being a 2009 purchase of mobile specialist Starent Networks that resulted in ASR5000 product line.

Throughout the mid-2000s, Cisco also built a significant presence in India, establishing its Globalization Centre East in Bengaluru for $1 billion, and planning that 20% of Cisco's leaders would be based there.

However, Cisco continued to be challenged by both domestic Alcatel-Lucent, Juniper Networks and overseas competitors Huawei. Due to lower-than-expected profit in 2011, Cisco was forced to reduce annual expenses by $1 billion. The company cut around 3,000 employees with an early-retirement program who accepted buyout and planned to eliminate as many as 10,000 jobs (around 14 percent of the 73,400 total employees before curtailment). During the 2011 analyst call, Cisco's CEO John Chambers called out several competitors by name, including Juniper and HP.

On 24 July 2012, Cisco received approval from the EU to acquire NDS (a TV software developer) for USD 5 billion. This acquisition signaled the end of the "The Human Network" strategy as Cisco found itself backing off from household hardware like Linksys and Flip into the cloud and software market.

Present Day

Portuguese President Aníbal Cavaco Silva, John T. Chambers,
and Senior Director of Corporate Innovation Helder Antunes, 2011.

On July 23, 2013, Cisco Systems announced a definitive agreement to acquire Sourcefire for $2.7 billion.

On August 14, 2013, Cisco Systems announced it would cut 4,000 jobs from its workforce, which was roughly 6% starting in 2014.

At the end of 2013, Cisco announced poor revenue due to depressed sales in emerging markets, caused by economic uncertainty and by fears of the National Security Agency planting backdoors in its products.

In April, 2014, Cisco Systems announced $150 million to fund early-stage firms around the globe to focus on the Internet of Everything. The investment fund was allocated to investments in IoT accelerators and startups such as The Alchemist Accelerator, Ayla Networks and EVRYTHNG. After the announcement, The Alchemist Accelerator announced Cisco as a strategic partner and launched an individual program specifically focused on advancing the growth of IoT startups. This new funding increased Cisco Investments' thematic investing to $250 million total, adding to the previously announced $100 million commitment to startups focused on the emerging Internet of Everything (IoE) market opportunity.

On August 13, 2014, the company announced it was laying off another 6,000 workers or 8% of its global workforce, as part of a second restructuring.

On May 4, 2015, Cisco announced CEO and Chairman John Chambers would step down as CEO on July 26, 2015, but remain chairman. Chuck Robbins, senior vice president of worldwide sales & operations and 17-year Cisco veteran, will become CEO.

On July 23, 2015, Cisco announced the divesture of its television set-top-box and cable modem business to Technicolor SA for $600 million, a division originally formed by Cisco's $6.9 billion purchase of Scientific Atlanta. The deal came as part of Cisco's gradual exit from the consumer market, and as part of an effort by Cisco's new leadership to focus on cloud-based products in enterprise segments. Cisco indicated that it would still collaborate with Technicolor on video products.

On November 19, 2015, Cisco, alongside ARM Holdings, Dell, Intel, Microsoft, and Princeton University, founded the OpenFog Consortium, to promote interests and development in fog computing. Cisco Sr. Managing-Director Helder Antunes became the consortium's first chairman.

In January 2016, Cisco invested in VeloCloud, a software-defined WAN (SD-WAN) start-up with a cloud offering for configuring and optimizing branch office networks. Cisco contributed to VeloCloud's $27 million Series C round, led by March Capital Partners. Cisco is one of two strategic investors.

Corporate Structure

Cisco Jasper, a Cisco IoT and cloud business platform subsidiary.

Cisco Meraki, a Cisco network security and connectivity subsidiary.

CloudLock, a Cisco cloud computing security subsidiary.

Acquisitions and Subsidiaries

Cisco acquired a variety of companies to spin products and talent into the company. In 1995–1996 the company completed 11 acquisitions. Several acquisitions, such as Stratacom, were the biggest deals in the industry when they occurred. During the Internet boom in 1999, the company acquired Cerent Corporation, a start-up company located in Petaluma, California, for about US$7 billion. It was the most expensive acquisition made by Cisco to that date, and only the acquisition of Scientific Atlanta has been larger. In 1999 Cisco also acquired stake for $1 Billion in KPMG Consulting to enable establishing Internet firm Metrius founded by Keyur Patel of Fuse. Several acquired companies have grown into $1Bn+ business units for Cisco, including LAN switching, Enterprise Voice over Internet Protocol (VOIP) platform Webex and home networking. The latter came as result of Cisco acquiring Linksys in 2003 and in 2010 was supplemented with new product line dubbed Cisco Valet.

Cisco announced on January 12, 2005, that it would acquire Airespace for US$450 million to reinforce the wireless controller product lines.

Cisco announced on January 4, 2007, that it would buy IronPort in a deal valued at US$830 million and completed the acquisition on June 25, 2007. IronPort was best known for its IronPort AntiSpam, its SenderBase email reputation service and its email security appliances. Accordingly, IronPort was integrated into the Cisco Security business unit. Ironport's Senderbase was renamed as Sensorbase to take account of the input into this database that other Cisco devices provide. SensorBase allows these devices to build a risk profile on IP addresses, therefore allowing risk profiles to be dynamically created on http sites and SMTP email sources.

Cisco announced on March 15, 2012, that it would acquire NDS Group for $5bn. The transaction was completed on July 30, 2012.

In more recent merger deals, Cisco bought Starent Networks (a mobile packet core company) and Moto Development Group, a product design consulting firm that helped develop Cisco's Flip video camera. Also in 2010, Cisco became a key stakeholder in *e-Skills Week*. In March 2011, Cisco completed the acquisition of privately held network configuration and change management software company Pari Networks.

Although many buy-ins (such as Crescendo Networks in 1993, Tandberg in 2010) resulted in acquisition of flagship technology to Cisco, many others have failed—partially or completely. For instance, in 2010 Cisco occupied a meaningful share of the packet-optical market, revenues were still not on par with US$7 billion price tag paid in 1999 for Cerent. Some of acquired technologies (such as Flip from Pure Digital) saw their product lines terminated.

Cisco campuses in Bangalore, India (top), Berlin, Germany (middle), and Oslo, Norway (bottom).

In January 2013, Cisco Systems acquired Israeli software maker Intucell for around $475 million in cash, a move to expand its mobile network management offerings. In the same month, Cisco Systems acquired Cognitive Security, a company focused on Cyber Threat Protection. Cisco also acquired SolveDirect (cloud services) in March 2013 and Ubiquisys (mobile software) in April 2013.

Cisco acquired cyber-security firm Sourcefire, in October 2013. On June 16, 2014, Cisco announced that it has completed the acquisition of ThreatGRID, a company that provided dynamic malware analysis and threat intelligence technology.

On June 17, 2014, Cisco announced its intent to acquire privately held Tail-f Systems, a leader in multi-vendor network service orchestration solutions for traditional and virtualized networks.

On April 2, 2015, Cisco announced plans to buy Embrane, a software-defined networking startup. The deal will give Cisco Embrane's software platform, which provides layer 3–7 network services for things such as firewalls, VPN termination, server load balancers and SSL offload.

On May 7, 2015 Cisco announced plans to buy Tropo, a cloud API platform that simplifies the addition of real-time communications and collaboration capabilities within applications.

On June 30, 2015, Cisco acquired privately held OpenDNS, the company best known for its DNS service that adds a level of security by monitoring domain name requests.

On August 6, 2015, Cisco announced that it has completed the acquisition of privately held MaintenanceNet, the US-based company best known for its cloud-based contract management platform ServiceExchange. On the same month, Cisco acquired Pawaa, a privately held company in Bangalore, India that provides secure on-premises and cloud-based file-sharing software.

On September 30, 2015, Cisco announced its intent to acquire privately held Portcullis Computer Security, a UK-based company that provides cybersecurity services to enterprise clients and the government sectors.

On October 26, 2015, Cisco announced its intent to acquire ParStream, a privately held company based in Cologne, Germany, that provides an analytics database that allows companies to analyze large amounts of data and store it in near real time anywhere in the network.

On October 27, 2015, Cisco announced that it would acquire Lancope, a company that focuses on detecting threat activity, for $452.5 million in a cash-and-equity deal.

On June 28, 2016, Cisco announced its intent to acquire CloudLock, a privately held cloud security company, for $293 million. The deal is expected to close in the first quarter of 2017.

In August 2016, Cisco announced it is getting closer to making a deal to acquire Springpath, the startup whose technology is used in Cisco's HyperFlex Systems. Cisco already owns an undisclosed stake in the hyper-converged provider.

Products and Services

Cisco SG300-28 Rackmount switch (top) and Cisco EPC-3010 router (bottom).

Cisco's products and services focus upon three market segments—enterprise and service provider, small business and the home.

Cisco has grown increasingly popular in the Asia-Pacific region over the last three decades and is the dominant vendor in the Australian market with leadership across all market segments. It uses its Australian office as one of the main headquarters for the Asia-Pacific region, offering a diverse product portfolio for long-term stability, and integration is a sustainable competitive advantage.

VoIP Services

Cisco became a major provider of Voice over IP to enterprises, and is now moving into the home user market through its acquisitions of Scientific Atlanta and Linksys. Scientific Atlanta provides VoIP equipment to cable service providers such as Time Warner, Cablevision, Rogers Communications, UPC and others; Linksys has partnered with companies such as Skype, Microsoft and Yahoo! to integrate consumer VoIP services with wireless and cordless phones.

Hosted Collaboration Solution (HCS)

Cisco partners can offer cloud-based services based on Cisco's virtualized Unified Computing System (UCS). A part of the Cisco Unified Services Delivery Solution that includes hosted versions of Cisco Unified Communications Manager (UCM), Cisco Unified Contact Center, Cisco Unified Mobility, Cisco Unified Presence, Cisco Unity Connection (unified messaging) and Cisco Webex Meeting Center.

Network Emergency Response

A Cisco 8851 IP Phone

As part of its Tactical Operations initiative, Cisco maintains several Network Emergency Response Vehicles (NERV)s. The vehicles are maintained and deployed by Cisco employees during natural disasters and other public crises. The vehicles are self-contained and provide wired and wireless services including voice and radio interoperability, voice over IP, network-based video surveillance and secured high-definition video-conferencing for leaders and first responders in crisis areas with up to 3 Mbit/s of bandwidth (up and down) via a 1.8-meter satellite antenna.

NERVs are based at Cisco headquarters sites in San José, California and at Research Triangle

Park, North Carolina, allowing strategic deployment in North America. They can become fully operational within 15 minutes of arrival. High-capacity diesel fuel-tanks allow the largest vehicles to run for up to 72 hours continuously. The NERV has been deployed to incidents such as the October 2007 California wildfires; hurricanes Gustav, Ike and Katrina; the 2010 San Bruno gas pipeline explosion, tornado outbreaks in North Carolina and Alabama in 2011; and Hurricane Sandy in 2012.

The Tactical Operations team maintains and deploys smaller, more portable communication kits to emergencies outside of North America. In 2010, the team deployed to assist in earthquake recovery in Haiti and in Christchurch (New Zealand). In 2011, they deployed to flooding in Brazil, as well as in response to the 2011 earthquake and tsunami in Japan.

In 2011, Cisco received the Innovation Preparedness award from the American Red Cross Silicon Valley Chapter for its development and use of these vehicles in disasters.

Certifications

Cisco headquarters in San José, California in Silicon Valley.

Cisco Systems also sponsors a line of IT professional certifications for Cisco products. There are five levels of certification: Entry (CCENT), Associate (CCNA/CCDA), Professional (CCNP/CCDP), Expert (CCIE/CCDE) and recently Architect, as well as nine different paths, Routing & Switching, Design, Industrial Network, Network Security, Service Provider, Service Provider Operations, Storage Networking, Voice, Datacenter and Wireless.

A number of specialist technician, sales and datacenter certifications are also available.

Cisco also provides training for these certifications via a portal called the Cisco Networking Academy. Qualifying schools can become members of the Cisco Networking Academy and then provide CCNA level or other level courses. Cisco Academy Instructors must be CCNA certified to be a CCAI certified instructor.

Cisco often finds itself involved with technical education. With over 10,000 partnerships in over 65 countries Cisco Academy program operates in many exotic locations. For example, in March 2013, Cisco announced its interest in Myanmar by investing in two Cisco Networking Academies in Yangon and Mandalay and a channel partner network.

Corporate Affairs

Awards and Accolades

In 2010, Secretary of State Hillary Clinton awarded Cisco the Secretary of State's Award for Corporate Excellence, which was presented in Jerusalem by Ambassador James B. Cunningham to Cisco Senior Manager Zika Abzuk.

Cisco products, most notably IP phones and Telepresence, are frequently sighted in movies and TV series. The company itself and its history was featured in the documentary film *Something Ventured* which premiered in 2011.

Cisco was a 2002–03 recipient of the Ron Brown Award, a U.S. presidential honor to recognize companies "for the exemplary quality of their relationships with employees and communities". Cisco commonly stays on top of Fortune "100 Best Companies to work for", with position No. 20 in 2011.

According to a report by technology consulting firm LexInnova, Cisco is one of the leading recipients of network security-related patents with the largest portfolio within other companies (6,442 security-related patents).

Controversies

Cisco Live 2007 in Anaheim, California. Cisco Live is the company's annual exposition and conference.

Shareholder relations A class action lawsuit filed on April 20, 2001, accused Cisco of making misleading statements that "were relied on by purchasers of Cisco stock" and of insider trading. While Cisco denied all allegations in the suit, on August 18, 2006, Cisco's liability insurers, its directors and officers paid the plaintiffs US$91.75 million to settle the suit.

Intellectual property disputes On December 11, 2008, the Free Software Foundation filed suit against Cisco regarding Cisco's failure to comply with the GPL and LGPL license models and make the applicable source code publicly available. On May 20, 2009, Cisco settled this lawsuit by complying with FSF licensing terms and making a monetary contribution to the FSF.

Censorship in China Cisco has been criticized for its involvement in censorship in the People's Republic of China. According to author Ethan Gutmann, Cisco and other telecommunications equipment providers supplied the Chinese government with surveillance and Internet infrastructure equipment that is used to block Internet websites and track online activities in China. Cisco says that it does not customize or develop specialized or unique filtering capabilities to enable governments to block access to information and that it sells the same equipment in China as it sells worldwide.

Wired News had uncovered a leaked, confidential Cisco PowerPoint presentation that details the commercial opportunities of the Golden Shield Project of Internet control. In her article, journalist Sarah Stirland accuses Cisco of marketing its technology "specifically as a tool of repression."

In May 2011, a group of Falun Gong practitioners filed the lawsuit under the Alien Tort Statute alleging that Cisco knowingly developed and customized its product to assist the Chinese government in prosecution and abuse of Falun Gong practitioners. The presentation leaked from Cisco lists "Combat "Falun Gong" evil religion and other hostiles" as one of the benefits of the Cisco system. The lawsuit was dismissed in September 2014 by the United States District Court for the Northern District of California, which decision was appealed to United States Court of Appeals for the Ninth Circuit in September 2015.

Tax fraud investigation On October 16, 2007, the Brazilian Federal Police and Brazilian Receita Federal (equivalent to the American IRS), under the "Persona Operation", uncovered an alleged tax fraud scheme employed by Cisco Systems Brazil Chief Carlos Roberto Carnevali since 2002 that exempted the company from paying over R$1.5 billion (US$824 million) in taxes.

Antitrust lawsuit On December 1, 2008, Multiven filed an antitrust lawsuit against Cisco Systems, Inc. in an effort to open up the network maintenance services marketplace for Cisco equipment, promote competition and ensure consumer choice and value. Multiven's complaint alleges that Cisco harmed Multiven and consumers by bundling and tying bug fixes/patches and updates for its operating system software to its maintenance services (SMARTnet) and through a series of other illegal exclusionary and anticompetitive acts designed to maintain Cisco's alleged monopoly in the network maintenance services market for Cisco networking equipment. In May 2010 Cisco has accused the person who filed the antitrust suit, British-Nigerian technology entrepreneur Peter Alfred-Adekeye, with hacking and pressured the US government to extradite him from Canada. Alfred-Adekeye was arrested while in the middle of testifying against Cisco in an anti-trust hearing. Although he was released after 28 days on bail, the case has stretched for a year, because the U.S. Attorney's office was unable to present the evidence required for the extradition. The antitrust lawsuit has been settled 2 months after Alfred-Adekeye's arrest. In May 2011 the US extradition request has been denied. Canadian Supreme Court Justice Ronald McKinnon, who oversaw the extradition hearing, commented on the arrest saying "It is simply not done in a civilized jurisdiction that is bound by the rule of law". He also stated that the real reason for the extradition proceedings was because Alfred-Adekeye "dared to take on a multinational giant." Judge McKinnon has also condemned the US prosecutor for hiding the fact that Alfred-Adekeye was in legal proceedings against Cisco Systems, for stating that Alfred-Adekeye had left the USA in a time period when he had not and a formal request for extradition was not filed against Alfred-Adekeye when he was taken into custody. He described the information provided by Cisco and the US prosecutor as "full of innuendo, half-truths and falsehoods," adding that "This speaks volumes for Cisco's duplicity" and accused them of "unmitigated gall" in using such a heavy-handed move as an unsupportable arrest and jailing to pressure Alfred-Adekeye to drop or settle his civil antitrust complaint.

This case was eventually settled out of court and dismissed with prejudice in February 2011.

In March 2013 Multiven has filed a complaint both in Switzerland and the US accusing Cisco of stealing thousands of its proprietary and copyrighted data files from its knowledge base. The attack has allegedly taken place with the use of "automated cyber scraping software" with the perpetrating IPs assigned to Cisco. Cisco has denied the claims.

On July 20, 2015, Multiven CEO, Peter Alfred-Adekeye filed a libel lawsuit against Cisco for (1) falsely claiming that *'he or someone under his control at Multiven'* downloaded and *'stole'* Cisco software five times in 2006 from cisco.com (2) using this lie to orchestrate his illegal arrest in Vancouver, Canada in 2010 and (3) continuing to knowingly propagate this falsehood till today.

Remotely monitoring users' connections Cisco's Linksys E2700, E3500, E4500 devices have been reported to be remotely updated to a firmware version that forces users to register for a cloud service, allows Cisco to monitor their network use and ultimately shut down the cloud service account and thus render the affected router unusable.

Firewall backdoor developed by NSA According to the German magazine Der Spiegel the NSA has developed JETPLOW for gaining access to ASA (series 5505, 5510, 5520, 5540 and 5550) and 500-series PIX Firewalls.

Cisco's Chief Security Officer addressed the allegations publicly and denied working with any government to weaken Cisco products for exploitation or to implement security back doors.

A document included in the trove of National Security Agency files released with Glenn Greenwald's book *No Place to Hide* details how the agency's Tailored Access Operations (TAO) unit and other NSA employees intercept servers, routers and other network gear being shipped to organizations targeted for surveillance and install covert firmware onto them before they're delivered. These Trojan horse systems were described by an NSA manager as being "some of the most productive operations in TAO because they pre-position access points into hard target networks around the world."

Cisco denied the allegations in a customer document saying that no information was included about specific Cisco products, supply chain intervention or implant techniques, or new security vulnerabilities. Cisco's General Counsel also claimed that Cisco does not work with any government, including the United States Government, to weaken its products. The allegations are reported to have prompted the company's CEO to express concern to the President of the United States.

Spherix patent suit In March 2014 Cisco Systems was sued for patent infringement. Spherix asserts that over $43 billion of Cisco's sales infringe on old Nortel patents owned by Spherix. Officials with

Spherix are claiming that a wide range of Cisco products, from switches to routers, infringe on 11 former Nortel patents that the company now owns.

VyOS

VyOS is a fork of the now defunct Vyatta Core edition of routing software. VyOS is a Linux-based routing solution built on the Debian Linux distribution, and currently runs on x86 and x86-64 platforms.

VyOS provides a free and open source routing platform that competes directly with other commercially available solutions from well known network providers. Because VyOS runs on standard x86 systems, it is able to be used as a router and firewall platform for cloud deployments.

History

After Brocade Communications stopped development of the Vyatta Core Edition of the Vyatta Routing software, a small group of enthusiasts took the last Community Edition, and worked on building an Open Source fork to live on in place of the end of life VC.

Releases

VyOS version 1.0.0 (Hydrogen) was released on December 22, 2013. On October 9, 2014 version 1.1.0 (Helium) was released. All versions released thus far have been based on Debian 6.0 (Squeeze), and are available as a 32-bit images and 64-bit images for both physical and virtual machines.

Keeping with the naming convention the next release will be Lithium.

Release History

Release	Version	Date
Hydrogen	1.0.0	December 22, 2013
	1.0.1	January 17, 2014
	1.0.2	February 3, 2014
	1.0.3	May 9, 2014
	1.0.4	June 16, 2014
	1.0.5	September 26, 2014
Helium	1.1.0	October 9, 2014
	1.1.1	December 8, 2014
	1.1.3	January 28, 2015
	1.1.4	March 9, 2015
	1.1.5	March 25, 2015
	1.1.6	August 17, 2015
	1.1.7	February 17, 2016

VMware Support

The VyOS OVA image for VMware was released with the February 3rd 2014 maintenance release. It allows a convenient setup of VyOS on a VMware platform and includes all of the VMware tools. The OVA image can be downloaded from the standard download sites or from VMware.

Amazon EC2 Support

Starting with version 1.0.2, Amazon EC2 customers can select a VyOS AMI image.

Embedded Operating System

An embedded operating system is an operating system for embedded computer systems. These operating systems are designed to be compact, efficient at resource usage, and reliable, forsaking many functions that non-embedded computer operating systems provide, and which may not be used by the specialized applications they run. They are frequently also referred to as real-time operating systems, and the term *RTOS* is often used as a synonym for *embedded operating system*.

Usually, the hardware running an embedded operating system is very limited in resources such as RAM and ROM therefore systems made for embedded hardware tend to be very specific, which means that due to the available resources (low if compared to non-embedded systems) these systems are created to cover specific tasks or scopes. In order to get advantage of the processing power of the main (or only) CPU, system creators often write them in assembly. This *machine efficient* language "squeezes" the potentiality in terms of speed and determinism, which means maximizing the responsiveness of the operating system. Though, it is not an absolute rule that all embedded operating systems are written in assembly language, as many of them are written in more portable languages, like C.

An important difference between most embedded operating systems and desktop operating systems is that the application, including the operating system, is usually statically linked together into a single executable image. Unlike a desktop operating system, the embedded operating system does not load and execute applications. This means that the system is only able to run a single application.

Real-time Operating System

A real-time operating system (RTOS) is an operating system (OS) intended to serve real-time applications which process data as it comes in, typically without buffering delays. Processing time requirements (including any OS delay) are measured in tenths of seconds or shorter increments of time. They either are event driven or time sharing. Event driven system switches between task based on their priorities while time sharing switch the task based on clock interrupts.

A key characteristic of a RTOS is the level of its consistency concerning the amount of time it takes to accept and complete an application's task; the variability is *jitter*. A *hard* real-time operating system has less jitter than a *soft* real-time operating system. The chief design goal is not high throughput, but rather a guarantee of a soft or hard performance category. A RTOS that can usually or *generally* meet a *deadline* is a soft real-time OS, but if it can meet a deadline deterministically it is a hard real-time OS.

A RTOS has an advanced algorithm for scheduling. Scheduler flexibility enables a wider, computer-system orchestration of process priorities, but a real-time OS is more frequently dedicated to a narrow set of applications. Key factors in a real-time OS are minimal interrupt latency and minimal thread switching latency; a real-time OS is valued more for how quickly or how predictably it can respond than for the amount of work it can perform in a given period of time.

Examples

According to a 2014 Embedded Market Study, the following RTOSes are among the top 10 operating systems used in the embedded systems market:

- InHouse/Custom (18%)
- Android (17%)
- FreeRTOS (17%)
- Ubuntu (15%)
- Debian Linux (12%)
- Green Hills Software INTEGRITY (3%)
- Wind River VxWorks (8%)
- QNX Neutrino (5%)
- Micrium μC/OS-II, III (10%)
- Windows CE (8%)
- TI-RTOS Kernel (previously called DSP/BIOS) (7%)
- RTEMS open source RTOS designed for embedded systems, mainly used for missile and space probes control

Design Philosophies

The most common designs are:

- Event-driven – switches tasks only when an event of higher priority needs servicing; called preemptive priority, or priority scheduling.
- Time-sharing – switches tasks on a regular clocked interrupt, and on events; called round robin.

Time sharing designs switch tasks more often than strictly needed, but give smoother multitasking, giving the illusion that a process or user has sole use of a machine.

Early CPU designs needed many cycles to switch tasks, during which the CPU could do nothing else useful. For example, with a 20 MHz 68000 processor (typical of the late 1980s), task switch times are roughly 20 microseconds. (In contrast, a 100 MHz ARM CPU (from 2008) switches in less than 3 microseconds.) Because of this, early OSes tried to minimize wasting CPU time by avoiding unnecessary task switching.

Scheduling

In typical designs, a task has three states:

1. Running (executing on the CPU);

2. Ready (ready to be executed);

3. Blocked (waiting for an event, I/O for example).

Most tasks are blocked or ready most of the time because generally only one task can run at a time per CPU. The number of items in the ready queue can vary greatly, depending on the number of tasks the system needs to perform and the type of scheduler that the system uses. On simpler non-preemptive but still multitasking systems, a task has to give up its time on the CPU to other tasks, which can cause the ready queue to have a greater number of overall tasks in the ready to be executed state (resource starvation).

Usually the data structure of the ready list in the scheduler is designed to minimize the worst-case length of time spent in the scheduler's critical section, during which preemption is inhibited, and, in some cases, all interrupts are disabled. But the choice of data structure depends also on the maximum number of tasks that can be on the ready list.

If there are never more than a few tasks on the ready list, then a doubly linked list of ready tasks is likely optimal. If the ready list usually contains only a few tasks but occasionally contains more, then the list should be sorted by priority. That way, finding the highest priority task to run does not require iterating through the entire list. Inserting a task then requires walking the ready list until reaching either the end of the list, or a task of lower priority than that of the task being inserted.

Care must be taken not to inhibit preemption during this search. Longer critical sections should be divided into small pieces. If an interrupt occurs that makes a high priority task ready during the insertion of a low priority task, that high priority task can be inserted and run immediately before the low priority task is inserted.

The critical response time, sometimes called the flyback time, is the time it takes to queue a new ready task and restore the state of the highest priority task to running. In a well-designed RTOS, readying a new task will take 3 to 20 instructions per ready-queue entry, and restoration of the highest-priority ready task will take 5 to 30 instructions.

In more advanced systems, real-time tasks share computing resources with many non-real-time tasks, and the ready list can be arbitrarily long. In such systems, a scheduler ready list implemented as a linked list would be inadequate.

Algorithms

Some commonly used RTOS scheduling algorithms are:

- Cooperative scheduling
- Preemptive scheduling
    - Rate-monotonic scheduling
    - Round-robin scheduling
    - Fixed priority pre-emptive scheduling, an implementation of preemptive time slicing
    - Fixed-Priority Scheduling with Deferred Preemption
    - Fixed-Priority Non-preemptive Scheduling
    - Critical section preemptive scheduling
    - Static time scheduling
- Earliest Deadline First approach
- Stochastic digraphs with multi-threaded graph traversal

Intertask Communication and Resource Sharing

A multitasking operating system like Unix is poor at real-time tasks. The scheduler gives the highest priority to jobs with the lowest demand on the computer, so there is no way to ensure that a time-critical job will have access to enough resources. Multitasking systems must manage sharing data and hardware resources among multiple tasks. It is usually unsafe for two tasks to access the same specific data or hardware resource simultaneously. There are three common approaches to resolve this problem:

Temporarily Masking/Disabling Interrupts

General-purpose operating systems usually do not allow user programs to mask (disable) interrupts, because the user program could control the CPU for as long as it wishes. Some modern CPUs don't allow user mode code to disable interrupts as such control is considered a key operating system resource. Many embedded systems and RTOSs, however, allow the application itself to run in kernel mode for greater system call efficiency and also to permit the application to have greater control of the operating environment without requiring OS intervention.

On single-processor systems, an application running in kernel mode and masking interrupts is the lowest overhead method to prevent simultaneous access to a shared resource. While interrupts are masked and the current task does not make a blocking OS call, the current task has *exclusive* use of the CPU since no other task or interrupt can take control, so the critical section is protected. When the task exits its critical section, it must unmask interrupts; pending interrupts, if any, will then execute. Temporarily masking interrupts should only be done when the longest path through the critical section is shorter than the desired maximum interrupt latency. Typically this method of protection is used only when the critical section is just a few instructions and contains no loops. This method is ideal for protecting hardware bit-mapped registers when the bits are controlled by different tasks.

Binary Semaphores

When the shared resource must be reserved without blocking all other tasks (such as waiting for Flash memory to be written), it is better to use mechanisms also available on general-purpose operating systems, such as semaphores and OS-supervised interprocess messaging. Such mechanisms involve system calls, and usually invoke the OS's dispatcher code on exit, so they typically take hundreds of CPU instructions to execute, while masking interrupts may take as few as one instruction on some processors.

A binary semaphore is either locked or unlocked. When it is locked, tasks must wait for the semaphore to unlock. A binary semaphore is therefore equivalent to a mutex. Typically a task will set a timeout on its wait for a semaphore. There are several well-known problems with semaphore based designs such as priority inversion and deadlocks.

In priority inversion a high priority task waits because a low priority task has a semaphore, but the lower priority task is not given CPU time to finish its work. A typical solution is to have the task that owns a semaphore run at, or 'inherit,' the priority of the highest waiting task. But this simple approach fails when there are multiple levels of waiting: task A waits for a binary semaphore locked by task B, which waits for a binary semaphore locked by task C. Handling multiple levels of inheritance without introducing instability in cycles is complex and problematic.

In a deadlock, two or more tasks lock semaphores without timeouts and then wait forever for the other task's semaphore, creating a cyclic dependency. The simplest deadlock scenario occurs when two tasks alternately lock two semaphores, but in the opposite order. Deadlock is prevented by careful design or by having floored semaphores, which pass control of a semaphore to the higher priority task on defined conditions.

Message Passing

The other approach to resource sharing is for tasks to send messages in an organized message passing scheme. In this paradigm, the resource is managed directly by only one task. When another task wants to interrogate or manipulate the resource, it sends a message to the managing task. Although their real-time behavior is less crisp than semaphore systems, simple message-based systems avoid most protocol deadlock hazards, and are generally better-behaved than semaphore systems. However, problems like those of semaphores are possible. Priority inversion can occur when a task is working on a low-priority message and ignores a higher-priority message (or a message originating indirectly from a high priority task) in its incoming message queue. Protocol deadlocks can occur when two or more tasks wait for each other to send response messages.

Interrupt Handlers and the Scheduler

Since an interrupt handler blocks the highest priority task from running, and since real time operating systems are designed to keep thread latency to a minimum, interrupt handlers are typically kept as short as possible. The interrupt handler defers all interaction with the hardware if possible; typically all that is necessary is to acknowledge or disable the interrupt (so that it won't occur again when the interrupt handler returns) and notify a task that work needs to be done. This can be done by unblocking a driver task through releasing a semaphore, setting a flag or sending a message. A scheduler often provides the ability to unblock a task from interrupt handler context.

An OS maintains catalogues of objects it manages such as threads, mutexes, memory, and so on. Updates to this catalogue must be strictly controlled. For this reason it can be problematic when an interrupt handler calls an OS function while the application is in the act of also doing so. The OS function called from an interrupt handler could find the object database to be in an inconsistent state because of the application's update. There are two major approaches to deal with this problem: the unified architecture and the segmented architecture. RTOSs implementing the unified architecture solve the problem by simply disabling interrupts while the internal catalogue is updated. The downside of this is that interrupt latency increases, potentially losing interrupts. The segmented architecture does not make direct OS calls but delegates the OS related work to a separate handler. This handler runs at a higher priority than any thread but lower than the interrupt handlers. The advantage of this architecture is that it adds very few cycles to interrupt latency. As a result, OSes which implement the segmented architecture are more predictable and can deal with higher interrupt rates compared to the unified architecture.

Memory Allocation

Memory allocation is more critical in a real-time operating system than in other operating systems.

First, for stability there cannot be memory leaks (memory that is allocated, then unused but never freed). The device should work indefinitely, without ever needing a reboot. For this reason, dynamic memory allocation is frowned upon. Whenever possible, all required memory allocation is specified statically at compile time.

Another reason to avoid dynamic memory allocation is memory fragmentation. With frequent allocation and releasing of small chunks of memory, a situation may occur when the memory is divided into several sections, in which case the RTOS cannot allocate a large continuous block of memory, although there is enough free memory. Secondly, speed of allocation is important. A standard memory allocation scheme scans a linked list of indeterminate length to find a suitable free memory block, which is unacceptable in an RTOS since memory allocation has to occur within a certain amount of time.

Because mechanical disks have much longer and more unpredictable response times, swapping to disk files is not used for the same reasons as RAM allocation discussed above.

The simple fixed-size-blocks algorithm works quite well for simple embedded systems because of its low overhead.

Unix

Unix is a family of multitasking, multiuser computer operating systems that derive from the original AT&T Unix, developed in the 1970s at the Bell Labs research center by Ken Thompson, Dennis Ritchie, and others.

Initially intended for use inside the Bell System, AT&T licensed Unix to outside parties from the late 1970s, leading to a variety of both academic and commercial variants of Unix from vendors such as the University of California, Berkeley (BSD), Microsoft (Xenix), IBM (AIX) and Sun Microsystems (Solaris). AT&T finally sold its rights in Unix to Novell in the early 1990s, which then sold its Unix business to the Santa Cruz Operation (SCO) in 1995, but the UNIX trademark passed to the industry standards consortium The Open Group, which allows the use of the mark for certified operating systems compliant with the Single UNIX Specification (SUS). Among these is Apple's macOS, which is the Unix version with the largest installed base as of 2014.

From the power user's or programmer's perspective, Unix systems are characterized by a modular design that is sometimes called the "Unix philosophy", meaning that the operating system provides a set of simple tools that each perform a limited, well-defined function, with a unified filesystem as the main means of communication and a shell scripting and command language to combine the tools to perform complex workflows. Aside from the modular design, Unix also distinguishes itself from its predecessors as the first portable operating system: almost the entire operating system is written in the C programming language that allowed Unix to reach numerous platforms.

Many clones of Unix have arisen over the years, of which Linux is the most popular, having displaced SUS-certified Unix on many server platforms since its inception in the early 1990s.

Overview

Version 7 Unix, the Research Unix ancestor of all modern Unix systems

Unix was originally meant to be a convenient platform for programmers developing software to be run on it and on other systems, rather than for non-programmer users. The system grew larger as the operating system started spreading in academic circles, as users added their own tools to the system and shared them with colleagues.

Unix was designed to be portable, multi-tasking and multi-user in a time-sharing configuration. Unix systems are characterized by various concepts: the use of plain text for storing data; a hierarchical file system; treating devices and certain types of inter-process communication (IPC) as files; and the use of a large number of software tools, small programs that can be strung together through a command-line interpreter using pipes, as opposed to using a single monolithic program that includes all of the same functionality. These concepts are collectively known as the "Unix philosophy". Brian Kernighan and Rob Pike summarize this in *The Unix Programming Environment* as "the idea that the power of a system comes more from the relationships among programs than from the programs themselves".

By the early 1980s users began seeing Unix as a potential universal operating system, suitable for computers of all sizes. The Unix environment and the client–server program model were essential elements in the development of the Internet and the reshaping of computing as centered in networks rather than in individual computers.

Both Unix and the C programming language were developed by AT&T and distributed to government and academic institutions, which led to both being ported to a wider variety of machine families than any other operating system.

Under Unix, the operating system consists of many utilities along with the master control program, the kernel. The kernel provides services to start and stop programs, handles the file system and other common "low-level" tasks that most programs share, and schedules access to avoid conflicts when programs try to access the same resource or device simultaneously. To mediate such access, the kernel has special rights, reflected in the division between user space and kernel space.

The microkernel concept was introduced in an effort to reverse the trend towards larger kernels and return to a system in which most tasks were completed by smaller utilities. In an era when a standard computer consisted of a hard disk for storage and a data terminal for input and output (I/O), the Unix file model worked quite well, as most I/O was linear. However, modern systems include networking and other new devices. As graphical user interfaces developed, the file model proved inadequate to the task of handling asynchronous events such as those generated by a mouse. In the 1980s, non-blocking I/O and the set of inter-process communication mechanisms were augmented with Unix domain sockets, shared memory, message queues, and semaphores. In microkernel implementations, functions such as network protocols could be moved out of the kernel, while conventional (monolithic) Unix implementations have network protocol stacks as part of the kernel.

History

Ken Thompson (sitting) and Dennis Ritchie working together at a PDP-11

The pre-history of Unix dates back to the mid-1960s when the Massachusetts Institute of Technology, Bell Labs, and General Electric were developing an innovative time-sharing operating system called Multics for the GE-645 mainframe. Multics introduced many innovations, but had many problems. Frustrated by the size and complexity of Multics but not by the aims, Bell Labs slowly pulled out of the project. Their last researchers to leave Multics, Ken Thompson, Dennis Ritchie, M. D. McIlroy, and J. F. Ossanna, decided to redo the work on a much smaller scale.

The name *Unics* (Uniplexed Information and Computing Service, pronounced as "eunuchs"), a pun on *Multics* (Multiplexed Information and Computer Services), was initially suggested for the project in 1970: the new operating system was an emasculated Multics. Peter H. Salus credits Peter Neumann with the pun, while Brian Kernighan claims the coining for himself, and adds that "no one can remember" who came up with the final spelling Unix. Dennis Ritchie also credits Kernighan.

In 1972, Unix was rewritten in the C programming language. The migration from assembly to the higher-level language C resulted in much more portable software, requiring only a relatively small amount of machine-dependent code to be replaced when porting Unix to other computing platforms. Bell Labs produced several versions of Unix that are collectively referred to as Research Unix. In 1975, the first source license for UNIX was sold to faculty at the University of Illinois Department of Computer Science. UIUC graduate student Greg Chesson (who had worked on the UNIX kernel at Bell Labs) was instrumental in negotiating the terms of this license.

During the late 1970s and early 1980s, the influence of Unix in academic circles led to large-scale adoption of Unix (BSD and System V) by commercial startups, including Sequent, HP-UX, Solaris, AIX, and Xenix. In the late 1980s, AT&T Unix System Laboratories and Sun Microsystems developed System V Release 4 (SVR4), which was subsequently adopted by many commercial Unix vendors.

In the 1990s, Unix-like systems grew in popularity as Linux and BSD distributions were developed through collaboration by a worldwide network of programmers. In 2000, Apple released Darwin that became the core of the macOS operating system.

Unix operating systems are widely used in modern servers, workstations, and mobile devices.

Standards

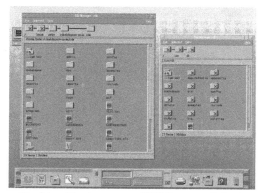

The Common Desktop Environment (CDE), part of the COSE initiative

Beginning in the late 1980s, an open operating system standardization effort now known as POSIX provided a common baseline for all operating systems; IEEE based POSIX around the common structure of the major competing variants of the Unix system, publishing the first POSIX standard in 1988. In the early 1990s, a separate but very similar effort was started by an industry consortium, the Common Open Software Environment (COSE) initiative, which eventually became the Single UNIX Specification (SUS) administered by The Open Group. Starting in 1998, the Open Group and IEEE started the Austin Group, to provide a common definition of POSIX and the Single UNIX Specification, which, by 2008, had become the Open Group Base Specification.

In 1999, in an effort towards compatibility, several Unix system vendors agreed on SVR4's Executable and Linkable Format (ELF) as the standard for binary and object code files. The common format allows substantial binary compatibility among Unix systems operating on the same CPU architecture.

The Filesystem Hierarchy Standard was created to provide a reference directory layout for Unix-like operating systems, and has mainly been used in Linux.

Components

The Unix system is composed of several components that were originally packaged together. By including the development environment, libraries, documents and the portable, modifiable source code for all of these components, in addition to the kernel of an operating system, Unix was a self-contained software system. This was one of the key reasons it emerged as an important teaching and learning tool and has had such a broad influence.

The inclusion of these components did not make the system large – the original V7 UNIX distribution, consisting of copies of all of the compiled binaries plus all of the source code and documentation occupied less than 10 MB and arrived on a single nine-track magnetic tape. The printed documentation, typeset from the on-line sources, was contained in two volumes.

The names and filesystem locations of the Unix components have changed substantially across the history of the system. Nonetheless, the V7 implementation is considered by many to have the canonical early structure:

- *Kernel* – source code in /usr/sys, composed of several sub-components:
    - *conf* – configuration and machine-dependent parts, including boot code
    - *dev* – device drivers for control of hardware (and some pseudo-hardware)
    - *sys* – operating system "kernel", handling memory management, process scheduling, system calls, etc.
    - *h* – header files, defining key structures within the system and important system-specific invariables
- *Development environment* – early versions of Unix contained a development environment sufficient to recreate the entire system from source code:
    - *cc* – C language compiler (first appeared in V3 Unix)
    - *as* – machine-language assembler for the machine

- o *ld* – linker, for combining object files

- o *lib* – object-code libraries (installed in /lib or /usr/lib). *libc*, the system library with C run-time support, was the primary library, but there have always been additional libraries for such things as mathematical functions (*libm*) or database access. V7 Unix introduced the first version of the modern "Standard I/O" library *stdio* as part of the system library. Later implementations increased the number of libraries significantly.

- o *make* – build manager (introduced in PWB/UNIX), for effectively automating the build process

- o *include* – header files for software development, defining standard interfaces and system invariants

- o *Other languages* – V7 Unix contained a Fortran-77 compiler, a programmable arbitrary-precision calculator (*bc, dc*), and the awk scripting language; later versions and implementations contain many other language compilers and toolsets. Early BSD releases included Pascal tools, and many modern Unix systems also include the GNU Compiler Collection as well as or instead of a proprietary compiler system.

- o *Other tools* – including an object-code archive manager (*ar*), symbol-table lister (*nm*), compiler-development tools (e.g. *lex* & *yacc*), and debugging tools.

- • *Commands* – Unix makes little distinction between commands (user-level programs) for system operation and maintenance (e.g. *cron*), commands of general utility (e.g. *grep*), and more general-purpose applications such as the text formatting and typesetting package. Nonetheless, some major categories are:

  - o *sh* – the "shell" programmable command-line interpreter, the primary user interface on Unix before window systems appeared, and even afterward (within a "command window").

  - o *Utilities* – the core toolkit of the Unix command set, including *cp, ls, grep, find* and many others. Subcategories include:

    - ▪ *System utilities* – administrative tools such as *mkfs, fsck*, and many others.

    - ▪ *User utilities* – environment management tools such as *passwd, kill*, and others.

  - o *Document formatting* – Unix systems were used from the outset for document preparation and typesetting systems, and included many related programs such as *nroff, troff, tbl, eqn, refer*, and *pic*. Some modern Unix systems also include packages such as TeX and Ghostscript.

  - o *Graphics* – the *plot* subsystem provided facilities for producing simple vector plots in a device-independent format, with device-specific interpreters to display such files. Modern Unix systems also generally include X11 as a standard windowing system and GUI, and many support OpenGL.

o   *Communications* – early Unix systems contained no inter-system communication, but did include the inter-user communication programs *mail* and *write*. V7 introduced the early inter-system communication system UUCP, and systems beginning with BSD release 4.1c included TCP/IP utilities.

- *Documentation* – Unix was the first operating system to include all of its documentation online in machine-readable form. The documentation included:

  o   *man* – manual pages for each command, library component, system call, header file, etc.

  o   *doc* – longer documents detailing major subsystems, such as the C language and troff

Impact

Ken Thompson and Dennis Ritchie, principal developers of Research Unix

Photo from USENIX 1984, including Dennis Ritchie (center)

The Unix system had significant impact on other operating systems. It achieved its reputation by its interactivity, by providing the software at a nominal fee for educational use, by running on inexpensive hardware, and by being easy to adapt and move to different machines. Unix was originally written in assembly language (which had been thought necessary for system implementations on early computers), but was soon rewritten in C, a high-level programming language. Although this followed the lead of Multics and Burroughs, it was Unix that popularized the idea.

Unix had a drastically simplified file model compared to many contemporary operating systems: treating all kinds of files as simple byte arrays. The file system hierarchy contained machine services and devices (such as printers, terminals, or disk drives), providing a uniform interface, but at the expense of occasionally requiring additional mechanisms such as ioctl and mode flags to access features of the hardware that did not fit the simple "stream of bytes" model. The Plan 9 operating system pushed this model even further and eliminated the need for additional mechanisms.

Unix also popularized the hierarchical file system with arbitrarily nested subdirectories, originally introduced by Multics. Other common operating systems of the era had ways to divide a storage device into multiple directories or sections, but they had a fixed number of levels, often only one level. Several major proprietary operating systems eventually added recursive subdirectory capabilities also patterned after Multics. DEC's RSX-11M's "group, user" hierarchy evolved into VMS directories, CP/M's volumes evolved into MS-DOS 2.0+ subdirectories, and HP's MPE group.account hierarchy and IBM's SSP and OS/400 library systems were folded into broader POSIX file systems.

Making the command interpreter an ordinary user-level program, with additional commands provided as separate programs, was another Multics innovation popularized by Unix. The Unix shell used the same language for interactive commands as for scripting (shell scripts — there was no separate job control language like IBM's JCL). Since the shell and OS commands were "just another program", the user could choose (or even write) his own shell. New commands could be added without changing the shell itself. Unix's innovative command-line syntax for creating modular chains of producer-consumer processes (pipelines) made a powerful programming paradigm (coroutines) widely available. Many later command-line interpreters have been inspired by the Unix shell.

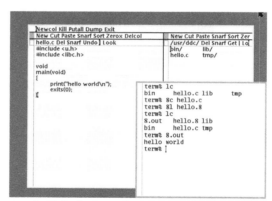

Plan 9 from Bell Labs extends Unix design principles, and was developed as a successor to Unix

A fundamental simplifying assumption of Unix was its focus on newline-delimited text for nearly all file formats. There were no "binary" editors in the original version of Unix — the entire system was configured using textual shell command scripts. The common denominator in the I/O system was the byte — unlike "record-based" file systems. The focus on text for representing nearly everything made Unix pipes especially useful, and encouraged the development of simple, general tools that could be easily combined to perform more complicated *ad hoc* tasks. The focus on text and bytes made the system far more scalable and portable than other systems. Over time, text-based applications have also proven popular in application areas, such as printing languages (PostScript, ODF), and at the application layer of the Internet protocols, e.g., FTP, SMTP, HTTP, SOAP, and SIP.

Unix popularized a syntax for regular expressions that found widespread use. The Unix programming interface became the basis for a widely implemented operating system interface standard. The C programming language soon spread beyond Unix, and is now ubiquitous in systems and applications programming.

Early Unix developers were important in bringing the concepts of modularity and reusability into software engineering practice, spawning a "software tools" movement. Over time, the leading developers of Unix (and programs that ran on it) established a set of cultural norms for developing software, norms which became as important and influential as the technology of Unix itself; this has been termed the Unix philosophy.

The TCP/IP networking protocols were quickly implemented on the Unix versions widely used on relatively inexpensive computers, which contributed to the Internet explosion of worldwide real-time connectivity, and which formed the basis for implementations on many other platforms.

The Unix policy of extensive on-line documentation and (for many years) ready access to all system source code raised programmer expectations, and contributed to the 1983 launch of the free software movement.

Free Unix and Unix-Like Variants

Console screenshots of Debian (top, a popular Linux distribution)
and FreeBSD (bottom, a popular Unix-like operating system)

In 1983, Richard Stallman announced the GNU project, an ambitious effort to create a free software Unix-like system; "free" in the sense that everyone who received a copy would be free to use, study, modify, and redistribute it. The GNU project's own kernel development project, GNU Hurd, had not produced a working kernel, but in 1991 Linus Torvalds released the Linux kernel as free software under the GNU General Public License. In addition to their use in the Linux operating system, many GNU packages – such as the GNU Compiler Collection (and the rest of the GNU toolchain), the GNU C library and the GNU core utilities – have gone on to play central roles in other free Unix systems as well.

Linux distributions, consisting of the Linux kernel and large collections of compatible software have become popular both with individual users and in business. Popular distributions include Red Hat Enterprise Linux, Fedora, SUSE Linux Enterprise, openSUSE, Debian GNU/Linux, Ubuntu, Linux Mint, Mandriva Linux, Slackware Linux, and Gentoo.

A free derivative of BSD Unix, 386BSD, was released in 1992 and led to the NetBSD and FreeBSD projects. With the 1994 settlement of a lawsuit brought against the University of California and Berkeley Software Design Inc. (USL v. BSDi) by UNIX Systems Laboratories, it was clarified that Berkeley had the right to distribute BSD Unix for free, if it so desired. Since then, BSD Unix has been developed in several different product branches, including OpenBSD and DragonFly BSD.

Linux and BSD are increasingly filling the market needs traditionally served by proprietary Unix operating systems, as well as expanding into new markets such as the consumer desktop and mobile and embedded devices. Because of the modular design of the Unix model, sharing components is relatively common; consequently, most or all Unix and Unix-like systems include at least some BSD code, and some systems also include GNU utilities in their distributions.

In a 1999 interview, Dennis Ritchie voiced his opinion that Linux and BSD operating systems are a continuation of the basis of the Unix design, and are derivatives of Unix:

I think the Linux phenomenon is quite delightful, because it draws so strongly on the basis that Unix provided. Linux seems to be the among the healthiest of the direct Unix derivatives, though there are also the various BSD systems as well as the more official offerings from the workstation and mainframe manufacturers.

In the same interview, he states that he views both Unix and Linux as "the continuation of ideas that were started by Ken and me and many others, many years ago."

OpenSolaris was the open-source counterpart to Solaris developed by Sun Microsystems, which included a CDDL-licensed kernel and a primarily GNU userland. However, Oracle discontinued the project upon their acquisition of Sun, which prompted a group of former Sun employees and members of the OpenSolaris community to fork OpenSolaris into the illumos kernel. As of 2014, illumos remains the only active open-source System V derivative.

Arpanet

In May 1975, RFC 681 described the development of *Network Unix* by the Center for Advanced Computation at the University of Illinois. The system was said to "present several interesting capabilities as an ARPANET mini-host". At the time Unix required a license from Bell Laboratories that at $20,000(US) was very expensive for non-university users, while an educational license cost just $150. It was noted that Bell was "open to suggestions" for an ARPANET-wide license.

Specific features found beneficial were the local processing facilities, compilers, editors, a document preparation system, efficient file system and access control, mountable and unmountable volumes, unified treatment of peripherals as special files, integration of the network control program (NCP) within the Unix file system, treatment of network connections as special files that can be accessed through standard Unix I/O calls, closing of all files on program exit, and the decision to be "desirable to minimize the amount of code added to the basic Unix kernel".

Branding

In October 1993, Novell, the company that owned the rights to the Unix System V source at the time, transferred the trademarks of Unix to the X/Open Company (now The Open Group), and in 1995 sold the related business operations to Santa Cruz Operation (SCO). Whether Novell also sold the copyrights to the actual software was the subject of a 2006 federal lawsuit, SCO v. Novell, which Novell won. The case was appealed, but on August 30, 2011, the United States Court of Appeals for the Tenth Circuit affirmed the trial decisions, closing the case. Unix vendor SCO Group Inc. accused Novell of slander of title.

Promotional license plate by Digital Equipment Corporation

HP9000 workstation running HP-UX, a certified Unix operating system

The present owner of the trademark *UNIX* is The Open Group, an industry standards consortium. Only systems fully compliant with and certified to the Single UNIX Specification qualify as "UNIX" (others are called "Unix system-like" or "Unix-like").

By decree of The Open Group, the term "UNIX" refers more to a class of operating systems than to a specific implementation of an operating system; those operating systems which meet The Open Group's Single UNIX Specification should be able to bear the UNIX 98 or UNIX 03 trademarks today, after the operating system's vendor pays a substantial certification fee and annual trademark royalties to The Open Group. Systems licensed to use the UNIX trademark include AIX, HP-UX, Inspur K-UX, IRIX, Solaris, Tru64 UNIX (formerly "Digital UNIX", or OSF/1), macOS, and a part of z/OS. Notably, Inspur K-UX is a Linux distribution certified as UNIX 03 compliant.

Sometimes a representation like *Un*x*, **NIX*, or **N?X* is used to indicate all operating systems similar to Unix. This comes from the use of the asterisk (*) and the question mark characters as wildcard indicators in many utilities. This notation is also used to describe other Unix-like systems that have not met the requirements for UNIX branding from the Open Group.

The Open Group requests that *UNIX* is always used as an adjective followed by a generic term such as *system* to help avoid the creation of a genericized trademark.

Unix was the original formatting, but the usage of *UNIX* remains widespread because it was once typeset in small caps (*Unix*). according to Dennis Ritchie, when presenting the original Unix paper to the third Operating Systems Symposium of the American Association for Computing Machinery (ACM), "we had a new typesetter and *troff* had just been invented and we were intoxicated by being able to produce small caps." Many of the operating system's predecessors and contemporaries used all-uppercase lettering, so many people wrote the name in upper case due to force of habit. It is not an acronym.

Several plural forms of Unix are used casually to refer to multiple brands of Unix and Unix-like systems. Most common is the conventional *Unixes*, but *Unices*, treating Unix as a Latin noun of the third declension, is also popular. The pseudo-Anglo-Saxon plural form *Unixen* is not common, although occasionally seen. Trademark names can be registered by different entities in different countries and trademark laws in some countries allow the same trademark name to be controlled by two different entities if each entity uses the trademark in easily distinguishable categories. The result is that Unix has been used as a brand name for various products including book shelves, ink pens, bottled glue, diapers, hair driers and food containers.

Berkeley Software Distribution

Berkeley Software Distribution (BSD) is a Unix operating system derivative developed and distributed by the Computer Systems Research Group (CSRG) of the University of California, Berkeley, from 1977 to 1995. Today the term "BSD" is often used non-specifically to refer to any of the BSD descendants which together form a branch of the family of Unix-like operating systems. Operating systems derived from the original BSD code remain actively developed and widely used.

Historically, BSD has been considered a branch of Unix, Berkeley Unix, because it shared the initial codebase and design with the original AT&T Unix operating system. In the 1980s, BSD was widely adopted by vendors of workstation-class systems in the form of proprietary Unix variants such as DEC ULTRIX and Sun Microsystems SunOS. This can be attributed to the ease with which it could be licensed, and the familiarity the founders of many technology companies of the time had with it.

Although these proprietary BSD derivatives were largely superseded by the UNIX System V Release 4 and OSF/1 systems in the 1990s (both of which incorporated BSD code and are the basis of other modern Unix systems), later BSD releases provided a basis for several open source development projects that are ongoing, e.g., FreeBSD, OpenBSD, NetBSD, Darwin, and PC-BSD. These, in turn, have been incorporated in whole or in part in modern proprietary operating systems, e.g., the TCP/IP networking code in Windows NT 3.1 and most of the foundation of Apple's macOS and iOS.

History

1BSD (PDP-11)

The earliest distributions of Unix from Bell Labs in the 1970s included the source code to the operating system, allowing researchers at universities to modify and extend Unix. The operating system arrived at Berkeley in 1974, at the request of computer science professor Bob Fabry who had been on the program committee for the Symposium on Operating Systems Principles where

Unix was first presented. A PDP-11/45 was bought to run the system, but for budgetary reasons, this machine was shared with the mathematics and statistics groups at Berkeley, who used RSTS, so that Unix only ran on the machine eight hours per day (sometimes during the day, sometimes during the night). A larger PDP-11/70 was installed at Berkeley the following year, using money from the Ingres database project.

Also in 1975, Ken Thompson took a sabbatical from Bell Labs and came to Berkeley as a visiting professor. He helped to install Version 6 Unix and started working on a Pascal implementation for the system. Graduate students Chuck Haley and Bill Joy improved Thompson's Pascal and implemented an improved text editor, ex. Other universities became interested in the software at Berkeley, and so in 1977 Joy started compiling the first Berkeley Software Distribution (1BSD), which was released on March 9, 1978. 1BSD was an add-on to Version 6 Unix rather than a complete operating system in its own right. Some thirty copies were sent out.

2BSD (PDP-11)

The Second Berkeley Software Distribution (2BSD), released in May 1979, included updated versions of the 1BSD software as well as two new programs by Joy that persist on Unix systems to this day: the vi text editor (a visual version of ex) and the C shell. Some 75 copies of 2BSD were sent out by Bill Joy. A further feature was a networking package called Berknet, developed by Eric Schmidt as part of his master's thesis work, that could connect up to twenty-six computers and provided email and file transfer.

After 3BSD had came out for the VAX line of computers, new releases of 2BSD for the PDP-11 were still issued and distributed through USENIX; for example, 1982's 2.8.1BSD included a collection of fixes for performance problems in Version 7 Unix, and later releases contained ports of changes from the VAX-based releases of BSD back to the PDP-11 architecture. 2.9BSD from 1983 included code from 4.1cBSD, and was the first release that was a full OS (a modified V7 Unix) rather than a set of applications and patches. The most recent release, 2.11BSD, was first issued in 1992. As of 2008, maintenance updates from volunteers are still continuing, with patch 448 being released on June 17, 2012.

3BSD

The DEC VT100 terminal, widely used for Unix timesharing

The VAX-11/780, a typical minicomputer used for early BSD timesharing systems

VAX-11/780 internals

A VAX computer was installed at Berkeley in 1978, but the port of Unix to the VAX architecture, UNIX/32V, did not take advantage of the VAX's virtual memory capabilities. The kernel of 32V was largely rewritten by Berkeley students to include a virtual memory implementation, and a complete operating system including the new kernel, ports of the 2BSD utilities to the VAX, and the utilities from 32V was released as 3BSD at the end of 1979. 3BSD was also alternatively called Virtual VAX/UNIX or VMUNIX (for Virtual Memory Unix), and BSD kernel images were normally called /vmunix until 4.4BSD.

The success of 3BSD was a major factor in the Defense Advanced Research Projects Agency's (DARPA) decision to fund Berkeley's Computer Systems Research Group (CSRG), which would develop a standard Unix platform for future DARPA research in the VLSI Project.

4BSD

4BSD (November 1980) offered a number of enhancements over 3BSD, notably job control in the previously released csh, delivermail (the antecedent of sendmail), "reliable" signals, and the Curses programming library. In a 1985 review of BSD releases, John Quarterman *et al.*, wrote:

4BSD was the operating system of choice for VAXs from the beginning until the release of System III (1979–1982) [...] Most organizations would buy a 32V license and order 4BSD from Berkeley without ever bothering to get a 32V tape. Many installations inside the Bell System ran 4.1BSD (many still do, and many others run 4.2BSD).

4.1BSD

4.1BSD (June 1981) was a response to criticisms of BSD's performance relative to the dominant VAX operating system, VMS. The 4.1BSD kernel was systematically tuned up by Bill Joy until it could perform as well as VMS on several benchmarks. The release would have been called *5BSD*, but after objections from AT&T the name was changed; AT&T feared confusion with AT&T's UNIX System V.

4.2BSD

4.2BSD (August 1983) would take over two years to implement and contained several major overhauls. Before its official release came three intermediate versions: *4.1a* incorporated a modified version of BBN's preliminary TCP/IP implementation; *4.1b* included the new Berkeley Fast File System, implemented by Marshall Kirk McKusick; and *4.1c* was an interim release during the last few months of 4.2BSD's development. Back at Bell Labs, 4.1cBSD became the basis of the 8th Edition of Research Unix, and a commercially supported version was available from mtXinu.

To guide the design of 4.2BSD, Duane Adams of DARPA formed a "steering committee" consisting of Bob Fabry, Bill Joy and Sam Leffler from UCB, Alan Nemeth and Rob Gurwitz from BBN, Dennis Ritchie from Bell Labs, Keith Lantz from Stanford, Rick Rashid from Carnegie-Mellon, Bert Halstead from MIT, Dan Lynch from ISI, and Gerald J. Popek of UCLA. The committee met from April 1981 to June 1983.

Apart from the Fast File System, several features from outside contributors were accepted, including disk quotas and job control. Sun Microsystems provided testing on its Motorola 68000 machines prior to release, ensuring portability of the system.

The official 4.2BSD release came in August 1983. It was notable as the first version released after the 1982 departure of Bill Joy to co-found Sun Microsystems; Mike Karels and Marshall Kirk McKusick took on leadership roles within the project from that point forward. On a lighter note, it also marked the debut of BSD's daemon mascot in a drawing by John Lasseter that appeared on the cover of the printed manuals distributed by USENIX.

4.3BSD

4.3BSD was released in June 1986. Its main changes were to improve the performance of many of the new contributions of 4.2BSD that had not been as heavily tuned as the 4.1BSD code. Prior to the release, BSD's implementation of TCP/IP had diverged considerably from BBN's official implementation. After several months of testing, DARPA determined that the 4.2BSD version was superior and would remain in 4.3BSD.

After 4.3BSD, it was determined that BSD would move away from the aging VAX platform. The

Power 6/32 platform (codenamed "Tahoe") developed by Computer Consoles Inc. seemed promising at the time, but was abandoned by its developers shortly thereafter. Nonetheless, the 4.3BSD-Tahoe port (June 1988) proved valuable, as it led to a separation of machine-dependent and machine-independent code in BSD which would improve the system's future portability.

"4.3 BSD UNIX" from the University of Wisconsin circa 1987. System startup and login.

4.3 BSD from the University of Wisconsin. Browsing "/usr/ucb" and "/usr/games"

Apart from portability, the CSRG worked on an implementation of the OSI network protocol stack, improvements to the kernel virtual memory system and (with Van Jacobson of LBL) new TCP/IP algorithms to accommodate the growth of the Internet.

Until then, all versions of BSD incorporated proprietary AT&T Unix code and were, therefore, subject to an AT&T software license. Source code licenses had become very expensive and several outside parties had expressed interest in a separate release of the networking code, which had been developed entirely outside AT&T and would not be subject to the licensing requirement. This led to Networking Release 1 (Net/1), which was made available to non-licensees of AT&T code and was freely redistributable under the terms of the BSD license. It was released in June 1989.

4.3BSD-Reno came in early 1990. It was an interim release during the early development of 4.4BSD, and its use was considered a "gamble", hence the naming after the gambling center of Reno, Nevada. This release was explicitly moving towards POSIX compliance, and, according to some, away from the BSD philosophy (as POSIX is very much based on System V, and Reno was quite bloated compared to previous releases). Among the new features were an NFS implementation from the University of Guelph and support for the HP 9000 range of computers, originating in the University of Utah's "HPBSD" port.

In August 2006, *InformationWeek* magazine rated 4.3BSD as the "Greatest Software Ever Written". They commented: "BSD 4.3 represents the single biggest theoretical undergirder of the Internet."

Net/2 and Legal Troubles

Installation of 386BSD. 386BSD was an early port of BSD to the Intel 80386 architecture.

After Net/1, BSD developer Keith Bostic proposed that more non-AT&T sections of the BSD system be released under the same license as Net/1. To this end, he started a project to reimplement most of the standard Unix utilities without using the AT&T code. For example, vi, which had been based on the original Unix version of ed, was rewritten as nvi (new vi). Within eighteen months, all of the AT&T utilities had been replaced, and it was determined that only a few AT&T files remained in the kernel. These files were removed, and the result was the June 1991 release of Networking Release 2 (Net/2), a nearly complete operating system that was freely distributable.

Net/2 was the basis for two separate ports of BSD to the Intel 80386 architecture: the free 386BSD by William Jolitz and the proprietary BSD/386 (later renamed BSD/OS) by Berkeley Software Design (BSDi). 386BSD itself was short-lived, but became the initial code base of the NetBSD and FreeBSD projects that were started shortly thereafter.

BSDi soon found itself in legal trouble with AT&T's Unix System Laboratories (USL) subsidiary, then the owners of the System V copyright and the Unix trademark. The *USL v. BSDi* lawsuit was filed in 1992 and led to an injunction on the distribution of Net/2 until the validity of USL's copyright claims on the source could be determined.

The lawsuit slowed development of the free-software descendants of BSD for nearly two years while their legal status was in question, and as a result systems based on the Linux kernel, which did not have such legal ambiguity, gained greater support. Although not released until 1992, development of 386BSD predated that of Linux. Linus Torvalds has said that if 386BSD or the GNU kernel had been available at the time, he probably would not have created Linux.

4.4BSD and Descendants

The lawsuit was settled in January 1994, largely in Berkeley's favor. Of the 18,000 files in the Berkeley distribution, only three had to be removed and 70 modified to show USL copyright notices. A further condition of the settlement was that USL would not file further lawsuits against users and distributors of the Berkeley-owned code in the upcoming 4.4BSD release. Marshall Kirk McKusick summarizes the lawsuit and its outcome:

Code copying and theft of trade secrets was alleged. The actual infringing code was not identified for nearly two years. The lawsuit could have dragged on for much longer but for the fact that Novell bought USL from AT&T and sought a settlement. In the end, three files were removed from the

18,000 that made up the distribution, and a number of minor changes were made to other files. In addition, the University agreed to add USL copyrights to about 70 files, with the stipulation that those files continued to be freely redistributed.

In June 1994, 4.4BSD was released in two forms: the freely distributable 4.4BSD-Lite contained no AT&T source, whereas 4.4BSD-Encumbered was available, as earlier releases had been, only to AT&T licensees.

The final release from Berkeley was 1995's 4.4BSD-Lite Release 2, after which the CSRG was dissolved and development of BSD at Berkeley ceased. Since then, several variants based directly or indirectly on 4.4BSD-Lite (such as FreeBSD, NetBSD, OpenBSD and DragonFly BSD) have been maintained.

In addition, the permissive nature of the BSD license has allowed many other operating systems, both free and proprietary, to incorporate BSD code. For example, Microsoft Windows has used BSD-derived code in its implementation of TCP/IP and bundles recompiled versions of BSD's command-line networking tools since Windows 2000. Also Darwin, the system on which Apple's macOS is built, is a derivative of 4.4BSD-Lite2 and FreeBSD. Various commercial Unix operating systems, such as Solaris, also contain varying amounts of BSD code.

Relationship to Research Unix

Starting with the 8th Edition, versions of Research Unix at Bell Labs had a close relationship to BSD. This began when 4.1cBSD for the VAX was used as the basis for Research Unix 8th Edition. This continued in subsequent versions, such as the 9th Edition, which incorporated source code and improvements from 4.3BSD. The result was that these later versions of Research Unix were closer to BSD than they were to System V. In a Usenet posting from 2000, Dennis Ritchie described this relationship between BSD and Research Unix:

Research Unix 8th Edition started from (I think) BSD 4.1c, but with enormous amounts scooped out and replaced by our own stuff. This continued with 9th and 10th. The ordinary user command-set was, I guess, a bit more BSD-flavored than SysVish, but it was pretty eclectic.

Relationship to System V

Eric S. Raymond summarizes the longstanding relationship between System V and BSD, stating, "The divide was roughly between longhairs and shorthairs; programmers and technical people tended to line up with Berkeley and BSD, more business-oriented types with AT&T and System V."

In 1989, David A. Curry wrote about the differences between BSD and System V. He characterized System V as being often regarded as the "standard Unix." However, he described BSD as more popular among university and government computer centers, due to its advanced features and performance:

Most university and government computer centers that use UNIX use Berkeley UNIX, rather than System V. There are several reasons for this, but perhaps the two most significant are that Berkeley UNIX provides networking capabilities that until recently (Release 3.0) were completely unavailable in System V, and that Berkeley UNIX is much more suited to a research environment, which requires a faster file system, better virtual memory handling, and a larger variety of programming languages.

Technology

Berkeley Sockets

4.3 BSD from the University of Wisconsin. Displaying the man page for Franz Lisp

Tape for SunOS 4.1.1, a 4.3BSD derivative

Sony NEWS workstation running the BSD-based NEWS-OS operating system

Berkeley's Unix was the first Unix to include libraries supporting the Internet Protocol stacks: *Berkeley sockets*. A Unix implementation of IP's predecessor, the ARPAnet's NCP, with FTP and Telnet clients, had been produced at U. Illinois in 1975, and was available at Berkeley. However, the memory scarcity on the PDP-11 forced a complicated design and performance problems.

By integrating sockets with the Unix operating system's file descriptors, it became almost as easy to read and write data across a network as it was to access a disk. The AT&T laboratory eventually released their own STREAMS library, which incorporated much of the same functionality in a software stack with a different architecture, but the wide distribution of the existing sockets library reduced the impact of the new API. Early versions of BSD were used to form Sun Microsystems' SunOS, founding the first wave of popular Unix workstations.

Binary Compatibility

BSD operating systems can run much native software of several other operating systems on the same architecture, using a binary compatibility layer. Much simpler and faster than emulation, this allows, for instance, applications intended for Linux to be run at effectively full speed. This makes BSDs not only suitable for server environments, but also for workstation ones, given the increasing availability of commercial or closed-source software for Linux only. This also allows administrators to migrate legacy commercial applications, which may have only supported commercial Unix variants, to a more modern operating system, retaining the functionality of such applications until they can be replaced by a better alternative.

Standards Adherence

Current BSD operating system variants support many of the common IEEE, ANSI, ISO, and POSIX standards, while retaining most of the traditional BSD behavior. Like AT&T Unix, the BSD kernel is monolithic, meaning that device drivers in the kernel run in privileged mode, as part of the core of the operating system.

Significant BSD Descendants

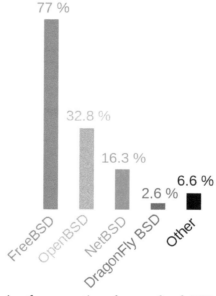

Bar chart showing the proportion of users of each BSD variant from a
BSD usage survey in 2005. Each participant was permitted to indicate multiple BSD variants

BSD has been the base of a large number of operating systems. Most notable among these today are perhaps the major open source BSDs: FreeBSD, NetBSD and OpenBSD, which are all derived from 386BSD and 4.4BSD-Lite by various routes. Both NetBSD and FreeBSD started life in 1993, initially derived from 386BSD, but in 1994 migrating to a 4.4BSD-Lite code base. OpenBSD was forked in 1995 from NetBSD. The three most notable descendants in current use—sometimes known as *the BSDs*—have themselves spawned a number of children, including DragonFly BSD, FreeSBIE, MirOS BSD, DesktopBSD, and PC-BSD. They are targeted at an array of systems for different purposes and are common in government facilities, universities and in commercial use.

A number of commercial operating systems are also partly or wholly based on BSD or its descendants, including Sun's SunOS and Apple Inc.'s macOS.

Most of the current BSD operating systems are open source and available for download, free of charge, under the BSD License, the most notable exception being macOS. They also generally use a monolithic kernel architecture, apart from macOS and DragonFly BSD which feature hybrid kernels. The various open source BSD projects generally develop the kernel and userland programs and libraries together, the source code being managed using a single central source repository.

In the past, BSD was also used as a basis for several proprietary versions of Unix, such as Sun's SunOS, Sequent's Dynix, NeXT's NeXTSTEP, DEC's Ultrix and OSF/1 AXP (now Tru64 UNIX). Parts of NeXT's software became the foundation for macOS, among the most commercially successful BSD variants in the general market.

A selection of significant Unix versions and Unix-like operating systems that descend from BSD includes:

- FreeBSD, an open source general purpose operating system.

    o NeXT NEXTSTEP and OpenStep, based on the Mach kernel and 4BSD; the ancestor of macOS

        ▪ Apple Inc.'s Darwin, the core of macOS and iOS; built on the XNU kernel (part Mach, part FreeBSD, part Apple-derived code) and a userland much of which comes from FreeBSD

    o TrueOS, GhostBSD and DesktopBSD, distributions of FreeBSD with emphasis on ease of use and user friendly interfaces for the desktop/laptop PC user.

    o MidnightBSD, another fork of FreeBSD

    o DragonFly BSD, a fork of FreeBSD to follow an alternative design, particularly related to SMP.

    o NextBSD, new BSD distribution derived from FreeBSD 10.1 and various macOS components.

    o FreeNAS a free network-attached storage server based on a minimal version of FreeBSD.

    o NAS4Free fork of 0.7 FreeNAS version, Network attached storage server.

    o Nokia IPSO (IPSO SB variant), the FreeBSD-based OS used in Nokia Firewall Appliances.

    o The OS for the Netflix Open Connect Appliance.

    o Junos, the operating system for Juniper routers, a customized version of FreeBSD, and a variety of other embedded operating systems

- o Isilon Systems' OneFS, the operating system used on Isilon IQ-series clustered storage systems, is a heavily customized version of FreeBSD.

- o NetApp's Data ONTAP, the operating system for NetApp filers, is a customized version of FreeBSD with the ONTAP architecture built on top.

- o monowall, a FreeBSD distribution tweaked for usage as a firewall.

- o pfSense free open source FreeBSD based firewall/router.

- o Coyote Point Systems EQ/OS, a hardened high-performance runtime for server load balancing.

- NetBSD, an open source BSD focused on clean design and portability.

  - o OpenBSD, a 1995 fork of NetBSD, focused on security.

    - MirOS BSD, a fork of OpenBSD with additional features such as European localizations.

    - ekkoBSD, a discontinued fork of OpenBSD, now partially merged with MirOS.

    - MicroBSD, an OpenBSD-based operating system with a small memory footprint.

  - o Force10 FTOS, the operating system for Force 10 and Dell datacenter network switches.

    - Dell DNOS version 9 and above, the successor to FTOS.

- TrustedBSD

- F5 Networks, F5 BIGIP Appliances used a BSD OS as the management OS until version 9.0 was released, which is built on top of Linux.

- DEC's Ultrix, the official version of Unix for its PDP-11, VAX, and DECstation systems

- Sony NEWS-OS, a BSD-based operating system for their network engineering workstations

- OSF/1, a microkernel-based Unix developed by the Open Software Foundation, incorporating the Mach kernel and parts of 4BSD

  - o Tru64 UNIX (formerly DEC OSF/1 AXP or Digital UNIX), the port of OSF/1 for DEC Alpha-based systems from DEC, Compaq and HP.

- Pre-5.0 versions of Sun Microsystems SunOS, an enhanced version of 4BSD for the Sun Motorola 68k-based Sun-2 and Sun-3 systems, SPARC-based systems, and x86-based Sun386i systems (SunOS 5.0 and later versions are System V Release 4-based)

- 386BSD, the first open source BSD-based operating system and the ancestor of most current BSD systems

- DEMOS, a Soviet BSD clone

- BSD/OS, a (now defunct) proprietary BSD for PCs

- RetroBSD, a fork of BSD 2.11 designed to run on microcontrollers such as the PIC32

macOS

macOS (originally named Mac OS X until 2012, then rebranded to OS X until 2016) is the current series of Unix-based graphical operating systems developed and marketed by Apple Inc. designed to run on Apple's Macintosh computers, having been preinstalled on all Macs since 2002. Within the market of desktop, laptop and home computers, and by web usage, it is the second most widely used desktop OS after Microsoft Windows.

Launched in 2001 as Mac OS X, the series is the latest in the family of Macintosh operating systems. Mac OS X succeeded the "classic" Mac OS, which was introduced in 1984, and the final release of which was Mac OS 9 in 1999. An initial, early version of the system, Mac OS X Server 1.0, was released in 1999. The first desktop version, Mac OS X 10.0, followed in March 2001. In 2012, Apple rebranded Mac OS X to OS X. Releases were code named after big cats from the original release up until OS X 10.8 Mountain Lion. Beginning in 2013 with OS X 10.9 Mavericks, Apple names macOS releases after landmarks in California. In 2016, Apple rebranded OS X to macOS, adopting the nomenclature that it uses for their other operating systems, iOS, watchOS, and tvOS. The latest version of macOS is macOS 10.12 Sierra, which was publicly released on September 20, 2016.

macOS is based on technologies developed at NeXT between 1985 until 1997, when Apple acquired the company. The "X" in Mac OS X and OS X is pronounced "ten", as it is the Roman numeral for the number 10. The X was a prominent part of the operating system's brand identity, and was used to showcase its Unix compatibility; UNIX 03 certification was achieved for the Intel version of Mac OS X 10.5 Leopard and all releases from Mac OS X 10.6 Snow Leopard up to the current version also have UNIX 03 certification. macOS shares its Unix-based core, named Darwin, and many of its frameworks with iOS, tvOS and watchOS. A heavily modified version of Mac OS X 10.4 Tiger was used for the first-generation Apple TV.

Apple also used to have a separate line of releases of macOS designed for servers. Beginning with Mac OS X 10.7 Lion, the server functions were made available as a separate package on the Mac App Store.

Releases of Mac OS X from 1999 to 2005 can run only on the PowerPC-based Macs from the time period. After Apple announced that they were switching to Intel CPUs from 2006 onwards, a separate version Mac OS X 10.4 Tiger was made and distributed exclusively with early Intel-based Macs; it included an emulator known as Rosetta, which allowed users to run most PowerPC applications on Intel-based Macs. Mac OS X 10.5 Leopard was released as a Universal binary, meaning the installer disc supported both Intel and PowerPC processors. In 2009, Apple released Mac OS X 10.6 Snow Leopard, which ran exclusively on Intel-based Macs. In 2011, Apple released Mac OS X 10.7 Lion, which no longer supported 32-bit Intel processors and also did not include Rosetta. All versions of the system released since then run exclusively on 64-bit Intel CPUs and do not support PowerPC applications.

History

Development

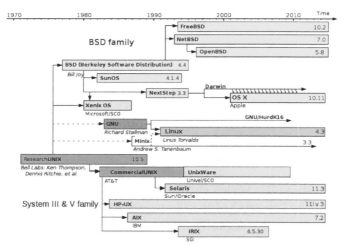

Simplified history of Unix-like operating systems

The heritage of what would become macOS had originated at NeXT, a company founded by Steve Jobs following his departure from Apple in 1985. There, the Unix-like NeXTSTEP operating system was developed, and then launched in 1989. The kernel of NeXTSTEP is based upon the Mach kernel, which was originally developed at Carnegie Mellon University, with additional kernel layers and low-level user space code derived from parts of BSD. Its graphical user interface was built on top of an object-oriented GUI toolkit using the Objective-C programming language.

Throughout the early 1990s, Apple had tried to create a "next-generation" OS to succeed its classic Mac OS through the Taligent, Copland and Gershwin projects, but all of them were eventually abandoned. This led Apple to purchase NeXT in 1996, allowing NeXTSTEP, then called OPEN-STEP, to serve as the basis for Apple's next generation operating system. This purchase also led to Steve Jobs returning to Apple as an interim, and then the permanent CEO, shepherding the transformation of the programmer-friendly OPENSTEP into a system that would be adopted by Apple's primary market of home users and creative professionals. The project was first code named "Rhapsody" and then officially named Mac OS X.

Mac OS X

Launch of Mac OS X

Mac OS X was originally presented as the tenth major version of Apple's operating system for Macintosh computers; current versions of macOS retain the major version number "10". Previous Macintosh operating systems (versions of the classic Mac OS) were named using Arabic numerals, e.g. Mac OS 8 and Mac OS 9. The letter "X" in Mac OS X's name refers to the number 10, a Roman numeral. It is therefore correctly pronounced "ten" /ˈtɛn/ in this context. However, a common mispronunciation is "X" /ˈɛks/.

The first version of Mac OS X, Mac OS X Server 1.0, was a transitional product, featuring an interface resembling the classic Mac OS, though it was not compatible with software designed for the older system. Consumer releases of Mac OS X included more backward compatibility. Mac OS applications could be rewritten to run natively via the Carbon API; many could also be run directly through the Classic Environment with a reduction in performance.

The consumer version of Mac OS X was launched in 2001 with Mac OS X 10.0. Reviews were variable, with extensive praise for its sophisticated, glossy Aqua interface but criticizing it for sluggish performance. With Apple's popularity at a low, the makers of several classic Mac applications such as FrameMaker and PageMaker declined to develop new versions of their software for Mac OS X. *Ars Technica* columnist John Siracusa, who reviewed every major OS X release up to 10.10, described the early releases in retrospect as 'dog-slow, feature poor' and Aqua as 'unbearably slow and a huge resource hog'.

Following Releases

Apple rapidly developed several new releases of Mac OS X. Siracusa's review of version 10.3, Panther, noted "It's strange to have gone from years of uncertainty and vaporware to a steady annual supply of major new operating system releases." Version 10.4, Tiger, reportedly shocked executives at Microsoft by offering a number of features, such as fast file searching and improved graphics processing, that Microsoft had spent several years struggling to add to Windows with acceptable performance.

In 2006, the first Intel Macs released used a specialized version of Mac OS X 10.4 Tiger. In 2007, Mac OS X 10.5 Leopard was the first to run on both PowerPC and Intel Macs with the use of universal binaries. Mac OS X 10.6 Snow Leopard was the first version of OS X to drop support for PowerPC Macs.

As the operating system evolved, it moved away from the classic Mac OS, with applications being added and removed. Targeting the consumer and media markets, Apple emphasized its new "digital lifestyle" applications such as the iLife suite, integrated home entertainment through the Front Row media center and the Safari web browser. With increasing popularity of the internet, Apple offered additional online services, including the .Mac, MobileMe and most recently iCloud products. It also began selling third-party applications through the Mac App Store.

Newer versions of Mac OS X also included modifications to the general interface, moving away from the striped gloss and transparency of the initial versions. Some applications began to use a brushed metal appearance, or non-pinstriped titlebar appearance in version 10.4. In Leopard, Apple announced a unification of the interface, with a standardized gray-gradient window style.

A key development for the system was the announcement and release of the iPhone from 2007 onwards. While Apple's previous iPod media players used a minimal operating system, the iPhone used an operating system based on Mac OS X, which would later be called "iPhone OS" and then iOS. The simultaneous release of two operating systems based on the same frameworks placed tension on Apple, which cited the iPhone as forcing it to delay Mac OS X 10.5 Leopard. However, after Apple opened the iPhone to third-party developers its commercial success drew attention to Mac OS X, with many iPhone software developers showing interest in Mac development.

In two succeeding versions, Lion and Mountain Lion, Apple moved some applications to a highly skeumorphic style of design inspired by contemporary versions of iOS, at the same time simplifying some elements by making controls such as scroll bars fade out when not in use. This direction was, like brushed metal interfaces, unpopular with some users, although it continued a trend of greater animation and variety in the interface previously seen in design aspects such as the Time Machine backup utility, which presented past file versions against a swirling nebula, and the glossy translucent dock of Leopard and Snow Leopard. In addition, with Mac OS X 10.7 Lion, Apple ceased to release separate server versions of Mac OS X, selling server tools as a separate downloadable application through the Mac App Store. A review described the trend in the server products as becoming "cheaper and simpler... shifting its focus from large businesses to small ones."

OS X

In 2012, with the release of OS X 10.8 Mountain Lion, the name of the system was shortened from Mac OS X to OS X. That year, Apple removed the head of OS X development, Scott Forstall, and design was changed towards a more minimal direction. Apple's new user interface design, using deep color saturation, text-only buttons and a minimal, 'flat' interface, was debuted with iOS 7 in 2013. With OS X engineers reportedly working on iOS 7, the version released in 2013, OS X 10.9 Mavericks, was something of a transitional release, with some of the skeuomorphic design removed, however the general interface of Mavericks remained largely unchanged. The next version, OS X 10.10 Yosemite, adopted a design similar to iOS 7 but with greater complexity suitable for an interface controlled with a mouse.

From 2012 onwards, the system has shifted to an annual release schedule similar to that of iOS. It also steadily cut the cost of updates from Snow Leopard onwards, before removing upgrade fees altogether from 2013 onwards. Some journalists and third-party software developers have suggested that this decision, while allowing more rapid feature release, meant less opportunity to focus on stability, with no version of OS X recommendable for users requiring stability and performance above new features. Apple's 2015 update, OS X 10.11 El Capitan, was announced to focus specifically on stability and performance improvements.

macOS

In 2016, with the release of macOS 10.12 Sierra, the name was changed from OS X to macOS. macOS 10.12 Sierra's main features are the long-awaited introduction of Siri to the Mac, Optimized Storage, improvements to included applications, greater integration with Apple's mobile devices. A new file system, Apple File System, is coming in a later update, designed to address the problems and limitations with the current filesystem, HFS Plus (commonly referred to as Mac OS Extended by Apple).

Architecture

macOS's core is a POSIX compliant operating system built on top of the XNU kernel, with standard Unix facilities available from the command line interface. Apple has released this family of software as a free and open source operating system named Darwin. On top of Darwin, Apple layered a number of components, including the Aqua interface and the Finder, to complete the GUI-based operating system which is macOS.

With its original introduction as Mac OS X, the system brought a number of new capabilities to provide a more stable and reliable platform than its predecessor, the classic Mac OS. For example, pre-emptive multitasking and memory protection improved the system's ability to run multiple applications simultaneously without them interrupting or corrupting each other. Many aspects of macOS's architecture are derived from OPENSTEP, which was designed to be portable, to ease the transition from one platform to another. For example, NeXTSTEP was ported from the original 68k-based NeXT workstations to x86 and other architectures before NeXT was purchased by Apple, and OPENSTEP was later ported to the PowerPC architecture as part of the Rhapsody project.

macOS's default file system is HFS+, which it inherited from the classic Mac OS. Operating system designer Linus Torvalds has criticized HFS+, saying it is "probably the worst file system ever", whose design is "actively corrupting user data". He criticized the case insensitivity of file names, a design made worse when Apple extended the file system to support Unicode. Initially, HFS+ was designed for classic Mac OS, which runs on big-endian 68K and PowerPC systems. When Apple switched Macintosh to little-endian Intel processors, it continued to use big-endian byte order on HFS+ file systems. As a result, macOS on current Macs must do byte swap when it reads file system data. These concerns are being addressed with the new Apple File System, which will be included in a later update.

The Darwin subsystem in macOS is in charge of managing the file system, which includes the Unix permissions layer. In 2003 and 2005, two Macworld editors expressed criticism of the permission scheme; Ted Landau called misconfigured permissions "the most common frustration" in macOS, while Rob Griffiths suggested that some users may even have to reset permissions every day, a process which can take up to 15 minutes. More recently, another Macworld editor, Dan Frakes, called the procedure of repairing permissions vastly overused. He argues that macOS typically handles permissions properly without user interference, and resetting permissions should just be tried when problems emerge.

The architecture of macOS incorporates a layered design: the layered frameworks aid rapid development of applications by providing existing code for common tasks. Apple provides its own software development tools, most prominently an integrated development environment called Xcode. Xcode provides interfaces to compilers that support several programming languages including C, C++, Objective-C, and Swift. For the Apple–Intel transition, it was modified so that developers could build their applications as a universal binary, which provides compatibility with both the Intel-based and PowerPC-based Macintosh lines. First and third-party applications can be controlled programatically using the AppleScript framework, retained from the classic Mac OS, or using the newer Automator application that offers pre-written tasks that do not require programming knowledge.

Software Compatibility

Apple offered two main APIs to develop software natively for macOS: Cocoa and Carbon. Cocoa was a descendant of APIs inherited from OPENSTEP with no ancestry from the classic Mac OS, while Carbon was an adaptation of classic Mac OS APIs, allowing Mac software to be minimally rewritten in order to run natively on Mac OS X.

The Cocoa API was created as the result of a 1993 collaboration between NeXT Computer and Sun Microsystems. This heritage is highly visible for Cocoa developers, since the "NS" prefix is ubiquitous in the framework, standing variously for **NeXTSTEP** or **NeXT/S**un. The official OPENSTEP API, published in September 1994, was the first to split the API between Foundation and ApplicationKit and the first to use the "NS" prefix. Traditionally, Cocoa programs have been mostly written in Objective-C, with Java as an alternative. However, on July 11, 2005, Apple announced that "features added to Cocoa in Mac OS X versions later than 10.4 will not be added to the Cocoa-Java programming interface." macOS also used to support the Java Platform as a "preferred software package"—in practice this means that applications written in Java fit as neatly into the operating system as possible while still being cross-platform compatible, and that graphical user interfaces written in Swing look almost exactly like native Cocoa interfaces. Since 2014, Apple has promoted its new programming language Swift as the preferred language for software development on Apple platforms.

Apple's original plan with macOS was to require all developers to rewrite their software into the Cocoa APIs. This caused much outcry among existing Mac developers, who threatened to abandon the platform rather than invest in a costly rewrite, and the idea was shelved. To permit a smooth transition from Mac OS 9 to Mac OS X, the Carbon Application Programming Interface (API) was created. Applications written with Carbon were initially able to run natively on both classic Mac OS and Mac OS X, although this ability was later dropped as Mac OS X developed. Carbon was not included in the first product sold as Mac OS X: the little-used original release of Mac OS X Server 1.0, which also did not include the Aqua interface. Apple limited further development of Carbon from the release of Leopard onwards, announcing Carbon applications would not receive the ability to run at 64-bit. As of 2015, a small number of older Mac OS X apps with heritage dating back to the classic Mac OS still used Carbon, including Microsoft Office. Early versions of macOS could also run some classic Mac OS applications through the Classic Environment with performance limitations; this feature was removed from 10.5 onwards and all Macs using Intel processors.

Because macOS is POSIX compliant, many software packages written for the other Unix-like systems such as Linux can be recompiled to run on it, including much scientific and technical software. Third-party projects such as Homebrew, Fink, MacPorts and pkgsrc provide pre-compiled or pre-formatted packages. Apple and others have provided versions of the X Window System graphical interface which can allow these applications to run with an approximation of the macOS look-and-feel. The current Apple-endorsed method is the open-source XQuartz project; earlier versions could use the X11 application provided by Apple, or before that the XDarwin project.

Applications can be distributed to Macs and installed by the user from any source and by any method such as downloading (with or without code signing, available via an Apple developer account) or through the Mac App Store, a marketplace of software maintained by Apple by way of a process requiring the company's approval. Apps installed through the Mac App Store run within a sandbox, restricting their ability to exchange information with other applications or modify the core operating system and its features. This has been cited as an advantage, by allowing users to install apps with confidence that they should not be able to damage their system, but also as a disadvantage, by blocking the Mac App Store's use by professional applications that require elevated privileges. Applications without any code signature cannot be run by default except from a computer's administrator account.

Apple produces macOS applications, some of which are included and some sold separately. This includes iWork, Final Cut Pro, Logic Pro, iLife, and the database application FileMaker. Numerous other developers also offer software for macOS.

Hardware Compatibility

List of macOS versions, the supported systems on which they run, and their RAM requirements

Operating system	Supported systems	RAM requirement
10.12	Intel Macs (64-bit) released in: 2009 (iMac and main MacBook line), 2010 (other) or later	2 GB
10.8 – 10.11	Intel Macs (64-bit) released in: 2007 (prosumer and iMac), 2008 (other consumer), 2009 (Xserve) or later	
10.7	Intel Macs (64-bit) Rosetta support dropped from 10.7 and newer.	
10.6	Intel Macs (32-bit or 64-bit)	1 GB
10.5	G4, G5 and Intel Macs (32-bit or 64-bit) at 867 MHz or faster Classic support dropped from 10.5 and newer.	512 MB
10.4	Macs with built-in FireWire and either a New World ROM or Intel processor	256 MB
10.3	Macs with a New World ROM	128 MB
10.0 – 10.2	G3, G4 and G5 iBook and PowerBook, Power Mac and iMac (except PowerBook G3 "Kanga")	

Tools such as XPostFacto and patches applied to the installation media have been developed by third parties to enable installation of newer versions of macOS on systems not officially supported by Apple. This includes a number of pre-G3 Power Macintosh systems that can be made to run up to and including Mac OS X 10.2 Jaguar, all G3-based Macs which can run up to and including Tiger, and sub-867 MHz G4 Macs can run Leopard by removing the restriction from the installation DVD or entering a command in the Mac's Open Firmware interface to tell the Leopard Installer that it has a clock rate of 867 MHz or greater. Except for features requiring specific hardware (e.g. graphics acceleration or DVD writing), the operating system offers the same functionality on all supported hardware.

As most Mac hardware components, or components similar to those, since the Intel transition are available for purchase, some technology-capable groups have developed software to install macOS on non-Apple computers. These are referred to as Hackintoshes, a portmanteau of the words "hack" and "Macintosh". This violates Apple's EULA (and is therefore unsupported by Apple technical support, warranties etc.), but communities that cater to personal users, who do not install for resale and profit, have generally been ignored by Apple. These self-made computers allow more flexibility and customization of hardware, but at a cost of leaving the user more responsible for their own machine, such as on matter of data integrity or security. Psystar, a business that attempted to profit from selling macOS on non-Apple certified hardware, was sued by Apple in 2008.

Specifics

Below are lists of exact versions released for every Intel computer Apple has made.

iMac

iMac	Date introduced	Original Mac OS X included	Later Mac OS X included	OS X Build(s)
iMac (Retina 5K, 27-inch, Late 2015)	Oct 2015	10.11	10.11.1	15A4310, 15B42
iMac (Retina 4K, 21.5-inch, Late 2015)	Oct 2015	10.11	10.11.1	15A2301, 15B42
iMac (21.5-inch, Late 2015)	Oct 2015	10.11	10.11.1	15A2301, 15B42
iMac (Retina 5k, 27-inch, Mid 2015)	May 2015	10.10.2	-	14C500
iMac (Retina 5K, 27-inch, Late 2014)	Oct 2014	10.10	10.10.2	14A389, 14C109
iMac (21.5-inch, Mid 2014)	June 2014	10.9.3	10.9.4, 10.10.2	13D2061, 13E28, 14C109
iMac (21.5-inch, Late 2013)	Sept 2013	10.8.4	10.9, 10.9.2, 10.9.4, 10.10.2	12E4022, 13A603, 13C64, 13E28, 14C109
iMac (27-inch, Late 2013)	Sept 2013	10.8.4	10.9, 10.9.2, 10.9.4, 10.10.2	12E4022, 13A603, 13A1900, 13C64, 13E28, 14C109
iMac (27-inch, Late 2012)	Dec 2012	10.8.2	10.8.3	12C2034,12C3103, 12C2037, 12D78
iMac (21.5 inch, Late 2012)	Nov 2012	10.8.1	10.8.2, 10.8.3	12B2517, 12C2034, 12D78
iMac (Late 2011)	Sep 2011	10.7.3	10.8	11D2001, 12A269
iMac (Mid 2011)	May 2011	10.6.6	10.6.7, 10.7, 10.7.2, 10.7.3	10J4026, 10J4139, 11A511a, 11C74, 11D2001
iMac (Mid 2010)	Jul 2010	10.6.3	10.6.4	10D2322a, 10F2056, 10F2061, 10F2090, 10F2108
iMac (27-inch, Quad Core, Late 2009)	Nov 2009	10.6.2	-	10C2234
iMac (21.5-inch, Late 2009)	Oct 2009	10.6.1	10.6.2	10A2155, 10C2234
iMac (27-inch, Late 2009)	Oct 2009	10.6.1	10.6.2	10A2155, 10C2234
iMac (20-inch, Mid 2009)	Apr 2009	10.5.6	10.6	9G3556, 10A432
iMac (Early 2009	Mar 2009	10.5.6	10.6	9G2030, 9G3610, 10A432
iMac (Early 2008)	Apr 2008	10.5.2	10.5.4	9C2028, 9E25
iMac (Mid 2007)	Aug 2007	10.4.10	10.5, 10.5.2	8R4031, 9A581, 9A3129, 9C3033
iMac (Late 2006, 20-inch)	Sep 2006	10.4.7	10.4.8	8K1106, 8N1430
iMac (Late 2006, 24-inch)	Sep 2006	10.4.7	10.4.8	8K1123, 8N1430
iMac (Late 2006, 17-inch CD)	Sep 2006	10.4.7	10.4.8, 10.4.10, 10.5.4	8K1106, 8N1430, 8R3032, 9E25
iMac (Late 2006, 17-inch)	Sep 2006	10.4.7	10.4.8	8K1106, 8N1430
iMac (Mid 2006, 17-inch)	Jul 2006	10.4.6	-	8I2057
iMac (Early 2006)	Jan 2006	10.4.4	10.4.6	8G1165, 8G1171, 8G1172, 8I2040

Mac Mini

Mac mini	Date introduced	Original OS X included	Later OS X included	OS X Build(s)
Mac mini (Late 2014)	Oct 2014	10.10	10.10.2, 10.11, 10.11.1, 10.11.2	14A389, 14C109, 15A284, 15B42, 15C50
Mac mini (Late 2012)	Oct 2012	10.8.1	10.8.2, 10.8.3, 10.9, 10.9.2	12B2100, 12C2034, 12D78, 13A603, 13C64
Mac mini (Mid 2011)	Jul 2011	10.7	10.7.2, 10.7.3, 10.8	11A2061, 11C74, 11D2001, 12A269
Mac mini Server (Mid 2011)	Jul 2011	10.7 (Server)	10.7.2, 10.7.3 (Server)	11A2061, 11C74, 11D2001 (Server)
Mac mini (Mid 2010)	Jun 2010	10.6.3	10.6.4	10D2235, 10F2108
Mac mini with Snow Leopard Server (Mid 2010)	Jun 2010	10.6.3 (Server)	-	10D2235
Mac mini (Late 2009)	Oct 2009	10.6	10.6.2	10A432, 10C2234
Mac mini with Snow Leopard Server (Late 2009)	Oct 2009	10.6 (Server)	-	10A433
Mac mini (Early 2009)	Mar 2009	10.5.6	10.6	9G2030, 10A432
Mac mini (Mid 2007)	Aug 2007	10.4.10	10.5, 10.5.2, 10.5.4	8R3014, 8R3050, 8R4088, 9A581, 9A3129, 9C3033, 9E25
Mac mini (Late 2006)	Sep 2006	10.4.7	10.4.8	8J2135, 8N1430
Mac mini (Early 2006)	Mar 2006	10.4.5	10.4.6	8H1619, 8I2025

Mac Pro

Mac Pro	Date introduced	Original OS X included	Later OS X included	OS X Build(s)
Mac Pro (Late 2013)	Dec 2013	10.9	10.9.2, 10.9.4, 10.11, 10.11.1, 10.11.2	13A4023, 13C64, 13E28, 15A284, 15B42, 15C50
Mac Pro (Mid 2012)	Jun 2012	10.7.3	10.8, 10.8.3	11D2001, 12A269, 12D78
Mac Pro (Mid 2010)	Aug 2010	10.6.4	10.7, 10.7.2, 10.7.3	10F2521, 10F2554, 11A511a, 11C74, 11D2001
Mac Pro with Mac OS X Server (Mid 2010)	Aug 2010	10.6.4	10.7, 10.7.2, 10.7.3 (Server)	10F2522, 11A511a, 11C74, 11D2001 (Server)
Mac Pro (Early 2009)	Mar 2009	10.5.6	10.6	9G3553, 10A432
Mac Pro (Early 2008)	Jan 2008	10.5.1	10.5.2, 10.5.4	9B2117, 9C2031, 9E25
Mac Pro	Aug 2006	10.4.7	10.4.8, 10.4.9, 10.4.10, 10.5	8K1079, 8N1430, 8N1250, 8K1124, 8P4037, 8R3032, 8R3041, 9A581, 9A3129

MacBook Pro

MacBook Pro	Date introduced	Original OS X included	Later OS X included	OS X Build(s)
MacBook Pro (Retina, 15-inch, Mid 2015)	May 2015	10.10.3	10.11, 10.11.1, 10.11.2	14D2134, 15A284, 15B42, 15C50
MacBook Pro (Retina, 13-inch, Early 2015)	Mar 2015	10.10.2	10.11, 10.11.1, 10.11.2	14C2055, 15A284, 15B42, 15C50
MacBook Pro (Retina, 13-inch, Mid 2014)	Jul 2014	10.9.4	-	13E28
MacBook Pro (Retina, 15-inch, Mid 2014)	Jul 2014	10.9.4	10.10.2	13E28, 14C109
MacBook Pro (Retina, 13-inch, Late 2013)	Oct 2013	10.9	10.9.2, 10.9.4	13A2093, 13C64, 13E28
MacBook Pro (Retina, 15-inch, Late 2013)	Oct 2013	10.9	10.9.2, 10.9.4	13A3017, 13C64, 13E28
MacBook Pro (Retina, 13-inch, Early 2013)	Feb 2013	10.8.2	10.8.3	12C3103, 12D78
MacBook Pro (Retina, 15-inch, Early 2013)	Feb 2013	10.8.2	10.8.3	12C3103, 12D78
MacBook Pro (Retina, 13-inch, Late 2012)	Oct 2012	10.8.1	10.8.2	12B2100, 12C2034, 12C3103
MacBook Pro (Retina, Mid 2012)	Jun 2012	10.7.4	10.7.4, 10.8	11E2068, 11E2617, 12A269, 12C2032,12C2034,12C3103
MacBook Pro (15-inch, Mid 2012)	Jun 2012	10.7.3	10.7.4, 10.8	11D2097, 11E2617, 12A269
MacBook Pro (13-inch, Mid 2012)	Jun 2012	10.7.3	10.7.4, 10.8, 10.9, 10.10.2, 10.11, 10.11.1, 10.11.2	11D2515, 11E2617, 12A269, 13A603, 14C109, 15A284, 15B42, 15C50
MacBook Pro (13-inch, Late 2011)	Oct 2011	10.7.2	10.7.3	11C74, 11C2002, 11D2001
MacBook Pro (15-inch, Late 2011)	Oct 2011	10.7.2	10.7.3	11C74, 11C2002, 11D2001
MacBook Pro (17-inch, Late 2011)	Oct 2011	10.7.2	10.7.3	11C74, 11C2002, 11D2001
MacBook Pro (13-inch, Early 2011)	Feb 2011	10.6.6	10.6.7, 10.7, 10.7.2	10J3210, 10J3331a, 10J4139, 11A511a, 11C74
MacBook Pro (15-inch, Early 2011)	Feb 2011	10.6.6	10.6.7, 10.7, 10.7.2	10J3210, 10J3331a, 10J4139, 11A511a, 11C74
MacBook Pro (17-inch, Early 2011)	Feb 2011	10.6.6	10.6.7, 10.7, 10.7.2	10J3210, 10J3331a, 10J4139, 11A511a, 11C74
MacBook Pro (13-inch, Mid 2010)	Apr 2010	10.6.3	10.6.4	10D2125, 10F2108

MacBook Pro (15-inch, Mid 2010)	Apr 2010	10.6.3	10.6.4	10D2063a, 10D2094, 10D2101a, 10F2108
MacBook Pro (17-inch, Mid 2010)	Apr 2010	10.6.3	10.6.4	10D2063a, 10D2094, 10D2101a, 10F2108
MacBook Pro (15-inch, Mid 2009)	Jun 2009	10.5.7	10.6	9J3050, 10A432
MacBook Pro (15-inch, 2.53 GHz, Mid 2009)	Jun 2009	10.5.7	10.6	9J3050, 10A432
MacBook Pro (17-inch, Mid 2009)	Jun 2009	10.5.7	10.6, 10.6.2	9J3050, 10A432, 10C2306
MacBook Pro (13-inch, Mid 2009)	Jun 2009	10.5.7	10.6	9J3050, 10A432
MacBook Pro (17-inch, Early 2009)	Jan 2009	10.5.6	-	9G2141
MacBook Pro (17-inch, Late 2008)	Oct 2008	10.5.4	-	9E27
MacBook Pro (15-inch, Late 2008)	Oct 2008	10.5.5	10.5.6	9F2088, 9F2533, 9G2133
MacBook Pro (Early 2008)	Feb 2008	10.5.2	10.5.4	9C2018, 9C2028, 9E25
MacBook Pro (2.4/2.2 GHz)	Jun 2007	10.4.9	10.4.10, 10.5	8Q1058, 8R4049, 9A581, 9A3129
MacBook Pro (Core 2 Duo)	Oct 2006	10.4.8	-	8N1037, 8N1051, 8N1430
MacBook Pro (17-inch)	Apr 2006	10.4.6	-	8I2032
MacBook Pro	Feb 2006	10.4.5	10.4.6	8G1453, 8I1121

MacBook Air

MacBook Air	Date introduced	Original OS X included	Later OS X included	OS X Build(s)
MacBook Air (11-inch, Early 2015)	Mar 2015	10.10.2	10.11, 10.11.1, 10.11.2	14C2043, 15A284, 15B42, 15C50
MacBook Air (13-inch, Early 2015)	Mar 2015	10.10.2	10.11, 10.11.1, 10.11.2	14C2043, 15A284, 15B42, 15C50
MacBook Air (11-inch, Early 2014)	April 2014	10.9.2	10.9, 10.9.2, 10.9.4	13C64, 13E28
MacBook Air (13-inch, Early 2014)	April 2014	10.9.2	10.9, 10.9.2, 10.9.4	13C64, 13E28
MacBook Air (11-inch, Mid 2013)	Jun 2013	10.8.4	10.9, 10.9.2	12E3067, 13A603, 13C64
MacBook Air (13-inch, Mid 2013)	Jun 2013	10.8.4	10.9, 10.9.2	12E3067, 13A603, 13C64

MacBook Air (11-inch, Mid 2012)	Jun 2012	10.7.4	10.8, 10.8.3	11E2520, 11E2702, 12A269, 12D78
MacBook Air (13-inch, Mid 2012)	Jun 2012	10.7.4	10.8, 10.8.3	11E2520, 11E2702, 12A269, 12D78
MacBook Air (11-inch, Mid 2011)	Jul 2011	10.7	10.7.2, 10.7.3	11A2063, 11C74, 11D2001
MacBook Air (13-inch, Mid 2011)	Jul 2011	10.7	10.7.2, 10.7.3	11A2063, 11C74, 11D2001
MacBook Air (11-inch, Late 2010)	Oct 2010	10.6.4	10.6.5	10F3061,10H717
MacBook Air (13-inch, Late 2010)	Oct 2010	10.6.4	10.6.5	10F3061,10H717
MacBook Air (Mid 2009)	Jun 2009	10.5.6	10.6	9G2152, 10A432
MacBook Air (Late 2008)	Nov 2008	10.5.5	10.5.6	9F2523, 9F2533, 9G2133
MacBook Air (Early 2008)	Jan 2008	10.5.1	10.5.2, 10.5.4	9B2324, 9C3033, 9E25

MacBook

MacBook	Date introduced	Original OS X included	Later OS X included	OS X Build(s)
MacBook (Retina, 12-inch, Early 2015)	April 2015	10.10.2	10.11, 10.11.1, 10.11.2	14C2061, 15A284, 15B42, 15C50
MacBook (13-inch, Mid 2010)	May 2010	10.6.3	10.6.4, 10.7.2	10D2162, 10F2108, 11C74
MacBook (13-inch, Late 2009)	Oct 2009	10.6	10.6.1	10A2047, 10A2062, 10F2108
MacBook (13-inch, Mid 2009)	Jun 2009	10.5.6	10.6	9G2110, 10A432
MacBook (13-inch, Early 2009)	Jan 2009	10.5.6	-	9G2110
MacBook (13-inch, Aluminum, Late 2008)	Oct 2008	10.5.5	10.5.6	9F2088, 9F2533, 9G2133
MacBook (13-inch, Late 2008)	Oct 2008	10.5.4	-	9E27, 9E29
MacBook (13-inch Early 2008)	Feb 2008	10.5.2	10.5.4	9C2015, 9C2028, 9E25
MacBook (13-inch Late 2007)	Oct 2007	10.5	-	9A3111, 9A3115A
MacBook (13-inch Mid 2007)	May 2007	10.4.9	10.4.10	8P4112, 8R3025, 8R3032, 8R3050
MacBook (Late 2007)	Nov 2007	10.5	-	9A3110, 9A3111, 9A3115a
MacBook (Late 2006)	Nov 2006	10.4.8	-	8N1108, 8N1150, 8N1430
MacBook	May 2006	10.4.6	-	8I2025

Xserve

Xserve	Date Introduced	Original OS X Server Included	Latest OS x Server Included	OS X Builds
Xserve (Early 2009)	Apr 2009	10.5.6	10.6.1	9G4008, 10A2054
Xserve (Early 2008)	Jan 2008	10.5.1	10.5.4	9B2117, 9E26
Xserve (Late 2006)	Nov 2006	10.4.8	10.4.10	8N1215, 8R3031

PowerPC–Intel Transition

Steve Jobs talks about the transition to Intel processors

In April 2002, eWeek announced a rumor that Apple had a version of Mac OS X code-named Marklar, which ran on Intel x86 processors. The idea behind Marklar was to keep Mac OS X running on an alternative platform should Apple become dissatisfied with the progress of the Power-PC platform. These rumors subsided until late in May 2005, when various media outlets, such as *The Wall Street Journal* and CNET, announced that Apple would unveil Marklar in the coming months.

On June 6, 2005, Steve Jobs announced in his keynote address at the annual Apple Worldwide Developers Conference that Apple would be making the transition from PowerPC to Intel processors over the following two years, and that Mac OS X would support both platforms during the transition. Jobs also confirmed rumors that Apple had versions of Mac OS X running on Intel processors for most of its developmental life. Intel-based Macs would run a new recompiled version of OS X along with Rosetta, a binary translation layer which enables software compiled for PowerPC Mac OS X to run on Intel Mac OS X machines. The system was included with Mac OS X versions up to version 10.6.8. Apple dropped support for Classic mode on the new Intel Macs. Third party emulation software such as Mini vMac, Basilisk II and SheepShaver provided support for some early versions of Mac OS. A new version of Xcode and the underlying command-line compilers supported building universal binaries that would run on either architecture.

PowerPC-only software is supported with Apple's official emulation software, Rosetta, though applications eventually had to be rewritten to run properly on the newer versions released for Intel processors. Apple initially encouraged developers to produce universal binaries with support for both PowerPC and Intel. There is a performance penalty when PowerPC binaries run on Intel Macs through Rosetta. Moreover, some PowerPC software, such as kernel extensions and System Preferences plugins, are not supported on Intel Macs at all. Some PowerPC applications would not run on macOS at all. Plugins for Safari need to be compiled for the same platform as Safari, so when Safari is running on Intel it requires plug-ins that have been compiled as Intel-only or universal binaries, so PowerPC-only plug-ins will not work. While Intel Macs are able to run PowerPC, Intel, and universal binaries; PowerPC Macs support only universal and PowerPC builds.

Support for the PowerPC platform was dropped following the transition. In 2009, Apple announced at its Worldwide Developers Conference that Mac OS X 10.6 Snow Leopard would drop support for PowerPC processors and be Intel-only. Rosetta continued to be offered as an optional download or installation choice in Snow Leopard before it was discontinued with Mac OS X 10.7 Lion. In addition, new versions of Mac OS X first- and third-party software increasingly required Intel processors, including new versions of iLife, iWork, Aperture and Logic Pro.

Features

Aqua User Interface

The original Aqua user interface as seen in the Mac OS X Public Beta from 2000

One of the major differences between the classic Mac OS and the current macOS was the addition of Aqua, a graphical user interface with water-like elements, in the first major release of Mac OS X. Every window element, text, graphic, or widget is drawn on-screen using spatial anti-aliasing technology. ColorSync, a technology introduced many years before, was improved and built into the core drawing engine, to provide color matching for printing and multimedia professionals. Also, drop shadows were added around windows and isolated text elements to provide a sense of depth. New interface elements were integrated, including sheets (dialog boxes attached to specific windows) and drawers, which would slide out and provide options.

The use of soft edges, translucent colors, and pinstripes, similar to the hardware design of the first iMacs, brought more texture and color to the user interface when compared to what Mac OS 9 and Mac OS X Server 1.0's "Platinum" appearance had offered. According to John Siracusa, an editor of Ars Technica, the introduction of Aqua and its departure from the then conventional look "hit like a ton of bricks." Bruce Tognazzini (who founded the original Apple Human Interface Group) said that the Aqua interface in Mac OS X 10.0 represented a step backwards in usability compared with the original Mac OS interface. Third-party developers started producing skins for customizable applications and other operating systems which mimicked the Aqua appearance. To some extent, Apple has used the successful transition to this new design as leverage, at various times threatening legal action against people who make or distribute software with an interface the company says is derived from its copyrighted design.

Apple has continued to change aspects of the macOS appearance and design, particularly with tweaks to the appearance of windows and the menu bar. Since 2012, Apple has sold many of its Mac models with high-resolution Retina displays, and macOS and its APIs have extensive support for resolution-independent development on supporting high-resolution displays. Reviewers have described Apple's support for the technology as superior to that on Windows.

The human interface guidelines published by Apple for macOS are followed by many applications, giving them consistent user interface and keyboard shortcuts. In addition, new services for applications are included, which include spelling and grammar checkers, special characters palette, color picker, font chooser and dictionary; these global features are present in every Cocoa application, adding consistency. The graphics system OpenGL composites windows onto the screen to allow hardware-accelerated drawing. This technology, introduced in version 10.2, is called Quartz Extreme, a component of Quartz. Quartz's internal imaging model correlates well with the Portable Document Format (PDF) imaging model, making it easy to output PDF to multiple devices. As a side result, PDF viewing and creating PDF documents from any application are built-in features. Reflecting its popularity with design users, macOS also has system support for a variety of professional video and image formats and includes an extensive pre-installed font library, featuring many prominent brand-name designs.

Components

The Finder is a file browser allowing quick access to all areas of the computer, which has been modified throughout subsequent releases of macOS. Quick Look is part of the Finder since version 10.5. It allows for dynamic previews of files, including videos and multi-page documents without opening any other applications. Spotlight, a file searching technology which has been integrated into the Finder since version 10.4, allows rapid real-time searches of data files; mail messages; photos; and other information based on item properties (metadata) and/or content. macOS makes use of a Dock, which holds file and folder shortcuts as well as minimized windows.

Apple added "Exposé" in version 10.3 (called Mission Control since version 10.7), a feature which includes three functions to help accessibility between windows and desktop. Its functions are to instantly display all open windows as thumbnails for easy navigation to different tasks, display all open windows as thumbnails from the current application, and hide all windows to access the desktop. Also, FileVault was introduced, which is an optional encryption of the user's files with the 128-bit Advanced Encryption Standard (AES-128).

Features introduced in version 10.4 include Automator, an application designed to create an automatic workflow for different tasks; Dashboard, a full-screen group of small applications called desktop widgets that can be called up and dismissed in one keystroke; and Front Row, a media viewer interface accessed by the Apple Remote. Moreover, the Sync Services were included, which is a system that allows applications to access a centralized extensible database for various elements of user data, including calendar and contact items. The operating system then managed conflicting edits and data consistency.

All system icons are scalable up to 512×512 pixels as of version 10.5 to accommodate various places where they appear in larger size, including for example the Cover Flow view, a three-dimensional graphical user interface included with iTunes, the Finder, and other Apple products for visually skimming through files and digital media libraries via cover artwork. That version also introduced Spaces, a virtual desktop implementation which enables the user to have more than one desktop and display them in an Exposé-like interface; an automatic backup technology called Time Machine, which provides the ability to view and restore previous versions of files and application data; and Screen Sharing was built in for the first time.

In more recent releases, Apple has developed support for emoji characters by including the proprietary Apple Color Emoji font. Apple has also connected macOS with social networks such as Twitter and Facebook through the addition of share buttons for content such as pictures and text. Apple has brought several applications and features that originally debuted in iOS, its mobile operating system, to macOS in recent releases, notably the intelligent personal assistant Siri, which was introduced in version 10.12 of macOS.

Multilingual Support

There are 34 system languages available in macOS for the user at the moment of installation; the system language is used throughout the entire operating system environment. Input methods for typing in dozens of scripts can be chosen independently of the system language. Recent updates have added increasing support for Chinese characters and interconnections with popular social networks in China.

Updating Methods

macOS can be updated using the Mac App Store application or the softwareupdate command line utility. Until OS X 10.8 Mountain Lion, a separate Software Update application performed this functionality. In Mountain Lion and later, this was merged into the Mac App Store application, although the underlying update mechanism remains unchanged and is fundamentally different than the download mechanism used when purchasing an App Store application.

Box/Mac App Store artwork for every version of macOS. Left to right: Cheetah/Puma (1), Jaguar (2), Panther (3), Tiger (4), Leopard (5), Snow Leopard (6), Lion (7), Mountain Lion (8), Mavericks (9), Yosemite (10), El Capitan (11), Sierra (12).

Mac OS X, OS X, and macOS version information

Version	Code-name	Darwin version	Processor support	Application support	Kernel	Date announced	Release date	Most recent version
Rhapsody Developer Release	Grail1Z4 / Titan1U		32-bit PowerPC	32-bit PowerPC	32-bit	Unknown	August 31, 1997	DR2 (May 14, 1998)
Mac OS X Server 1.0	Hera					Unknown	March 16, 1999	1.2v3 (October 27, 2000)
Mac OS X Developer Preview	Unknown					May 11, 1998	March 16, 1999	DP4 (April 5, 2000)
Mac OS X Public Beta	Kodiak	1.2.1				Unknown	September 13, 2000	N/A
Mac OS X 10.0	Cheetah	1.3.1				Unknown	March 24, 2001	10.0.4 (June 22, 2001)
Mac OS X 10.1	Puma	1.4.1 / 5				July 18, 2001	September 25, 2001	10.1.5 (June 6, 2002)
Mac OS X 10.2	Jaguar	6	32/64-bit PowerPC			May 6, 2002	August 24, 2002	10.2.8 (October 3, 2003)
Mac OS X 10.3	Panther	7	32/64-bit PowerPC			June 23, 2003	October 24, 2003	10.3.9 (April 15, 2005)
Mac OS X 10.4	Tiger	8	32/64-bit PowerPC and Intel	32/64-bit PowerPC and Intel		May 4, 2004	April 29, 2005	10.4.11 (November 14, 2007)
Mac OS X 10.5	Leopard	9		32/64-bit PowerPC and Intel		June 26, 2006	October 26, 2007	10.5.8 (August 5, 2009)
Mac OS X 10.6	Snow Leopard	10	32/64-bit Intel	32/64-bit Intel 32-bit PowerPC	32/64-bit	June 9, 2008	August 28, 2009	10.6.8 v1.1 (July 25, 2011)
Mac OS X 10.7	Lion	11	64-bit Intel	32/64-bit Intel		October 20, 2010	July 20, 2011	10.7.5 (September 19, 2012)
OS X 10.8	Mountain Lion	12			64-bit	February 16, 2012	July 25, 2012	10.8.5 (12F45) (October 3, 2013)
OS X 10.9	Mavericks	13				June 10, 2013	October 22, 2013	10.9.5 (13F1112) (September 18, 2014)
OS X 10.10	Yosemite	14				June 2, 2014	October 16, 2014	10.10.5 (14F27) (August 13, 2015)
OS X 10.11	El Capitan	15				June 8, 2015	September 30, 2015	10.11.6 (15G31) (July 18, 2016)
macOS 10.12	Sierra	16				June 13, 2016	September 20, 2016	10.12 (16A323) (September 20, 2016)

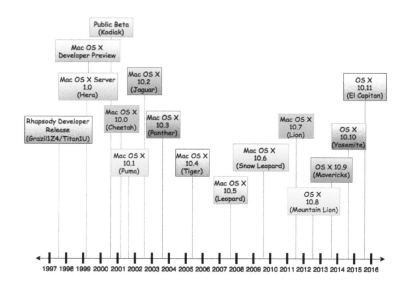

Timeline of versions (not including 2016's macOS Sierra)

With the exception of Mac OS X Server 1.0 and the original public beta, OS X versions were named after big cats until OS X 10.9 Mavericks, when Apple switched to using California locations. Prior to its release, Mac OS X 10.0 was code named "Cheetah" internally at Apple, and Mac OS X 10.1 was code named internally as "Puma". After the immense buzz surrounding Mac OS X 10.2, code-named "Jaguar", Apple's product marketing began openly using the code names to promote the operating system. Mac OS X 10.3 was marketed as "Panther", Mac OS X 10.4 as "Tiger", Mac OS X 10.5 as "Leopard", Mac OS X 10.6 as "Snow Leopard", Mac OS X 10.7 as "Lion", OS X 10.8 as "Mountain Lion", and OS X 10.9 as "Mavericks".

"Panther", "Tiger" and "Leopard" are registered as trademarks of Apple, but "Cheetah", "Puma" and "Jaguar" have never been registered. Apple has also registered "Lynx" and "Cougar" as trademarks, though these were allowed to lapse. Computer retailer Tiger Direct sued Apple for its use of the name "Tiger". On May 16, 2005 a US federal court in the Southern District of Florida ruled that Apple's use did not infringe on Tiger Direct's trademark.

Mac OS X Public Beta

On September 13, 2000, Apple released a $29.95 "preview" version of Mac OS X internally code-named Kodiak in order to gain feedback from users.

The "PB" as it was known marked the first public availability of the Aqua interface and Apple made many changes to the UI based on customer feedback. Mac OS X Public Beta expired and ceased to function in Spring 2001.

Mac OS X 10.0 Cheetah

On March 24, 2001, Apple released Mac OS X 10.0 (internally codenamed Cheetah). The initial version was slow, incomplete, and had very few applications available at the time of its launch, mostly from independent developers. While many critics suggested that the operating system was not ready for mainstream adoption, they recognized the importance of its initial launch as a base on which to improve. Simply releasing Mac OS X was received by the Macintosh community as a great accomplishment, for attempts to completely overhaul the Mac OS had been underway since 1996, and delayed by countless setbacks. Following some bug fixes, kernel panics became much less frequent.

Screenshot of OS X 10.0

Mac OS X 10.1 Puma

Later that year on September 25, 2001, Mac OS X 10.1 (internally codenamed Puma) was released. It featured increased performance and provided missing features, such as DVD playback. Apple released 10.1 as a free upgrade CD for 10.0 users, in addition to the US$129 boxed version for people running Mac OS 9. It was discovered that the upgrade CDs were full install CDs that could be used with Mac OS 9 systems by removing a specific file; Apple later re-released the CDs in an actual stripped-down format that did not facilitate installation on such systems. On January 7, 2002, Apple announced that Mac OS X was to be the default operating system for all Macintosh products by the end of that month.

Mac OS X 10.2 Jaguar

On August 23, 2002, Apple followed up with Mac OS X 10.2 Jaguar, the first release to use its code name as part of the branding. It brought great raw performance improvements, a sleeker look, and many powerful user-interface enhancements (over 150, according to Apple), including Quartz Extreme for compositing graphics directly on an ATI Radeon or Nvidia GeForce2 MX AGP-based video card with at least 16 MB of VRAM, a system-wide repository for contact information in the new Address Book, and an instant messaging client named iChat. The Happy Mac which had appeared during the Mac OS startup sequence for almost 18 years was replaced with a large grey Apple logo with the introduction of Mac OS X v10.2.

Mac OS X 10.3 Panther

Mac OS X v10.3 Panther was released on October 24, 2003. In addition to providing much improved performance, it also incorporated the most extensive update yet to the user interface. Panther included as many or more new features as Jaguar had the year before, including an updated Finder, incorporating a brushed-metal interface, Fast user switching, Exposé (Window manager), FileVault, Safari, iChat AV (which added videoconferencing features to iChat), improved Portable Document Format (PDF) rendering and much greater Microsoft Windows interoperability. Support for some early G3 computers such as "beige" Power Macs and "WallStreet" PowerBooks was discontinued.

Mac OS X 10.4 Tiger

Screenshot of Tiger

Mac OS X 10.4 Tiger was released on April 29, 2005. Apple stated that Tiger contained more than 200 new features. As with Panther, certain older machines were no longer supported; Tiger requires a Mac with 256 MB and a built-in FireWire port. Among the new features, Tiger introduced Spotlight, Dashboard, Smart Folders, updated Mail program with Smart Mailboxes, QuickTime 7, Safari 2, Automator, VoiceOver, Core Image and Core Video. The initial release of the Apple TV used a modified version of Tiger with a different graphical interface and fewer applications and services. On January 10, 2006, Apple released the first Intel-based Macs along with the 10.4.4 update to Tiger. This operating system functioned identically on the PowerPC-based Macs and the new Intel-based machines, with the exception of the Intel release dropping support for the Classic environment.

Mac OS X 10.5 Leopard

Mac OS X 10.5 Leopard was released on October 26, 2007. It was called by Apple "the largest update of Mac OS X". It brought more than 300 new features. Leopard supports both PowerPC- and Intel x86-based Macintosh computers; support for the G3 processor was dropped and the G4 processor required a minimum clock rate of 867 MHz, and at least 512 MB of RAM to be installed. The single DVD works for all supported Macs (including 64-bit machines). New features include a new look, an updated Finder, Time Machine, Spaces, Boot Camp pre-installed, full support for 64-bit applications (including graphical applications), new features in Mail and iChat, and a number of new security features. Leopard is an Open Brand UNIX 03 registered product on the Intel platform. It was also the first BSD-based OS to receive UNIX 03 certification. Leopard dropped support for the Classic Environment and all Classic applications. It was the final version of Mac OS X to support the PowerPC architecture.

Mac OS X 10.6 Snow Leopard

Mac OS X 10.6 Snow Leopard was released on August 28, 2009. Rather than delivering big changes to the appearance and end user functionality like the previous releases of Mac OS X, Snow

Leopard focused on "under the hood" changes, increasing the performance, efficiency, and stability of the operating system. For most users, the most noticeable changes were: the disk space that the operating system frees up after a clean install compared to Mac OS X 10.5 Leopard, a more responsive Finder rewritten in Cocoa, faster Time Machine backups, more reliable and user friendly disk ejects, a more powerful version of the Preview application, as well as a faster Safari web browser. Snow Leopard only supported machines with Intel CPUs, required at least 1 GB of RAM, and dropped default support for applications built for the PowerPC architecture (Rosetta could be installed as an additional component to retain support for PowerPC-only applications).

Snow Leopard also featured new 64-bit technology capable of supporting greater amounts of RAM, improved support for multi-core processors through Grand Central Dispatch, and advanced GPU performance with OpenCL.

An update introduced support for the Mac App Store, Apple's digital distribution platform for macOS applications.

Mac OS X Lion was announced at WWDC 2011 at Moscone West

Mac OS X 10.7 Lion

Mac OS X 10.7 Lion was released on July 20, 2011. It brought developments made in Apple's iOS, such as an easily navigable display of installed applications called Launchpad and a greater use of multi-touch gestures, to the Mac. This release removed Rosetta, making it incompatible with PowerPC applications.

Changes made to the GUI include auto-hiding scrollbars that only appear when they are being used, and Mission Control which unifies Exposé, Spaces, Dashboard, and full-screen applications within a single interface. Apple also made changes to applications: they resume in the same state as they were before they were closed, similar to iOS. Documents auto-save by default.

OS X 10.8 Mountain Lion

OS X 10.8 Mountain Lion was released on July 25, 2012. It incorporates some features seen in iOS 5, which include Game Center, support for iMessage in the new Messages messaging application, and Reminders as a to-do list app separate from iCal (which is renamed as Calendar, like the iOS app). It also includes support for storing iWork documents in iCloud. Notification Center, which makes its debut in Mountain Lion, is a desktop version similar to the one in iOS 5.0 and higher.

Application pop-ups are now concentrated on the corner of the screen, and the Center itself is pulled from the right side of the screen. Mountain Lion also includes more Chinese features including support for Baidu as an option for Safari search engine, QQ, 163.com and 126.com services for Mail, Contacts and Calendar, Youku, Tudou and Sina Weibo are integrated into share sheets.

Starting with Mountain Lion, Apple software updates (including the OS) are distributed via the App Store. This updating mechanism replaced the Apple Software Update utility.

A screenshot of OS X Mavericks

OS X 10.9 Mavericks

OS X 10.9 Mavericks was released on October 22, 2013. It was a free upgrade to all users running Snow Leopard or later with a 64-bit Intel processor. Its changes include the addition of the previously iOS-only Maps and iBooks applications, improvements to the Notification Center, enhancements to several applications, and many under-the-hood improvements.

OS X 10.10 Yosemite

OS X 10.10 Yosemite was released on October 16, 2014. It features a redesigned user interface similar to that of iOS 7, intended to feature a more minimal, text-based 'flat' design, with use of translucency effects and intensely saturated colors. Apple's showcase new feature in Yosemite is Handoff, which enables users with iPhones running iOS 8.1 or later to answer phone calls, receive and send SMS messages, and complete unfinished iPhone emails on their Mac.

OS X 10.11 El Capitan

Screenshot of El Capitan

OS X 10.11 El Capitan was released on September 30, 2015. Similar to Mac OS X 10.6 Snow Leopard, Apple described this release as containing "refinements to the Mac experience" and "improvements to system performance" rather than new features. Refinements include public transport built into the Maps application, GUI improvements to the Notes application, adopting San Francisco as the system font for clearer legibility, and the introduction of System Integrity Protection. The Metal API, first introduced in iOS 8, was also included in this operating system for "all Macs since 2012".

macOS 10.12 Sierra

During the keynote at WWDC on June 13, 2016, Apple announced that OS X would be renamed macOS to stylistically match Apple's other operating systems, such as iOS, watchOS, and tvOS.

macOS 10.12 Sierra was released to the public on September 20, 2016. New features include the addition of Siri, Optimized Storage, and updates to Photos, Messages, and iTunes.

Reception

Usage Share

As of July 2016, macOS is the second-most-active general-purpose desktop client operating system in use on the World Wide Web following Microsoft Windows, with a 4.90% usage share according to statistics compiled by Wikimedia. It is the most successful Unix-like desktop operating system on the web, estimated at approximately 5 times the usage of Linux (which has 1.01%). Usage share generally continues to shift away from the desktop and toward mobile operating systems such as iOS and Android.

Malware and Spyware

In its earlier years, Mac OS X enjoyed a near-absence of the types of malware and spyware that have affected Microsoft Windows users. macOS has a smaller usage share compared to Windows, but it also has traditionally more secure Unix roots. Worms, as well as potential vulnerabilities, were noted in 2006, which led some industry analysts and anti-virus companies to issue warnings that Apple's Mac OS X is not immune to malware. Increasing market share coincided with additional reports of a variety of attacks. In early 2011, Mac OS X experienced a large increase in malware attacks, and malware such as Mac Defender, MacProtector, and MacGuard were seen as an increasing problem for Mac users. At first, the malware installer required the user to enter the administrative password, but later versions were able to install without user input. Initially, Apple support staff were instructed not to assist in the removal of the malware or admit the existence of the malware issue, but as the malware spread, a support document was issued. Apple announced an OS X update to fix the problem. An estimated 100,000 users were affected. Apple releases security updates for macOS regularly.

Promotion

As a devices company, most large-scale Apple promotion for macOS has been part of the sale of Macs, with promotion of macOS updates generally focused on existing users, promotion at Apple Store and other retail partners, or through events for developers. In larger scale advertising campaigns, Apple specifically promoted macOS as better for handling media and other home-user applications, and comparing Mac OS X (especially versions Tiger and Leopard) with the heavy criticism Microsoft received for the long-awaited Windows Vista operating system.

Linux

Linux is a Unix-like computer operating system assembled under the model of free and open-source software development and distribution. The defining component of Linux is the Linux kernel, an operating system kernel first released on September 17, 1991 by Linus Torvalds. The Free Software Foundation uses the name GNU/Linux to describe the operating system, which has led to some controversy; while they explicitly have no controversy over the name Android (they object to it on proprietary grounds however), as GNU isn't a part of it.

Linux was originally developed for personal computers based on the Intel x86 architecture, but has since been ported to more platforms than any other operating system. Because of the dominance of Android on smartphones, Linux has the largest installed base of all general-purpose operating systems. Linux is also the leading operating system on servers and other big iron systems such as mainframe computers and on 99.6% of the fastest (TOP500) supercomputers, but is used on only around 2.3% of desktop computers; not including Chrome OS, used in Chromebooks, that are dominating the US K–12 education market, while overall in the US are at about 5% and representing nearly 20% of the sub-$300 notebook sales. Linux also runs on embedded systems, which are devices whose operating system is typically built into the firmware and is highly tailored to the system; this includes smartphones and tablet computers running Android and other Linux derivatives, TiVo and similar DVR devices, network routers, facility automation controls, televisions, video game consoles and smartwatches.

The development of Linux is one of the most prominent examples of free and open-source software collaboration. The underlying source code may be used, modified and distributed—commercially or non-commercially—by anyone under the terms of its respective licenses, such as the GNU General Public License. Typically, Linux is packaged in a form known as a *Linux distribution* (or *distro* for short) for both desktop and server use. Some of the most popular mainstream Linux distributions are Arch Linux, CentOS, Debian, Fedora, Gentoo Linux, Linux Mint, Mageia, openSUSE and Ubuntu, together with commercial distributions such as Red Hat Enterprise Linux and SUSE Linux Enterprise Server. Distributions include the Linux kernel, supporting utilities and libraries, many of which are provided by the GNU Project, and usually a large amount of application software to fulfil the distribution's intended use.

Desktop Linux distributions include a windowing system, such as X11, Mir or a Wayland implementation, and an accompanying desktop environment such as GNOME or the KDE Software Compilation; some distributions may also include a less resource-intensive desktop, such as LXDE or Xfce. Distributions intended to run on servers may omit all graphical environments from the standard install, and instead include other software to set up and operate a solution stack such as LAMP. Because Linux is freely redistributable, anyone may create a distribution for any intended use.

History

Antecedents

The Unix operating system was conceived and implemented in 1969 at AT&T's Bell Laboratories in the United States by Ken Thompson, Dennis Ritchie, Douglas McIlroy, and Joe Ossanna.

First released in 1971, Unix was written entirely in assembly language, as was common practice at the time. Later, in a key pioneering approach in 1973, it was rewritten in the C programming language by Dennis Ritchie (with exceptions to the kernel and I/O). The availability of a high-level language implementation of Unix made its porting to different computer platforms easier.

Linus Torvalds, principal author of the Linux kernel

Due to an earlier antitrust case forbidding it from entering the computer business, AT&T was required to license the operating system's source code to anyone who asked. As a result, Unix grew quickly and became widely adopted by academic institutions and businesses. In 1984, AT&T divested itself of Bell Labs; freed of the legal obligation requiring free licensing, Bell Labs began selling Unix as a proprietary product.

The GNU Project, started in 1983 by Richard Stallman, has the goal of creating a "complete Unix-compatible software system" composed entirely of free software. Work began in 1984. Later, in 1985, Stallman started the Free Software Foundation and wrote the GNU General Public License (GNU GPL) in 1989. By the early 1990s, many of the programs required in an operating system (such as libraries, compilers, text editors, a Unix shell, and a windowing system) were completed, although low-level elements such as device drivers, daemons, and the kernel were stalled and incomplete.

Linus Torvalds has stated that if the GNU kernel had been available at the time (1991), he would not have decided to write his own.

Although not released until 1992 due to legal complications, development of 386BSD, from which NetBSD, OpenBSD and FreeBSD descended, predated that of Linux. Torvalds has also stated that if 386BSD had been available at the time, he probably would not have created Linux.

MINIX was created by Andrew S. Tanenbaum, a computer science professor, and released in 1987 as a minimal Unix-like operating system targeted at students and others who wanted to learn the operating system principles. Although the complete source code of MINIX was freely available, the licensing terms prevented it from being free software until the licensing changed in April 2000.

Creation

In 1991, while attending the University of Helsinki, Torvalds became curious about operating systems and frustrated by the licensing of MINIX, which at the time limited it to educational use only. He began to work on his own operating system kernel, which eventually became the Linux kernel.

Torvalds began the development of the Linux kernel on MINIX and applications written for MINIX were also used on Linux. Later, Linux matured and further Linux kernel development took place on Linux systems. GNU applications also replaced all MINIX components, because it was advantageous to use the freely available code from the GNU Project with the fledgling operating system; code licensed under the GNU GPL can be reused in other computer programs as long as they also are released under the same or a compatible license. Torvalds initiated a switch from his original license, which prohibited commercial redistribution, to the GNU GPL. Developers worked to integrate GNU components with the Linux kernel, making a fully functional and free operating system.

Naming

5.25-inch floppy disks holding a very early version of Linux

Linus Torvalds had wanted to call his invention "Freax", a portmanteau of "free", "freak", and "x" (as an allusion to Unix). During the start of his work on the system, some of the project's makefiles included the name "Freax" for about half a year. Torvalds had already considered the name "Linux", but initially dismissed it as too egotistical.

In order to facilitate development, the files were uploaded to the FTP server (ftp.funet.fi) of FUNET in September 1991. Ari Lemmke, Torvald's coworker at the Helsinki University of Technology (HUT), who was one of the volunteer administrators for the FTP server at the time, did not think that "Freax" was a good name. So, he named the project "Linux" on the server without consulting Torvalds. Later, however, Torvalds consented to "Linux".

Commercial and Popular Uptake

Ubuntu, a popular Linux distribution

Nexus 5X running Android

Adoption of Linux in production environments, rather than being used only by hobbyists, started to take off first in the mid-1990s in the supercomputing community, where organizations such as NASA started to replace their increasingly expensive machines with clusters of inexpensive commodity computers running Linux. Commercial use followed when Dell and IBM, followed by Hewlett-Packard, started offering Linux support to escape Microsoft's monopoly in the desktop operating system market.

Today, Linux systems are used throughout computing, from embedded systems to supercomputers, and have secured a place in server installations such as the popular LAMP application stack. Use of Linux distributions in home and enterprise desktops has been growing. Linux distributions have also become popular in the netbook market, with many devices shipping with customized Linux distributions installed, and Google releasing their own Chrome OS designed for netbooks.

Linux's greatest success in the consumer market is perhaps the mobile device market, with Android being one of the most dominant operating systems on smartphones and very popular on tablets and, more recently, on wearables. Linux gaming is also on the rise with Valve showing its support for Linux and rolling out its own gaming oriented Linux distribution. Linux distributions have also gained popularity with various local and national governments, such as the federal government of Brazil.

Current Development

Torvalds continues to direct the development of the kernel. Stallman heads the Free Software Foundation, which in turn supports the GNU components. Finally, individuals and corporations develop third-party non-GNU components. These third-party components comprise a vast body of work and may include both kernel modules and user applications and libraries.

Linux vendors and communities combine and distribute the kernel, GNU components, and non-GNU components, with additional package management software in the form of Linux distributions.

Design

A Linux-based system is a modular Unix-like operating system, deriving much of its basic design from principles established in Unix during the 1970s and 1980s. Such a system uses a monolithic kernel, the Linux kernel, which handles process control, networking, access to the peripherals, and file systems. Device drivers are either integrated directly with the kernel, or added as modules that are loaded while the system is running.

Separate projects that interface with the kernel provide much of the system's higher-level functionality. The GNU userland is an important part of most Linux-based systems, providing the most common implementation of the C library, a popular CLI shell, and many of the common Unix tools which carry out many basic operating system tasks. The graphical user interface (or GUI) used by most Linux systems is built on top of an implementation of the X Window System. More recently, the Linux community seeks to advance to Wayland as the new display server protocol in place of X11; Ubuntu, however, develops Mir instead of Wayland.

Various layers within Linux, also showing separation between the userland and kernel space

User mode	**User applications**	For example, bash, LibreOffice, Apache OpenOffice, Blender, 0 A.D., Mozilla Firefox, etc.			
	Low-level system components:	System daemons: *systemd, runit, logind, networkd, soundd, ...*	Windowing system: *X11, Wayland, Mir, SurfaceFlinger (Android)*	Other libraries: *GTK+, Qt, EFL, SDL, SFML, FLTK,* GNUstep, etc.	Graphics: *Mesa, AMD Catalyst, ...*
	C standard library	open(), exec(), sbrk(), socket(), fopen(), calloc(), ... (up to 2000 subroutines) *glibc* aims to be POSIX/SUS-compatible, *uClibc* targets embedded systems, *bionic* written for Android, etc.			
Kernel mode	Linux kernel	stat, splice, dup, read, open, ioctl, write, mmap, close, exit, etc. (about 380 system calls) The Linux kernel System Call Interface (SCI, aims to be POSIX/SUS-compatible)			
		Process scheduling subsystem	IPC subsystem	Memory management subsystem	Virtual files subsystem / Network subsystem
		Other components: ALSA, DRI, evdev, LVM, device mapper, Linux Network Scheduler, Netfilter Linux Security Modules: *SELinux, TOMOYO, AppArmor, Smack*			
		Hardware (CPU, main memory, data storage devices, etc.)			

Installed components of a Linux system include the following:

- A bootloader, for example GNU GRUB, LILO, SYSLINUX, or Gummiboot. This is a program that loads the Linux kernel into the computer's main memory, by being executed by the computer when it is turned on and after the firmware initialization is performed.

- An init program, such as the traditional sysvinit and the newer systemd, OpenRC and Upstart. This is the first process launched by the Linux kernel, and is at the root of the process tree: in other terms, all processes are launched through init. It starts processes such as system services and login prompts (whether graphical or in terminal mode).

- Software libraries, which contain code that can be used by running processes. On Linux systems using ELF-format executable files, the dynamic linker that manages use of dynamic libraries is known as ld-linux.so. If the system is set up for the user to compile software themselves, header files will also be included to describe the interface of installed libraries. Besides the most commonly used software library on Linux systems, the GNU C Library (glibc), there are numerous other libraries.

  - C standard library is the library needed to run standard C programs on a computer system, with the GNU C Library being the most commonly used. Several alternatives are available, such as the EGLIBC (which was used by Debian for some time) and uClibc (which was designed for uClinux).

  - Widget toolkits are the libraries used to build graphical user interfaces (GUIs) for software applications. Numerous widget toolkits are available, including GTK+ and Clutter developed by the GNOME project, Qt developed by the Qt Project and led by Digia, and Enlightenment Foundation Libraries (EFL) developed primarily by the Enlightenment team.

- User interface programs such as command shells or windowing environments.

User Interface

The user interface, also known as the shell, is either a command-line interface (CLI), a graphical user interface (GUI), or through controls attached to the associated hardware, which is common for embedded systems. For desktop systems, the default mode is usually a graphical user interface, although the CLI is available through terminal emulator windows or on a separate virtual console.

CLI shells are text-based user interfaces, which use text for both input and output. The dominant shell used in Linux is the Bourne-Again Shell (bash), originally developed for the GNU project. Most low-level Linux components, including various parts of the userland, use the CLI exclusively. The CLI is particularly suited for automation of repetitive or delayed tasks, and provides very simple inter-process communication.

On desktop systems, the most popular user interfaces are the GUI shells, packaged together with extensive desktop environments, such as the K Desktop Environment (KDE), GNOME, MATE, Cinnamon, Unity, LXDE, Pantheon and Xfce, though a variety of additional user interfaces exist. Most popular user interfaces are based on the X Window System, often simply called "X". It provides network transparency and permits a graphical application running on one system to be displayed on another where a user may interact with the application; however, certain extensions of the X Window System are not capable of working over the network. Several X display servers exist, with the reference implementation, X.Org Server, being the most popular.

Several types of window managers exist for X11, including tiling, dynamic, stacking and compositing. Window managers provide means to control the placement and appearance of individual application windows, and interact with the X Window System. Simpler X window managers such as dwm or ratpoison provide a minimalist functionality, while more elaborate window managers such as FVWM, Enlightenment or Window Maker provide more features such as a built-in taskbar and themes, but are still lightweight when compared to desktop environments. Desktop environments include window managers as part of their standard installations, such as Mutter (GNOME), KWin (KDE) or Xfwm (xfce), although users may choose to use a different window manager if preferred.

Wayland is a display server protocol intended as a replacement for the X11 protocol; as of 2014, it has not received wider adoption. Unlike X11, Wayland does not need an external window manager and compositing manager. Therefore, a Wayland compositor takes the role of the display server, window manager and compositing manager. Weston is the reference implementation of Wayland, while GNOME's Mutter and KDE's KWin are being ported to Wayland as standalone display servers. Enlightenment has already been successfully ported since version 19.

Video Input Infrastructure

Linux currently has two modern kernel-userspace APIs for handing video input devices: V4L2 API for video streams and radio, and DVB API for digital TV reception.

Due to the complexity and diversity of different devices, and due to the large amount of formats and standards handled by those APIs, this infrastructure needs to evolve to better fit other devices. Also, a good userspace device library is the key of the success for having userspace applications to be able to work with all formats supported by those devices.

Development

The primary difference between Linux and many other popular contemporary operating systems is that the Linux kernel and other components are free and open-source software. Linux is not the only such operating system, although it is by far the most widely used. Some free and open-source software licenses are based on the principle of copyleft, a kind of reciprocity: any work derived from a copyleft piece of software must also be copyleft itself. The most common free software license, the GNU General Public License (GPL), is a form of copyleft, and is used for the Linux kernel and many of the components from the GNU Project.

Linux based distributions are intended by developers for interoperability with other operating systems and established computing standards. Linux systems adhere to POSIX, SUS, LSB, ISO, and ANSI standards where possible, although to date only one Linux distribution has been POSIX.1 certified, Linux-FT.

Free software projects, although developed through collaboration, are often produced independently of each other. The fact that the software licenses explicitly permit redistribution, however, provides a basis for larger scale projects that collect the software produced by stand-alone projects and make it available all at once in the form of a Linux distribution.

Many Linux distributions, or "distros", manage a remote collection of system software and application software packages available for download and installation through a network connection. This allows users to adapt the operating system to their specific needs. Distributions are maintained by individuals, loose-knit teams, volunteer organizations, and commercial entities. A distribution is responsible for the default configuration of the installed Linux kernel, general system security, and more generally integration of the different software packages into a coherent whole. Distributions typically use a package manager such as apt, yum, zypper, pacman or portage to install, remove, and update all of a system's software from one central location.

Community

A distribution is largely driven by its developer and user communities. Some vendors develop and fund their distributions on a volunteer basis, Debian being a well-known example. Others maintain a community version of their commercial distributions, as Red Hat does with Fedora, and SUSE does with openSUSE.

In many cities and regions, local associations known as Linux User Groups (LUGs) seek to promote their preferred distribution and by extension free software. They hold meetings and provide free demonstrations, training, technical support, and operating system installation to new users. Many Internet communities also provide support to Linux users and developers. Most distributions and free software / open-source projects have IRC chatrooms or newsgroups. Online forums are another means for support, with notable examples being LinuxQuestions.org and the various distribution specific support and community forums, such as ones for Ubuntu, Fedora, and Gentoo. Linux distributions host mailing lists; commonly there will be a specific topic such as usage or development for a given list.

There are several technology websites with a Linux focus. Print magazines on Linux often bundle cover disks that carry software or even complete Linux distributions.

Although Linux distributions are generally available without charge, several large corporations sell, support, and contribute to the development of the components of the system and of free software. An analysis of the Linux kernel showed 75 percent of the code from December 2008 to January 2010 was developed by programmers working for corporations, leaving about 18 percent to volunteers and 7% unclassified. Major corporations that provide contributions include Dell, IBM, HP, Oracle, Sun Microsystems (now part of Oracle) and Nokia. A number of corporations, notably Red Hat, Canonical and SUSE, have built a significant business around Linux distributions.

The free software licenses, on which the various software packages of a distribution built on the Linux kernel are based, explicitly accommodate and encourage commercialization; the relationship between a Linux distribution as a whole and individual vendors may be seen as symbiotic. One common business model of commercial suppliers is charging for support, especially for business users. A number of companies also offer a specialized business version of their distribution, which adds proprietary support packages and tools to administer higher numbers of installations or to simplify administrative tasks.

Another business model is to give away the software in order to sell hardware. This used to be the norm in the computer industry, with operating systems such as CP/M, Apple DOS and versions of Mac OS prior to 7.6 freely copyable (but not modifiable). As computer hardware standardized throughout the 1980s, it became more difficult for hardware manufacturers to profit from this tactic, as the OS would run on any manufacturer's computer that shared the same architecture.

Programming on Linux

Linux distributions support dozens of programming languages. The original development tools used for building both Linux applications and operating system programs are found within the GNU toolchain, which includes the GNU Compiler Collection (GCC) and the GNU Build System. Amongst others, GCC provides compilers for Ada, C, C++, Go and Fortran. Many programming languages have a cross-platform reference implementation that supports Linux, for example PHP, Perl, Ruby, Python, Java, Go, Rust and Haskell. First released in 2003, the LLVM project provides an alternative cross-platform open-source compiler for many languages. Proprietary compilers for Linux include the Intel C++ Compiler, Sun Studio, and IBM XL C/C++ Compiler. BASIC in the form of Visual Basic is supported in such forms as Gambas, FreeBASIC, and XBasic, and in terms of terminal programming or QuickBASIC or Turbo BASIC programming in the form of QB64.

A common feature of Unix-like systems, Linux includes traditional specific-purpose programming languages targeted at scripting, text processing and system configuration and management in general. Linux distributions support shell scripts, awk, sed and make. Many programs also have an embedded programming language to support configuring or programming themselves. For example, regular expressions are supported in programs like grep, or locate, while advanced text editors, like GNU Emacs, have a complete Lisp interpreter built-in.

Most distributions also include support for PHP, Perl, Ruby, Python and other dynamic languages. While not as common, Linux also supports C# (via Mono), Vala, and Scheme. A number of Java Virtual Machines and development kits run on Linux, including the original Sun Microsystems JVM (HotSpot), and IBM's J2SE RE, as well as many open-source projects like Kaffe and JikesRVM.

GNOME and KDE are popular desktop environments and provide a framework for developing applications. These projects are based on the GTK+ and Qt widget toolkits, respectively, which can also be used independently of the larger framework. Both support a wide variety of languages. There are a number of Integrated development environments available including Anjuta, Code::-Blocks, CodeLite, Eclipse, Geany, ActiveState Komodo, KDevelop, Lazarus, MonoDevelop, NetBeans, and Qt Creator, while the long-established editors Vim, nano and Emacs remain popular.

Hardware Support

The Linux kernel is a widely ported operating system kernel, available for devices ranging from mobile phones to supercomputers; it runs on a highly diverse range of computer architectures, including the hand-held ARM-based iPAQ and the IBM mainframes System z9 or System z10. Specialized distributions and kernel forks exist for less mainstream architectures; for example, the ELKS kernel fork can run on Intel 8086 or Intel 80286 16-bit microprocessors, while the µClinux kernel fork may run on systems without a memory management unit. The kernel also runs on architectures that were only ever intended to use a manufacturer-created operating system, such as Macintosh computers (with both PowerPC and Intel processors), PDAs, video game consoles, portable music players, and mobile phones.

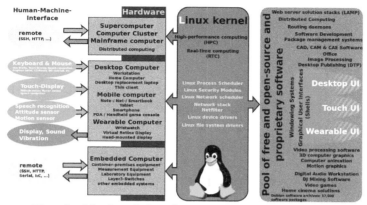

Linux is ubiquitously found on various types of hardware.

There are several industry associations and hardware conferences devoted to maintaining and improving support for diverse hardware under Linux, such as FreedomHEC. Over time, support for different hardware has improved in Linux, resulting in any off-the-shelf purchase having a "good chance" of being compatible.

Uses

Beside the Linux distributions designed for general-purpose use on desktops and servers, distributions may be specialized for different purposes including: computer architecture support, embedded systems, stability, security, localization to a specific region or language, targeting of specific user groups, support for real-time applications, or commitment to a given desktop environment. Furthermore, some distributions deliberately include only free software. As of 2015, over four hundred Linux distributions are actively developed, with about a dozen distributions being most popular for general-purpose use.

Desktop

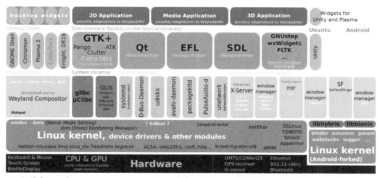

Visible software components of the Linux desktop stack include the
display server, widget engines, and some of the more widespread widget toolkits.
There are also components not directly visible to end users, including D-Bus and PulseAudio.

The popularity of Linux on standard desktop computers and laptops has been increasing over the years. Most modern distributions include a graphical user environment, with, as of February 2015, the two most popular environments being the KDE Plasma Desktop and Xfce.

No single official Linux desktop exists: rather desktop environments and Linux distributions select components from a pool of free and open-source software with which they construct a GUI implementing some more or less strict design guide. GNOME, for example, has its human interface guidelines as a design guide, which gives the human–machine interface an important role, not just when doing the graphical design, but also when considering people with disabilities, and even when focusing on security.

The collaborative nature of free software development allows distributed teams to perform language localization of some Linux distributions for use in locales where localizing proprietary systems would not be cost-effective. For example, the Sinhalese language version of the Knoppix distribution became available significantly before Microsoft translated Windows XP into Sinhalese. In this case the Lanka Linux User Group played a major part in developing the localized system by combining the knowledge of university professors, linguists, and local developers.

Performance and Applications

The performance of Linux on the desktop has been a controversial topic; for example in 2007 Con Kolivas accused the Linux community of favoring performance on servers. He quit Linux kernel development out of frustration with this lack of focus on the desktop, and then gave a "tell all" interview on the topic. Since then a significant amount of development has focused on improving the desktop experience. Projects such as Upstart and systemd aim for a faster boot time; the Wayland and Mir projects aim at replacing X11 while enhancing desktop performance, security and appearance.

Many popular applications are available for a wide variety of operating systems. For example, Mozilla Firefox, OpenOffice.org/LibreOffice and Blender have downloadable versions for all major operating systems. Furthermore, some applications initially developed for Linux, such as Pidgin, and GIMP, were ported to other operating systems (including Windows and Mac OS X) due to their popularity. In addition, a growing number of proprietary desktop applications are also supported on Linux, such as Autodesk Maya, Softimage XSI and Apple Shake in the high-end field of animation and visual effects; see the list of proprietary software for Linux for more details. There are also several companies that have ported their own or other companies' games to Linux, with Linux also being a supported platform on both the popular Steam and Desura digital-distribution services.

Many other types of applications available for Microsoft Windows and Mac OS X also run on Linux. Commonly, either a free software application will exist which does the functions of an application found on another operating system, or that application will have a version that works on Linux, such as with Skype and some video games like Dota 2 and Team Fortress 2. Furthermore, the Wine project provides a Windows compatibility layer to run unmodified Windows applications on Linux. It is sponsored by commercial interests including CodeWeavers, which produces a commercial version of the software. Since 2009, Google has also provided funding to the Wine project. CrossOver, a proprietary solution based on the open-source Wine project, supports running Windows versions of Microsoft Office, Intuit applications such as Quicken and QuickBooks, Adobe Photoshop versions through CS2, and many popular games such as *World of Warcraft*. In other cases, where there is no Linux port of some software in areas such as desktop publishing and professional audio, there is equivalent software available on Linux.

Components and Installation

Besides externally visible components, such as X window managers, a non-obvious but quite central role is played by the programs hosted by freedesktop.org, such as D-Bus or PulseAudio; both major desktop environments (GNOME and KDE) include them, each offering graphical front-ends written using the corresponding toolkit (GTK+ or Qt). A display server is another component, which for the longest time has been communicating in the X11 display server protocol with its clients; prominent software talking X11 includes the X.Org Server and Xlib. Frustration over the cumbersome X11 core protocol, and especially over its numerous extensions, has led to the creation of a new display server protocol, Wayland.

Installing, updating and removing software in Linux is typically done through the use of package managers such as the Synaptic Package Manager, PackageKit, and Yum Extender. While most major Linux distributions have extensive repositories, often containing tens of thousands of packages, not all the software that can run on Linux is available from the official repositories. Alternatively, users can install packages from unofficial repositories, download pre-compiled packages directly from websites, or compile the source code by themselves. All these methods come with different degrees of difficulty; compiling the source code is in general considered a challenging process for new Linux users, but it is hardly needed in modern distributions and is not a method specific to Linux.

- Samples of graphical desktop interfaces

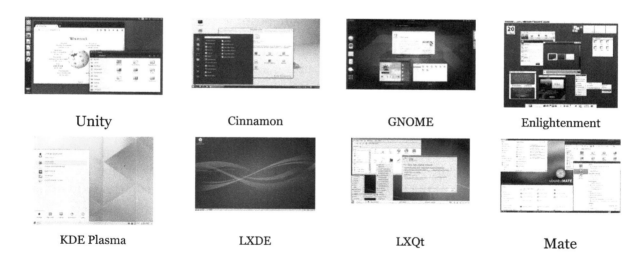

| Unity | Cinnamon | GNOME | Enlightenment |

| KDE Plasma | LXDE | LXQt | Mate |

Netbooks

Linux distributions have also become popular in the netbook market, with many devices such as the Asus Eee PC and Acer Aspire One shipping with customized Linux distributions installed.

In 2009, Google announced its Chrome OS as a minimal Linux-based operating system, using the Chrome browser as the main user interface. Chrome OS does not run any non-web applications, except for the bundled file manager and media player (a certain level of support for Android applications was added in later versions). The netbooks that shipped with the operating system, termed Chromebooks, started appearing on the market in June 2011.

Servers, Mainframes and Supercomputers

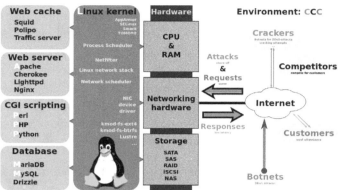

Broad overview of the LAMP software bundle, displayed here together with Squid.
A high-performance and high-availability web server solution providing security in a hostile environment.

Linux distributions have long been used as server operating systems, and have risen to prominence in that area; Netcraft reported in September 2006, that eight of the ten most reliable internet hosting companies ran Linux distributions on their web servers. In June 2008, Linux distributions represented five of the top ten, FreeBSD three of ten, and Microsoft two of ten; since February 2010, Linux distributions represented six of the top ten, FreeBSD two of ten, and Microsoft one of ten.

Linux distributions are the cornerstone of the LAMP server-software combination (Linux, Apache, MariaDB/MySQL, Perl/PHP/Python) which has achieved popularity among developers, and which is one of the more common platforms for website hosting.

Linux distributions have become increasingly popular on mainframes, partly due to pricing and the open-source model. In December 2009, computer giant IBM reported that it would predominantly market and sell mainframe-based Enterprise Linux Server. At LinuxCon North America 2015, IBM announced LinuxONE, a series of mainframes specifically designed to run Linux and open-source software.

Linux distributions are also most commonly used as operating systems for supercomputers; in the decade since the Earth Simulator supercomputer, all the fastest supercomputers have used Linux. As of November 2016, 99.6% of the world's 500 fastest supercomputers run some variant of Linux, including the top 280.

Smart Devices

Android smartphones

Several operating systems for smart devices, such as smartphones, tablet computers, smart TVs, and in-vehicle infotainment (IVI) systems, are based on Linux. Major platforms for such systems include Android, Firefox OS, Mer and Tizen.

Android has become the dominant mobile operating system for smartphones, running on 79.3% of units sold worldwide during the second quarter of 2013. Android is also a popular operating system for tablets, and Android smart TVs and in-vehicle infotainment systems have also appeared in the market.

Cellphones and PDAs running Linux on open-source platforms became more common from 2007; examples include the Nokia N810, Openmoko's Neo1973, and the Motorola ROKR E8. Continuing the trend, Palm (later acquired by HP) produced a new Linux-derived operating system, webOS, which is built into its line of Palm Pre smartphones.

Nokia's Maemo, one of the earliest mobile operating systems, was based on Debian. It was later merged with Intel's Moblin, another Linux-based operating system, to form MeeGo. The project was later terminated in favor of Tizen, an operating system targeted at mobile devices as well as IVI. Tizen is a project within The Linux Foundation. Several Samsung products are already running Tizen, Samsung Gear 2 being the most significant example. Samsung Z smartphones will use Tizen instead of Android.

As a result of MeeGo's termination, the Mer project forked the MeeGo codebase to create a basis for mobile-oriented operating systems. In July 2012, Jolla announced Sailfish OS, their own mobile operating system built upon Mer technology.

Mozilla's Firefox OS consists of the Linux kernel, a hardware abstraction layer, a web-standards-based runtime environment and user interface, and an integrated web browser.

Canonical has released Ubuntu Touch, aiming to bring convergence to the user experience on this mobile operating system and its desktop counterpart, Ubuntu. The operating system also provides a full Ubuntu desktop when connected to an external monitor.

Embedded Devices

The Jolla Phone has the Linux-based Sailfish OS

In-car entertainment system of the Tesla Model S is based on Ubuntu

Nokia X, a smartphone that runs Linux kernel

Due to its low cost and ease of customization, Linux is often used in embedded systems. In the non-mobile telecommunications equipment sector, the majority of customer-premises equipment (CPE) hardware runs some Linux-based operating system. OpenWrt is a community driven example upon which many of the OEM firmwares are based.

For example, the popular TiVo digital video recorder also uses a customized Linux, as do several network firewalls and routers from such makers as Cisco/Linksys. The Korg OASYS, the Korg KRONOS, the Yamaha Motif XS/Motif XF music workstations, Yamaha S90XS/S70XS, Yamaha MOX6/MOX8 synthesizers, Yamaha Motif-Rack XS tone generator module, and Roland RD-700GX digital piano also run Linux. Linux is also used in stage lighting control systems, such as the WholeHogIII console.

Gaming

There had been several games that run on traditional desktop Linux, and many of which originally written for desktop OS. However, due to most game developers not paying attention to such a small market as desktop Linux, only a few prominent games have been available for desktop Linux. On the other hand, as a popular mobile platform, Android has gained much developer interest and there are many games available for Android.

On February 14, 2013, Valve released a Linux version of Steam, a popular game distribution platform on PC. Many Steam games were ported to Linux. On December 13, 2013, Valve released SteamOS, a gaming oriented OS based on Debian, for beta testing, and has plans to ship Steam Machines as a gaming and entertainment platform. Valve has also developed VOGL, an OpenGL debugger intended to aid video game development, as well as porting its Source game engine to desktop Linux. As a result of Valve's effort, several prominent games such as DotA 2, Team Fortress 2, Portal, Portal 2 and Left 4 Dead 2 are now natively available on desktop Linux.

On July 31, 2013, Nvidia released Shield as an attempt to use Android as a specialized gaming platform.

Specialized Uses

Due to the flexibility, customizability and free and open-source nature of Linux, it becomes possible to highly tune Linux for a specific purpose. There are two main methods for creating a specialized Linux distribution: building from scratch or from a general-purpose distribution as a base. The distributions often used for this purpose include Debian, Fedora, Ubuntu (which is itself based on Debian), Arch Linux, Gentoo, and Slackware. In contrast, Linux distributions built from scratch do not have general-purpose bases; instead, they focus on the JeOS philosophy by including only necessary components and avoiding resource overhead caused by components considered redundant in the distribution's use cases.

Home Theater PC

A home theater PC (HTPC) is a PC that is mainly used as an entertainment system, especially a Home theater system. It is normally connected to a television, and often an additional audio system.

OpenELEC, a Linux distribution that incorporates the media center software Kodi, is an OS tuned specifically for an HTPC. Having been built from the ground up adhering to the JeOS principle, the OS is very lightweight and very suitable for the confined usage range of an HTPC.

There are also special editions of Linux distributions that include the MythTV media center software, such as Mythbuntu, a special edition of Ubuntu.

Digital security

Kali Linux is a Debian-based Linux distribution designed for digital forensics and penetration testing. It comes preinstalled with several software applications for penetration testing and identifying security exploits. The Ubuntu derivative BackBox provides pre-installed security and network analysis tools for ethical hacking.

There are many Linux distributions created with privacy, secrecy, network anonymity and information security in mind, including Tails, Tin Hat Linux and Tinfoil Hat Linux. Lightweight Portable Security is a distribution based on Arch Linux and developed by the United States Department of Defense. Tor-ramdisk is a minimal distribution created solely to host the network anonymity software Tor.

System Rescue

Linux Live CD sessions have long been used as a tool for recovering data from a broken computer system and for repairing the system. Building upon that idea, several Linux distributions tailored for this purpose have emerged, most of which use GParted as a partition editor, with additional data recovery and system repair software:

- GParted Live – a Debian-based distribution developed by the GParted project.

- Parted Magic – a commercial Linux distribution.

- SystemRescueCD – a Gentoo-based distribution with support for editing Windows registry.

In Space

SpaceX uses multiple redundant flight computers in a fault-tolerant design in the Falcon 9 rocket. Each Merlin engine is controlled by three voting computers, with two physical processors per computer that constantly check each other's operation. Linux is not inherently fault-tolerant (no operating system is, as it is a function of the whole system including the hardware), but the flight computer software makes it so for its purpose. For flexibility, commercial off-the-shelf parts and system-wide "radiation-tolerant" design are used instead of radiation hardened parts. As of June 2015, SpaceX has made 19 launches of the Falcon 9 since 2010, out of which 18 have successfully delivered their primary payloads to Earth orbit, including some support missions for the International Space Station.

In addition, Windows was used as an operating system on non-mission critical systems—laptops used on board the space station, for example—but it has been replaced with Linux; the first Linux-powered humanoid robot is also undergoing in-flight testing.

The Jet Propulsion Laboratory has used Linux for a number of years "to help with projects relating to the construction of unmanned space flight and deep space exploration"; NASA uses Linux in robotics in the Mars rover, and Ubuntu Linux to "save data from satellites".

Education

Linux distributions have been created to provide hands-on experience with coding and source code to students, on devices such as the Raspberry Pi. In addition to producing a practical device, the intention is to show students "how things work under the hood".

The Ubuntu derivatives Edubuntu and The Linux Schools Project, as well as the Debian derivative Skolelinux, provide education-oriented software packages. They also include tools for administering and building school computer labs and computer-based classrooms, such as the Linux Terminal Server Project (LTSP).

Others

Instant WebKiosk and Webconverger are browser-based Linux distributions often used in web kiosks and digital signage. Thinstation is a minimalist distribution designed for thin clients. Rocks Cluster Distribution is tailored for high-performance computing clusters.

There are general-purpose Linux distributions that target a specific audience, such as users of a specific language or geographical area. Such examples include Ubuntu Kylin for Chinese language users and BlankOn targeted at Indonesians. Profession-specific distributions include Ubuntu Studio for media creation and DNALinux for bioinformatics. There is also a Muslim-oriented distribution of the name Sabily, as well as an Arabic-focused distribution called Ojuba Linux that consequently also provides some Islamic tools. Certain organizations use slightly specialized Linux distributions internally, including GendBuntu used by the French National Gendarmerie, Goobuntu used internally by Google, and Astra Linux developed specifically for the Russian army.

Market Share and Uptake

Many quantitative studies of free/open-source software focus on topics including market share and reliability, with numerous studies specifically examining Linux. The Linux market is growing rapidly, and the revenue of servers, desktops, and packaged software running Linux was expected to exceed $35.7 billion by 2008. Analysts and proponents attribute the relative success of Linux to its security, reliability, low cost, and freedom from vendor lock-in.

Desktops and laptops

According to web server statistics, as of June 2016, the estimated market share of Linux on desktop computers is around 1.8%. In comparison, Microsoft Windows has a market share of around 89.7%, while Mac OS covers around 8.5%.

Web servers

W3Cook publishes stats that use the top 1,000,000 Alexa domains, which as of May 2015 estimate that 96.55% of web servers run Linux, 1.73% run Windows, and 1.72% run FreeBSD.

W3Techs publishes stats that use the top 10,000,000 Alexa domains, updated monthly and as of November 2016 estimate that 66.7% of web servers run Linux/Unix, and 33.4% run Microsoft Windows.

In September 2008, Microsoft's CEO Steve Ballmer stated that 60% of web servers ran Linux, versus 40% that ran Windows Server.

IDC's Q1 2007 report indicated that Linux held 12.7% of the overall server market at that time; this estimate was based on the number of Linux servers sold by various companies, and did not include server hardware purchased separately that had Linux installed on it later.

Mobile devices

Android, which is based on the Linux kernel, has become the dominant operating system for smartphones. During the second quarter of 2013, 79.3% of smartphones sold worldwide used Android. Android is also a popular operating system for tablets, being responsible for more than 60% of tablet sales as of 2013. According to web server statistics, as of December 2014 Android has a market share of about 46%, with iOS holding 45%, and the remaining 9% attributed to various niche platforms.

Film production

For years Linux has been the platform of choice in the film industry. The first major film produced on Linux servers was 1997's *Titanic*. Since then major studios including Dream-Works Animation, Pixar, Weta Digital, and Industrial Light & Magic have migrated to Linux. According to the Linux Movies Group, more than 95% of the servers and desktops at large animation and visual effects companies use Linux.

Use in government

Linux distributions have also gained popularity with various local and national governments. The federal government of Brazil is well known for its support for Linux. News of the Russian military creating its own Linux distribution has also surfaced, and has come to fruition as the G.H.ost Project. The Indian state of Kerala has gone to the extent of mandating that all state high schools run Linux on their computers. China uses Linux exclusively as the operating system for its Loongson processor family to achieve technology independence. In Spain, some regions have developed their own Linux distributions, which are widely used in education and official institutions, like gnuLinEx in Extremadura and Guadalinex in Andalusia. France and Germany have also taken steps toward the adoption of Linux. North Korea's Red Star OS, developed since 2002, is based on a version of Fedora Linux.

Copyright, Trademark, and Naming

Linux kernel is licensed under the GNU General Public License (GPL), version 2. The GPL requires that anyone who distributes software based on source code under this license, must make the originating source code (and any modifications) available to the recipient under the same terms. Other key components of a typical Linux distribution are also mainly licensed under the GPL, but they may use other licenses; many libraries use the GNU Lesser General Public License (LGPL), a more permissive variant of the GPL, and the X.org implementation of the X Window System uses the MIT License.

Torvalds states that the Linux kernel will not move from version 2 of the GPL to version 3. He specifically dislikes some provisions in the new license which prohibit the use of the software in digital rights management. It would also be impractical to obtain permission from all the copyright holders, who number in the thousands.

A 2001 study of Red Hat Linux 7.1 found that this distribution contained 30 million source lines of code. Using the Constructive Cost Model, the study estimated that this distribution required about eight thousand man-years of development time. According to the study, if all this software had been developed by conventional proprietary means, it would have cost about $1.49 billion (2016 US dollars) to develop in the United States. Most of the source code (71%) was written in the C programming language, but many other languages were used, including C++, Lisp, assembly language, Perl, Python, Fortran, and various shell scripting languages. Slightly over half of all lines of code were licensed under the GPL. The Linux kernel itself was 2.4 million lines of code, or 8% of the total.

In a later study, the same analysis was performed for Debian version 4.0 (etch, which was released in 2007). This distribution contained close to 283 million source lines of code, and the study estimated that it would have required about seventy three thousand man-years and cost US$8.2 billion (in 2016 dollars) to develop by conventional means.

The name "Linux" is also used for a laundry detergent made by Swiss company Rösch.

In the United States, the name *Linux* is a trademark registered to Linus Torvalds. Initially, nobody registered it, but on August 15, 1994, William R. Della Croce, Jr. filed for the trademark *Linux*, and then demanded royalties from Linux distributors. In 1996, Torvalds and some affected organizations sued him to have the trademark assigned to Torvalds, and, in 1997, the case was settled. The licensing of the trademark has since been handled by the Linux Mark Institute (LMI). Torvalds has stated that he trademarked the name only to prevent someone else from using it. LMI originally charged a nominal sublicensing fee for use of the Linux name as part of trademarks, but later changed this in favor of offering a free, perpetual worldwide sublicense.

The Free Software Foundation (FSF) prefers *GNU/Linux* as the name when referring to the operating system as a whole, because it considers Linux distributions to be variants of the GNU operating system initiated in 1983 by Richard Stallman, president of the FSF.

A minority of public figures and software projects other than Stallman and the FSF, notably Debian (which had been sponsored by the FSF up to 1996), also use *GNU/Linux* when referring to the operating system as a whole. Most media and common usage, however, refers to this family of operating systems simply as *Linux*, as do many large Linux distributions (for example, SUSE Linux and Red Hat Enterprise Linux). In contrast Linux distributions containing only free software use "GNU/Linux" or simply "GNU", such as Trisquel GNU/Linux, Parabola GNU/Linux-libre, BLAG Linux and GNU, and gNewSense.

As of May 2011, about 8% to 13% of a modern Linux distribution is made of GNU components (the range depending on whether GNOME is considered part of GNU), as determined by counting lines of source code making up Ubuntu's "Natty" release; meanwhile, 6% is taken by the Linux kernel, and 9% by the Linux kernel and its direct dependencies.

Just Enough Operating System

Just Enough Operating System (JeOS, pronounced "juice") is a paradigm for customizing operating systems to fit the needs of a particular application such as for a software appliance. The platform only includes the operating system components required to support a particular application and any other third-party components contained in the appliance, (e.g., the kernel). This makes the appliance smaller, faster (to boot and to execute the particular application) and potentially more secure than an application running under a full general-purpose OS.

Common Implementations

Typically, a JeOS will consist of the following:

- JeOS media (OS core {kernel, virtual drives, login})

- OS minimum maintenance tools

- Minimum user space tools

- Packages repository (DVD or network based)

It is important to differentiate between true fully *minimalized OS* install profiles forced, for example, with security hardening tools or representing Recovery Console images and *JeOS* richer install profiles which are designed and built for wider audience usage, so VM/VA creators and their users can easily perform needed installation or configuration tasks.

BareMetal

BareMetal is an exokernel-based single address space operating system (OS) created by Return Infinity.

It is written in assembly to achieve high-performance computing with minimal footprint with a JeOS approach. The operating system is primarily targeted towards virtualized environments for cloud computing, or HPCs due to its design as a lightweight kernel (LWK). It could be used as a unikernel.

It was inspired by another OS written in assembly, MikeOS, and it is a current-day example of an operating system that is not written in C or C++, nor based on Unix-like kernels.

Overview

Hardware Requirements

- Intel/AMD-based 64-bit computer
- Memory: 4 MB (plus 2 MB for every additional core)
- Hard Disk: 32 MB

One Task Per Core

Multitasking on BareMetal is unusual for operating systems in this day and age. BareMetal uses an internal work queue that all CPU cores poll. A task added to the work queue will be processed by any available CPU core in the system and will execute until completion, which results in no context switch overhead.

Programming

API

An API is documented but, in line with its philosophy, the OS does not enforce entry points for system calls (e.g.: no call gates or other safety mechanisms).

C

BareMetal OS has a build script to pull the latest code, make the needed changes, and then compile C code using the Newlib C standard library.

C++

A mostly-complete C++11 Standard Library was designed and developed for working in ring 0.

The main goal of such library is providing, on a library level, an alternative to hardware memory protection used in classical OSes, with help of carefully designed classes.

Rust

A Rust program demonstration was added to the programs in November 2014, demonstrating the ability to write Rust programs for BareMetal OS.

Networking

TCP/IP stack

A TCP/IP stack was *the #1 feature request*. A port of lwIP written in C was announced in October 2014.

OpenELEC

OpenELEC (short for Open Embedded Linux Entertainment Center) is a Linux distribution designed for home theater PCs and based on the Kodi (formerly XBMC) media player.

OpenELEC applies the "just enough operating system" principle. It is designed to consume relatively few resources and to boot quickly from flash memory. OpenELEC disk images for the Raspberry Pi series and Freescale i.MX6 based devices are also available.

The OpenELEC team released OpenELEC 4.0 on 5 May 2014, and this version features updated XBMC 13.0 with further updated important parts of the operating system as well as the Linux kernel updated to version 3.14 and additional device drivers. OpenELEC 4.0 also switched its init system to systemd.

Description

OpenELEC provides a complete media center software suite that comes with a pre-configured version of Kodi and third-party addons with retro video game console emulators and DVR plugins. OpenELEC is an extremely small and very fast booting Linux based distribution, primarily designed to be booted from flash memory card such as CompactFlash or a solid-state drive, similar to that of the XBMCbuntu (formerly XBMC Live) distribution but specifically targeted to a minimum set-top box hardware setup based on an ARM SoCs or Intel x86 processor and graphics.

History

Since 2011, the OpenELEC team usually releases a new major version, following the Kodi release schedule.

Since 2014, specifics builds supporting a set of Graphics/GPU chipsets (ION, Fusion, Intel,...) are deprecated. And since version 6, x86 builds are deprecated too. Builds are currently available for x86-64 systems (as "Generic Build"), Raspberry Pi, Raspberry Pi 2, Raspberry Pi 3 and the first generation Apple TV.

	OpenELEC version	Release date	Kodi version		Kernel
1	1.0	20 October 2011	10.1	Dharma	
2	2.0	16 October 2012	11.0	Eden	3.2.31
3	3.0	24 March 2013	12.1	Frodo	
	3.0.6	15 June 2013	12.1		
	3.2	13 September 2013	12.2		3.10
	3.2.4	28 November 2013	12.2		3.10.20
4	4.0	5 May 2014	13.0	Gotham	3.14
	4.0.7	9 July 2014	13.1		3.14.11
	4.2	26 September 2014	13.2		3.16
5	5.0	28 December 2014	14.0	Helix	3.17
	5.0.7	29 March 2015	14.2		3.17
6	6.0	1 November 2015	15.2	Isengard	4.1
	6.0.3	1 March 2016	15.2		4.1

Systems

On 5 February 2013, OpenELEC announced that they had jointly developed, with Arctic, a manufacturer of computer cooling systems based in Switzerland, a passively cooled entertainment system – the MC001 media centre, based on the Kodi 12 (OpenELEC 3.0) platform. They also announced plans to provide further builds for the ARCTIC MC001 systems on their next release.

Pulse-Eight sells both custom and off the shelf hardware products primarily designed for Kodi, such as remote controls, HTPC systems and accessories, including a HTPC PVR set-top-box pre-installed with Kodi that they call *"PulseBox"* Pulse-Eight also offers free performance tuned embedded versions of Kodi that they call *"Pulse"* which is based on OpenELEC and a custom PVR-build of Kodi that is meant to run on dedicated HTPC systems.

Xtreamer Ultra and Xtreamer Ultra 2, manufactured by the South Korean company Unicorn Information Systems, are nettops based on Nvidia graphics and Intel Atom processors which comes with OpenELEC and Kodi software pre-installed. The first-generation Xtreamer Ultra uses Nvidia Ion chipset with a 1.80 GHz Dual-Core Intel Atom D525 CPU, while the Xtreamer Ultra 2 uses discrete GeForce GT 520M graphics with a 2.13 GHz Dual-Core Intel Atom D2700 CPU.

OpenSolaris

OpenSolaris is a discontinued, open source computer operating system based on Solaris created by Sun Microsystems. It was also the name of the project initiated by Sun to build a developer and user community around the software. After the acquisition of Sun Microsystems in 2010, Oracle decided to discontinue open development of the core software, and replaced the OpenSolaris distribution model with the proprietary Solaris Express.

Prior to Oracle's moving of core development "behind closed doors", a group of former OpenSolaris developers decided to fork the core software under the name OpenIndiana. The OpenIndiana project, a part of the illumos Foundation, aims to continue the development and distribution of the OpenSolaris codebase. Since then many more illumos distributions are available for use, continuing development in open or offering support.

OpenSolaris is a descendant of the UNIX System V Release 4 (SVR4) code base developed by Sun and AT&T in the late 1980s. It is the only version of the System V variant of UNIX available as open source. OpenSolaris was developed as a combination of several software *consolidations* that were open sourced subsequent to Solaris 10. It includes a variety of free software, including popular desktop and server software. On Friday, August 13, 2010, details started to emerge relating to the discontinuation of the OpenSolaris project and the pending release of a new closed-source, proprietary version of Solaris, Solaris 11.

History

OpenSolaris was based on Solaris, which was originally released by Sun in 1991. Solaris is a version of UNIX System V Release 4 (SVR4), jointly developed by Sun and AT&T to merge features from several existing Unix systems. It was licensed by Sun from Novell to replace SunOS.

Planning for OpenSolaris started in early 2004. A pilot program was formed in September 2004 with 18 non-Sun community members and ran for 9 months growing to 145 external participants. Sun submitted the CDDL (Common Development and Distribution License) to the OSI, which approved it on January 14, 2005.

The first part of the Solaris code base to be open sourced was the Solaris Dynamic Tracing facility (commonly known as DTrace), a tool that aids in the analysis, debugging, and tuning of applications and systems. DTrace was released under the CDDL on January 25, 2005 on the newly launched *opensolaris.org* website. The bulk of the Solaris system code was released on June 14, 2005. There remains some system code that is not open sourced, and is available only as pre-compiled binary files.

To direct the newly fledged project, a Community Advisory Board was announced on April 4, 2005: two were elected by the pilot community, two were employees appointed by Sun, and one was appointed from the broader free software community by Sun. The members were Roy Fielding, Al Hopper, Rich Teer, Casper Dik, and Simon Phipps. On February 10, 2006 Sun approved *The OpenSolaris Charter*, which reestablished this body as the independent OpenSolaris Governing Board. The task of creating a governance document or "constitution" for this organization was given to the OGB and three invited members: Stephen Hahn and Keith Wesolowski (developers in Sun's Solaris organization) and Ben Rockwood (a prominent OpenSolaris community member). The former next-generation Solaris OS version under development by Sun to eventually succeed Solaris 10 was codenamed 'Nevada', and was derived from what was the OpenSolaris codebase and this new code was then pulled into new OpenSolaris 'Nevada' snapshot builds. *"While under Sun Microsystems' control, there were bi-weekly snapshots of Solaris Nevada (the codename for the next-generation Solaris OS to eventually succeed Solaris 10) and this new code was then pulled into new OpenSolaris preview snapshots available at Genunix.org. The stable releases of OpenSolaris are based on these Nevada builds."*

Initially, Sun's *Solaris Express* program provided a distribution based on the OpenSolaris code in combination with software found only in Solaris releases. The first independent distribution was released on June 17, 2005, and many others have emerged since.

On March 19, 2007, Sun announced that it had hired Ian Murdock, founder of Debian, to head *Project Indiana,* an effort to produce a complete OpenSolaris distribution, with GNOME and userland tools from GNU, plus a network-based package management system. The new distribution was planned to refresh the user experience, and would become the successor to Solaris Express as the basis for future releases of Solaris.

On May 5, 2008, OpenSolaris 2008.05 was released in a format that could be booted as a Live CD or installed directly. It uses the GNOME desktop environment as the primary user interface. The later OpenSolaris 2008.11 release included a GUI for ZFS' snapshotting capabilities, known as Time Slider, that provides functionality similar to macOS's Time Machine.

In December 2008, Sun Microsystems and Toshiba America Information Systems announced plans to distribute Toshiba laptops pre-installed with OpenSolaris. On April 1, 2009, the Tecra M10 and Portégé R600 came preinstalled with OpenSolaris 2008.11 release and several supplemental software packages.

On June 1, 2009, OpenSolaris 2009.06 was released, with support for the SPARC platform.

On January 6, 2010, it was announced that Solaris Express program would be closed while an OpenSolaris binary release was scheduled to be released March 26 of 2010. The OpenSolaris 2010.03 release never appeared.

On August 13, 2010, Oracle was rumored to have discontinued the OpenSolaris binary distribution to focus on the Solaris Express binary distribution program. Source code would continue to be accepted from the community and Oracle source code would continue to be released into Open Source, but Oracle code releases would occur only after binary releases. Internal email was released by an OpenSolaris kernel developer but was unconfirmed by Oracle.

There was a post confirming the leak posted to the OpenSolaris Forums on August 13, 2010. Upstream contributions will continue through a new Oracle web site, downstream source code publishing will continue, binary distribution will continue under the old Solaris Express model, but release of source code will occur after binary cuts, and binary cuts will become less frequent.

On September 14, 2010, OpenIndiana was formally launched at the JISC Centre in London. While OpenIndiana is a fork in the technical sense, it is a continuation of OpenSolaris in spirit: the project intends to deliver a System V family operating system which is binary-compatible with the Oracle products Solaris 11 and Solaris 11 Express. However, rather than being based around the OS/Net consolidation like OpenSolaris was, OpenIndiana became a distribution based on illumos (the first release is still based around OS/Net). The project uses the same IPS package management system as OpenSolaris.

On November 12, 2010, a final build of OpenSolaris (134b) was published by Oracle to the /release repository to serve as an upgrade path to Solaris 11 Express.

Oracle Solaris 11 Express 2010.11, a preview of Solaris 11 and the first release of the post-OpenSolaris distribution from Oracle, was released on November 15, 2010.

Version History

Color	Meaning
Red	Release no longer supported
Green	Release still supported

Version	Build	Release date	End of support phase		
			General Availability (GA)	Post End of Version (EOV)	SunSpectrum End of Service Life (SS-EOSL)
2008.05	86	13 May 2008	13 November 2008	13 May 2011	-
2008.11	101b	25 November 2008	25 May 2009	25 November 2011	-
2009.06	111b	1 June 2009	1 December 2009	1 June 2012	1 June 2014

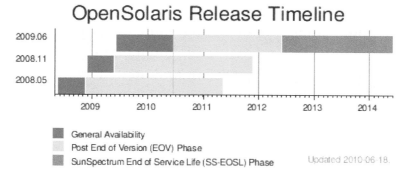

OpenSolaris Release Timeline

General Availability
Post End of Version (EOV) Phase
SunSpectrum End of Service Life (SS-EOSL) Phase

Updated 2010-06-18.

Release Model

OpenSolaris 2009.06 x86 LiveCD GNOME with terminal.

OpenSolaris is offered as both development (unstable) and production (stable) releases.

- Development releases are built from the latest OpenSolaris codebase (consolidations) and include newer technologies, security updates and bug fixes, and more applications, but may not have undergone extensive testing.

- Production releases are branched from a snapshot of the development codebase (following a code freeze) and undergo a QA process that includes backporting security updates and bug fixes.

OpenSolaris can be installed from CD-ROM, USB drives, or over a network with the Automated Installer. CD, USB, and network install images are made available for both types of releases.

Repositories

OpenSolaris uses a network-aware package management system called the *Image Packaging System* (also known as pkg(5)) to add, remove, and manage installed software and to update to newer releases.

Packages for development releases of OpenSolaris are published by Oracle typically every two weeks to the */dev* repository. Production releases use the */release* repository which does not receive updates until the next production release. Only Sun customers with paid support contracts have access to updates for production releases.

Paid support for production releases which allows access to security updates and bug fixes is offered by Sun through the */support* repository on *pkg.sun.com*.

Documentation

A hardware compatibility list (HCL) for OpenSolaris can be consulted when choosing hardware for OpenSolaris deployment.

Extensive OpenSolaris administration, usage, and development documentation is available online, including community-contributed information.

License

Sun has released most of the Solaris source code under the *Common Development and Distribution License* (CDDL), which is based on the Mozilla Public License (MPL) version 1.1. The CDDL was approved as an open source license by the Open Source Initiative (OSI) in January 2005. Files licensed under the CDDL can be combined with files licensed under other licenses, whether open source or proprietary.

During Sun's announcement of Java's release under the GNU General Public License (GPL), Jonathan Schwartz and Rich Green both hinted at the possibility of releasing Solaris under the GPL, with Green saying he was "certainly not" averse to relicensing under the GPL. When Schwartz pressed him (jokingly), Green said Sun would "take a very close look at it." In January 2007, eWeek reported that anonymous sources at Sun had told them OpenSolaris would be dual-licensed under CDDL and GPLv3. Green responded in his blog the next day that the article was incorrect, saying that although Sun is giving "very serious consideration" to such a dual-licensing arrangement, it would be subject to agreement by the rest of the OpenSolaris community.

Conferences

The first annual OpenSolaris Developer Conference (abbreviated as OSDevCon) was organized by the German Unix User Group (GUUG) and took place from February 27 to March 2, 2007 at the Freie Universität Berlin in Germany. The 2008 OSDevCon was a joint effort of the GUUG and the

Czech OpenSolaris User Group (CZOSUG) and look place June 25–27, 2008 in Prague, Czech Republic. The 2009 OSDevCon look place October 27–30, 2009, in Dresden, Germany.

In 2007, Sun Microsystems organized the first OpenSolaris Developer Summit, which was held on the weekend of October 13, 2007, at the University of California, Santa Cruz in the United States. The 2008 OpenSolaris Developer Summit returned to UCSC on May 2–3, 2008, and took place immediately prior to the launch of Sun's new OpenSolaris distribution on May 5, 2008, at the CommunityOne conference in San Francisco, California.

The first OpenSolaris Storage Summit was organized by Sun and held September 21, 2008, preceding the SNIA Storage Developer Conference (SDC), in Santa Clara, California. The second OpenSolaris Storage Summit preceded the USENIX Conference on File and Storage Technologies (FAST) on February 23, 2009, in San Francisco, United States.

On November 3, 2009, a Solaris/OpenSolaris Security Summit was held by Sun in the Inner Harbor area of Baltimore, Maryland, preceding the Large Installation System Administration Conference (LISA).

Ports

- PowerPC Port: Project Polaris, experimental PowerPC port, based on the previous porting effort, Project Pulsar from Sun Labs.

- OpenSolaris for System z, for IBM mainframes: Project Sirius, developed by Sine Nomine Associates, named as an analogy to Polaris.

- OpenSolaris on ARM Port

- OpenSolaris on MIPS Port

Derivatives

- illumos, a fully open source fork of the project, started in 2010 by a community of Sun OpenSolaris engineers and the NexentaOS support. Note that OpenSolaris was not 100% open source: Some drivers and some libraries were property of other companies that Sun (now Oracle) licensed and was not able to release.

- OpenIndiana, a project under the illumos umbrella aiming "... *to become the defacto OpenSolaris distribution installed on production servers where security and bug fixes are required free of charge.*"

- SchilliX, the first LiveCD released after OpenSolaris code was opened to public.

- MartUX is the first SPARC distribution of OpenSolaris, with an alpha prototype released by Martin Bochnig in April 2006. It was distributed as a Live CD but is later available only on DVD as it has had the Blastwave community software added. Its goal was to become a desktop operating system. The first SPARC release was a small Live CD, released as marTux_0.2 Live CD in summer of 2006, the first straight OpenSolaris distribution for SPARC. It was later re-branded as MartUX and the next releases included full SPARC installers in addition to the Live media. Much later, MartUX was re-branded as OpenSXCE when it moved to the first OpenSolaris release to support both SPARC and Intel architectures after Sun was acquired by Oracle.

- MilaX, small Live CD/Live USB with minimal set of packages to fit a 90 MB image

- EON ZFS Storage, a NAS implementation targeted at embedded systems

- Jaris OS, Live DVD and also installable. Pronounced according to the IPA but in English as Yah-Rees. This distribution has been heavily modified to fully support a version of Wine called Madoris that can install and run Windows programs at native speed. Jaris stands for "Japanese Solaris". Madoris is a combination of the Japanese word for Windows "mado" and Solaris.

- napp-it, free Browser managed internet/ san/ nas/ project, based on nexenta3 or eon/ opensolaris

- OpenSXCE, an OpenSolaris distribution release for both 32-bit and 64-bit x86 platforms and SPARC microprocessors, initially produced from OpenSolaris source code repository, ported to the illumos source code repository to form OpenIndiana's first SPARC distribution. Notably, the first OpenSolaris distribution with illumos source for SPARC based upon OpenIndiana, OpenSXCE finally moved to a new source code repository, based upon DilOS, where new releases continue.

- NexentaStor, optimized for storage workloads, based on Nexenta OS

- OSDyson: illumos kernel with GNU userland and packages from Debian. Strives to become an official Debian port.

- SmartOS: Virtualization centered derivative from Joyent.

Discontinued

- Nexenta OS (discontinued October 31, 2012), first distribution based on Ubuntu userland with Solaris-derived kernel

- *StormOS, stormos.org*, a lightweight desktop OS based on Nexenta OS and Xfce.

Ubuntu JeOS

Ubuntu JeOS (pronounced "juice") was a variant of Ubuntu that is described as "an efficient variant ... configured specifically for virtual appliances." It is a concept for what an operating system should look like in the context of a virtual appliance. JeOS stands for "Just enough Operating System."

Its first release was Ubuntu JeOS 7.10, and since the release of Ubuntu 8.10 it has been included as an option as part of the standard Ubuntu Server Edition.

Supported Platforms

The latest version of JeOS is optimized for virtualization technologies by VMware, Inc. and the Linux Kernel-based Virtual Machine.

Specifications

Specifications for version 8.10 and above include:

- Part of the standard Ubuntu Server ISO image

- Less than 380 MB installed footprint

- Specialized server kernel

- Intended for VMware ESX, VMware Server, libvirt and KVM

- 128 MB minimum memory

- No graphical environment preloaded

Distributed Operating System

A distributed operating system is a software over a collection of independent, networked, communicating, and physically separate computational nodes. Each individual node holds a specific software subset of the global aggregate operating system. Each subset is a composite of two distinct service provisioners. The first is a ubiquitous minimal kernel, or microkernel, that directly controls that node's hardware. Second is a higher-level collection of *system management components* that coordinate the node's individual and collaborative activities. These components abstract microkernel functions and support user applications.

The microkernel and the management components collection work together. They support the system's goal of integrating multiple resources and processing functionality into an efficient and stable system. This seamless integration of individual nodes into a global system is referred to as *transparency*, or *single system image*; describing the illusion provided to users of the global system's appearance as a single computational entity.

Description

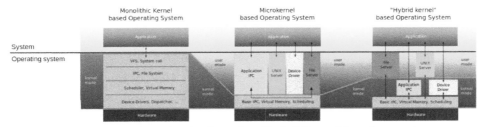

Structure of monolithic kernel, microkernel and hybrid kernel-based operating systems

A distributed OS provides the same essential services and functionality required of an OS but adds attributes and particular configurations to allow it to support additional requirements such as increased scale and availability. To a user, a distributed OS works in a manner similar to a single-node, monolithic operating system. That is, although it consists of multiple nodes, it appears to users and applications as a single-node.

Separating minimal system-level functionality from additional user-level modular services provides a "separation of mechanism and policy." Mechanism and policy can be simply interpreted as "what something is done" versus "how something is done," respectively. This separation increases flexibility and scalability.

Overview

The kernel

At each locale (typically a node), the kernel provides a minimally complete set of node-level utilities necessary for operating a node's underlying hardware and resources. These mechanisms include allocation, management, and disposition of a node's resources, processes, communication, and input/output management support functions. Within the kernel, the communications sub-system is of foremost importance for a distributed OS.

In a distributed OS, the kernel often supports a minimal set of functions, including low-level address space management, thread management, and inter-process communication (IPC). A kernel of this design is referred to as a *microkernel*. Its modular nature enhances reliability and security, essential features for a distributed OS. It is common for a kernel to be identically replicated over all nodes in a system and therefore that the nodes in a system use similar hardware. The combination of minimal design and ubiquitous node coverage enhances the global system's extensibility, and the ability to dynamically introduce new nodes or services.

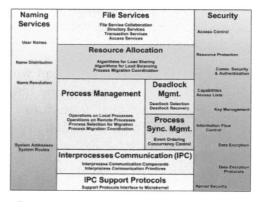

System management components overview

System Management

System management components are software processes that define the node's *policies*. These components are the part of the OS outside the kernel. These components provide higher-level communication, process and resource management, reliability, performance and security. The components match the functions of a single-entity system, adding the transparency required in a distributed environment.

The distributed nature of the OS requires additional services to support a node's responsibilities to the global system. In addition, the system management components accept the "defensive" responsibilities of reliability, availability, and persistence. These responsibilities can conflict with each other. A consistent approach, balanced perspective, and a deep understanding of the overall system can assist in identifying diminishing returns. Separation of policy and mechanism mitigates such conflicts.

Working Together as an Operating System

The architecture and design of a distributed operating system must realize both individual node and global system goals. Architecture and design must be approached in a manner consistent with separating policy and mechanism. In doing so, a distributed operating system attempts to provide an efficient and reliable distributed computing framework allowing for an absolute minimal user awareness of the underlying command and control efforts.

The multi-level collaboration between a kernel and the system management components, and in turn between the distinct nodes in a distributed operating system is the functional challenge of the distributed operating system. This is the point in the system that must maintain a perfect harmony of purpose, and simultaneously maintain a complete disconnect of intent from implementation. This challenge is the distributed operating system's opportunity to produce the foundation and framework for a reliable, efficient, available, robust, extensible, and scalable system. However, this opportunity comes at a very high cost in complexity.

The Price of Complexity

In a distributed operating system, the exceptional degree of inherent complexity could easily render the entire system an anathema to any user. As such, the logical price of realizing a distributed operation system must be calculated in terms of overcoming vast amounts of complexity in many areas, and on many levels. This calculation includes the depth, breadth, and range of design investment and architectural planning required in achieving even the most modest implementation.

These design and development considerations are critical and unforgiving. For instance, a deep understanding of a distributed operating system's overall architectural and design detail is required at an exceptionally early point. An exhausting array of design considerations are inherent in the development of a distributed operating system. Each of these design considerations can potentially affect many of the others to a significant degree. This leads to a massive effort in balanced approach, in terms of the individual design considerations, and many of their permutations. As an aid in this effort, most rely on documented experience and research in distributed computing.

History

Research and experimentation efforts began in earnest in the 1970s and continued through 1990s, with focused interest peaking in the late 1980s. A number of distributed operating systems were introduced during this period; however, very few of these implementations achieved even modest commercial success.

Fundamental and pioneering implementations of primitive distributed operating system component concepts date to the early 1950s. Some of these individual steps were not focused directly on distributed computing, and at the time, many may not have realized their important impact. These pioneering efforts laid important groundwork, and inspired continued research in areas related to distributed computing.

In the mid-1970s, research produced important advances in distributed computing. These breakthroughs provided a solid, stable foundation for efforts that continued through the 1990s.

The accelerating proliferation of multi-processor and multi-core processor systems research led to a resurgence of the distributed OS concept.

1950s

The DYSEAC

One of the first efforts was the DYSEAC, a general-purpose synchronous computer. In one of the earliest publications of the Association for Computing Machinery, in April 1954, a researcher at the National Bureau of Standards – now the National Institute of Standards and Technology (NIST) – presented a detailed specification of the DYSEAC. The introduction focused upon the requirements of the intended applications, including flexible communications, but also mentioned other computers:

Finally, the external devices could even include other full-scale computers employing the same digital language as the DYSEAC. For example, the SEAC or other computers similar to it could be harnessed to the DYSEAC and by use of coordinated programs could be made to work together in mutual cooperation on a common task... Consequently[,] the computer can be used to coordinate the diverse activities of all the external devices into an effective ensemble operation.

—ALAN L. LEINER, System Specifications for the DYSEAC

The specification discussed the architecture of multi-computer systems, preferring peer-to-peer rather than master-slave.

Each member of such an interconnected group of separate computers is free at any time to initiate and dispatch special control orders to any of its partners in the system. As a consequence, the supervisory control over the common task may initially be loosely distributed throughout the system and then temporarily concentrated in one computer, or even passed rapidly from one machine to the other as the need arises. ...it should be noted that the various interruption facilities which have been described are based on mutual cooperation between the computer and the external devices subsidiary to it, and do not reflect merely a simple master-slave relationship.

—ALAN L. LEINER, System Specifications for the DYSEAC

This is one of the earliest examples of a computer with distributed control. The Dept. of the Army reports certified it reliable and that it passed all acceptance tests in April 1954. It was completed and delivered on time, in May 1954. This was a "portable computer", housed in a tractor-trailer, with 2 attendant vehicles and 6 tons of refrigeration capacity.

Lincoln TX-2

Described as an experimental input-output system, the Lincoln TX-2 emphasized flexible, simultaneously operational input-output devices, i.e., multiprogramming. The design of the TX-2 was modular, supporting a high degree of modification and expansion.

The system employed The Multiple-Sequence Program Technique. This technique allowed multiple program counters to each associate with one of 32 possible sequences of program code. These explicitly prioritized sequences could be interleaved and executed concurrently, affecting not only the computation in process, but also the control flow of sequences and switching of devices as well. Much discussion related to device sequencing.

Similar to DYSEAC the TX-2 separately programmed devices can operate simultaneously, increasing throughput. The full power of the central unit was available to any device. The TX-2 was another example of a system exhibiting distributed control, its central unit not having dedicated control.

Intercommunicating Cells

One early effort at abstracting memory access was Intercommunicating Cells, where a cell was composed of a collection of memory elements. A memory element was basically a binary electronic flip-flop or relay. Within a cell there were two types of elements, *symbol* and *cell*. Each cell structure stores data in a string of symbols, consisting of a name and a set of parameters. Information is linked through cell associations.

Intercommunicating Cells fundamentally broke from tradition in that it had no counters or any concept of addressing memory. The theory contended that addressing is a wasteful and non-valuable level of indirection. Information was accessed in two ways, direct and cross-retrieval. Direct retrieval accepts a name and returns a parameter set. Cross-retrieval projects through parameter sets and returns a set of names containing the given subset of parameters. This was similar to a modified hash table data structure that allowed multiple values (parameters) for each key (name).

Cellular memory would have many advantages:

- A major portion of a system's logic is distributed within the associations of information stored in the cells,

- This flow of information association is somewhat guided by the act of storing and retrieving,

- The time required for storage and retrieval is mostly constant and completely unrelated to the size and fill-factor of the memory

- Cells are logically indistinguishable, making them both flexible to use and relatively simple to extend in size

This configuration was ideal for distributed systems. The constant-time projection through memory for storing and retrieval was inherently atomic and exclusive. The cellular memory's intrinsic distributed characteristics would be invaluable. The impact on the user, hardware/device, or Application programming interfaces was indirect. The authors were considering distributed systems, stating:

We wanted to present here the basic ideas of a distributed logic system with... the macroscopic concept of logical design, away from scanning, from searching, from addressing, and from counting, is equally important. We must, at all cost, free ourselves from the burdens of detailed local problems which only befit a machine low on the evolutionary scale of machines.

— Chung-Yeol (C. Y.) Lee, Intercommunicating Cells, Basis for a Distributed Logic Computer

Foundational Work

Coherent Memory Abstraction

Algorithms for scalable synchronization on shared-memory multiprocessors

File System Abstraction

Measurements of a distributed file system
Memory coherence in shared virtual memory systems

Transaction Abstraction

Transactions Sagas

Transactional Memory
Composable memory transactions
Transactional memory: architectural support for lock-free data structures
Software transactional memory for dynamic-sized data structures
Software transactional memory

Persistence Abstraction

OceanStore: an architecture for global-scale persistent storage

Coordinator Abstraction

Weighted voting for replicated data
Consensus in the presence of partial synchrony

Reliability Abstraction

Sanity checks
The Byzantine Generals Problem
Fail-stop processors: an approach to designing fault-tolerant computing systems

Recoverability
Distributed snapshots: determining global states of distributed systems
Optimistic recovery in distributed systems

Distributed Computing Models

Three Basic Distributions

To better illustrate this point, examine three system architectures; centralized, decentralized, and distributed. In this examination, consider three structural aspects: organization, connection, and control. Organization describes a system's physical arrangement characteristics. Connection covers the communication pathways among nodes. Control manages the operation of the earlier two considerations.

Organization

A centralized system has one level of structure, where all constituent elements directly depend upon a single control element. A decentralized system is hierarchical. The bottom level unites subsets of a system's entities. These entity subsets in turn combine at higher levels, ultimately culminating at a central master element. A distributed system is a collection of autonomous elements with no concept of levels.

Connection

Centralized systems connect constituents directly to a central master entity in a hub and spoke fashion. A decentralized system (aka network system) incorporates direct and indirect paths between constituent elements and the central entity. Typically this is configured as a hierarchy with only one shortest path between any two elements. Finally, the distributed operating system requires no pattern; direct and indirect connections are possible between any two elements. Consider the 1970s phenomena of "string art" or a spirograph drawing as a fully connected system, and the spider's web or the Interstate Highway System between U.S. cities as examples of a *partially connected system*.

Control

Centralized and decentralized systems have directed flows of connection to and from the central entity, while distributed systems communicate along arbitrary paths. This is the pivotal notion of the third consideration. Control involves allocating tasks and data to system elements balancing efficiency, responsiveness and complexity.

Centralized and decentralized systems offer more control, potentially easing administration by limiting options. Distributed systems are more difficult to explicitly control, but scale better horizontally and offer fewer points of system-wide failure. The associations conform to the needs imposed by its design but not by organizational limitations.

Design Considerations

Transparency

Transparency or *single-system image* refers to the ability of an application to treat the system on which it operates without regard to whether it is distributed and without regard to hardware or other implementation details. Many areas of a system can benefit from transparency, including access, location, performance, naming, and migration. The consideration of transparency directly affects decision making in every aspect of design of a distributed operating system. Transparency can impose certain requirements and/or restrictions on other design considerations.

Systems can optionally violate transparency to varying degrees to meet specific application requirements. For example, a distributed operating system may present a hard drive on one computer as "C:" and a drive on another computer as "G:". The user does not require any knowledge of device drivers or the drive's location; both devices work the same way, from the application's perspective. A less transparent interface might require the application to know which computer hosts the drive. Transparency domains:

- *Location transparency* – Location transparency comprises two distinct aspects of transparency, naming transparency and user mobility. Naming transparency requires that nothing in the physical or logical references to any system entity should expose any indication of the entity's location, or its local or remote relationship to the user or application. User mobility requires the consistent referencing of system entities, regardless of the system location from which the reference originates.

- *Access transparency* – Local and remote system entities must remain indistinguishable when viewed through the user interface. The distributed operating system maintains this perception through the exposure of a single access mechanism for a system entity, regardless of that entity being local or remote to the user. Transparency dictates that any differences in methods of accessing any particular system entity—either local or remote—must be both invisible to, and undetectable by the user.

- *Migration transparency* – Resources and activities migrate from one element to another controlled solely by the system and without user/application knowledge or action.

- *Replication transparency* – The process or fact that a resource has been duplicated on another element occurs under system control and without user/application knowledge or intervention.

- *Concurrency transparency* – Users/applications are unaware of and unaffected by the presence/activities of other users.

- *Failure transparency* – The system is responsible for detection and remediation of system failures. No user knowledge/action is involved other than waiting for the system to resolve the problem.

- *Performance Transparency* – The system is responsible for the detection and remediation of local or global performance shortfalls. Note that system policies may prefer some users/user classes/tasks over others. No user knowledge or interaction. is involved.

- *Size/Scale transparency* – The system is responsible for managing its geographic reach, number of nodes, level of node capability without any required user knowledge or interaction.

- *Revision transparency* – The system is responsible for upgrades and revisions and changes to system infrastructure without user knowledge or action.

- *Control transparency* – The system is responsible for providing all system information, constants, properties, configuration settings, etc. in a consistent appearance, connotation, and denotation to all users and applications.

- *Data transparency* – The system is responsible for providing data to applications without user knowledge or action relating to where the system stores it.

- *Parallelism transparency* – The system is responsible for exploiting any ability to parallelize task execution without user knowledge or interaction. Arguably the most difficult aspect of transparency, and described by Tanenbaum as the "Holy grail" for distributed system designers.

Inter-process Communication

Inter-Process Communication (IPC) is the implementation of general communication, process interaction, and dataflow between threads and/or processes both within a node, and between nodes in a distributed OS. The intra-node and inter-node communication requirements drive low-level IPC design, which is the typical approach to implementing communication functions that support transparency. In this sense, Inter process communication is the greatest underlying concept in the low-level design considerations of a distributed operating system.

Process Management

Process management provides policies and mechanisms for effective and efficient sharing of resources between distributed processes. These policies and mechanisms support operations involving the allocation and de-allocation of processes and ports to processors, as well as mechanisms to run, suspend, migrate, halt, or resume process execution. While these resources and operations can be either local or remote with respect to each other, the distributed OS maintains state and synchronization over all processes in the system.

As an example, load balancing is a common process management function. Load balancing monitors node performance and is responsible for shifting activity across nodes when the system is out of balance. One load balancing function is picking a process to move. The kernel may employ several selection mechanisms, including priority-based choice. This mechanism chooses a process based on a policy such as 'newest request'. The system implements the policy

Resource Management

Systems resources such as memory, files, devices, etc. are distributed throughout a system, and at any given moment, any of these nodes may have light to idle workloads. *Load sharing* and load balancing require many policy-oriented decisions, ranging from finding idle CPUs, when to move, and which to move. Many algorithms exist to aid in these decisions; however, this calls for a second level of decision making policy in choosing the algorithm best suited for the scenario, and the conditions surrounding the scenario.

Reliability

Distributed OS can provide the necessary resources and services to achieve high levels of *reliability*, or the ability to prevent and/or recover from errors. Faults are physical or logical defects that can cause errors in the system. For a system to be reliable, it must somehow overcome the adverse effects of faults.

The primary methods for dealing with faults include *fault avoidance*, fault tolerance, and *fault detection and recovery*. Fault avoidance covers proactive measures taken to minimize the occurrence of faults. These proactive measures can be in the form of *transactions*, replication and backups. Fault tolerance is the ability of a system to continue operation in the presence of a fault. In the event, the system should detect and recover full functionality. In any event, any actions taken should make every effort to preserve the *single system image*.

Availability

Availability is the fraction of time during which the system can respond to requests.

Performance

Many benchmark metrics quantify performance; throughput, response time, job completions per unit time, system utilization, etc. With respect to a distributed OS, performance most often distills to a balance between process parallelism and IPC. Managing the task granularity of parallelism in a sensible relation to the messages required for support is extremely effective. Also, identifying when it is more beneficial to migrate a process to its data, rather than copy the data, is effective as well.

Synchronization

Cooperating concurrent processes have an inherent need for synchronization, which ensures that changes happen in a correct and predictable fashion. Three basic situations that define the scope of this need:

- one or more processes must synchronize at a given point for one or more other processes to continue,

- one or more processes must wait for an asynchronous condition in order to continue,

- or a process must establish exclusive access to a shared resource.

Improper synchronization can lead to multiple failure modes including loss of atomicity, consistency, isolation and durability, deadlock, livelock and loss of serializability.

Flexibility

Flexibility in a distributed operating system is enhanced through the modular and characteristics of the distributed OS, and by providing a richer set of higher-level services. The completeness and quality of the kernel/microkernel simplifies implementation of such services, and potentially enables service providers greater choice of providers for such services.

Research

Replicated Model Extended to a Component Object Model

Architectural Design of E1 Distributed Operating System
The Cronus distributed operating system
Design and development of MINIX distributed operating system

Complexity/Trust Exposure Through Accepted Responsibility

Scale and performance in the Denali isolation kernel.

Multi/Many-core Focused Systems

The multikernel: a new OS architecture for scalable multicore systems.

Corey: an Operating System for Many Cores.

Almos: Advanced Locality Management Operating System for cc-NUMA Many-Cores.

Distributed Processing over Extremes in Heterogeneity

Helios: heterogeneous multiprocessing with satellite kernels.

Effective and Stable in Multiple Levels of Complexity

Tessellation: Space-Time Partitioning in a Manycore Client OS.

Microsoft Windows

Microsoft Windows (or simply Windows) is a metafamily of graphical operating systems developed, marketed, and sold by Microsoft. It consists of several families of operating systems, each of which cater to a certain sector of the computing industry with the OS typically associated with IBM PC compatible architecture. Active Windows families include Windows NT, Windows Embedded and Windows Phone; these may encompass subfamilies, e.g. Windows Embedded Compact (Windows CE) or Windows Server. Defunct Windows families include Windows 9x; Windows 10 Mobile is an active product, unrelated to the defunct family Windows Mobile.

Microsoft introduced an operating environment named *Windows* on November 20, 1985, as a graphical operating system shell for MS-DOS in response to the growing interest in graphical user interfaces (GUIs). Microsoft Windows came to dominate the world's personal computer (PC) market with over 90% market share, overtaking Mac OS, which had been introduced in 1984. Apple came to see Windows as an unfair encroachment on their innovation in GUI development as implemented on products such as the Lisa and Macintosh (eventually settled in court in Microsoft's favor in 1993). On PCs, Windows is still the most popular operating system. However, in 2014, Microsoft admitted losing the majority of the overall operating system market to Android, because of the massive growth in sales of Android smartphones. In 2014, the number of Windows devices sold were less than 25% of Android devices sold. This comparisons, however, may not be fully relevant as the two operating systems traditionally targeted different platforms.

As of September 2016, the most recent version of Windows for PCs, tablets, smartphones and embedded devices is Windows 10. The most recent versions for server computers is Windows Server 2016. A specialized version of Windows runs on the Xbox One game console.

Genealogy

By Marketing Role

Microsoft, the developer of Windows, has registered several trademarks each of which denote a family of Windows operating systems that target a specific sector of the computing industry. As of 2014, the following Windows families are being actively developed:

- Windows NT: Started as a family of operating system with Windows NT 3.1, an operating system for server computers and workstations. It now consists of three operating system subfamilies that are released almost at the same time and share the same kernel. It is almost impossible for someone unfamiliar with the subject to identify the members of this family by name because they do not adhere to any specific rule; e.g. Windows Vista, Windows 7, Windows 8/8.1 and Windows RT are members of this family but Windows 3.1 is not.

  o Windows: The operating system for mainstream personal computers, tablets and smartphones. The latest version is Windows 10. The main competitor of this family is macOS by Apple Inc. for personal computers and Android for mobile devices (c.f. Usage share of operating systems § Market share by category).

  o Windows Server: The operating system for server computers. The latest version is Windows Server 2016. Unlike its clients sibling, it has adopted a strong naming scheme. The main competitor of this family is Linux. (c.f. Usage share of operating systems § Market share by category)

  o Windows PE: A lightweight version of its Windows sibling meant to operate as a live operating system, used for installing Windows on bare-metal computers (especially on many computers at once), recovery or troubleshooting purposes. The latest version is Windows PE 10.0.10586.0.

- Windows Embedded: Initially, Microsoft developed Windows CE as a general-purpose operating system for every device that was too resource-limited to be called a full-fledged computer. Eventually, however, Windows CE was renamed Windows Embedded Compact and was folded under Windows Compact trademark which also consists of Windows Embedded Industry, Windows Embedded Professional, Windows Embedded Standard, Windows Embedded Handheld and Windows Embedded Automotive.

The following Windows families are no longer being developed:

- Windows 9x: An operating system that targeted consumers market. Discontinued because of suboptimal performance. (*PC World* called its last version, Windows ME, one of the worst products of all times.) Microsoft now caters to the consumers market with Windows NT.

- Windows Mobile: The predecessor to Windows Phone, it was a mobile phone operating system. The first version was called Pocket PC 2000; the third version, Windows Mobile 2003 is the first version to adopt the Windows Mobile trademark. The last version is Windows Mobile 6.5.

- Windows Phone: An operating system sold only to manufacturers of smartphones. The first version was Windows Phone 7, followed by Windows Phone 8, and the last version Windows Phone 8.1. It was succeeded by Windows 10 Mobile.

Version History

The term *Windows* collectively describes any or all of several generations of Microsoft operating system products. These products are generally categorized as follows:

Early Versions

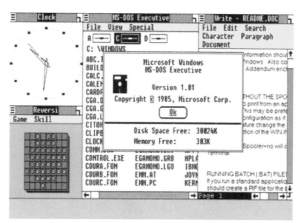

Windows 1.0, the first version, released in 1985

The history of Windows dates back to September 1981, when Chase Bishop, a computer scientist, designed the first model of an electronic device and project Interface Manager was started. It was announced in November 1983 (after the Apple Lisa, but before the Macintosh) under the name "Windows", but Windows 1.0 was not released until November 1985. Windows 1.0 was to compete with Apple's operating system, but achieved little popularity. Windows 1.0 is not a complete operating system; rather, it extends MS-DOS. The shell of Windows 1.0 is a program known as the MS-DOS Executive. Components included Calculator, Calendar, Cardfile, Clipboard viewer, Clock, Control Panel, Notepad, Paint, Reversi, Terminal and Write. Windows 1.0 does not allow overlapping windows. Instead all windows are tiled. Only modal dialog boxes may appear over other windows.

Windows 2.0 was released in December 1987, and was more popular than its predecessor. It features several improvements to the user interface and memory management. Windows 2.03 changed the OS from tiled windows to overlapping windows. The result of this change led to Apple Computer filing a suit against Microsoft alleging infringement on Apple's copyrights. Windows 2.0 also introduced more sophisticated keyboard shortcuts and could make use of expanded memory.

Windows 2.1 was released in two different versions: Windows/286 and Windows/386. Windows/386 uses the virtual 8086 mode of the Intel 80386 to multitask several DOS programs and the paged memory model to emulate expanded memory using available extended memory. Windows/286, in spite of its name, runs on both Intel 8086 and Intel 80286 processors. It runs in real mode but can make use of the high memory area.

In addition to full Windows-packages, there were runtime-only versions that shipped with early Windows software from third parties and made it possible to run their Windows software on MS-DOS and without the full Windows feature set.

The early versions of Windows are often thought of as graphical shells, mostly because they ran on top of MS-DOS and use it for file system services. However, even the earliest Windows versions already assumed many typical operating system functions; notably, having their own executable file format and providing their own device drivers (timer, graphics, printer, mouse, keyboard and sound). Unlike MS-DOS, Windows allowed users to execute multiple graphical applications at the same time, through cooperative multitasking. Windows implemented an elaborate, segment-based, software virtual memory scheme, which allows it to run applications larger than available memory: code segments and resources are swapped in and thrown away when memory became scarce; data segments moved in memory when a given application had relinquished processor control.

Windows 3.x

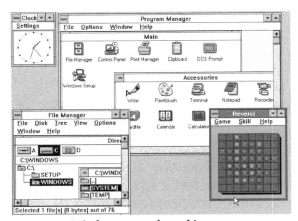

Windows 3.0, released in 1990

Windows 3.0, released in 1990, improved the design, mostly because of virtual memory and loadable virtual device drivers (VxDs) that allow Windows to share arbitrary devices between multitasked DOS applications. Windows 3.0 applications can run in protected mode, which gives them access to several megabytes of memory without the obligation to participate in the software virtual memory scheme. They run inside the same address space, where the segmented memory provides a degree of protection. Windows 3.0 also featured improvements to the user interface. Microsoft rewrote critical operations from C into assembly. Windows 3.0 is the first Microsoft Windows version to achieve broad commercial success, selling 2 million copies in the first six months.

Windows 3.1, made generally available on March 1, 1992, featured a facelift. In August 1993, Windows for Workgroups, a special version with integrated peer-to-peer networking features and a version number of 3.11, was released. It was sold along Windows 3.1. Support for Windows 3.1 ended on December 31, 2001.

Windows 3.2, released 1994, is an updated version of the Chinese version of Windows 3.1. The update was limited to this language version, as it fixed only issues related to the complex writing system of the Chinese language. Windows 3.2 was generally sold by computer manufacturers with a ten-disk version of MS-DOS that also had Simplified Chinese characters in basic output and some translated utilities.

Windows 9x

The next major consumer-oriented release of Windows, Windows 95, was released on August 24, 1995. While still remaining MS-DOS-based, Windows 95 introduced support for native 32-bit applications, plug and play hardware, preemptive multitasking, long file names of up to 255 characters, and provided increased stability over its predecessors. Windows 95 also introduced a redesigned, object oriented user interface, replacing the previous Program Manager with the

Start menu, taskbar, and Windows Explorer shell. Windows 95 was a major commercial success for Microsoft; Ina Fried of CNET remarked that "by the time Windows 95 was finally ushered off the market in 2001, it had become a fixture on computer desktops around the world." Microsoft published four OEM Service Releases (OSR) of Windows 95, each of which was roughly equivalent to a service pack. The first OSR of Windows 95 was also the first version of Windows to be bundled with Microsoft's web browser, Internet Explorer. Mainstream support for Windows 95 ended on December 31, 2000, and extended support for Windows 95 ended on December 31, 2001.

Windows 95 was followed up with the release of Windows 98 on June 25, 1998, which introduced the Windows Driver Model, support for USB composite devices, support for ACPI, hibernation, and support for multi-monitor configurations. Windows 98 also included integration with Internet Explorer 4 through Active Desktop and other aspects of the Windows Desktop Update (a series of enhancements to the Explorer shell which were also made available for Windows 95). In May 1999, Microsoft released Windows 98 Second Edition, an updated version of Windows 98. Windows 98 SE added Internet Explorer 5.0 and Windows Media Player 6.2 amongst other upgrades. Mainstream support for Windows 98 ended on June 30, 2002, and extended support for Windows 98 ended on July 11, 2006.

On September 14, 2000, Microsoft released Windows ME (Millennium Edition), the last DOS-based version of Windows. Windows ME incorporated visual interface enhancements from its Windows NT-based counterpart Windows 2000, had faster boot times than previous versions (which however, required the removal of the ability to access a real mode DOS environment, removing compatibility with some older programs), expanded multimedia functionality (including Windows Media Player 7, Windows Movie Maker, and the Windows Image Acquisition framework for retrieving images from scanners and digital cameras), additional system utilities such as System File Protection and System Restore, and updated home networking tools. However, Windows ME was faced with criticism for its speed and instability, along with hardware compatibility issues and its removal of real mode DOS support. *PC World* considered Windows ME to be one of the worst operating systems Microsoft had ever released, and the 4th worst tech product of all time.

Windows NT

Early Versions

In November 1988, a new development team within Microsoft (which included former Digital Equipment Corporation developers Dave Cutler and Mark Lucovsky) began work on a revamped version of IBM and Microsoft's OS/2 operating system known as "NT OS/2". NT OS/2 was intended to be a secure, multi-user operating system with POSIX compatibility and a modular, portable kernel with preemptive multitasking and support for multiple processor architectures. However, following the successful release of Windows 3.0, the NT development team decided to rework the project to use an extended 32-bit port of the Windows API known as Win32 instead of those of OS/2. Win32 maintained a similar structure to the Windows APIs (allowing existing Windows applications to easily be ported to the platform), but also supported the capabilities of the existing NT kernel. Following its approval by Microsoft's staff, development continued on what was now Windows NT, the first 32-bit version of Windows. However, IBM objected to the changes, and ultimately continued OS/2 development on its own.

The first release of the resulting operating system, Windows NT 3.1 (named to associate it with Windows 3.1) was released in July 1993, with versions for desktop workstations and servers. Windows NT 3.5 was released in September 1994, focusing on performance improvements and support for Novell's NetWare, and was followed up by Windows NT 3.51 in May 1995, which included additional improvements and support for the PowerPC architecture. Windows NT 4.0 was released in June 1996, introducing the redesigned interface of Windows 95 to the NT series. On February 17, 2000, Microsoft released Windows 2000, a successor to NT 4.0. The Windows NT name was dropped at this point in order to put a greater focus on the Windows brand.

Home Versions of Windows NT

The next major version of Windows NT, Windows XP, was released on October 25, 2001. The introduction of Windows XP aimed to unify the consumer-oriented Windows 9x series with the architecture introduced by Windows NT, a change which Microsoft promised would provide better performance over its DOS-based predecessors. Windows XP would also introduce a redesigned user interface (including an updated Start menu and a "task-oriented" Windows Explorer), streamlined multimedia and networking features, Internet Explorer 6, integration with Microsoft's .NET Passport services, modes to help provide compatibility with software designed for previous versions of Windows, and Remote Assistance functionality.

At retail, Windows XP was now marketed in two main editions: the "Home" edition was targeted towards consumers, while the "Professional" edition was targeted towards business environments and power users, and included additional security and networking features. Home and Professional were later accompanied by the "Media Center" edition (designed for home theater PCs, with an emphasis on support for DVD playback, TV tuner cards, DVR functionality, and remote controls), and the "Tablet PC" edition (designed for mobile devices meeting its specifications for a tablet computer, with support for stylus pen input and additional pen-enabled applications). Mainstream support for Windows XP ended on April 14, 2009. Extended support ended on April 8, 2014.

After Windows 2000, Microsoft also changed its release schedules for server operating systems; the server counterpart of Windows XP, Windows Server 2003, was released in April 2003. It was followed in December 2005, by Windows Server 2003 R2.

Windows Vista

After a lengthy development process, Windows Vista was released on November 30, 2006, for volume licensing and January 30, 2007, for consumers. It contained a number of new features, from a redesigned shell and user interface to significant technical changes, with a particular focus on security features. It was available in a number of different editions, and has been subject to some criticism, such as drop of performance, longer boot time, criticism of new UAC, and stricter license agreement. Vista's server counterpart, Windows Server 2008 was released in early 2008.

Windows 7

On July 22, 2009, Windows 7 and Windows Server 2008 R2 were released as RTM (release to manufacturing) while the former was released to the public 3 months later on October 22, 2009.

Unlike its predecessor, Windows Vista, which introduced a large number of new features, Windows 7 was intended to be a more focused, incremental upgrade to the Windows line, with the goal of being compatible with applications and hardware with which Windows Vista was already compatible. Windows 7 has multi-touch support, a redesigned Windows shell with an updated taskbar, a home networking system called HomeGroup, and performance improvements.

Windows 8 and 8.1

Windows 8, the successor to Windows 7, was released generally on October 26, 2012. A number of significant changes were made on Windows 8, including the introduction of a user interface based around Microsoft's Metro design language with optimizations for touch-based devices such as tablets and all-in-one PCs. These changes include the Start screen, which uses large tiles that are more convenient for touch interactions and allow for the display of continually updated information, and a new class of apps which are designed primarily for use on touch-based devices. Other changes include increased integration with cloud services and other online platforms (such as social networks and Microsoft's own OneDrive (formerly SkyDrive) and Xbox Live services), the Windows Store service for software distribution, and a new variant known as Windows RT for use on devices that utilize the ARM architecture. An update to Windows 8, called Windows 8.1, was released on October 17, 2013, and includes features such as new live tile sizes, deeper OneDrive integration, and many other revisions. Windows 8 and Windows 8.1 has been subject to some criticism, such as removal of Start Menu.

Windows 10

On September 30, 2014, Microsoft announced Windows 10 as the successor to Windows 8.1. It was released on July 29, 2015, and addresses shortcomings in the user interface first introduced with Windows 8. Changes include the return of the Start Menu, a virtual desktop system, and the ability to run Windows Store apps within windows on the desktop rather than in full-screen mode. Windows 10 is said to be available to update from qualified Windows 7 with SP1 and Windows 8.1 computers from the Get Windows 10 Application (for Windows 7, Windows 8.1) or Windows Update (Windows 7).

On November 12, 2015, an update to Windows 10, version 1511, was released. This update can be activated with a Windows 7, 8 or 8.1 product key as well as Windows 10 product keys. Features include new icons and right-click context menus, default printer management, four times as many tiles allowed in the Start menu, Find My Device, and Edge updates.

Multilingual Support

Multilingual support is built into Windows. The language for both the keyboard and the interface can be changed through the Region and Language Control Panel. Components for all supported input languages, such as Input Method Editors, are automatically installed during Windows installation (in Windows XP and earlier, files for East Asian languages, such as Chinese, and right-to-left scripts, such as Arabic, may need to be installed separately, also from the said Control Panel). Third-party IMEs may also be installed if a user feels that the provided one is insufficient for their needs.

Interface languages for the operating system are free for download, but some languages are limited to certain editions of Windows. Language Interface Packs (LIPs) are redistributable and may be downloaded from Microsoft's Download Center and installed for any edition of Windows (XP or later) – they translate most, but not all, of the Windows interface, and require a certain base language (the language which Windows originally shipped with). This is used for most languages in emerging markets. Full Language Packs, which translates the complete operating system, are only available for specific editions of Windows (Ultimate and Enterprise editions of Windows Vista and 7, and all editions of Windows 8, 8.1 and RT except Single Language). They do not require a specific base language, and are commonly used for more popular languages such as French or Chinese. These languages cannot be downloaded through the Download Center, but available as optional updates through the Windows Update service (except Windows 8).

The interface language of installed applications are not affected by changes in the Windows interface language. Availability of languages depends on the application developers themselves.

Windows 8 and Windows Server 2012 introduces a new Language Control Panel where both the interface and input languages can be simultaneously changed, and language packs, regardless of type, can be downloaded from a central location. The PC Settings app in Windows 8.1 and Windows Server 2012 R2 also includes a counterpart settings page for this. Changing the interface language also changes the language of preinstalled Windows Store apps (such as Mail, Maps and News) and certain other Microsoft-developed apps (such as Remote Desktop). The above limitations for language packs are however still in effect, except that full language packs can be installed for any edition except Single Language, which caters to emerging markets.

Platform Support

Windows NT included support for several different platforms before the x86-based personal computer became dominant in the professional world. Windows NT 4.0 and its predecessors supported PowerPC, DEC Alpha and MIPS R4000. (Although some these platforms implement 64-bit computing, the operating system treated them as 32-bit.) However, Windows 2000, the successor of Windows NT 4.0, dropped support for all platforms except the third generation x86 (known as IA-32) or newer in 32-bit mode. The client line of Window NT family still runs on IA-32, although the Windows Server line has ceased supporting this platform with the release of Windows Server 2008 R2.

With the introduction of the Intel Itanium architecture (IA-64), Microsoft released new versions of Windows to support it. Itanium versions of Windows XP and Windows Server 2003 were released at the same time as their mainstream x86 counterparts. Windows XP 64-Bit Edition, released in 2005, is the last Windows client operating systems to support Itanium. Windows Server line continues to support this platform until Windows Server 2012; Windows Server 2008 R2 is the last Windows operating system to support Itanium architecture.

On April 25, 2005, Microsoft released Windows XP Professional x64 Edition and Windows Server 2003 x64 Editions to support the x86-64 (or simply x64), the eighth generation of x86 architecture. Windows Vista was the first client version of Windows NT to be released simultaneously in IA-32 and x64 editions. x64 is still supported.

An edition of Windows 8 known as Windows RT was specifically created for computers with ARM architecture and while ARM is still used for Windows smartphones with Windows 10, tablets with Windows RT will not be updated.

Windows CE

The latest current version of Windows CE, Windows Embedded Compact 7, displaying a concept media player UI

Windows CE (officially known as *Windows Embedded Compact*), is an edition of Windows that runs on minimalistic computers, like satellite navigation systems and some mobile phones. Windows Embedded Compact is based on its own dedicated kernel, dubbed Windows CE kernel. Microsoft licenses Windows CE to OEMs and device makers. The OEMs and device makers can modify and create their own user interfaces and experiences, while Windows CE provides the technical foundation to do so.

Windows CE was used in the Dreamcast along with Sega's own proprietary OS for the console. Windows CE was the core from which Windows Mobile was derived. Its successor, Windows Phone 7, was based on components from both Windows CE 6.0 R3 and Windows CE 7.0. Windows Phone 8 however, is based on the same NT-kernel as Windows 8.

Windows Embedded Compact is not to be confused with Windows XP Embedded or Windows NT 4.0 Embedded, modular editions of Windows based on Windows NT kernel.

Xbox OS

Xbox OS is an unofficial name given to the version of Windows that runs on the Xbox One. It is a more specific implementation with an emphasis on virtualization (using Hyper-V) as it is three operating systems running at once, consisting of the core operating system, a second implemented for games and a more Windows-like environment for applications. Microsoft updates Xbox One's OS every month, and these updates can be downloaded from the Xbox Live service to the Xbox and subsequently installed, or by using offline recovery images downloaded via a PC. The Windows 10-based Core had replaced the Windows 8-based one in this update, and the new system is sometimes referred to as "Windows 10 on Xbox One" or "OneCore". Xbox One's system also allows backward compatibility with Xbox 360, and the Xbox 360's system is backwards compatible with the original Xbox.

Timeline of Releases

Product name	Latest version	General availability date	Codename	Support until		Latest version of		
				Mainstream	Extended	IE	DirectX	Edge
Windows 1.0	1.01	November 20, 1985	Interface Manager	December 31, 2001		N/A	N/A	N/A
Windows 2.0	2.03	December 9, 1987	N/A	December 31, 2001		N/A	N/A	N/A
Windows 2.1	2.11	May 27, 1988	N/A	December 31, 2001		N/A	N/A	N/A
Windows 3.0	3.0	May 22, 1990	N/A	December 31, 2001		N/A	N/A	N/A
Windows 3.1	3.1	April 6, 1992	Janus	December 31, 2001		5	N/A	N/A
Windows For Workgroups 3.1	3.1	October 1992	Sparta, Winball	December 31, 2001		5	N/A	N/A
Windows NT 3.1	NT 3.1.528	July 27, 1993	N/A	December 31, 2001		5	N/A	N/A
Windows For Workgroups 3.11	3.11	August 11, 1993	Sparta, Winball	December 31, 2001		5	N/A	N/A
Windows 3.2	3.2	November 22, 1993	N/A	December 31, 2001		5	N/A	N/A
Windows NT 3.5	NT 3.5.807	September 21, 1994	Daytona	December 31, 2001		5	N/A	N/A
Windows NT 3.51	NT 3.51.1057	May 30, 1995	N/A	December 31, 2001		5	N/A	N/A
Windows 95	4.0.950	August 24, 1995	Chicago, 4.0	December 31, 2000	December 31, 2001	5.5	6.1	N/A
Windows NT 4.0	NT 4.0.1381	July 31, 1996	Cairo	December 31, 2000	December 31, 2001	5	N/A	N/A
Windows 98	4.10.1998	June 25, 1998	Memphis, 97, 4.1	June 30, 2002	July 11, 2006	6	6.1	N/A
Windows 98 SE	4.10.2222	May 5, 1999	N/A	June 30, 2002	July 11, 2006	6	6.1	N/A
Windows 2000	NT 5.0.2195	December 15, 1999	N/A	June 30, 2005	July 13, 2010	5	N/A	N/A
Windows ME	4.90.3000	September 14, 2000	Millenium, 4.9	December 31, 2003	July 11, 2006	6	9.0c	N/A
Windows XP	NT 5.1.2600	October 25, 2001	Whistler	April 14, 2009	April 8, 2014	8	9.0c	N/A
Windows XP 64-bit Edition	NT 5.2.3790	March 28, 2003	N/A	April 14, 2009	April 8, 2014	6	9.0c	N/A
Windows Server 2003	NT 5.2.3790	April 24, 2003	N/A	July 13, 2010	July 14, 2015	8	9.0c	N/A

Windows XP Professional x64 Edition	NT 5.2.3790	April 25, 2005	N/A	April 14, 2009	April 8, 2014	8	9.0c	N/A
Windows Fundamentals for Legacy PCs	NT 5.1.2600	July 8, 2006	Eiger, Mönch	April 14, 2009	April 8, 2014	8	9.0c	N/A
Windows Vista	NT 6.0.6002	January 30, 2007	Longhorn	April 10, 2012	April 11, 2017	9	11	N/A
Windows Home Server	NT 5.2.4500	November 4, 2007	N/A	January 8, 2013		8	9.0c	N/A
Windows Server 2008	NT 6.0.6002	February 27, 2008	Longhorn Server	January 13, 2015	January 14, 2020	9	11	N/A
Windows 7	NT 6.1.7601	October 22, 2009	Blackcomb, Vienna	January 13, 2015	January 14, 2020	11	11	N/A
Windows Server 2008 R2	NT 6.1.7601	October 22, 2009	N/A	January 13, 2015	January 14, 2020	11	11	N/A
Windows Home Server 2011	NT 6.1.8400	April 6, 2011	Vail	April 12, 2016		9	11	N/A
Windows Server 2012	NT 6.2.9200	September 4, 2012	N/A	January 9, 2018	January 10, 2023	10	11.1	N/A
Windows 8	NT 6.2.9200	October 26, 2012	N/A	January 12, 2016		10	11.1	N/A
Windows 8.1	NT 6.3.9600	October 17, 2013	Blue	January 9, 2018	January 10, 2023	11	11.2	N/A
Windows Server 2012 R2	NT 6.3.9600	October 18, 2013	Server Blue	January 9, 2018	January 10, 2023	11	11.2	N/A
Windows 10	NT 10.0.14393	July 29, 2015	Threshold, Restone	October 13, 2020	October 14, 2025	11	12	25
Windows Server 2016	NT 10.0.14393	TBA	N/A	TBA	TBA	11	12	25

Windows timeline: Bar chart

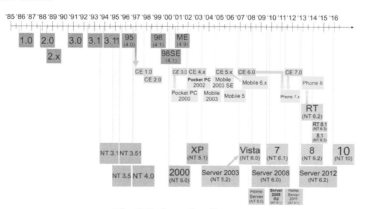

The Windows family tree

Usage Share and Device Sales

This box:

Market share overview According to Net Applications and StatCounter data from September 2016

Desktop OS	Net Applications	StatCounter
Windows XP	9.11%	5.44%
Windows Vista	1.09%	1.15%
Windows 7	48.27%	39.40%
Windows 8	1.78%	2.31%
Windows 8.1	7.83%	8.50%
Windows 10	22.53%	24.42%
All listed versions	90.61%	81.22%

Mobile OS	Net Applications	StatCounter
Windows RT 8.1	–	0.05%
Windows Phone 7.5	0.06%	1.46%
Windows Phone 8	0.38%	1.46%
Windows Phone 8.1	1.41%	1.46%
Windows 10 Mobile	0.45%	1.46%
All listed versions	**2.30%**	**1.51%**

According to Net Applications, that tracks use based on web use, Windows is the most-used operating system family for personal computers as of June 2016 with close to 90% usage share. When including both personal computers of all kinds, e.g. mobile devices, in July 2016, according to StatCounter, that also tracks use based on web use, Windows OSes accounted for 46.87% of usage share, compared to 36.48% for Android, 12.26% for iOS, and 4.81% for OS X. The below 50% usage share of Windows, also applies to developed countries, such as the US, the UK and Ireland. These numbers are easiest (monthly numbers) to find that track real use, but they may not mirror installed base or sales numbers (in recent years) of devices.

In terms of the number of devices shipped with the operating system installed, on smartphones, Windows Phone was the third-most-shipped OS (2.6%) after Android (82.8%) and iOS (13.9%) in the second quarter of 2015 according IDC. Across both PCs and mobile devices, in 2014, Windows OSes were the second-most-shipped (333 million devices, or 14%) after Android (1.2 billion, 49%) and ahead of iOS and macOS combined (263 million, 11%).

Security

Consumer versions of Windows were originally designed for ease-of-use on a single-user PC without a network connection, and did not have security features built in from the outset. However, Windows NT and its successors are designed for security (including on a network) and multi-user PCs, but were not initially designed with Internet security in mind as much, since, when it was first developed in the early 1990s, Internet use was less prevalent.

These design issues combined with programming errors (e.g. buffer overflows) and the popularity of Windows means that it is a frequent target of computer worm and virus writers. In June 2005, Bruce Schneier's *Counterpane Internet Security* reported that it had seen over 1,000 new viruses and worms in the previous six months. In 2005, Kaspersky Lab found around 11,000 malicious programs—viruses, Trojans, back-doors, and exploits written for Windows.

Microsoft releases security patches through its Windows Update service approximately once a month (usually the second Tuesday of the month), although critical updates are made available at shorter intervals when necessary. In versions of Windows after and including Windows 2000 SP3 and Windows XP, updates can be automatically downloaded and installed if the user selects to do so. As a result, Service Pack 2 for Windows XP, as well as Service Pack 1 for Windows Server 2003, were installed by users more quickly than it otherwise might have been.

While the Windows 9x series offered the option of having profiles for multiple users, they had no concept of access privileges, and did not allow concurrent access; and so were not true multi-user operating systems. In addition, they implemented only partial memory protection. They were accordingly widely criticised for lack of security.

The Windows NT series of operating systems, by contrast, are true multi-user, and implement absolute memory protection. However, a lot of the advantages of being a true multi-user operating system were nullified by the fact that, prior to Windows Vista, the first user account created during the setup process was an administrator account, which was also the default for new accounts. Though Windows XP did have limited accounts, the majority of home users did not change to an account type with fewer rights – partially due to the number of programs which unnecessarily required administrator rights – and so most home users ran as administrator all the time.

Windows Vista changes this by introducing a privilege elevation system called User Account Control. When logging in as a standard user, a logon session is created and a token containing only the most basic privileges is assigned. In this way, the new logon session is incapable of making changes that would affect the entire system. When logging in as a user in the Administrators group, two separate tokens are assigned. The first token contains all privileges typically awarded to an administrator, and the second is a restricted token similar to what a standard user would receive. User applications, including the Windows shell, are then started with the restricted token, resulting in a reduced privilege environment even under an Administrator account. When an application requests higher privileges or "Run as administrator" is clicked, UAC will prompt for confirmation and, if consent is given (including administrator credentials if the account requesting the elevation is not a member of the administrators group), start the process using the unrestricted token.

File Permissions

All Windows versions from Windows NT 3 have been based on a file system permission system referred to as AGLP (Accounts, Global, Local, Permissions) AGDLP which in essence where file permissions are applied to the file/folder in the form of a 'local group' which then has other 'global groups' as members. These global groups then hold other groups or users depending on different Windows versions used. This system varies from other vendor products such as Linux and NetWare due to the 'static' allocation of permission being applied directory to the file or folder. However using this process of AGLP/AGDLP/AGUDLP allows a small number of static permissions to be applied and allows for easy changes to the account groups without reapplying the file permissions on the files and folders.

Windows Defender

On January 6, 2005, Microsoft released a Beta version of Microsoft AntiSpyware, based upon the previously released Giant AntiSpyware. On February 14, 2006, Microsoft AntiSpyware became Windows Defender with the release of Beta 2. Windows Defender is a freeware program designed to protect against spyware and other unwanted software. Windows XP and Windows Server 2003 users who have genuine copies of Microsoft Windows can freely download the program from Microsoft's web site, and Windows Defender ships as part of Windows Vista and 7. In Windows 8, Windows Defender and Microsoft Security Essentials have been combined into a single program, named Windows Defender. It is based on Microsoft Security Essentials, borrowing its features and user interface. Although it is enabled by default, it can be turned off to use another anti-virus solution. Windows Malicious Software Removal Tool and the optional Microsoft Safety Scanner are two other free security products offered by Microsoft.

Third-party Analysis

In an article based on a report by Symantec, internetnews.com has described Microsoft Windows as having the "fewest number of patches and the shortest average patch development time of the five operating systems it monitored in the last six months of 2006."

A study conducted by Kevin Mitnick and marketing communications firm Avantgarde in 2004, found that an unprotected and unpatched Windows XP system with Service Pack 1 lasted only four minutes on the Internet before it was compromised, and an unprotected and also unpatched Windows Server 2003 system was compromised after being connected to the internet for 8 hours. The computer that was running Windows XP Service Pack 2 was not compromised. The AOL National Cyber Security Alliance Online Safety Study of October 2004, determined that 80% of Windows users were infected by at least one spyware/adware product. Much documentation is available describing how to increase the security of Microsoft Windows products. Typical suggestions include deploying Microsoft Windows behind a hardware or software firewall, running anti-virus and anti-spyware software, and installing patches as they become available through Windows Update.

Alternative Implementations

Owing to the operating system's popularity, a number of applications have been released that aim to provide compatibility with Windows applications, either as a compatibility layer for another operating system, or as a standalone system that can run software written for Windows out of the box. These include:

- Wine – a free and open-source implementation of the Windows API, allowing one to run many Windows applications on x86-based platforms, including UNIX, Linux and OS X. Wine developers refer to it as a "compatibility layer" and use Windows-style APIs to emulate Windows environment.

    o CrossOver – a Wine package with licensed fonts. Its developers are regular contributors to Wine, and focus on Wine running officially supported applications.

    o Cedega – a proprietary fork of Wine by TransGaming Technologies, designed specifically for running Microsoft Windows games on Linux. A version of Cedega known as Cider allows Windows games to run on OS X. Since Wine was licensed under the LGPL, Cedega has been unable to port the improvements made to Wine to their proprietary codebase. Cedega ceased its service in February 2011.

- o Darwine – a port of Wine for OS X and Darwin. Operates by running Wine on QEMU.

- o Linux Unified Kernel – a set of patches to the Linux kernel allowing many Windows executable files in Linux (using Wine DLLs); and some Windows drivers to be used.

- ReactOS – an open-source OS intended to run the same software as Windows, originally designed to simulate Windows NT 4.0, now aiming at Windows 7 compatibility. It has been in the development stage since 1996.

- Linspire – formerly LindowsOS, a commercial Linux distribution initially created with the goal of running major Windows software. Changed its name to Linspire after *Microsoft v. Lindows*. Discontinued in favor of Xandros Desktop, that was also later discontinued.

- Freedows OS – an open-source attempt at creating a Windows clone for x86 platforms, intended to be released under the GNU General Public License. Started in 1996, by Reece K. Sellin, the project was never completed, getting only to the stage of design discussions which featured a number of novel concepts until it was suspended in 2002.

References

- Begun, Daniel A. (March 2011) [2011]. "Dealing with fragmentation on Android devices". Amazing Android Apps. For Dummies. Wiley. p. 7. ISBN 978-0-470-93629-0. Retrieved May 22, 2013.[

- Saylor, Michael (2012). The Mobile Wave: How Mobile Intelligence Will Change Everything. Vanguard Press. p. 33. ISBN 1-59315-720-7.

- Segal, Adam (January 10, 2011). "Chapter 8 – Promoting Innovation at Home". Advantage: How American Innovation Can Overcome the Asian Challenge. W. W. Norton. p. 191. ISBN 978-0-393-06878-8.

- Tanenbaum, Andrew (2008). Modern Operating Systems. Upper Saddle River, NJ: Pearson/Prentice Hall. p. 160. ISBN 978-0-13-600663-3.

- Raymond, Eric (2003-09-19). The Art of Unix Programming. Addison-Wesley. ISBN 0-13-142901-9. Retrieved 2009-02-09.

- Stuart, Brian L. (2009). Principles of operating systems: design & applications. Boston, Massachusetts: Thompson Learning. p. 23. ISBN 1-4188-3769-5.

- Troy, Douglas (1990). UNIX Systems. Computing Fundamentals. Benjamin/Cumming Publishing Company. p. 4. ISBN 0-201-19827-4.

- Shacklette, Mark (2004). "Unix Operating System". The Internet Encyclopedia. Wiley. p. 497. ISBN 9780471222019.

- Torvalds, Linus and Diamond, David, Just for Fun: The Story of an Accidental Revolutionary, 2001, ISBN 0-06-662072-4

- Sinha, Pradeep Kumar (1997). Distributed Operating Systems: Concepts and Design. IEEE Press. ISBN 978-0-7803-1119-0.

Components of Operating Systems

The components of an operating system are vital for the different parts of a computer to work together. The different components of an operating system are kernel, process, interrupt, protected mode, virtual memory, device driver etc. The topics discussed in the chapter are of great importance to broaden the existing knowledge on operating systems.

Kernel (Operating System)

The kernel (also called nucleus) is a computer program that constitutes the central core of a computer's operating system. It has complete control over everything that occurs in the system. As such, it is the first program loaded on startup, and then manages the remainder of the startup, as well as input/output requests from software, translating them into data processing instructions for the central processing unit. It is also responsible for managing memory, and for managing and communicating with computing peripherals, like printers, speakers, etc. The kernel is a fundamental part of a modern computer's operating system.

The critical code of the kernel is usually loaded into a *protected area* of memory, which prevents it from being overwritten by other, less frequently used parts of the operating system or by applications. The kernel performs its tasks, such as executing processes and handling interrupts, in *kernel space*, whereas everything a user normally does, such as writing text in a text editor or running programs in a GUI (graphical user interface), is done in *user space*. This separation prevents user data and kernel data from interfering with each other and thereby diminishing performance or causing the system to become unstable (and possibly crashing).

When a *process* makes requests of the kernel, the request is called a system call. Various kernel designs differ in how they manage system calls and resources. For example, a monolithic kernel executes all the operating system instructions in the same address space in order to improve the performance of the system. A microkernel runs most of the operating system's background processes in user space, to make the operating system more modular and, therefore, easier to maintain.

The kernel's interface is a low-level abstraction layer.

Functions of the Kernel

The kernel's primary function is to mediate access to the computer's resources, including:

The central processing unit

> This central component of a computer system is responsible for *running* or *executing* programs. The kernel takes responsibility for deciding at any time which of the many running

programs should be allocated to the processor or processors (each of which can usually run only one program at a time).

Random-access memory

Random-access memory is used to store both program instructions and data. Typically, both need to be present in memory in order for a program to execute. Often multiple programs will want access to memory, frequently demanding more memory than the computer has available. The kernel is responsible for deciding which memory each process can use, and determining what to do when not enough memory is available.

Input/output (I/O) devices

I/O devices include such peripherals as keyboards, mice, disk drives, printers, network adapters, and display devices. The kernel allocates requests from applications to perform I/O to an appropriate device and provides convenient methods for using the device (typically abstracted to the point where the application does not need to know implementation details of the device).

Key aspects necessary in resource management are the definition of an execution domain (address space) and the protection mechanism used to mediate the accesses to the resources within a domain.

Kernels also usually provide methods for synchronization and communication between processes called inter-process communication (IPC).

A kernel may implement these features itself, or rely on some of the processes it runs to provide the facilities to other processes, although in this case it must provide some means of IPC to allow processes to access the facilities provided by each other.

Finally, a kernel must provide running programs with a method to make requests to access these facilities.

Memory Management

The kernel has full access to the system's memory and must allow processes to safely access this memory as they require it. Often the first step in doing this is virtual addressing, usually achieved by paging and/or segmentation. Virtual addressing allows the kernel to make a given physical address appear to be another address, the virtual address. Virtual address spaces may be different for different processes; the memory that one process accesses at a particular (virtual) address may be different memory from what another process accesses at the same address. This allows every program to behave as if it is the only one (apart from the kernel) running and thus prevents applications from crashing each other.

On many systems, a program's virtual address may refer to data which is not currently in memory. The layer of indirection provided by virtual addressing allows the operating system to use other data stores, like a hard drive, to store what would otherwise have to remain in main memory (RAM). As a result, operating systems can allow programs to use more memory than the system has physically available. When a program needs data which is not currently in RAM, the CPU signals to the kernel that this has happened, and the kernel responds by writing the contents of an inactive memory block to disk (if necessary) and replacing it with the data requested by the program. The program can then be resumed from the point where it was stopped. This scheme is generally known as demand paging.

Virtual addressing also allows creation of virtual partitions of memory in two disjointed areas, one being reserved for the kernel (kernel space) and the other for the applications (user space). The applications are not permitted by the processor to address kernel memory, thus preventing an application from damaging the running kernel. This fundamental partition of memory space has contributed much to the current designs of actual general-purpose kernels and is almost universal in such systems, although some research kernels (e.g. Singularity) take other approaches.

Device Management

To perform useful functions, processes need access to the peripherals connected to the computer, which are controlled by the kernel through device drivers. A device driver is a computer program that enables the operating system to interact with a hardware device. It provides the operating system with information of how to control and communicate with a certain piece of hardware. The driver is an important and vital piece to a program application. The design goal of a driver is abstraction; the function of the driver is to translate the OS-mandated function calls (programming calls) into device-specific calls. In theory, the device should work correctly with the suitable driver. Device drivers are used for such things as video cards, sound cards, printers, scanners, modems, and LAN cards. The common levels of abstraction of device drivers are:

1. On the hardware side:

    *   Interfacing directly.

    *   Using a high level interface (Video BIOS).

    *   Using a lower-level device driver (file drivers using disk drivers).

    *   Simulating work with hardware, while doing something entirely different.

2. On the software side:

    *   Allowing the operating system direct access to hardware resources.

    *   Implementing only primitives.

    *   Implementing an interface for non-driver software (Example: TWAIN).

    *   Implementing a language, sometimes high-level (Example PostScript).

For example, to show the user something on the screen, an application would make a request to the kernel, which would forward the request to its display driver, which is then responsible for actually plotting the character/pixel.

A kernel must maintain a list of available devices. This list may be known in advance (e.g. on an embedded system where the kernel will be rewritten if the available hardware changes), configured by the user (typical on older PCs and on systems that are not designed for personal use) or detected by the operating system at run time (normally called plug and play). In a plug and play system, a device manager first performs a scan on different hardware buses, such as Peripheral Component Interconnect (PCI) or Universal Serial Bus (USB), to detect installed devices, then searches for the appropriate drivers.

As device management is a very OS-specific topic, these drivers are handled differently by each kind of kernel design, but in every case, the kernel has to provide the I/O to allow drivers to physically access their devices through some port or memory location. Very important decisions have to be made when designing the device management system, as in some designs accesses may involve context switches, making the operation very CPU-intensive and easily causing a significant performance overhead.

System Calls

In computing, a system call is how a program requests a service from an operating system's kernel that it does not normally have permission to run. System calls provide the interface between a process and the operating system. Most operations interacting with the system require permissions not available to a user level process, e.g. I/O performed with a device present on the system, or any form of communication with other processes requires the use of system calls.

A system call is a mechanism that is used by the application program to request a service from the operating system. They use a machine-code instruction that causes the processor to change mode. An example would be from supervisor mode to protected mode. This is where the operating system performs actions like accessing hardware devices or the memory management unit. Generally the operating system provides a library that sits between the operating system and normal programs. Usually it is a C library such as Glibc or Windows API. The library handles the low-level details of passing information to the kernel and switching to supervisor mode. System calls include close, open, read, wait and write.

To actually perform useful work, a process must be able to access the services provided by the kernel. This is implemented differently by each kernel, but most provide a C library or an API, which in turn invokes the related kernel functions.

The method of invoking the kernel function varies from kernel to kernel. If memory isolation is in use, it is impossible for a user process to call the kernel directly, because that would be a violation of the processor's access control rules. A few possibilities are:

- Using a software-simulated interrupt. This method is available on most hardware, and is therefore very common.

- Using a call gate. A call gate is a special address stored by the kernel in a list in kernel memory at a location known to the processor. When the processor detects a call to that address, it instead redirects to the target location without causing an access violation. This requires hardware support, but the hardware for it is quite common.

- Using a special system call instruction. This technique requires special hardware support, which common architectures (notably, x86) may lack. System call instructions have been added to recent models of x86 processors, however, and some operating systems for PCs make use of them when available.

- Using a memory-based queue. An application that makes large numbers of requests but does not need to wait for the result of each may add details of requests to an area of memory that the kernel periodically scans to find requests.

Kernel Design Decisions

Issues of Kernel Support for Protection

An important consideration in the design of a kernel is the support it provides for protection from faults (fault tolerance) and from malicious behaviours (security). These two aspects are usually not clearly distinguished, and the adoption of this distinction in the kernel design leads to the rejection of a hierarchical structure for protection.

The mechanisms or policies provided by the kernel can be classified according to several criteria, including: static (enforced at compile time) or dynamic (enforced at run time); pre-emptive or post-detection; according to the protection principles they satisfy (e.g. Denning); whether they are hardware supported or language based; whether they are more an open mechanism or a binding policy; and many more.

Support for hierarchical protection domains is typically implemented using CPU modes.

Many kernels provide implementation of "capabilities", i.e. objects that are provided to user code which allow limited access to an underlying object managed by the kernel. A common example occurs in file handling: a file is a representation of information stored on a permanent storage device. The kernel may be able to perform many different operations (e.g. read, write, delete or execute the file content's) but a user level application may only be permitted to perform some of these operations (e.g. it may only be allowed to read the file). A common implementation of this is for the kernel to provide an object to the application (typically called a "file handle") which the application may then invoke operations on, the validity of which the kernel checks at the time the operation is requested. Such a system may be extended to cover all objects that the kernel manages, and indeed to objects provided by other user applications.

An efficient and simple way to provide hardware support of capabilities is to delegate the MMU the responsibility of checking access-rights for every memory access, a mechanism called capability-based addressing. Most commercial computer architectures lack such MMU support for capabilities.

An alternative approach is to simulate capabilities using commonly supported hierarchical domains; in this approach, each protected object must reside in an address space that the application does not have access to; the kernel also maintains a list of capabilities in such memory. When an application needs to access an object protected by a capability, it performs a system call and the kernel then checks whether the application's capability grants it permission to perform the requested action, and if it is permitted performs the access for it (either directly, or by delegating the request to another user-level process). The performance cost of address space switching limits the practicality of this approach in systems with complex interactions between objects, but it is used in current operating systems for objects that are not accessed frequently or which are not expected to perform quickly. Approaches where protection mechanism are not firmware supported but are instead simulated at higher levels (e.g. simulating capabilities by manipulating page tables on hardware that does not have direct support), are possible, but there are performance implications. Lack of hardware support may not be an issue, however, for systems that choose to use language-based protection.

An important kernel design decision is the choice of the abstraction levels where the security mechanisms and policies should be implemented. Kernel security mechanisms play a critical role in supporting security at higher levels.

One approach is to use firmware and kernel support for fault tolerance, and build the security policy for malicious behavior on top of that (adding features such as cryptography mechanisms where necessary), delegating some responsibility to the compiler. Approaches that delegate enforcement of security policy to the compiler and/or the application level are often called *language-based security*.

The lack of many critical security mechanisms in current mainstream operating systems impedes the implementation of adequate security policies at the application abstraction level. In fact, a common misconception in computer security is that any security policy can be implemented in an application regardless of kernel support.

Hardware-based or Language-based Protection

Typical computer systems today use hardware-enforced rules about what programs are allowed to access what data. The processor monitors the execution and stops a program that violates a rule (e.g., a user process that is about to read or write to kernel memory, and so on). In systems that lack support for capabilities, processes are isolated from each other by using separate address spaces. Calls from user processes into the kernel are regulated by requiring them to use one of the above-described system call methods.

An alternative approach is to use language-based protection. In a language-based protection system, the kernel will only allow code to execute that has been produced by a trusted language compiler. The language may then be designed such that it is impossible for the programmer to instruct it to do something that will violate a security requirement.

Advantages of this approach include:

- No need for separate address spaces. Switching between address spaces is a slow operation that causes a great deal of overhead, and a lot of optimization work is currently performed in order to prevent unnecessary switches in current operating systems. Switching is completely unnecessary in a language-based protection system, as all code can safely operate in the same address space.

- Flexibility. Any protection scheme that can be designed to be expressed via a programming language can be implemented using this method. Changes to the protection scheme (e.g. from a hierarchical system to a capability-based one) do not require new hardware.

Disadvantages include:

- Longer application start up time. Applications must be verified when they are started to ensure they have been compiled by the correct compiler, or may need recompiling either from source code or from bytecode.

- Inflexible type systems. On traditional systems, applications frequently perform operations that are not type safe. Such operations cannot be permitted in a language-based protection system, which means that applications may need to be rewritten and may, in some cases, lose performance.

Examples of systems with language-based protection include JX and Microsoft's Singularity.

Process Cooperation

Edsger Dijkstra proved that from a logical point of view, atomic lock and unlock operations operating on binary semaphores are sufficient primitives to express any functionality of process cooperation. However this approach is generally held to be lacking in terms of safety and efficiency, whereas a message passing approach is more flexible. A number of other approaches (either lower- or higher-level) are available as well, with many modern kernels providing support for systems such as shared memory and remote procedure calls.

I/O Devices Management

The idea of a kernel where I/O devices are handled uniformly with other processes, as parallel co-operating processes, was first proposed and implemented by Brinch Hansen (although similar ideas were suggested in 1967). In Hansen's description of this, the "common" processes are called *internal processes*, while the I/O devices are called *external processes*.

Similar to physical memory, allowing applications direct access to controller ports and registers can cause the controller to malfunction, or system to crash. With this, depending on the complexity of the device, some devices can get surprisingly complex to program, and use several different controllers. Because of this, providing a more abstract interface to manage the device is important. This interface is normally done by a Device Driver or Hardware Abstraction Layer. Frequently, applications will require access to these devices. The Kernel must maintain the list of these devices by querying the system for them in some way. This can be done through the BIOS, or through one of the various system buses (such as PCI/PCIE, or USB). When an application requests an operation on a device (Such as displaying a character), the kernel needs to send this request to the current active video driver. The video driver, in turn, needs to carry out this request. This is an example of Inter Process Communication (IPC).

Kernel-wide Design Approaches

Naturally, the above listed tasks and features can be provided in many ways that differ from each other in design and implementation.

The principle of *separation of mechanism and policy* is the substantial difference between the philosophy of micro and monolithic kernels. Here a *mechanism* is the support that allows the implementation of many different policies, while a policy is a particular "mode of operation". For instance, a mechanism may provide for user log-in attempts to call an authorization server to determine whether access should be granted; a policy may be for the authorization server to request a password and check it against an encrypted password stored in a database. Because the mechanism is generic, the policy could more easily be changed (e.g. by requiring the use of a security token) than if the mechanism and policy were integrated in the same module.

In minimal microkernel just some very basic policies are included, and its mechanisms allows what is running on top of the kernel (the remaining part of the operating system and the other applications) to decide which policies to adopt (as memory management, high level process scheduling, file system management, etc.). A monolithic kernel instead tends to include many policies, therefore restricting the rest of the system to rely on them.

Per Brinch Hansen presented arguments in favour of separation of mechanism and policy. The failure to properly fulfill this separation is one of the major causes of the lack of substantial innovation in existing operating systems, a problem common in computer architecture. The monolithic design is induced by the "kernel mode"/"user mode" architectural approach to protection (technically called hierarchical protection domains), which is common in conventional commercial systems; in fact, every module needing protection is therefore preferably included into the kernel. This link between monolithic design and "privileged mode" can be reconducted to the key issue of mechanism-policy separation; in fact the "privileged mode" architectural approach melts together the protection mechanism with the security policies, while the major alternative architectural approach, capability-based addressing, clearly distinguishes between the two, leading naturally to a microkernel design.

While monolithic kernels execute all of their code in the same address space (kernel space) microkernels try to run most of their services in user space, aiming to improve maintainability and modularity of the codebase. Most kernels do not fit exactly into one of these categories, but are rather found in between these two designs. These are called hybrid kernels. More exotic designs such as nanokernels and exokernels are available, but are seldom used for production systems. The Xen hypervisor, for example, is an exokernel.

Monolithic Kernels

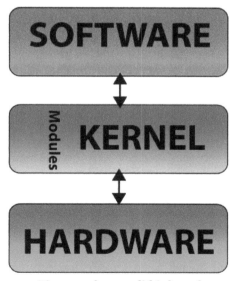

Diagram of a monolithic kernel

In a monolithic kernel, all OS services run along with the main kernel thread, thus also residing in the same memory area. This approach provides rich and powerful hardware access. Some developers, such as UNIX developer Ken Thompson, maintain that it is "easier to implement a monolithic kernel" than microkernels. The main disadvantages of monolithic kernels are the dependencies between system components – a bug in a device driver might crash the entire system – and the fact that large kernels can become very difficult to maintain.

Monolithic kernels, which have traditionally been used by Unix-like operating systems, contain all the operating system core functions and the device drivers (small programs that allow the operating system to interact with hardware devices, such as disk drives, video cards and printers). This is the traditional design of UNIX systems. A monolithic kernel is one single program that contains all of the code necessary to perform every kernel related task. Every part which is to be accessed by most programs which cannot be put in a library is in the kernel space: Device drivers, Scheduler, Memory handling, File systems, Network stacks. Many system calls are provided to applications, to allow them to access all those services. A monolithic kernel, while initially loaded with subsystems that may not be needed, can be tuned to a point where it is as fast as or faster than the one that was specifically designed for the hardware, although more relevant in a general sense. Modern monolithic kernels, such as those of Linux and FreeBSD, both of which fall into the category of Unix-like operating systems, feature the ability to load modules at runtime, thereby allowing easy extension of the kernel's capabilities as required, while helping to minimize the amount of code running in kernel space. In the monolithic kernel, some advantages hinge on these points:

- Since there is less software involved it is faster.

- As it is one single piece of software it should be smaller both in source and compiled forms.

- Less code generally means fewer bugs which can translate to fewer security problems.

Most work in the monolithic kernel is done via system calls. These are interfaces, usually kept in a tabular structure, that access some subsystem within the kernel such as disk operations. Essentially calls are made within programs and a checked copy of the request is passed through the system call. Hence, not far to travel at all. The monolithic Linux kernel can be made extremely small not only because of its ability to dynamically load modules but also because of its ease of customization. In fact, there are some versions that are small enough to fit together with a large number of utilities and other programs on a single floppy disk and still provide a fully functional operating system (one of the most popular of which is muLinux). This ability to miniaturize its kernel has also led to a rapid growth in the use of Linux in embedded systems.

These types of kernels consist of the core functions of the operating system and the device drivers with the ability to load modules at runtime. They provide rich and powerful abstractions of the underlying hardware. They provide a small set of simple hardware abstractions and use applications called servers to provide more functionality. This particular approach defines a high-level virtual interface over the hardware, with a set of system calls to implement operating system services such as process management, concurrency and memory management in several modules that run in supervisor mode. This design has several flaws and limitations:

- Coding in kernel can be challenging, in part because one cannot use common libraries (like a full-featured libc), and because one needs to use a source-level debugger like gdb. Rebooting the computer is often required. This is not just a problem of convenience to the developers. When debugging is harder, and as difficulties become stronger, it becomes more likely that code will be "buggier".

- Bugs in one part of the kernel have strong side effects; since every function in the kernel has all the privileges, a bug in one function can corrupt data structure of another, totally unrelated part of the kernel, or of any running program.

- Kernels often become very large and difficult to maintain.

- Even if the modules servicing these operations are separate from the whole, the code integration is tight and difficult to do correctly.

- Since the modules run in the same address space, a bug can bring down the entire system.

- Monolithic kernels are not portable; therefore, they must be rewritten for each new architecture that the operating system is to be used on.

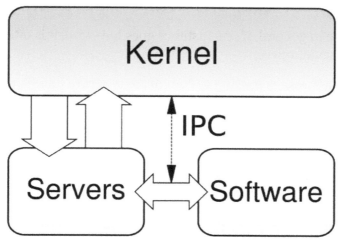

In the microkernel approach, the kernel itself only provides basic functionality that allows the execution of servers, separate programs that assume former kernel functions, such as device drivers, GUI servers, etc.

Microkernels

Microkernel (also abbreviated μK or uK) is the term describing an approach to operating system design by which the functionality of the system is moved out of the traditional "kernel", into a set of "servers" that communicate through a "minimal" kernel, leaving as little as possible in "system space" and as much as possible in "user space". A microkernel that is designed for a specific platform or device is only ever going to have what it needs to operate. The microkernel approach consists of defining a simple abstraction over the hardware, with a set of primitives or system calls to implement minimal OS services such as memory management, multitasking, and inter-process communication. Other services, including those normally provided by the kernel, such as networking, are implemented in user-space programs, referred to as *servers*. Microkernels are easier to maintain than monolithic kernels, but the large number of system calls and context switches might slow down the system because they typically generate more overhead than plain function calls.

Only parts which really require being in a privileged mode are in kernel space: IPC (Inter-Process Communication), basic scheduler, or scheduling primitives, basic memory handling, basic I/O primitives. Many critical parts are now running in user space: The complete scheduler, memory handling, file systems, and network stacks. Micro kernels were invented as a reaction to traditional "monolithic" kernel design, whereby all system functionality was put in a one static program running in a special "system" mode of the processor. In the microkernel, only the most fundamental of tasks are performed such as being able to access some (not necessarily all) of the hardware, manage memory and coordinate message passing between the processes. Some systems that use micro kernels are QNX and the HURD. In the case of QNX and Hurd user sessions can be entire snapshots of the system itself or views as it is referred to. The very essence of the microkernel architecture illustrates some of its advantages:

- Maintenance is generally easier.

- Patches can be tested in a separate instance, and then swapped in to take over a production instance.

- Rapid development time and new software can be tested without having to reboot the kernel.

- More persistence in general, if one instance goes hay-wire, it is often possible to substitute it with an operational mirror.

Most micro kernels use a message passing system of some sort to handle requests from one server to another. The message passing system generally operates on a port basis with the microkernel. As an example, if a request for more memory is sent, a port is opened with the microkernel and the request sent through. Once within the microkernel, the steps are similar to system calls. The rationale was that it would bring modularity in the system architecture, which would entail a cleaner system, easier to debug or dynamically modify, customizable to users' needs, and more performing. They are part of the operating systems like AIX, BeOS, Hurd, Mach, macOS, MINIX, QNX. Etc. Although micro kernels are very small by themselves, in combination with all their required auxiliary code they are, in fact, often larger than monolithic kernels. Advocates of monolithic kernels also point out that the two-tiered structure of microkernel systems, in which most of the operating system does not interact directly with the hardware, creates a not-insignificant cost in terms of system efficiency. These types of kernels normally provide only the minimal services such as defining memory address spaces, Inter-process communication (IPC) and the process management. The other functions such as running the hardware processes are not handled directly by micro kernels. Proponents of micro kernels point out those monolithic kernels have the disadvantage that an error in the kernel can cause the entire system to crash. However, with a microkernel, if a kernel process crashes, it is still possible to prevent a crash of the system as a whole by merely restarting the service that caused the error.

Other services provided by the kernel such as networking are implemented in user-space programs referred to as *servers*. Servers allow the operating system to be modified by simply starting and stopping programs. For a machine without networking support, for instance, the networking server is not started. The task of moving in and out of the kernel to move data between the various applications and servers creates overhead which is detrimental to the efficiency of micro kernels in comparison with monolithic kernels.

Disadvantages in the microkernel exist however. Some are:

- Larger running memory footprint

- More software for interfacing is required, there is a potential for performance loss.

- Messaging bugs can be harder to fix due to the longer trip they have to take versus the one off copy in a monolithic kernel.

- Process management in general can be very complicated.

The disadvantages for micro kernels are extremely context based. As an example, they work well for small single purpose (and critical) systems because if not many processes need to run, then the complications of process management are effectively mitigated.

A microkernel allows the implementation of the remaining part of the operating system as a normal application program written in a high-level language, and the use of different operating systems on top of the same unchanged kernel. It is also possible to dynamically switch among operating systems and to have more than one active simultaneously.

Monolithic Kernels Vs. Microkernels

As the computer kernel grows, so grows the size and vulnerability of its trusted computing base; and, besides reducing security, there is the problem of enlarging the memory footprint. This is mitigated to some degree by perfecting the virtual memory system, but not all computer architectures have virtual memory support. To reduce the kernel's footprint, extensive editing has to be performed to carefully remove unneeded code, which can be very difficult with non-obvious interdependencies between parts of a kernel with millions of lines of code.

By the early 1990s, due to the various shortcomings of monolithic kernels versus microkernels, monolithic kernels were considered obsolete by virtually all operating system researchers. As a result, the design of Linux as a monolithic kernel rather than a microkernel was the topic of a famous debate between Linus Torvalds and Andrew Tanenbaum. There is merit on both sides of the argument presented in the Tanenbaum–Torvalds debate.

Performance

Monolithic kernels are designed to have all of their code in the same address space (kernel space), which some developers argue is necessary to increase the performance of the system. Some developers also maintain that monolithic systems are extremely efficient if well written. The monolithic model tends to be more efficient through the use of shared kernel memory, rather than the slower IPC system of microkernel designs, which is typically based on message passing.

The performance of microkernels was poor in both the 1980s and early 1990s. However, studies that empirically measured the performance of these microkernels did not analyze the reasons of such inefficiency. The explanations of this data were left to "folklore", with the assumption that they were due to the increased frequency of switches from "kernel-mode" to "user-mode", to the increased frequency of inter-process communication and to the increased frequency of context switches.

In fact, as guessed in 1995, the reasons for the poor performance of microkernels might as well have been: (1) an actual inefficiency of the whole microkernel *approach*, (2) the particular *con-*

cepts implemented in those microkernels, and (3) the particular *implementation* of those concepts. Therefore it remained to be studied if the solution to build an efficient microkernel was, unlike previous attempts, to apply the correct construction techniques.

On the other end, the hierarchical protection domains architecture that leads to the design of a monolithic kernel has a significant performance drawback each time there's an interaction between different levels of protection (i.e. when a process has to manipulate a data structure both in 'user mode' and 'supervisor mode'), since this requires message copying by value.

By the mid-1990s, most researchers had abandoned the belief that careful tuning could reduce this overhead dramatically, but recently, newer microkernels, optimized for performance, such as L4 and K42 have addressed these problems.

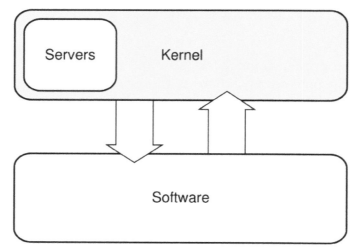

The hybrid kernel approach combines the speed and simpler design of
a monolithic kernel with the modularity and execution safety of a microkernel.

Hybrid (or Modular) Kernels

Hybrid kernels are used in most commercial operating systems such as Microsoft Windows NT 3.1, NT 3.5, NT 3.51, NT 4.0, 2000, XP, Vista, 7, 8, 8.1 and 10. Apple Inc's own macOS uses a hybrid kernel called XNU which is based upon code from Carnegie Mellon's Mach kernel and FreeBSD's monolithic kernel. They are similar to micro kernels, except they include some additional code in kernel-space to increase performance. These kernels represent a compromise that was implemented by some developers before it was demonstrated that pure micro kernels can provide high performance. These types of kernels are extensions of micro kernels with some properties of monolithic kernels. Unlike monolithic kernels, these types of kernels are unable to load modules at runtime on their own. Hybrid kernels are micro kernels that have some "non-essential" code in kernel-space in order for the code to run more quickly than it would were it to be in user-space. Hybrid kernels are a compromise between the monolithic and microkernel designs. This implies running some services (such as the network stack or the filesystem) in kernel space to reduce the performance overhead of a traditional microkernel, but still running kernel code (such as device drivers) as servers in user space.

Many traditionally monolithic kernels are now at least adding (if not actively exploiting) the module capability. The most well known of these kernels is the Linux kernel. The modular kernel essentially can have parts of it that are built into the core kernel binary or binaries that load into memory on demand. It is important to note that a code tainted module has the potential to destabilize a running kernel. Many people become confused on this point when discussing micro kernels. It is possible to write a driver for a microkernel in a completely separate memory space and test it before "going" live. When a kernel module is loaded, it accesses the monolithic portion's memory space by adding to it what it needs, therefore, opening the doorway to possible pollution. A few advantages to the modular (or) Hybrid kernel are:

- Faster development time for drivers that can operate from within modules. No reboot required for testing (provided the kernel is not destabilized).

- On demand capability versus spending time recompiling a whole kernel for things like new drivers or subsystems.

- Faster integration of third party technology (related to development but pertinent unto itself nonetheless).

Modules, generally, communicate with the kernel using a module interface of some sort. The interface is generalized (although particular to a given operating system) so it is not always possible to use modules. Often the device drivers may need more flexibility than the module interface affords. Essentially, it is two system calls and often the safety checks that only have to be done once in the monolithic kernel now may be done twice. Some of the disadvantages of the modular approach are:

- With more interfaces to pass through, the possibility of increased bugs exists (which implies more security holes).

- Maintaining modules can be confusing for some administrators when dealing with problems like symbol differences.

Nanokernels

A nanokernel delegates virtually all services – including even the most basic ones like interrupt controllers or the timer – to device drivers to make the kernel memory requirement even smaller than a traditional microkernel.

Exokernels

Exokernels are a still-experimental approach to operating system design. They differ from the other types of kernels in that their functionality is limited to the protection and multiplexing of the raw hardware, providing no hardware abstractions on top of which to develop applications. This separation of hardware protection from hardware management enables application developers to determine how to make the most efficient use of the available hardware for each specific program.

Exokernels in themselves are extremely small. However, they are accompanied by library operating systems, providing application developers with the functionalities of a conventional operating system. A major advantage of exokernel-based systems is that they can incorporate multiple library operating systems, each exporting a different API, for example one for high level UI development and one for real-time control.

History of Kernel Development

Early Operating System Kernels

Strictly speaking, an operating system (and thus, a kernel) is not *required* to run a computer. Programs can be directly loaded and executed on the "bare metal" machine, provided that the authors of those programs are willing to work without any hardware abstraction or operating system support. Most early computers operated this way during the 1950s and early 1960s, which were reset and reloaded between the execution of different programs. Eventually, small ancillary programs such as program loaders and debuggers were left in memory between runs, or loaded from ROM. As these were developed, they formed the basis of what became early operating system kernels. The "bare metal" approach is still used today on some video game consoles and embedded systems, but in general, newer computers use modern operating systems and kernels.

In 1969, the RC 4000 Multiprogramming System introduced the system design philosophy of a small nucleus "upon which operating systems for different purposes could be built in an orderly manner", what would be called the microkernel approach.

Time-sharing Operating Systems

In the decade preceding Unix, computers had grown enormously in power – to the point where computer operators were looking for new ways to get people to use their spare time on their machines. One of the major developments during this era was time-sharing, whereby a number of users would get small slices of computer time, at a rate at which it appeared they were each connected to their own, slower, machine.

The development of time-sharing systems led to a number of problems. One was that users, particularly at universities where the systems were being developed, seemed to want to hack the system to get more CPU time. For this reason, security and access control became a major focus of the Multics project in 1965. Another ongoing issue was properly handling computing resources: users spent most of their time staring at the screen and thinking instead of actually using the resources of the computer, and a time-sharing system should give the CPU time to an active user during these periods. Finally, the systems typically offered a memory hierarchy several layers deep, and partitioning this expensive resource led to major developments in virtual memory systems.

Amiga

The Commodore Amiga was released in 1985, and was among the first – and certainly most successful – home computers to feature an advanced kernel architecture. The AmigaOS kernel's executive component, *exec.library*, uses a microkernel message-passing design, but there are other kernel components, like *graphics.library*, that have direct access to the hardware. There is no memory protection, and the kernel is almost always running in user mode. Only special actions are executed in kernel mode, and user-mode applications can ask the operating system to execute their code in kernel mode.

Unix

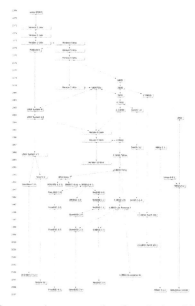

A diagram of the predecessor/successor family relationship for Unix-like systems

During the design phase of Unix, programmers decided to model every high-level device as a file, because they believed the purpose of computation was data transformation.

For instance, printers were represented as a "file" at a known location – when data was copied to the file, it printed out. Other systems, to provide a similar functionality, tended to virtualize devices at a lower level – that is, both devices *and* files would be instances of some lower level concept. Virtualizing the system at the file level allowed users to manipulate the entire system using their existing file management utilities and concepts, dramatically simplifying operation. As an extension of the same paradigm, Unix allows programmers to manipulate files using a series of small programs, using the concept of pipes, which allowed users to complete operations in stages, feeding a file through a chain of single-purpose tools. Although the end result was the same, using smaller programs in this way dramatically increased flexibility as well as ease of development and use, allowing the user to modify their workflow by adding or removing a program from the chain.

In the Unix model, the *operating system* consists of two parts; first, the huge collection of utility programs that drive most operations, the other the kernel that runs the programs. Under Unix, from a programming standpoint, the distinction between the two is fairly thin; the kernel is a program, running in supervisor mode, that acts as a program loader and supervisor for the small utility programs making up the rest of the system, and to provide locking and I/O services for these programs; beyond that, the kernel didn't intervene at all in user space.

Over the years the computing model changed, and Unix's treatment of everything as a file or byte stream no longer was as universally applicable as it was before. Although a terminal could be treated as a file or a byte stream, which is printed to or read from, the same did not seem to be true for a graphical user interface. Networking posed another problem. Even if network communication can be compared to file access, the low-level packet-oriented architecture dealt with discrete chunks of data and not with whole files. As the capability of computers grew, Unix became increasingly cluttered with code. It is also because the modularity of the Unix kernel is extensively scalable. While kernels might have had 100,000 lines of code in the seventies and eighties, kernels of modern Unix successors like Linux have more than 13 million lines.

Modern Unix-derivatives are generally based on module-loading monolithic kernels. Examples of this are the QNX, a microkernel owned by BlackBerry, Linux kernel in its many distributions as well as the Berkeley software distribution variant kernels such as FreeBSD, DragonflyBSD, OpenBSD, NetBSD,and macOS. Apart from these alternatives, amateur developers maintain an active operating system development community, populated by self-written hobby kernels which mostly end up sharing many features with Linux, FreeBSD, DragonflyBSD, OpenBSD or NetBSD kernels and/or being compatible with them.

Mac OS

Apple first launched its classic Mac OS in 1984, bundled with its Macintosh personal computer. Apple moved to a nanokernel design in Mac OS 8.6. Against this, the modern macOS (originally named Mac OS X) is based on Darwin, which uses a hybrid kernel called XNU, which was created combining the 4.3BSD kernel and the Mach kernel.

Microsoft Windows

Microsoft Windows was first released in 1985 as an add-on to MS-DOS. Because of its dependence on another operating system, initial releases of Windows, prior to Windows 95, were considered an operating environment). This product line continued to evolve through the 1980s and 1990s, culminating with release of the Windows 9x series (upgrading the system's capabilities to 32-bit addressing and pre-emptive multitasking) through the mid-1990s and ending with the release of Windows Me in 2000. Microsoft also developed Windows NT, an operating system intended for high-end and business users. This line started with the release of Windows NT 3.1 in 1993, and has continued through the years of 2010 with Windows 8 and Windows Server 2012.

The release of Windows XP in October 2001 brought the NT kernel version of Windows to general users, replacing Windows 9x with a completely different operating system. The architecture of Windows NT's kernel is considered a hybrid kernel because the kernel itself contains tasks such as the Window Manager and the IPC Managers, with a client/server layered subsystem model.

Development of Microkernels

Although Mach, developed at Carnegie Mellon University from 1985 to 1994, is the best-known general-purpose microkernel, other microkernels have been developed with more specific aims. The L4 microkernel family (mainly the L3 and the L4 kernel) was created to demonstrate that microkernels are not necessarily slow. Newer implementations such as Fiasco and Pistachio are able to run Linux next to other L4 processes in separate address spaces.

Additionally, QNX is a microkernel which is principally used in embedded systems.

Process (Computing)

A list of processes as displayed by htop

In computing, a process is an instance of a computer program that is being executed. It contains the program code and its current activity. Depending on the operating system (OS), a process may be made up of multiple threads of execution that execute instructions concurrently.

A computer program is a passive collection of instructions, while a process is the actual execution of those instructions. Several processes may be associated with the same program; for example, opening up several instances of the same program often means more than one process is being executed.

Multitasking is a method to allow multiple processes to share processors (CPUs) and other system resources. Each CPU executes a single task at a time. However, multitasking allows each processor to switch between tasks that are being executed without having to wait for each task to finish. Depending on the operating system implementation, switches could be performed when tasks perform input/output operations, when a task indicates that it can be switched, or on hardware interrupts.

A common form of multitasking is time-sharing. Time-sharing is a method to allow fast response for interactive user applications. In time-sharing systems, context switches are performed rapidly, which makes it seem like multiple processes are being executed simultaneously on the same processor. This seeming execution of multiple processes simultaneously is called concurrency.

For security and reliability, most modern operating systems prevent direct communication between independent processes, providing strictly mediated and controlled inter-process communication functionality.

Representation

In general, a computer system process consists of (or is said to *own*) the following resources:

- An *image* of the executable machine code associated with a program.

- Memory (typically some region of virtual memory); which includes the executable code, process-specific data (input and output), a call stack (to keep track of active subroutines and/or other events), and a heap to hold intermediate computation data generated during run time.

- Operating system descriptors of resources that are allocated to the process, such as file descriptors (Unix terminology) or handles (Windows), and data sources and sinks.

- Security attributes, such as the process owner and the process' set of permissions (allowable operations).

- Processor state (context), such as the content of registers and physical memory addressing. The *state* is typically stored in computer registers when the process is executing, and in memory otherwise.

The operating system holds most of this information about active processes in data structures called process control blocks. Any subset of the resources, typically at least the processor state, may be associated with each of the process' threads in operating systems that support threads or *child* (*daughter*) processes.

The operating system keeps its processes separate and allocates the resources they need, so that they are less likely to interfere with each other and cause system failures (e.g., deadlock or thrashing). The operating system may also provide mechanisms for inter-process communication to enable processes to interact in safe and predictable ways.

Multitasking and Process Management

A multitasking operating system may just switch between processes to give the appearance of many processes executing simultaneously (that is, in parallel), though in fact only one process can be executing at any one time on a single CPU (unless the CPU has multiple cores, then multithreading or other similar technologies can be used).

It is usual to associate a single process with a main program, and child processes with any spin-off, parallel processes, which behave like asynchronous subroutines. A process is said to *own* resources, of which an *image* of its program (in memory) is one such resource. However, in multiprocessing systems *many* processes may run off of, or share, the same reentrant program at the same location in memory, but each process is said to own its own *image* of the program.

Processes are often called "tasks" in embedded operating systems. The sense of "process" (or task) is "something that takes up time", as opposed to "memory", which is "something that takes up space".

The above description applies to both processes managed by an operating system, and processes as defined by process calculi.

If a process requests something for which it must wait, it will be blocked. When the process is in the blocked state, it is eligible for swapping to disk, but this is transparent in a virtual memory system, where regions of a process's memory may be really on disk and not in main memory at any time. Note that even *unused* portions of active processes/tasks (executing programs) are eligible for swapping to disk. *All parts of an executing program and its data do not have to be in physical memory for the associated process to be active.*

Process States

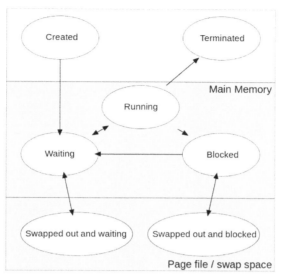

The various process states, displayed in a state diagram, with arrows indicating possible transitions between states.

An operating system kernel that allows multitasking needs processes to have certain states. Names for these states are not standardised, but they have similar functionality.

- First, the process is "created" by being loaded from a secondary storage device (hard disk drive, CD-ROM, etc.) into main memory. After that the process scheduler assigns it the "waiting" state.

- While the process is "waiting", it waits for the scheduler to do a so-called context switch and load the process into the processor. The process state then becomes "running", and the processor executes the process instructions.

- If a process needs to wait for a resource (wait for user input or file to open, for example), it is assigned the "blocked" state. The process state is changed back to "waiting" when the process no longer needs to wait (in a blocked state).

- Once the process finishes execution, or is terminated by the operating system, it is no longer needed. The process is removed instantly or is moved to the "terminated" state. When removed, it just waits to be removed from main memory.

Inter-process Communication

When processes communicate with each other it is called "Inter-process communication" (IPC). Processes frequently need to communicate, for instance in a shell pipeline, the output of the first process need to pass to the second one, and so on to the other process. It is preferred in a well-structured way not using interrupts.

It is even possible for the two processes to be running on different machines. The operating system

(OS) may differ from one process to the other, therefore some mediator(s) (called protocols) are needed.

History

By the early 1960s, computer control software had evolved from monitor control software, for example IBSYS, to executive control software. Over time, computers got faster while computer time was still neither cheap nor fully utilized; such an environment made multiprogramming possible and necessary. Multiprogramming means that several programs run concurrently. At first, more than one program ran on a single processor, as a result of underlying uniprocessor computer architecture, and they shared scarce and limited hardware resources; consequently, the concurrency was of a *serial* nature. On later systems with multiple processors, multiple programs may run concurrently in *parallel*.

Programs consist of sequences of instructions for processors. A single processor can run only one instruction at a time: it is impossible to run more programs at the same time. A program might need some resource, such as an input device, which has a large delay, or a program might start some slow operation, such as sending output to a printer. This would lead to processor being "idle" (unused). To keep the processor busy at all times, the execution of such a program is halted and the operating system switches the processor to run another program. To the user, it will appear that the programs run at the same time (hence the term "parallel").

Shortly thereafter, the notion of a "program" was expanded to the notion of an "executing program and its context". The concept of a process was born, which also became necessary with the invention of re-entrant code. Threads came somewhat later. However, with the advent of concepts such as time-sharing, computer networks, and multiple-CPU shared memory computers, the old "multiprogramming" gave way to true multitasking, multiprocessing and, later, multithreading.

Interrupt

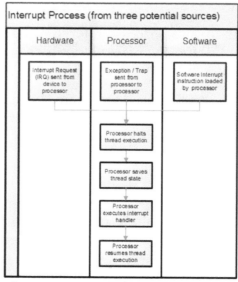

interrupt sources and processor handling

In system programming, an interrupt is a signal to the processor emitted by hardware or software indicating an event that needs immediate attention. An interrupt alerts the processor to a high-priority condition requiring the interruption of the current code the processor is executing. The processor responds by suspending its current activities, saving its state, and executing a function called an *interrupt handler* (or an interrupt service routine, ISR) to deal with the event. This interruption is temporary, and, after the interrupt handler finishes, the processor resumes normal activities. There are two types of interrupts: hardware interrupts and software interrupts.

Hardware interrupts are used by devices to communicate that they require attention from the operating system. Internally, hardware interrupts are implemented using electronic alerting signals that are sent to the processor from an external device, which is either a part of the computer itself, such as a disk controller, or an external peripheral. For example, pressing a key on the keyboard or moving the mouse triggers hardware interrupts that cause the processor to read the keystroke or mouse position. Unlike the software type (described below), hardware interrupts are asynchronous and can occur in the middle of instruction execution, requiring additional care in programming. The act of initiating a hardware interrupt is referred to as an interrupt request (IRQ).

A software interrupt is caused either by an exceptional condition in the processor itself, or a special instruction in the instruction set which causes an interrupt when it is executed. The former is often called a *trap* or *exception* and is used for errors or events occurring during program execution that are exceptional enough that they cannot be handled within the program itself. For example, a divide-by-zero exception will be thrown if the processor's arithmetic logic unit is commanded to divide a number by zero as this instruction is in error and impossible. The operating system will catch this exception, and can choose to abort the instruction. Software interrupt instructions can also function similarly to subroutine calls and be used for a variety of purposes, such as to request services from device drivers, like interrupts sent to and from a disk controller to request reading or writing of data to and from the disk.

Each interrupt has its own interrupt handler. The number of hardware interrupts is limited by the number of interrupt request (IRQ) lines to the processor, but there may be hundreds of different software interrupts. Interrupts are a commonly used technique for computer multitasking, especially in real-time computing. Such a system is said to be interrupt-driven.

Overview

Hardware interrupts were introduced as an optimization, eliminating unproductive waiting time in polling loops, waiting for external events. They may be implemented in hardware as a distinct system with control lines, or they may be integrated into the memory subsystem.

If implemented in hardware, an interrupt controller circuit such as the IBM PC's Programmable Interrupt Controller (PIC) may be connected between the interrupting device and the processor's interrupt pin to multiplex several sources of interrupt onto the one or two CPU lines typically available. If implemented as part of the memory controller, interrupts are mapped into the system's memory address space.

Interrupts can be categorized into these different types:

- *Maskable interrupt* (IRQ): a hardware interrupt that may be ignored by setting a bit in an interrupt mask register's (IMR) bit-mask.

- *Non-maskable interrupt* (NMI): a hardware interrupt that lacks an associated bit-mask, so that it can never be ignored. NMIs are used for the highest priority tasks such as timers, especially watchdog timers.

- *Inter-processor interrupt* (IPI): a special case of interrupt that is generated by one processor to interrupt another processor in a multiprocessor system.

- *Software interrupt*: an interrupt generated within a processor by executing an instruction. Software interrupts are often used to implement system calls because they result in a subroutine call with a CPU ring level change.

- *Spurious interrupt*: a hardware interrupt that is unwanted. They are typically generated by system conditions such as electrical interference on an interrupt line or through incorrectly designed hardware.

Processors typically have an internal *interrupt mask* which allows software to ignore all external hardware interrupts while it is set. Setting or clearing this mask may be faster than accessing an interrupt mask register (IMR) in a PIC or disabling interrupts in the device itself. In some cases, such as the x86 architecture, disabling and enabling interrupts on the processor itself act as a memory barrier; however, it may actually be slower.

An interrupt that leaves the machine in a well-defined state is called a *precise interrupt*. Such an interrupt has four properties:

- The Program Counter (PC) is saved in a known place.

- All instructions before the one pointed to by the PC have fully executed.

- No instruction beyond the one pointed to by the PC has been executed (that is no prohibition on instruction beyond that in PC, it is just that any changes they make to registers or memory must be undone before the interrupt happens).

- The execution state of the instruction pointed to by the PC is known.

An interrupt that does not meet these requirements is called an *imprecise interrupt*.

The phenomenon where the overall system performance is severely hindered by excessive amounts of processing time spent handling interrupts is called an interrupt storm.

Types of Interrupts

Level-triggered

A *level-triggered interrupt* is an interrupt signalled by maintaining the interrupt line at a high or low level. A device wishing to signal a Level-triggered interrupt drives the interrupt request line to its active level (high or low), and then holds it at that level until it is serviced. It ceases asserting the line when the CPU commands it to or otherwise handles the condition that caused it to signal the interrupt.

Typically, the processor samples the interrupt input at predefined times during each bus cycle such as state T2 for the Z80 microprocessor. If the interrupt isn't active when the processor samples it, the CPU doesn't see it. One possible use for this type of interrupt is to minimize spurious signals from a noisy interrupt line: a spurious pulse will often be so short that it is not noticed.

Multiple devices may share a level-triggered interrupt line if they are designed to. The interrupt line must have a pull-down or pull-up resistor so that when not actively driven it settles to its inactive state. Devices actively assert the line to indicate an outstanding interrupt, but let the line float (do not actively drive it) when not signalling an interrupt. The line is then in its asserted state when any (one or more than one) of the sharing devices is signalling an outstanding interrupt.

Level-triggered interrupt is favored by some because it is easy to share the interrupt request line without losing the interrupts, when multiple shared devices interrupt at the same time. Upon detecting assertion of the interrupt line, the CPU must search through the devices sharing the interrupt request line until one who triggered the interrupt is detected. After servicing this device, the CPU may recheck the interrupt line status to determine whether any other devices also needs service. If the line is now de-asserted, the CPU avoids checking the remaining devices on the line. Since some devices interrupt more frequently than others, and other device interrupts are particularly expensive, a careful ordering of device checks is employed to increase efficiency. The original PCI standard mandated level-triggered interrupts because of this advantage of sharing interrupts.

There are also serious problems with sharing level-triggered interrupts. As long as any device on the line has an outstanding request for service the line remains asserted, so it is not possible to detect a change in the status of any other device. Deferring servicing a low-priority device is not an option, because this would prevent detection of service requests from higher-priority devices. If there is a device on the line that the CPU does not know how to service, then any interrupt from that device permanently blocks all interrupts from the other devices.

Edge-triggered

An *edge-triggered interrupt* is an interrupt signalled by a level transition on the interrupt line, either a falling edge (high to low) or a rising edge (low to high). A device, wishing to signal an interrupt, drives a pulse onto the line and then releases the line to its inactive state. If the pulse is too short to be detected by polled I/O then special hardware may be required to detect the edge.

Multiple devices may share an edge-triggered interrupt line if they are designed to. The interrupt line must have a pull-down or pull-up resistor so that when not actively driven it settles to one particular state. Devices signal an interrupt by briefly driving the line to its non-default state, and let the line float (do not actively drive it) when not signalling an interrupt. This type of connection is also referred to as open collector. The line then carries all the pulses generated by all the devices. (This is analogous to the pull cord on some buses and trolleys that any passenger can pull to signal the driver that they are requesting a stop.) However, interrupt pulses from different devices may merge if they occur close in time. To avoid losing interrupts the CPU must trigger on the trailing edge of the pulse (e.g. the rising edge if the line is pulled up and driven low). After detecting an interrupt the CPU must check all the devices for service requirements.

Edge-triggered interrupts do not suffer the problems that level-triggered interrupts have with sharing. Service of a low-priority device can be postponed arbitrarily, and interrupts will continue to be received from the high-priority devices that are being serviced. If there is a device that the CPU does not know how to service, it may cause a spurious interrupt, or even periodic spurious interrupts, but it does not interfere with the interrupt signalling of the other devices. However, it is fairly easy for an edge triggered interrupt to be missed - for example if interrupts have to be masked for a period - and unless there is some type of hardware latch that records the event it is impossible to recover. Such problems caused many "lockups" in early computer hardware because the processor did not know it was expected to do something. More modern hardware often has one or more interrupt status registers that latch the interrupt requests; well written edge-driven interrupt software often checks such registers to ensure events are not missed.

The elderly Industry Standard Architecture (ISA) bus uses edge-triggered interrupts, but does not mandate that devices be able to share them. The parallel port also uses edge-triggered interrupts. Many older devices assume that they have exclusive use of their interrupt line, making it electrically unsafe to share them. However, ISA motherboards include pull-up resistors on the IRQ lines, so well-behaved devices share ISA interrupts just fine.

Hybrid

Some systems use a hybrid of level-triggered and edge-triggered signalling. The hardware not only looks for an edge, but it also verifies that the interrupt signal stays active for a certain period of time.

A common use of a hybrid interrupt is for the NMI (non-maskable interrupt) input. Because NMIs generally signal major – or even catastrophic – system events, a good implementation of this signal tries to ensure that the interrupt is valid by verifying that it remains active for a period of time. This 2-step approach helps to eliminate false interrupts from affecting the system.

Message-signaled

A *message-signalled interrupt* does not use a physical interrupt line. Instead, a device signals its request for service by sending a short message over some communications medium, typically a computer bus. The message might be of a type reserved for interrupts, or it might be of some pre-existing type such as a memory write.

Message-signalled interrupts behave very much like edge-triggered interrupts, in that the interrupt is a momentary signal rather than a continuous condition. Interrupt-handling software treats the two in much the same manner. Typically, multiple pending message-signalled interrupts with the same message (the same virtual interrupt line) are allowed to merge, just as closely spaced edge-triggered interrupts can merge.

Message-signalled interrupt vectors can be shared, to the extent that the underlying communication medium can be shared. No additional effort is required.

Because the identity of the interrupt is indicated by a pattern of data bits, not requiring a separate physical conductor, many more distinct interrupts can be efficiently handled. This reduces the need for sharing. Interrupt messages can also be passed over a serial bus, not requiring any additional lines.

PCI Express, a serial computer bus, uses message-signalled interrupts exclusively.

Doorbell

In a push button analogy applied to computer systems, the term *doorbell* or *doorbell interrupt* is often used to describe a mechanism whereby a software system can signal or notify a computer hardware device that there is some work to be done. Typically, the software system will place data in some well-known and mutually agreed upon memory location(s), and "ring the doorbell" by writing to a different memory location. This different memory location is often called the doorbell region, and there may even be multiple doorbells serving different purposes in this region. It is this act of writing to the door-bell region of memory that "rings the bell" and notifies the hardware device that the data are ready and waiting. The hardware device would now know that the data are valid and can be acted upon. It would typically write the data to a hard disk drive, or send them over a network, or encrypt them, etc.

The term *doorbell interrupt* is usually a misnomer. It's similar to an interrupt, because it causes some work to be done by the device; however, the doorbell region is sometimes implemented as a polled region, sometimes the doorbell region writes through to physical device registers, and sometimes the doorbell region is hardwired directly to physical device registers. When either writing through or directly to physical device registers, this may cause a real interrupt to occur at the device's central processor unit (CPU), if it has one.

Doorbell interrupts can be compared to Message Signaled Interrupts, as they have some similarities.

Difficulty with Sharing Interrupt Lines

Multiple devices sharing an interrupt line (of any triggering style) all act as spurious interrupt sources with respect to each other. With many devices on one line the workload in servicing interrupts grows in proportion to the square of the number of devices. It is therefore preferred to spread devices evenly across the available interrupt lines. Shortage of interrupt lines is a problem in older system designs where the interrupt lines are distinct physical conductors. Message-signalled interrupts, where the interrupt line is virtual, are favored in new system architectures (such as PCI Express) and relieve this problem to a considerable extent.

Some devices with a poorly designed programming interface provide no way to determine whether they have requested service. They may lock up or otherwise misbehave if serviced when they do not want it. Such devices cannot tolerate spurious interrupts, and so also cannot tolerate sharing an interrupt line. ISA cards, due to often cheap design and construction, are notorious for this problem. Such devices are becoming much rarer, as hardware logic becomes cheaper and new system architectures mandate shareable interrupts.

Performance Issues

Interrupts provide low overhead and good latency at low load, but degrade significantly at high interrupt rate unless care is taken to prevent several pathologies. These are various forms of live-locks, when the system spends all of its time processing interrupts to the exclusion of other required tasks. Under extreme conditions, a large number of interrupts (like very high network traffic) may completely stall the system. To avoid such problems, an operating system must schedule network interrupt handling as carefully as it schedules process execution.

With multi-core processors, additional performance improvements in interrupt handling can be achieved through receive-side scaling (RSS) when multiqueue NICs are used. Such NICs provide multiple receive queues associated to separate interrupts; by routing each of those interrupts to different cores, processing of the interrupt requests triggered by the network traffic received by a single NIC can be distributed among multiple cores. Distribution of the interrupts among cores can be performed automatically by the operating system, or the routing of interrupts (usually referred to as *IRQ affinity*) can be manually configured.

A purely software-based implementation of the receiving traffic distribution, known as *receive packet steering* (RPS), distributes received traffic among cores later in the data path, as part of the interrupt handler functionality. Advantages of RPS over RSS include no requirements for specific hardware, more advanced traffic distribution filters, and reduced rate of interrupts produced by a NIC. As a downside, RPS increases the rate of inter-processor interrupts (IPIs). *Receive flow steering* (RFS) takes the software-based approach further by accounting for application locality; further performance improvements are achieved by processing interrupt requests by the same cores on which particular network packets will be consumed by the targeted application.

Typical Uses

Typical uses of interrupts include the following: system timers, disk I/O, power-off signals, and traps. Other interrupts exist to transfer data bytes using UARTs or Ethernet; sense key-presses; control motors; or anything else the equipment must do.

Another typical use is to generate periodic interrupts by dividing the output of a crystal oscillator and having an interrupt handler count the interrupts in order for a processor to keep time. These periodic interrupts are often used by the OS's task scheduler to reschedule the priorities of running processes. Some older computers generated periodic interrupts from the power line frequency because it was controlled by the utilities to eliminate long-term drift of electric clocks.

For example, a disk interrupt signals the completion of a data transfer from or to the disk peripheral; a process waiting to read or write a file starts up again. As another example, a power-off interrupt predicts or requests a loss of power, allowing the computer equipment to perform an orderly shut-down. Also, interrupts are used in typeahead features for buffering events like keystrokes.

Protected Mode

In computing, protected mode, also called protected virtual address mode, is an operational mode of x86-compatible central processing units (CPUs). It allows system software to use features such as virtual memory, paging and safe multi-tasking designed to increase an operating system's control over application software.

When a processor that supports x86 protected mode is powered on, it begins executing instructions in real mode, in order to maintain backward compatibility with earlier x86 processors. Protected mode may only be entered after the system software sets up several descriptor tables and enables the Protection Enable (PE) bit in the control register 0 (CR0).

Protected mode was first added to the x86 architecture in 1982, with the release of Intel's 80286 (286) processor, and later extended with the release of the 80386 (386) in 1985. Due to the enhancements added by protected mode, it has become widely adopted and has become the foundation for all subsequent enhancements to the x86 architecture, although many of those enhancements, such as added instructions and new registers, also brought benefits to the real mode.

History

The Intel 8086, the predecessor to the 286, was originally designed with a 20-bit address bus for its memory. This allowed the processor to access 2^{20} bytes of memory, equivalent to 1 megabyte. At the time, 1 megabyte was considered a relatively large amount of memory, so the designers of the IBM Personal Computer reserved the first 640 kilobytes for use by applications and the operating system and the remaining 384 kilobytes for the BIOS (Basic Input/Output System) and memory for add-on devices.

As the cost of memory decreased and memory use increased, the 1 MB limitation became a significant problem. Intel intended to solve this limitation along with others with the release of the 286.

The 286

The initial protected mode, released with the 286, was not widely used; for example, it was used by Microsoft Xenix (around 1984), Coherent and Minix. Several shortcomings such as the inability to access the BIOS or DOS calls due to inability to switch back to real mode without resetting the processor prevented widespread usage. Acceptance was additionally hampered by the fact that the 286 only allowed memory access in 16 bit segments via each of four segment registers, meaning only $4*2^{16}$ bytes, equivalent to 256 kilobytes, could be accessed at a time. Because changing a segment register in protected mode caused a 6-byte segment descriptor to be loaded into the CPU from memory, the segment register load instruction took many tens of processor cycles, making it much slower than on the 8086; therefore, the strategy of computing segment addresses on-the-fly in order to access data structures larger than 128 kilobytes (the combined size of the two data segments) became impractical, even for those few programmers who had mastered it on the 8086/8088.

The 286 maintained backwards compatibility with its precursor the 8086 by initially entering real mode on power up. Real mode functioned virtually identically to the 8086, allowing the vast majority of existing 8086 software to run unmodified on the newer 286. Real mode also served as a more basic mode in which protected mode could be set up, solving a sort of chicken-and-egg problem. To access the extended functionality of the 286, the operating system would set up some tables in memory that controlled memory access in protected mode, set the addresses of those tables into some special registers of the processor, and then set the processor into protected mode. This enabled 24 bit addressing which allowed the processor to access 2^{24} bytes of memory, equivalent to 16 megabytes.

The 386

With the release of the 386 in 1985, many of the issues preventing widespread adoption of the previous protected mode were addressed. The 386 was released with an address bus size of 32 bits, which allows for 2^{32} bytes of memory accessing, equivalent to 4 gigabytes. The segment sizes were also increased to 32 bits, meaning that the full address space of 4 gigabytes could be accessed without the need to switch between multiple segments. In addition to the increased size of the address bus and segment registers, many other new features were added with the intention of increasing operational security and stability. Protected mode is now used in virtually all modern operating systems which run on the x86 architecture, such as Microsoft Windows, Linux, and many others.

An Intel 80386 microprocessor

Furthermore, learning from the failures of the 286 protected mode to satisfy the needs for multiuser DOS, Intel added a separate virtual 8086 mode, which allowed multiple virtualized 8086 processors to be emulated on the 386. Hardware support required for virtualizing the protected mode itself, however, had to wait for another 20 years.

386 Additions to Protected Mode

With the release of the 386, the following additional features were added to protected mode:

- Paging

- 32-bit physical and virtual address space (The 32-bit physical address space is not present on the 80386SX, and other 386 processor variants which use the older 286 bus.)

- 32-bit segment offsets

- Ability to switch back to real mode without resetting

- Virtual 8086 mode

Entering and Exiting Protected Mode

Until the release of the 386, protected mode did not offer a direct method to switch back into real mode once protected mode was entered. IBM devised a workaround (implemented in the IBM

AT) which involved resetting the CPU via the keyboard controller and saving the system registers, stack pointer and often the interrupt mask in the real-time clock chip's RAM. This allowed the BIOS to restore the CPU to a similar state and begin executing code before the reset. Later, a triple fault was used to reset the 286 CPU, which was a lot faster and cleaner than the keyboard controller method (and does not depend on IBM AT-compatible hardware, but will work on any 80286 CPU in any system).

To enter protected mode, the Global Descriptor Table (GDT) must first be created with a minimum of three entries: a null descriptor, a code segment descriptor and data segment descriptor. In an IBM-compatible machine, the A20 line (21st address line) also must be enabled to allow the use of all the address lines so that the CPU can access beyond 1 megabyte of memory (Only the first 20 are allowed to be used after power-up, to guarantee compatibility with older software written for the Intel 8088-based IBM PC and PC/XT models). After performing those two steps, the PE bit must be set in the CR0 register and a far jump must be made to clear the prefetch input queue.

```
; set PE bit

mov eax, cr0

or eax, 1

mov cr0, eax

; far jump (cs = selector of code segment)

jmp cs:@pm

@pm:

; Now we are in PM.
```

With the release of the 386, protected mode could be exited by loading the segment registers with real mode values, disabling the A20 line and clearing the PE bit in the CR0 register, without the need to perform the initial setup steps required with the 286.

Features

Protected mode has a number of features designed to enhance an operating system's control over application software, in order to increase security and system stability. These additions allow the operating system to function in a way that would be significantly more difficult or even impossible without proper hardware support.

Privilege Levels

In protected mode, there are four privilege levels or rings, numbered from 0 to 3, with ring 0 being the most privileged and 3 being the least. The use of rings allows for system software to restrict tasks from accessing data, call gates or executing privileged instructions. In most environments, the operating system and some device drivers run in ring 0 and applications run in ring 3.

Real mode Application Compatibility

According to the *Intel 80286 Programmer's Reference Manual*,

> ...the 80286 remains upwardly compatible with most 8086 and 80186 application programs. Most 8086 application programs can be re-compiled or re-assembled and executed on the 80286 in Protected Mode.

For the most part, the binary compatibility with real-mode code, the ability to access up to 16 MB of physical memory, and 1 GB of virtual memory, were the most apparent changes to application programmers. This was not without its limitations, if an application utilized or relied on any of the techniques below it wouldn'trun:

- Segment arithmetic
- Privileged instructions
- Direct hardware access
- Writing to a code segment
- Executing data
- Overlapping segments
- Use of BIOS functions, due to the BIOS interrupts being reserved by Intel

In reality, almost all DOS application programs violated these rules. Due to these limitations, virtual 8086 mode was introduced with the 386. Despite such potential setbacks, Windows 3.0 and its successors can take advantage of the binary compatibility with real mode to run many Windows 2.x (Windows 2.0 and Windows 2.1x) applications, which run in real mode in Windows 2.x, in protected mode.

Virtual 8086 Mode

With the release of the 386, protected mode offers what the Intel manuals call *virtual 8086 mode*. Virtual 8086 mode is designed to allow code previously written for the 8086 to run unmodified and concurrently with other tasks, without compromising security or system stability.

Virtual 8086 mode, however, is not completely backwards compatible with all programs. Programs that require segment manipulation, privileged instructions, direct hardware access, or use self-modifying code will generate an exception that must be served by the operating system. In addition, applications running in virtual 8086 mode generate a trap with the use of instructions that involve input/output (I/O), which can negatively impact performance.

Due to these limitations, some programs originally designed to run on the 8086 cannot be run in virtual 8086 mode. As a result, system software is forced to either compromise system security or backwards compatibility when dealing with legacy software. An example of such a compromise can be seen with the release of Windows NT, which dropped backwards compatibility for "ill-behaved" DOS applications.

Segment Addressing

In real mode each logical address points directly into physical memory location, every logical address consists of two 16 bit parts: The segment part of the logical address contains the base address of a segment with a granularity of 16 bytes, i.e. a segments may start at physical address

0, 16, 32, ..., 2^{20}-16. The offset part of the logical address contains an offset inside the segment, i.e. the physical address can be calculated as physical_address : = segment_part × 16 + offset (if the address line A20 is enabled), respectively (segment_part × 16 + offset) mod 2^{20} (if A20 is off) Every segment has a size of 2^{16} bytes.

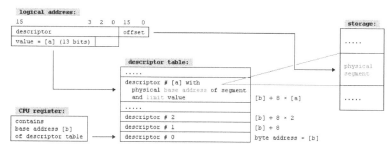

Virtual segments of 80286

Protected Mode

In protected mode, the segment_part is replaced by a 16-bit *selector*, in which the 13 upper bits (bit 3 to bit 15) contain the index of an *entry* inside a *descriptor table*. The next bit (bit 2) specifies whether the operation is used with the GDT or the LDT. The lowest two bits (bit 1 and bit 0) of the selector are combined to define the privilege of the request, where the values of 0 and 3 represent the highest and the lowest priority, respectively. This means that the byte offset of descriptors in the descriptor table is the same as the 16-bit selector, provided the lower three bits are zeroed.

The descriptor table entry defines the real *linear* address of the segment, a limit value for the segment size, and some attribute bits (flags).

286

The segment address inside the descriptor table entry has a length of 24 bits so every byte of the physical memory can be defined as bound of the segment. The limit value inside the descriptor table entry has a length of 16 bits so segment length can be between 1 byte and 2^{16} byte. The calculated linear address equals the physical memory address.

386

The segment address inside the descriptor table entry is expanded to 32 bits so every byte of the physical memory can be defined as bound of the segment. The limit value inside the descriptor table entry is expanded to 20 bits and completed with a granularity flag (G-bit, for short):

- If G-bit is zero limit has a granularity of 1 byte, i.e. segment size may be 1, 2, ..., 2^{20} bytes.

- If G-bit is one limit has a granularity of 2^{12} bytes, i.e. segment size may be 1×2^{12}, 2×2^{12}, ..., $2^{20} \times 2^{12}$ bytes. If paging is off, the calculated linear address equals the physical memory address. If paging is on, the calculated linear address is used as input of paging.

The 386 processor also uses 32 bit values for the address offset.

For maintaining compatibility with 286 protected mode a new default flag (D-bit, for short) was added. If the D-bit of a code segment is off (0) all commands inside this segment will be interpreted as 16-bit commands by default; if it is on (1), they will be interpreted as 32-bit commands.

Structure of Segment Descriptor Entry

B	Bits	80286	80386	B			Attribute flags #2
0	00..07, 0..7	limit	bits 0..15 of limit	0	52	4	unused, available for operating system
1	08..15, 0..7			1	53	5	reserved, should be zero
2	16..23, 0..7	base address	bits 0..23 of base address	2	54	6	default flag / D-bit
3	24..31, 0..7			3	55	7	granularity flag / G-bit
4	32..39, 0..7			4			
5	40..47, 0..7	attribute flags #1		5			
6	48..51, 0..3	unused	bits 16..19 of limit	6			
	52..55, 4..7		attribute flags #2				
7	56..63, 0..7		bits 24..31 of base address	7			

a. Byte offset inside entry.

b. First range is the bit offset inside entry; second range is the bit offset inside byte.

Paging

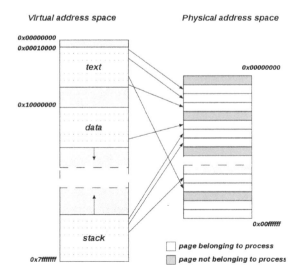

Common method of using paging to create a virtual address space

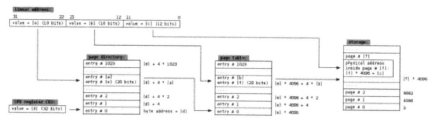

Paging (on Intel 80386) with page size of 4K

In addition to adding virtual 8086 mode, the 386 also added paging to protected mode. Through paging, system software can restrict and control a task's access to pages, which are sections of memory. In many operating systems, paging is used to create an independent virtual address space for each task, preventing one task from manipulating the memory of another. Paging also allows for pages to be moved out of primary storage and onto a slower and larger secondary storage, such as a hard disk drive. This allows for more memory to be used than physically available in primary storage.

The x86 architecture allows control of pages through two arrays: page directories and page tables. Originally, a page directory was the size of one page, four kilobytes, and contained 1,024 page directory entries (PDE), although subsequent enhancements to the x86 architecture have added the ability to use larger page sizes. Each PDE contained a pointer to a page table. A page table was also originally four kilobytes in size and contained 1,024 page table entries (PTE). Each PTE contained a pointer to the actual page's physical address and are only used when the four-kilobyte pages are used. At any given time, only one page directory may be in active use.

Multitasking

Through the use of the rings, privileged call gates, and the Task State Segment (TSS), introduced with the 286, preemptive multitasking was made possible on the x86 architecture. The TSS allows general-purpose registers, segment selector fields, and stacks to all be modified without affecting those of another task. The TSS also allows a task's privilege level, and I/O port permissions to be independent of another task's.

In many operating systems, the full features of the TSS are not used. This is commonly due to portability concerns or due to the performance issues created with hardware task switches. As a result, many operating systems use both hardware and software to create a multitasking system.

Operating Systems

Operating systems like OS/2 1.x try to switch the processor between protected and real modes. This is both slow and unsafe, because a real mode program can easily crash a computer. OS/2 1.x defines restrictive programming rules allowing a *Family API* or *bound* program to run in either real or protected mode. Some early Unix operating systems, OS/2 1.x, and Windows used this mode.

Windows 3.0 was able to run real mode programs in 16-bit protected mode; when switching to protected mode, it decided to preserve the single privilege level model that was used in real mode, which is why Windows applications and DLLs can hook interrupts and do direct hardware access. That lasted through the Windows 9x series. If a Windows 1.x or 2.x program is written properly and avoids segment arithmetic, it will run the same way in both real and protected modes. Windows programs generally avoid segment arithmetic because Windows implements a software virtual memory scheme, moving program code and data in memory when programs are not running, so manipulating absolute addresses is dangerous; programs should only keep handles to memory blocks when not running. Starting an old program while Windows 3.0 is running in protected mode triggers a warning dialog, suggesting to either run Windows in real mode or to obtain an updated version of the application. Updating well-behaved programs using the MARK utility with the MEMORY parameter avoids this dialog. It is not possible to have some GUI programs running in 16-bit protected mode and other GUI programs running in real mode. In Windows 3.1, real mode was no longer supported and could not be accessed.

In modern operating systems, 16-bit protected mode is still used for running applications, e.g. DPMI compatible DOS extender programs (through virtual DOS machines) or Windows 3.x applications (through the Windows on Windows subsystem) and certain classes of device drivers (e.g. for changing the screen-resolution using BIOS functionality) in OS/2 2.0 and later, all under control of a 32-bit kernel.

Memory Management

Memory management is a form of resource management applied to computer memory. The essential requirement of memory management is to provide ways to dynamically allocate portions of memory to programs at their request, and free it for reuse when no longer needed. This is critical to any advanced computer system where more than a single process might be underway at any time.

Several methods have been devised that increase the effectiveness of memory management. Virtual memory systems separate the memory addresses used by a process from actual physical addresses, allowing separation of processes and increasing the size of the virtual address space beyond the available amount of RAM using paging or swapping to secondary storage. The quality of the virtual memory manager can have an extensive effect on overall system performance.

Levels

Modern general-purpose computer systems manage memory at two levels:

- operating system level, and

- application level.

Application

Application-level memory management is generally categorized as either automatic memory management, usually involving garbage collection (computer science), or manual memory management.

Dynamic Memory Allocation

External fragmentation

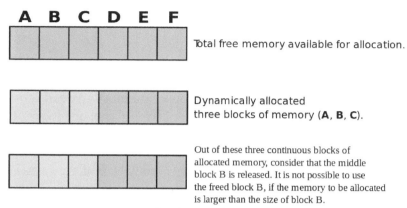

An example of external fragmentation

Details

The task of fulfilling an allocation request consists of locating a block of unused memory of sufficient size. Memory requests are satisfied by allocating portions from a large pool of memory called the *heap* or *free store*.[a] At any given time, some parts of the heap are in use, while some are "free" (unused) and thus available for future allocations.

Several issues complicate the implementation, such as external fragmentation, which arises when there are many small gaps between allocated memory blocks, which invalidates their use for an allocation request. The allocator's metadata can also inflate the size of (individually) small allocations. This is often managed by chunking. The memory management system must track outstanding allocations to ensure that they do not overlap and that no memory is ever "lost" as a memory leak.

Efficiency

The specific dynamic memory allocation algorithm implemented can impact performance significantly. A study conducted in 1994 by Digital Equipment Corporation illustrates the overheads involved for a variety of allocators. The lowest average instruction path length required to allocate a single memory slot was 52 (as measured with an instruction level profiler on a variety of software).

Implementations

Since the precise location of the allocation is not known in advance, the memory is accessed indirectly, usually through a pointer reference. The specific algorithm used to organize the memory area and allocate and deallocate chunks is interlinked with the kernel, and may use any of the following methods:

Fixed-size Blocks Allocation

Fixed-size blocks allocation, also called memory pool allocation, uses a free list of fixed-size blocks of memory (often all of the same size). This works well for simple embedded systems where no large objects need to be allocated, but suffers from fragmentation, especially with long memory addresses. However, due to the significantly reduced overhead this method can substantially improve performance for objects that need frequent allocation / de-allocation and is often used in video games.

Buddy Blocks

In this system, memory is allocated into several pools of memory instead of just one, where each pool represents blocks of memory of a certain power of two in size, or blocks of some other convenient size progression. All blocks of a particular size are kept in a sorted linked list or tree and all new blocks that are formed during allocation are added to their respective memory pools for later use. If a smaller size is requested than is available, the smallest available size is selected and split. One of the resulting parts is selected, and the process repeats until the request is complete. When a block is allocated, the allocator will start with the smallest sufficiently large block to avoid needlessly breaking blocks. When a block is freed, it is compared to its buddy. If they are both free, they are combined and placed in the correspondingly larger-sized buddy-block list.

Systems with Virtual Memory

Virtual memory is a method of decoupling the memory organization from the physical hardware. The applications operate memory via *virtual addresses*. Each time an attempt to access stored data is made, virtual memory data orders translate the virtual address to a *physical address*. In this way addition of virtual memory enables granular control over memory systems and methods of access.

In virtual memory systems the operating system limits how a process can access the memory. This feature, called memory protection, can be used to disallow a process to read or write to memory that is not allocated to it, preventing malicious or malfunctioning code in one program from interfering with the operation of another.

Even though the memory allocated for specific processes is normally isolated, processes sometimes need to be able to share information. Shared memory is one of the fastest techniques for inter-process communication.

Memory is usually classified by access rate into primary storage and secondary storage. Memory management systems, among other operations, also handle the moving of information between these two levels of memory.

Virtual Memory

In computing, virtual memory is a memory management technique that is implemented using both hardware and software. It maps memory addresses used by a program, called *virtual addresses*, into *physical addresses* in computer memory. Main storage as seen by a process or task appears as a contiguous address space or collection of contiguous segments. The operating system manages virtual address spaces and the assignment of real memory to virtual memory. Address translation hardware in the CPU, often referred to as a memory management unit or *MMU*, automatically translates virtual addresses to physical addresses. Software within the operating system may extend these capabilities to provide a virtual address space that can exceed the capacity of real memory and thus reference more memory than is physically present in the computer.

The primary benefits of virtual memory include freeing applications from having to manage a shared memory space, increased security due to memory isolation, and being able to conceptually use more memory than might be physically available, using the technique of paging.

Properties

Virtual memory makes application programming easier by hiding fragmentation of physical memory; by delegating to the kernel the burden of managing the memory hierarchy (eliminating the need for the program to handle overlays explicitly); and, when each process is run in its own dedicated address space, by obviating the need to relocate program code or to access memory with relative addressing.

Memory virtualization can be considered a generalization of the concept of virtual memory.

Usage

Virtual memory is an integral part of a modern computer architecture; implementations usually require hardware support, typically in the form of a memory management unit built into the CPU. While not necessary, emulators and virtual machines can employ hardware support to increase performance of their virtual memory implementations. Consequently, older operating systems, such as those for the mainframes of the 1960s, and those for personal computers of the early to mid-1980s (e.g., DOS), generally have no virtual memory functionality, though notable exceptions for mainframes of the 1960s include:

- the Atlas Supervisor for the Atlas
- THE multiprogramming system for the Electrologica X8 (software based virtual memory without hardware support)
- MCP for the Burroughs B5000
- MTS, TSS/360 and CP/CMS for the IBM System/360 Model 67
- Multics for the GE 645
- the Time Sharing Operating System for the RCA Spectra 70/46

and the operating system for the Apple Lisa is an example of a personal computer operating system of the 1980s that features virtual memory.

During the 1960s and early 70s, computer memory was very expensive. The introduction of virtual memory provided an ability for software systems with large memory demands to run on computers with less real memory. The savings from this provided a strong incentive to switch to virtual memory for all systems. The additional capability of providing virtual address spaces added another level of security and reliability, thus making virtual memory even more attractive to the market place.

Most modern operating systems that support virtual memory also run each process in its own dedicated address space. Each program thus appears to have sole access to the virtual memory. However, some older operating systems (such as OS/VS1 and OS/VS2 SVS) and even modern ones (such as IBM i) are single address space operating systems that run all processes in a single address space composed of virtualized memory.

Embedded systems and other special-purpose computer systems that require very fast and/or very consistent response times may opt not to use virtual memory due to decreased determinism; virtual memory systems trigger unpredictable traps that may produce unwanted "jitter" during I/O operations. This is because embedded hardware costs are often kept low by implementing all such operations with software (a technique called bit-banging) rather than with dedicated hardware.

History

In the 1940s and 1950s, all larger programs had to contain logic for managing primary and secondary storage, such as overlaying. Virtual memory was therefore introduced not only to extend primary memory, but to make such an extension as easy as possible for programmers to use. To allow for multiprogramming and multitasking, many early systems divided memory between multiple programs without virtual memory, such as early models of the PDP-10 via registers.

The concept of virtual memory was first developed by German physicist Fritz-Rudolf Güntsch at the Technische Universität Berlin in 1956 in his doctoral thesis, *Logical Design of a Digital Computer with Multiple Asynchronous Rotating Drums and Automatic High Speed Memory Operation*; it described a machine with 6 100-word blocks of primary core memory and an address space of 1,000 100-word blocks, with hardware automatically moving blocks between primary memory and secondary drum memory. Paging was first implemented at the University of Manchester as a way to extend the Atlas Computer's working memory by combining its 16 thousand words of primary core memory with an additional 96 thousand words of secondary drum memory. The first Atlas was commissioned in 1962 but working prototypes of paging had been developed by 1959.[p2] In 1961, the Burroughs Corporation independently released the first commercial computer with virtual memory, the B5000, with segmentation rather than paging.

Before virtual memory could be implemented in mainstream operating systems, many problems had to be addressed. Dynamic address translation required expensive and difficult to build specialized hardware; initial implementations slowed down access to memory slightly. There were worries that new system-wide algorithms utilizing secondary storage would be less effective than previously used application-specific algorithms. By 1969, the debate over virtual memory for commercial computers was over; an IBM research team led by David Sayre showed that their virtual memory overlay system consistently worked better than the best manually controlled systems. The first minicomputer to introduce virtual memory was the Norwegian NORD-1; during the 1970s, other minicomputers implemented virtual memory, notably VAX models running VMS.

Virtual memory was introduced to the x86 architecture with the protected mode of the Intel 80286 processor, but its segment swapping technique scaled poorly to larger segment sizes. The Intel

80386 introduced paging support underneath the existing segmentation layer, enabling the page fault exception to chain with other exceptions without double fault. However, loading segment descriptors was an expensive operation, causing operating system designers to rely strictly on paging rather than a combination of paging and segmentation.

Paged

Nearly all implementations of virtual memory divide a virtual address space into pages, blocks of contiguous virtual memory addresses. Pages on contemporary systems are usually at least 4 kilobytes in size; systems with large virtual address ranges or amounts of real memory generally use larger page sizes.

Page Tables

Page tables are used to translate the virtual addresses seen by the application into physical addresses used by the hardware to process instructions; such hardware that handles this specific translation is often known as the memory management unit. Each entry in the page table holds a flag indicating whether the corresponding page is in real memory or not. If it is in real memory, the page table entry will contain the real memory address at which the page is stored. When a reference is made to a page by the hardware, if the page table entry for the page indicates that it is not currently in real memory, the hardware raises a page fault exception, invoking the paging supervisor component of the operating system.

Systems can have one page table for the whole system, separate page tables for each application and segment, a tree of page tables for large segments or some combination of these. If there is only one page table, different applications running at the same time use different parts of a single range of virtual addresses. If there are multiple page or segment tables, there are multiple virtual address spaces and concurrent applications with separate page tables redirect to different real addresses.

Paging Supervisor

This part of the operating system creates and manages page tables. If the hardware raises a page fault exception, the paging supervisor accesses secondary storage, returns the page that has the virtual address that resulted in the page fault, updates the page tables to reflect the physical location of the virtual address and tells the translation mechanism to restart the request.

When all physical memory is already in use, the paging supervisor must free a page in primary storage to hold the swapped-in page. The supervisor uses one of a variety of page replacement algorithms such as least recently used to determine which page to free.

Pinned Pages

Operating systems have memory areas that are *pinned* (never swapped to secondary storage). Other terms used are *locked*, *fixed*, or *wired* pages. For example, interrupt mechanisms rely on an array of pointers to their handlers, such as I/O completion and page fault. If the pages containing these pointers or the code that they invoke were pageable, interrupt-handling would become far more complex and time-consuming, particularly in the case of page fault interruptions. Hence, some part of the page table structures is not pageable.

Some pages may be pinned for short periods of time, others may be pinned for long periods of time, and still others may need to be permanently pinned. For example:

- The paging supervisor code and drivers for secondary storage devices on which pages reside must be permanently pinned, as otherwise paging wouldn't even work because the necessary code wouldn't be available.

- Timing-dependent components may be pinned to avoid variable paging delays.

- Data buffers that are accessed directly by peripheral devices that use direct memory access or I/O channels must reside in pinned pages while the I/O operation is in progress because such devices and the buses to which they are attached expect to find data buffers located at physical memory addresses; regardless of whether the bus has a memory management unit for I/O, transfers cannot be stopped if a page fault occurs and then restarted when the page fault has been processed.

In IBM's operating systems for System/370 and successor systems, the term is "fixed", and such pages may be long-term fixed, or may be short-term fixed, or may be unfixed (i.e., pageable). System control structures are often long-term fixed (measured in wall-clock time, i.e., time measured in seconds, rather than time measured in fractions of one second) whereas I/O buffers are usually short-term fixed (usually measured in significantly less than wall-clock time, possibly for tens of milliseconds). Indeed, the OS has a special facility for "fast fixing" these short-term fixed data buffers (fixing which is performed without resorting to a time-consuming Supervisor Call instruction).

Multics used the term "wired". OpenVMS and Windows refer to pages temporarily made nonpageable (as for I/O buffers) as "locked", and simply "nonpageable" for those that are never pageable.

Virtual-real Operation

In OS/VS1 and similar OSes, some parts of systems memory are managed in "virtual-real" mode, called "V=R". In this mode every virtual address corresponds to the same real address. This mode is used for interrupt mechanisms, for the paging supervisor and page tables in older systems, and for application programs using non-standard I/O management. For example, IBM's z/OS has 3 modes (virtual-virtual, virtual-real and virtual-fixed).

Thrashing

When paging and page stealing are used, a problem called "thrashing" can occur, in which the computer spends an unsuitably large amount of time transferring pages to and from a backing store, hence slowing down useful work. A task's working set is the minimum set of pages that should be in memory in order for it to make useful progress. Thrashing occurs when there is insufficient memory available to store the working sets of all active programs. Adding real memory is the simplest response, but improving application design, scheduling, and memory usage can help. Another solution is to reduce the number of active tasks on the system. This reduces demand on real memory by swapping out the entire working set of one or more processes.

Segmented

Some systems, such as the Burroughs B5500, use segmentation instead of paging, dividing virtual address spaces into variable-length segments. A virtual address here consists of a segment number and an offset within the segment. The Intel 80286 supports a similar segmentation scheme as an option, but it is rarely used. Segmentation and paging can be used together by dividing each segment into pages; systems with this memory structure, such as Multics and IBM System/38, are usually paging-predominant, segmentation providing memory protection.

In the Intel 80386 and later IA-32 processors, the segments reside in a 32-bit linear, paged address space. Segments can be moved in and out of that space; pages there can "page" in and out of main memory, providing two levels of virtual memory; few if any operating systems do so, instead using only paging. Early non-hardware-assisted x86 virtualization solutions combined paging and segmentation because x86 paging offers only two protection domains whereas a VMM / guest OS / guest applications stack needs three. The difference between paging and segmentation systems is not only about memory division; segmentation is visible to user processes, as part of memory model semantics. Hence, instead of memory that looks like a single large space, it is structured into multiple spaces.

This difference has important consequences; a segment is not a page with variable length or a simple way to lengthen the address space. Segmentation that can provide a single-level memory model in which there is no differentiation between process memory and file system consists of only a list of segments (files) mapped into the process's potential address space.

This is not the same as the mechanisms provided by calls such as mmap and Win32's MapViewOf-File, because inter-file pointers do not work when mapping files into semi-arbitrary places. In Multics, a file (or a segment from a multi-segment file) is mapped into a segment in the address space, so files are always mapped at a segment boundary. A file's linkage section can contain pointers for which an attempt to load the pointer into a register or make an indirect reference through it causes a trap. The unresolved pointer contains an indication of the name of the segment to which the pointer refers and an offset within the segment; the handler for the trap maps the segment into the address space, puts the segment number into the pointer, changes the tag field in the pointer so that it no longer causes a trap, and returns to the code where the trap occurred, re-executing the instruction that caused the trap. This eliminates the need for a linker completely and works when different processes map the same file into different places in their private address spaces.

Address Space Swapping

Some operating systems provide for swapping entire address spaces, in addition to whatever facilities they have for paging and segmentation. When this occurs, the OS writes those pages and segments currently in real memory to swap files. In a swap-in, the OS reads back the data from the swap files but does not automatically read back pages that had been paged out at the time of the swap out operation.

IBM's MVS, from OS/VS2 Release 2 through z/OS, provides for marking an address space as unswappable; doing so does not pin any pages in the address space. This can be done for the duration of a job by entering the name of an eligible main program in the Program Properties Table with an unswappable flag. In addition, privileged code can temporarily make an address space unswappable With a SYSEVENT Supervisor Call instruction (SVC); certain changes in the address space properties require that the OS swap it out and then swap it back in, using SYSEVENT TRANSWAP.

Preemption (Computing)

In computing, preemption is the act of temporarily interrupting a task being carried out by a computer system, without requiring its cooperation, and with the intention of resuming the task at a later time. Such changes of the executed task are known as context switches. It is normally carried out by a privileged task or part of the system known as a preemptive scheduler, which has the power to preempt, or interrupt, and later resume, other tasks in the system.

User Mode and Kernel Mode

In any given system design, some operations performed by the system may not be preemptible. This usually applies to kernel functions and service interrupts which, if not permitted to run to completion, would tend to produce race conditions resulting in deadlock. Barring the scheduler from preempting tasks while they are processing kernel functions simplifies the kernel design at the expense of system responsiveness. The distinction between user mode and kernel mode, which determines privilege level within the system, may also be used to distinguish whether a task is currently preemptible.

Most modern systems have preemptive kernels, designed to permit tasks to be preempted even when in kernel mode. Examples of such systems are Solaris 2.0/SunOS 5.0, Windows NT, Linux kernel (2.6.x and newer), AIX and some BSD systems (NetBSD, since version 5).

Preemptive Multitasking

The term preemptive multitasking is used to distinguish a multitasking operating system, which permits preemption of tasks, from a cooperative multitasking system wherein processes or tasks must be explicitly programmed to yield when they do not need system resources.

In simple terms: Preemptive multitasking involves the use of an interrupt mechanism which suspends the currently executing process and invokes a scheduler to determine which process should execute next. Therefore, all processes will get some amount of CPU time at any given time.

In preemptive multitasking, the operating system kernel can also initiate a context switch to satisfy the scheduling policy's priority constraint, thus preempting the active task. In general, preemption means "prior seizure of". When the high priority task at that instance seizes the currently running task, it is known as preemptive scheduling.

The term "preemptive multitasking" is sometimes mistakenly used when the intended meaning is more specific, referring instead to the class of scheduling policies known as *time-shared scheduling*, or *time-sharing*.

Preemptive multitasking allows the computer system to more reliably guarantee each process a regular "slice" of operating time. It also allows the system to rapidly deal with important external events like incoming data, which might require the immediate attention of one or another process.

At any specific time, processes can be grouped into two categories: those that are waiting for input or output (called "I/O bound"), and those that are fully utilizing the CPU ("CPU bound"). In early systems, processes would often "poll", or "busywait" while waiting for requested input (such as disk, keyboard or network input). During this time, the process was not performing useful work, but still maintained complete control of the CPU. With the advent of interrupts and preemptive multitasking, these I/O bound processes could be "blocked", or put on hold, pending the arrival of the necessary data, allowing other processes to utilize the CPU. As the arrival of the requested data would generate an interrupt, blocked processes could be guaranteed a timely return to execution.

Although multitasking techniques were originally developed to allow multiple users to share a single machine, it soon became apparent that multitasking was useful regardless of the number of users. Many operating systems, from mainframes down to single-user personal computers and no-user control systems (like those in robotic spacecraft), have recognized the usefulness of multitasking support for a variety of reasons. Multitasking makes it possible for a single user to run multiple applications at the same time, or to run "background" processes while retaining control of the computer.

Time Slice

The period of time for which a process is allowed to run in a preemptive multitasking system is generally called the *time slice* or *quantum*; this relates to the instruction cycle, which is the quantum of hardware execution. The scheduler is run once every time slice to choose the next process to run. The length of each time slice can be critical to balancing system performance vs process responsiveness - if the time slice is too short then the scheduler will consume too much processing time, but if the time slice is too long, processes will take longer to respond to input.

An interrupt is scheduled to allow the operating system kernel to switch between processes when their time slices expire, effectively allowing the processor's time to be shared between a number of tasks, giving the illusion that it is dealing with these tasks simultaneously, or concurrently. The operating system which controls such a design is called a multi-tasking system.

System Support

Today, nearly all operating systems support preemptive multitasking, including the current versions of Windows, macOS, Linux (including Android) and iOS.

Some of the earliest operating systems available to home users featuring preemptive multitasking were Sinclair QDOS (1984) and Amiga OS (1985). These both ran on Motorola 68000-family microprocessors without memory management. Amiga OS used dynamic loading of relocatable code blocks ("hunks" in Amiga jargon) to multitask preemptively all processes in the same flat address space.

Early PC operating systems such as MS-DOS and PC DOS, did not support multitasking at all, however alternative operating systems such as MP/M-86 (1981) and Concurrent CP/M-86 did support preemptive multitasking. Other Unix-like systems including MINIX and Coherent provided preemptive multitasking on 1980s-era personal computers.

Later DOS versions natively supporting preemptive multitasking/multithreading include Concurrent DOS, Multiuser DOS, Novell DOS (later called Caldera OpenDOS and DR-DOS 7.02 and higher). Since Concurrent DOS 386, they could also run multiple DOS programs concurrently in virtual DOS machines.

The earliest version of Windows to support a limited form of preemptive multitasking was Windows 2.1x, which used the Intel 80386's Virtual 8086 mode to run DOS applications in virtual 8086 machines, commonly known as "DOS boxes", which could be preempted. In Windows 95, 98 and Me, 32-bit applications were made preemptive by running each one in a separate address space, but 16-bit applications remained cooperative for backward compatibility. In Windows 3.1x (protected mode), the kernel and virtual device drivers ran preemptively, but all 16-bit applications were non-preemptive and shared the same address space.

Preemptive multitasking has always been supported by Windows NT (all versions), OS/2 (native applications), Unix and Unix-like systems (such as Linux, BSD and macOS), VMS, OS/360, and many other operating systems designed for use in the academic and medium-to-large business markets.

Although there were plans to upgrade the cooperative multitasking found in the classic Mac OS to a preemptive model (and a preemptive API did exist in Mac OS 9, although in a limited sense), these were abandoned in favor of macOS that, as a hybrid of the old Mac System style and NeXT-STEP, is an operating system based on the Mach kernel and derived in part from BSD, which had always provided Unix-like preemptive multitasking.

Device Driver

In computing, a device driver (commonly referred to simply as a *driver*) is a computer program that operates or controls a particular type of device that is attached to a computer. A driver provides a software interface to hardware devices, enabling operating systems and other computer programs to access hardware functions without needing to know precise details of the hardware being used.

A driver communicates with the device through the computer bus or communications subsystem to which the hardware connects. When a calling program invokes a routine in the driver, the driver issues commands to the device. Once the device sends data back to the driver, the driver may invoke routines in the original calling program. Drivers are hardware dependent and operating-system-specific. They usually provide the interrupt handling required for any necessary asynchronous time-dependent hardware interface.

Purpose

The main purpose of Device drivers is to provide abstraction by acting as translator between a hardware device and the applications or operating systems that use it. Programmers can write the higher-level application code independently of whatever specific hardware the end-user is using.

For example, a high-level application for interacting with a serial port may simply have two functions for "send data" and "receive data". At a lower level, a device driver implementing these functions would communicate to the particular serial port controller installed on a user's computer. The commands needed to control a 16550 UART are much different from the commands needed to control an FTDI serial port converter, but each hardware-specific device driver abstracts these details into the same (or similar) software interface.

Development

Writing a device driver requires an in-depth understanding of how the hardware and the software works for a given platform function. Because drivers require low-level access to hardware functions in order to operate, drivers typically operate in a highly privileged environment and can cause system operational issues if something goes wrong. In contrast, most user-level software on modern operating systems can be stopped without greatly affecting the rest of the system. Even drivers executing in user mode can crash a system if the device is erroneously programmed. These factors make it more difficult and dangerous to diagnose problems.

The task of writing drivers thus usually falls to software engineers or computer engineers who work for hardware-development companies. This is because they have better information than most outsiders about the design of their hardware. Moreover, it was traditionally considered in the hardware manufacturer's interest to guarantee that their clients can use their hardware in an optimum way. Typically, the Logical Device Driver (LDD) is written by the operating system vendor, while the Physical Device Driver (PDD) is implemented by the device vendor. But in recent years non-vendors have written numerous device drivers, mainly for use with free and open source operating systems. In such cases, it is important that the hardware manufacturer provides information on how the device communicates. Although this information can instead be learned by reverse engineering, this is much more difficult with hardware than it is with software.

Microsoft has attempted to reduce system instability due to poorly written device drivers by creating a new framework for driver development, called Windows Driver Foundation (WDF). This includes User-Mode Driver Framework (UMDF) that encourages development of certain types of drivers—primarily those that implement a message-based protocol for communicating with their devices—as user-mode drivers. If such drivers malfunction, they do not cause system instability. The Kernel-Mode Driver Framework (KMDF) model continues to allow development of kernel-mode device drivers, but attempts to provide standard implementations of functions that are known to cause problems, including cancellation of I/O operations, power management, and plug and play device support.

Apple has an open-source framework for developing drivers on Mac OS X called the I/O Kit.

In Linux environments, programmers can build device drivers as parts of the kernel, separately as loadable modules, or as user-mode drivers (for certain types of devices where kernel interfaces exist, such as for USB devices). Makedev includes a list of the devices in Linux: ttyS (terminal), lp (parallel port), hd (disk), loop, sound (these include mixer, sequencer, dsp, and audio)...

The Microsoft Windows .sys files and Linux .ko modules contain loadable device drivers. The advantage of loadable device drivers is that they can be loaded only when necessary and then unloaded, thus saving kernel memory.

Kernel Mode Vs. User Mode

Device drivers, particularly on modern Microsoft Windows platforms, can run in kernel-mode (Ring 0 on x86 CPUs) or in user-mode (Ring 3 on x86 CPUs). The primary benefit of running a driver in user mode is improved stability, since a poorly written user mode device driver cannot crash the system by overwriting kernel memory. On the other hand, user/kernel-mode transitions usually impose a considerable performance overhead, thereby prohibiting user-mode drivers for low latency and high throughput requirements.

Kernel space can be accessed by user module only through the use of system calls. End user programs like the UNIX shell or other GUI-based applications are part of the user space. These applications interact with hardware through kernel supported functions.

Applications

Because of the diversity of modern hardware and operating systems, drivers operate in many different environments. Drivers may interface with:

- Printers
- Video adapters
- Network cards
- Sound cards
- Local buses of various sorts—in particular, for bus mastering on modern systems
- Low-bandwidth I/O buses of various sorts (for pointing devices such as mice, keyboards, USB, etc.)
- Computer storage devices such as hard disk, CD-ROM, and floppy disk buses (ATA, SATA, SCSI)
- Implementing support for different file systems
- Image scanners
- Digital cameras

Common levels of abstraction for device drivers include:

- For hardware:
    - Interfacing directly
    - Writing to or reading from a device control register
    - Using some higher-level interface (e.g. Video BIOS)
    - Using another lower-level device driver (e.g. file system drivers using disk drivers)
    - Simulating work with hardware, while doing something entirely different
- For software:

- ○ Allowing the operating system direct access to hardware resources

- ○ Implementing only primitives

- ○ Implementing an interface for non-driver software (e.g., TWAIN)

- ○ Implementing a language, sometimes quite high-level (e.g., PostScript)

So choosing and installing the correct device drivers for given hardware is often a key component of computer system configuration.

Virtual Device Drivers

Virtual device drivers represent a particular variant of device drivers. They are used to emulate a hardware device, particularly in virtualization environments, for example when a DOS program is run on a Microsoft Windows computer or when a guest operating system is run on, for example, a Xen host. Instead of enabling the guest operating system to dialog with hardware, virtual device drivers take the opposite role and emulate a piece of hardware, so that the guest operating system and its drivers running inside a virtual machine can have the illusion of accessing real hardware. Attempts by the guest operating system to access the hardware are routed to the virtual device driver in the host operating system as e.g., function calls. The virtual device driver can also send simulated processor-level events like interrupts into the virtual machine.

Virtual devices may also operate in a non-virtualized environment. For example, a virtual network adapter is used with a virtual private network, while a virtual disk device is used with iSCSI. A good example for virtual device drivers can be Daemon Tools.

There are several variants of virtual device drivers, such as VxDs, VLMs, VDDs.

Open Drivers

- Printers: CUPS

- RAIDs: CCISS (Compaq Command Interface for SCSI-3 Support)

- Scanners: SANE

- Video: Vidix, Direct Rendering Infrastructure

Solaris descriptions of commonly used device drivers

- fas: Fast/wide SCSI controller

- hme: Fast (10/100 Mbit/s) Ethernet

- isp: Differential SCSI controllers and the SunSwift card

- glm: (Gigabaud Link Module) UltraSCSI controllers

- scsi: Small Computer Serial Interface (SCSI) devices

- sf: soc+ or social Fiber Channel Arbitrated Loop (FCAL)

- soc: SPARC Storage Array (SSA) controllers and the control device

- social: Serial optical controllers for FCAL (soc+)

APIs

- Windows Display Driver Model (WDDM) – the graphic display driver architecture for Windows Vista, Windows 7, Windows 8, and Windows 10.

- Unified Audio Model(UAM)

- Windows Driver Foundation (WDF)

- Windows Driver Model (WDM)

- Network Driver Interface Specification (NDIS) – a standard network card driver API

- Advanced Linux Sound Architecture (ALSA) – as of 2009 the standard Linux sound-driver interface

- Scanner Access Now Easy (SANE) – a public-domain interface to raster-image scanner-hardware

- I/O Kit – an open-source framework from Apple for developing Mac OS X device drivers

- Installable File System (IFS) – a filesystem API for IBM OS/2 and Microsoft Windows NT

- Open Data-Link Interface (ODI) – a network card API similar to NDIS

- Uniform Driver Interface (UDI) – a cross-platform driver interface project

- Dynax Driver Framework (dxd) – C++ open source cross-platform driver framework for KMDF and IOKit

Identifiers

A device on the PCI bus or USB is identified by two IDs which consist of 4 hexadecimal numbers each. The vendor ID identifies the vendor of the device. The device ID identifies a specific device from that manufacturer/vendor.

A PCI device has often an ID pair for the main chip of the device, and also a subsystem ID pair which identifies the vendor, which may be different from the chip manufacturer.

Computer Security

Computer security, also known as cyber security or IT security, is the protection of computer systems from the theft or damage to the hardware, software or the information on them, as well as from disruption or misdirection of the services they provide.

It includes controlling physical access to the hardware, as well as protecting against harm that may come via network access, data and code injection, and due to malpractice by operators, whether intentional, accidental, or due to them being tricked into deviating from secure procedures.

The field is of growing importance due to the increasing reliance on computer systems and the Internet in most societies, wireless networks such as Bluetooth and Wi-Fi – and the growth of "smart" devices, including smartphones, televisions and tiny devices as part of the Internet of Things.

Vulnerabilities and Attacks

A vulnerability is a system susceptibility or flaw. Many vulnerabilities are documented in the Common Vulnerabilities and Exposures (CVE) database. An *exploitable* vulnerability is one for which at least one working attack or "exploit" exists.

To secure a computer system, it is important to understand the attacks that can be made against it, and these threats can typically be classified into one of the categories below:

Backdoors

A backdoor in a computer system, a cryptosystem or an algorithm, is any secret method of bypassing normal authentication or security controls. They may exist for a number of reasons, including by original design or from poor configuration. They may have been added by an authorized party to allow some legitimate access, or by an attacker for malicious reasons; but regardless of the motives for their existence, they create a vulnerability.

Denial-of-service Attack

Denial of service attacks (DoS) are designed to make a machine or network resource unavailable to its intended users. Attackers can deny service to individual victims, such as by deliberately entering a wrong password enough consecutive times to cause the victim account to be locked, or they may overload the capabilities of a machine or network and block all users at once. While a network attack from a single IP address can be blocked by adding a new firewall rule, many forms of Distributed denial of service (DDoS) attacks are possible, where the attack comes from a large number of points – and defending is much more difficult. Such attacks can originate from the zombie computers of a botnet, but a range of other techniques are possible including reflection and amplification attacks, where innocent systems are fooled into sending traffic to the victim.

Direct-access Attacks

An unauthorized user gaining physical access to a computer is most likely able to directly copy data from it. They may also compromise security by making operating system modifications, installing software worms, keyloggers, covert listening devices or using wireless mice. Even when the system is protected by standard security measures, these may be able to be by-passed by booting another operating system or tool from a CD-ROM or other bootable media. Disk encryption and Trusted Platform Module are designed to prevent these attacks.

Eavesdropping

Eavesdropping is the act of surreptitiously listening to a private conversation, typically between hosts on a network. For instance, programs such as Carnivore and NarusInsight have been used by the FBI and NSA to eavesdrop on the systems of internet service providers. Even machines that operate as a closed system (i.e., with no contact to the outside world) can be eavesdropped upon via monitoring the faint electro-magnetic transmissions generated by the hardware; TEMPEST is a specification by the NSA referring to these attacks.

Spoofing

Spoofing, in general, is a fraudulent or malicious practice in which communication is sent from an unknown source disguised as a source known to the receiver. Spoofing is most prevalent in communication mechanisms that lack a high level of security.

Tampering

Tampering describes a malicious modification of products. So-called "Evil Maid" attacks and security services planting of surveillance capability into routers are examples.

Privilege Escalation

Privilege escalation describes a situation where an attacker with some level of restricted access is able to, without authorization, elevate their privileges or access level. So for example a standard computer user may be able to fool the system into giving them access to restricted data; or even to "become root" and have full unrestricted access to a system.

Phishing

Phishing is the attempt to acquire sensitive information such as usernames, passwords, and credit card details directly from users. Phishing is typically carried out by email spoofing or instant messaging, and it often directs users to enter details at a fake website whose look and feel are almost identical to the legitimate one. Preying on a victim's trust, phishing can be classified as a form of social engineering.

Clickjacking

Clickjacking, also known as "UI redress attack" or "User Interface redress attack", is a malicious technique in which an attacker tricks a user into clicking on a button or link on another webpage while the user intended to click on the top level page. This is done using multiple transparent or opaque layers. The attacker is basically "hijacking" the clicks meant for the top level page and routing them to some other irrelevant page, most likely owned by someone else. A similar technique can be used to hijack keystrokes. Carefully drafting a combination of stylesheets, iframes, buttons and text boxes, a user can be led into believing that they are typing the password or other information on some authentic webpage while it is being channeled into an invisible frame controlled by the attacker.

Social Engineering

Social engineering aims to convince a user to disclose secrets such as passwords, card numbers, etc. by, for example, impersonating a bank, a contractor, or a customer.

A popular and profitable cyber scam involves fake CEO emails sent to accounting and finance departments. In early 2016, the FBI reported that the scam has cost US businesses more than $2bn in about two years.

In May 2016, the Milwaukee Bucks NBA team was the victim of this type of cyber scam with a perpetrator impersonating the team's president Peter Feigin, resulting in the handover of all the team's employees' 2015 W-2 tax forms.

Systems at Risk

Computer security is critical in almost any industry which uses computers. Currently, most electronic devices such as computers, laptops and cellphones come with built in firewall security software, but despite this, computers are not 100 percent accurate and dependable to protect our data (Smith, Grabosky & Urbas, 2004.) There are many different ways of hacking into computers. It can be done through a network system, clicking into unknown links, connecting to unfamiliar Wi-Fi, downloading software and files from unsafe sites, power consumption, electromagnetic radiation waves, and many more. However, computers can be protected through well built software and hardware. By having strong internal interactions of properties, software complexity can prevent software crash and security failure.

Financial Systems

Web sites and apps that accept or store credit card numbers, brokerage accounts, and bank account information are prominent hacking targets, because of the potential for immediate financial gain from transferring money, making purchases, or selling the information on the black market. In-store payment systems and ATMs have also been tampered with in order to gather customer account data and PINs.

Utilities and Industrial Equipment

Computers control functions at many utilities, including coordination of telecommunications, the power grid, nuclear power plants, and valve opening and closing in water and gas networks. The Internet is a potential attack vector for such machines if connected, but the Stuxnet worm demonstrated that even equipment controlled by computers not connected to the Internet can be vulnerable to physical damage caused by malicious commands sent to industrial equipment (in that case uranium enrichment centrifuges) which are infected via removable media. In 2014, the Computer Emergency Readiness Team, a division of the Department of Homeland Security, investigated 79 hacking incidents at energy companies. Vulnerabilities in smart meters (many of which use local radio or cellular communications) can cause problems with billing fraud.

Aviation

The aviation industry is very reliant on a series of complex system which could be attacked. A simple power outage at one airport can cause repercussions worldwide, much of the system relies on radio transmissions which could be disrupted, and controlling aircraft over oceans is especially dangerous because radar surveillance only extends 175 to 225 miles offshore. There is also potential for attack from within an aircraft.

In Europe, with the (Pan-European Network Service) and NewPENS, and in the US with the Next-Gen program, air navigation service providers are moving to create their own dedicated networks.

The consequences of a successful attack range from loss of confidentiality to loss of system integrity, which may lead to more serious concerns such as exfiltration of data, network and air traffic control outages, which in turn can lead to airport closures, loss of aircraft, loss of passenger life, damages on the ground and to transportation infrastructure. A successful attack on a military aviation system that controls munitions could have even more serious consequences.

Consumer Devices

Desktop computers and laptops are commonly infected with malware either to gather passwords or financial account information, or to construct a botnet to attack another target. Smart phones, tablet computers, smart watches, and other mobile devices such as Quantified Self devices like activity trackers have also become targets and many of these have sensors such as cameras, microphones, GPS receivers, compasses, and accelerometers which could be exploited, and may collect personal information, including sensitive health information. Wifi, Bluetooth, and cell phone networks on any of these devices could be used as attack vectors, and sensors might be remotely activated after a successful breach.

Home automation devices such as the Nest thermostat are also potential targets.

Large Corporations

Large corporations are common targets. In many cases this is aimed at financial gain through identity theft and involves data breaches such as the loss of millions of clients' credit card details by Home Depot, Staples, and Target Corporation. Medical records have been targeted for use in general identify theft, health insurance fraud, and impersonating patients to obtain prescription drugs for recreational purposes or resale.

Not all attacks are financially motivated however; for example security firm HBGary Federal suffered a serious series of attacks in 2011 from hacktivist group Anonymous in retaliation for the firm's CEO claiming to have infiltrated their group, and Sony Pictures was attacked in 2014 where the motive appears to have been to embarrass with data leaks, and cripple the company by wiping workstations and servers.

Automobiles

If access is gained to a car's internal controller area network, it is possible to disable the brakes and turn the steering wheel. Computerized engine timing, cruise control, anti-lock brakes, seat belt tensioners, door locks, airbags and advanced driver assistance systems make these disruptions possible, and self-driving cars go even further. Connected cars may use wifi and bluetooth to communicate with onboard consumer devices, and the cell phone network to contact concierge and emergency assistance services or get navigational or entertainment information; each of these networks is a potential entry point for malware or an attacker. Researchers in 2011 were even able to use a malicious compact disc in a car's stereo system as a successful attack vector, and cars with built-in voice recognition or remote assistance features have onboard microphones which could be used for eavesdropping.

A 2015 report by U.S. Senator Edward Markey criticized manufacturers' security measures as inadequate, and also highlighted privacy concerns about driving, location, and diagnostic data being collected, which is vulnerable to abuse by both manufacturers and hackers.

Government

Government and military computer systems are commonly attacked by activists and foreign powers. Local and regional government infrastructure such as traffic light controls, police and intelligence agency communications, personnel records, student records, and financial systems are also potential targets as they are now all largely computerized. Passports and government ID cards that control access to facilities which use RFID can be vulnerable to cloning.

Internet of Things and Physical Vulnerabilities

The Internet of Things (IoT) is the network of physical objects such as devices, vehicles, and buildings that are embedded with electronics, software, sensors, and network connectivity that enables them to collect and exchange data – and concerns have been raised that this is being developed without appropriate consideration of the security challenges involved.

While the IoT creates opportunities for more direct integration of the physical world into computer-based systems, it also provides opportunities for misuse. In particular, as the Internet of Things spreads widely, cyber attacks are likely to become an increasingly physical (rather than simply virtual) threat. If a front door's lock is connected to the Internet, and can be locked/unlocked from a phone, then a criminal could enter the home at the press of a button from a stolen or hacked phone. People could stand to lose much more than their credit card numbers in a world controlled by IoT-enabled devices. Thieves have also used electronic means to circumvent non-Internet-connected hotel door locks.

Medical devices have either been successfully attacked or had potentially deadly vulnerabilities demonstrated, including both in-hospital diagnostic equipment and implanted devices including pacemakers and insulin pumps.

Impact of Security Breaches

Serious financial damage has been caused by security breaches, but because there is no standard model for estimating the cost of an incident, the only data available is that which is made public by the organizations involved. "Several computer security consulting firms produce estimates of total worldwide losses attributable to virus and worm attacks and to hostile digital acts in general. The 2003 loss estimates by these firms range from $13 billion (worms and viruses only) to $226 billion (for all forms of covert attacks). The reliability of these estimates is often challenged; the underlying methodology is basically anecdotal."

However, reasonable estimates of the financial cost of security breaches can actually help organizations make rational investment decisions. According to the classic Gordon-Loeb Model analyzing the optimal investment level in information security, one can conclude that the amount a firm spends to protect information should generally be only a small fraction of the expected loss (i.e., the expected value of the loss resulting from a cyber/information security breach).

Attacker Motivation

As with physical security, the motivations for breaches of computer security vary between attackers. Some are thrill-seekers or vandals, others are activists or criminals looking for financial gain. State-sponsored attackers are now common and well resourced, but started with amateurs such as Markus Hess who hacked for the KGB, as recounted by Clifford Stoll, in *The Cuckoo's Egg*.

A standard part of threat modelling for any particular system is to identify what might motivate an attack on that system, and who might be motivated to breach it. The level and detail of precautions will vary depending on the system to be secured. A home personal computer, bank, and classified military network face very different threats, even when the underlying technologies in use are similar.

Computer Protection (Countermeasures)

In computer security a countermeasure is an action, device, procedure, or technique that reduces a threat, a vulnerability, or an attack by eliminating or preventing it, by minimizing the harm it can cause, or by discovering and reporting it so that corrective action can be taken.

Some common countermeasures are listed in the following sections:

Security by Design

Security by design, or alternately secure by design, means that the software has been designed from the ground up to be secure. In this case, security is considered as a main feature.

Some of the techniques in this approach include:

- The principle of least privilege, where each part of the system has only the privileges that are needed for its function. That way even if an attacker gains access to that part, they have only limited access to the whole system.

- Automated theorem proving to prove the correctness of crucial software subsystems.

- Code reviews and unit testing, approaches to make modules more secure where formal correctness proofs are not possible.

- Defense in depth, where the design is such that more than one subsystem needs to be violated to compromise the integrity of the system and the information it holds.

- Default secure settings, and design to "fail secure" rather than "fail insecure". Ideally, a secure system should require a deliberate, conscious, knowledgeable and free decision on the part of legitimate authorities in order to make it insecure.

- Audit trails tracking system activity, so that when a security breach occurs, the mechanism and extent of the breach can be determined. Storing audit trails remotely, where they can only be appended to, can keep intruders from covering their tracks.

- Full disclosure of all vulnerabilities, to ensure that the "window of vulnerability" is kept as short as possible when bugs are discovered.

Security Architecture

The Open Security Architecture organization defines IT security architecture as "the design artifacts that describe how the security controls (security countermeasures) are positioned, and how they relate to the overall information technology architecture. These controls serve the purpose to maintain the system's quality attributes: confidentiality, integrity, availability, accountability and assurance services".

Techopedia defines security architecture as "a unified security design that addresses the necessities and potential risks involved in a certain scenario or environment. It also specifies when and where to apply security controls. The design process is generally reproducible." The key attributes of security architecture are:

- the relationship of different components and how they depend on each other.

- the determination of controls based on risk assessment, good practice, finances, and legal matters.

- the standardization of controls.

Security Measures

A state of computer "security" is the conceptual ideal, attained by the use of the three processes: threat prevention, detection, and response. These processes are based on various policies and system components, which include the following:

- User account access controls and cryptography can protect systems files and data, respectively.

- Firewalls are by far the most common prevention systems from a network security perspective as they can (if properly configured) shield access to internal network services, and block certain kinds of attacks through packet filtering. Firewalls can be both hardware- or software-based.

- Intrusion Detection System (IDS) products are designed to detect network attacks in-progress and assist in post-attack forensics, while audit trails and logs serve a similar function for individual systems.

- "Response" is necessarily defined by the assessed security requirements of an individual system and may cover the range from simple upgrade of protections to notification of legal authorities, counter-attacks, and the like. In some special cases, a complete destruction of the compromised system is favored, as it may happen that not all the compromised resources are detected.

Today, computer security comprises mainly "preventive" measures, like firewalls or an exit procedure. A firewall can be defined as a way of filtering network data between a host or a network and another network, such as the Internet, and can be implemented as software running on the machine, hooking into the network stack (or, in the case of most UNIX-based operating systems such as Linux, built into the operating system kernel) to provide real time filtering and blocking. Another implementation is a so-called "physical firewall", which consists of a separate machine filtering network traffic. Firewalls are common amongst machines that are permanently connected to the Internet.

Some organizations are turning to big data platforms, such as Apache Hadoop, to extend data accessibility and machine learning to detect advanced persistent threats.

However, relatively few organisations maintain computer systems with effective detection systems, and fewer still have organised response mechanisms in place. As result, as Reuters points out: "Companies for the first time report they are losing more through electronic theft of data than physical stealing of assets". The primary obstacle to effective eradication of cyber crime could be traced to excessive reliance on firewalls and other automated "detection" systems. Yet it is basic evidence gathering by using packet capture appliances that puts criminals behind bars.

Vulnerability Management

Vulnerability management is the cycle of identifying, and remediating or mitigating vulnerabilities", especially in software and firmware. Vulnerability management is integral to computer security and network security.

Vulnerabilities can be discovered with a vulnerability scanner, which analyzes a computer system in search of known vulnerabilities, such as open ports, insecure software configuration, and susceptibility to malware

Beyond vulnerability scanning, many organisations contract outside security auditors to run regular penetration tests against their systems to identify vulnerabilities. In some sectors this is a contractual requirement.

Reducing Vulnerabilities

While formal verification of the correctness of computer systems is possible, it is not yet common. Operating systems formally verified include seL4, and SYSGO's PikeOS – but these make up a very small percentage of the market.

Cryptography properly implemented is now virtually impossible to directly break. Breaking them requires some non-cryptographic input, such as a stolen key, stolen plaintext (at either end of the transmission), or some other extra cryptanalytic information.

Two factor authentication is a method for mitigating unauthorized access to a system or sensitive information. It requires "something you know"; a password or PIN, and "something you have"; a card, dongle, cellphone, or other piece of hardware. This increases security as an unauthorized person needs both of these to gain access.

Social engineering and direct computer access (physical) attacks can only be prevented by non-computer means, which can be difficult to enforce, relative to the sensitivity of the information. Training is often involved to help mitigate this risk, but even in a highly disciplined environments (e.g. military organizations), social engineering attacks can still be difficult to foresee and prevent.

It is possible to reduce an attacker's chances by keeping systems up to date with security patches and updates, using a security scanner or/and hiring competent people responsible for security. The effects of data loss/damage can be reduced by careful backing up and insurance.

Hardware Protection Mechanisms

While hardware may be a source of insecurity, such as with microchip vulnerabilities maliciously introduced during the manufacturing process, hardware-based or assisted computer security also offers an alternative to software-only computer security. Using devices and methods such as dongles, trusted platform modules, intrusion-aware cases, drive locks, disabling USB ports, and mobile-enabled access may be considered more secure due to the physical access (or sophisticated backdoor access) required in order to be compromised. Each of these is covered in more detail below.

- USB dongles are typically used in software licensing schemes to unlock software capabilities, but they can also be seen as a way to prevent unauthorized access to a computer or other device's software. The dongle, or key, essentially creates a secure encrypted tunnel between the software application and the key. The principle is that an encryption scheme on the dongle, such as Advanced Encryption Standard (AES) provides a stronger measure of security, since it is harder to hack and replicate the dongle than to simply copy the native software to another machine and use it. Another security application for dongles is to use them for accessing web-based content such as cloud software or Virtual Private Networks (VPNs). In addition, a USB dongle can be configured to lock or unlock a computer.

- Trusted platform modules (TPMs) secure devices by integrating cryptographic capabilities onto access devices, through the use of microprocessors, or so-called computers-on-a-chip. TPMs used in conjunction with server-side software offer a way to detect and authenticate hardware devices, preventing unauthorized network and data access.

- Computer case intrusion detection refers to a push-button switch which is triggered when a computer case is opened. The firmware or BIOS is programmed to show an alert to the operator when the computer is booted up the next time.

- Drive locks are essentially software tools to encrypt hard drives, making them inaccessible to thieves. Tools exist specifically for encrypting external drives as well.

- Disabling USB ports is a security option for preventing unauthorized and malicious access to an otherwise secure computer. Infected USB dongles connected to a network from a computer inside the firewall are considered by the magazine Network World as the most common hardware threat facing computer networks.

- Mobile-enabled access devices are growing in popularity due to the ubiquitous nature of cell phones. Built-in capabilities such as Bluetooth, the newer Bluetooth low energy (LE), Near field communication (NFC) on non-iOS devices and biometric validation such as thumb print readers, as well as QR code reader software designed for mobile devices, offer new, secure ways for mobile phones to connect to access control systems. These control systems provide computer security and can also be used for controlling access to secure buildings.

Secure Operating Systems

One use of the term "computer security" refers to technology that is used to implement secure operating systems. In the 1980s the United States Department of Defense (DoD) used the "Orange Book" standards, but the current international standard ISO/IEC 15408, "Common Criteria" defines a number of progressively more stringent Evaluation Assurance Levels. Many common operating systems meet the EAL4 standard of being "Methodically Designed, Tested and Reviewed", but the formal verification required for the highest levels means that they are uncommon. An example of an EAL6 ("Semiformally Verified Design and Tested") system is Integrity-178B, which is used in the Airbus A380 and several military jets.

Secure Coding

In software engineering, secure coding aims to guard against the accidental introduction of security vulnerabilities. It is also possible to create software designed from the ground up to be secure. Such systems are "secure by design". Beyond this, formal verification aims to prove the correctness of the algorithms underlying a system; important for cryptographic protocols for example.

Capabilities and Access Control Lists

Within computer systems, two of many security models capable of enforcing privilege separation are access control lists (ACLs) and capability-based security. Using ACLs to confine programs has been proven to be insecure in many situations, such as if the host computer can be tricked into indirectly allowing restricted file access, an issue known as the confused deputy problem. It has also been shown that the promise of ACLs of giving access to an object to only one person can never be guaranteed in practice. Both of these problems are resolved by capabilities. This does not mean practical flaws exist in all ACL-based systems, but only that the designers of certain utilities must take responsibility to ensure that they do not introduce flaws.

Capabilities have been mostly restricted to research operating systems, while commercial OSs still use ACLs. Capabilities can, however, also be implemented at the language level, leading to a style of programming that is essentially a refinement of standard object-oriented design. An open source project in the area is the E language.

The most secure computers are those not connected to the Internet and shielded from any interference. In the real world, the most secure systems are operating systems where security is not an add-on.

Response to Breaches

Responding forcefully to attempted security breaches (in the manner that one would for attempted physical security breaches) is often very difficult for a variety of reasons:

- Identifying attackers is difficult, as they are often in a different jurisdiction to the systems they attempt to breach, and operate through proxies, temporary anonymous dial-up accounts, wireless connections, and other anonymising procedures which make backtracing difficult and are often located in yet another jurisdiction. If they successfully breach security, they are often able to delete logs to cover their tracks.

- The sheer number of attempted attacks is so large that organisations cannot spend time pursuing each attacker (a typical home user with a permanent (e.g., cable modem) connection will be attacked at least several times per day, so more attractive targets could be presumed to see many more). Note however, that most of the sheer bulk of these attacks are made by automated vulnerability scanners and computer worms.

- Law enforcement officers are often unfamiliar with information technology, and so lack the skills and interest in pursuing attackers. There are also budgetary constraints. It has been argued that the high cost of technology, such as DNA testing, and improved forensics mean less money for other kinds of law enforcement, so the overall rate of criminals not getting dealt with goes up as the cost of the technology increases. In addition, the identification of attackers across a network may require logs from various points in the network and in many countries, the release of these records to law enforcement (with the exception of being voluntarily surrendered by a network administrator or a system administrator) requires a search warrant and, depending on the circumstances, the legal proceedings required can be drawn out to the point where the records are either regularly destroyed, or the information is no longer relevant.

Notable Attacks and Breaches

Some illustrative examples of different types of computer security breaches are given below.

Robert Morris and the First Computer Worm

In 1988, only 60,000 computers were connected to the Internet, and most were mainframes, mini-computers and professional workstations. On November 2, 1988, many started to slow down, because they were running a malicious code that demanded processor time and that spread itself to other computers – the first internet "computer worm". The software was traced back to 23-year-old Cornell University graduate student Robert Tappan Morris, Jr. who said 'he wanted to count how many machines were connected to the Internet'.

Rome Laboratory

In 1994, over a hundred intrusions were made by unidentified crackers into the Rome Laboratory, the US Air Force's main command and research facility. Using trojan horses, hackers were able to obtain unrestricted access to Rome's networking systems and remove traces of their activities. The intruders were able to obtain classified files, such as air tasking order systems data and furthermore able to penetrate connected networks of National Aeronautics and Space Administration's Goddard Space Flight Center, Wright-Patterson Air Force Base, some Defense contractors, and other private sector organizations, by posing as a trusted Rome center user.

TJX Customer Credit Card Details

In early 2007, American apparel and home goods company TJX announced that it was the victim of an unauthorized computer systems intrusion and that the hackers had accessed a system that stored data on credit card, debit card, check, and merchandise return transactions.

Stuxnet Attack

The computer worm known as Stuxnet reportedly ruined almost one-fifth of Iran's nuclear centrifuges by disrupting industrial programmable logic controllers (PLCs) in a targeted attack generally believed to have been launched by Israel and the United States although neither has publicly acknowledged this.

Global Surveillance Disclosures

In early 2013, massive breaches of computer security by the NSA were revealed, including deliberately inserting a backdoor in a NIST standard for encryption and tapping the links between Google's data centres. These were disclosed by NSA contractor Edward Snowden.

Target and Home Depot Breaches

In 2013 and 2014, a Russian/Ukrainian hacking ring known as "Rescator" broke into Target Corporation computers in 2013, stealing roughly 40 million credit cards, and then Home Depot computers in 2014, stealing between 53 and 56 million credit card numbers. Warnings were delivered at both corporations, but ignored; physical security breaches using self checkout machines are believed to have played a large role. "The malware utilized is absolutely unsophisticated and uninteresting," says Jim Walter, director of threat intelligence operations at security technology company McAfee – meaning that the heists could have easily been stopped by existing antivirus software had administrators responded to the warnings. The size of the thefts has resulted in major attention from state and Federal United States authorities and the investigation is ongoing.

Ashley Madison Breach

In July 2015, a hacker group known as "The Impact Team" successfully breached the extramarital relationship website Ashley Madison. The group claimed that they had taken not only company data but user data as well. After the breach, The Impact Team dumped emails from the company's CEO, to prove their point, and threatened to dump customer data unless the website was taken down permanently. With this initial data release, the group stated "Avid Life Media has been instructed to take Ashley Madison and Established Men offline permanently in all forms, or we will release all customer records, including profiles with all the customers' secret sexual fantasies and matching credit card transactions, real names and addresses, and employee documents and emails. The other websites may stay online." When Avid Life Media, the parent company that created the Ashley Madison website, did not take the site offline, The Impact Group released two more compressed files, one 9.7GB and the second 20GB. After the second data dump, Avid Life Media CEO Noel Biderman resigned, but the website remained functional.

Legal Issues and Global Regulation

Conflict of laws in cyberspace has become a major cause of concern for computer security community. Some of the main challenges and complaints about the antivirus industry are the lack of global web regulations, a global base of common rules to judge, and eventually punish, cyber crimes and cyber criminals. There is no global cyber law and cybersecurity treaty that can be invoked for enforcing global cybersecurity issues.

International legal issues of cyber attacks are complicated in nature. Even if an antivirus firm locates the cyber criminal behind the creation of a particular virus or piece of malware or form of cyber attack, often the local authorities cannot take action due to lack of laws under which to prosecute. Authorship attribution for cyber crimes and cyber attacks is a major problem for all law enforcement agencies.

"[Computer viruses] switch from one country to another, from one jurisdiction to another — moving around the world, using the fact that we don't have the capability to globally police operations like this. So the Internet is as if someone [had] given free plane tickets to all the online criminals of the world." Use of dynamic DNS, fast flux and bullet proof servers have added own complexities to this situation.

Government

The role of the government is to make regulations to force companies and organizations to protect their systems, infrastructure and information from any cyber-attacks, but also to protect its own national infrastructure such as the national power-grid.

The question of whether the government should intervene or not in the regulation of the cyberspace is a very polemical one. Indeed, for as long as it has existed and by definition, the cyberspace is a virtual space free of any government intervention. Where everyone agree that an improvement on cybersecurity is more than vital, is the government the best actor to solve this issue? Many government officials and experts think that the government should step in and that there is a crucial need for regulation, mainly due to the failure of the private sector to solve efficiently the cybersecurity problem. R. Clarke said during a panel discussion at the RSA Security Conference in San Francisco, he believes that the "industry only responds when you threaten regulation. If industry doesn't respond (to the threat), you have to follow through." On the other hand, executives from the private sector agree that improvements are necessary, but think that the government intervention would affect their ability to innovate efficiently.

Actions and Teams in the US

Legislation

The 1986 18 U.S.C. § 1030, more commonly known as the Computer Fraud and Abuse Act is the key legislation. It prohibits unauthorized access or damage of "protected computers" as defined in 18 U.S.C. § 1030(e)(2).

Although various other measures have been proposed, such as the "Cybersecurity Act of 2010 – S. 773" in 2009, the "International Cybercrime Reporting and Cooperation Act – H.R.4962" and

"Protecting Cyberspace as a National Asset Act of 2010 – S.3480" in 2010 – none of these has succeeded.

Executive order 13636 *Improving Critical Infrastructure Cybersecurity* was signed February 12, 2013.

Agencies

The Department of Homeland Security has a dedicated division responsible for the response system, risk management program and requirements for cybersecurity in the United States called the National Cyber Security Division. The division is home to US-CERT operations and the National Cyber Alert System. The National Cybersecurity and Communications Integration Center brings together government organizations responsible for protecting computer networks and networked infrastructure.

The third priority of the Federal Bureau of Investigation (FBI) is to: *"Protect the United States against cyber-based attacks and high-technology crimes"*, and they, along with the National White Collar Crime Center (NW3C), and the Bureau of Justice Assistance (BJA) are part of the multi-agency task force, The Internet Crime Complaint Center, also known as IC3.

In addition to its own specific duties, the FBI participates alongside non-profit organizations such as InfraGard.

In the criminal division of the United States Department of Justice operates a section called the Computer Crime and Intellectual Property Section. The CCIPS is in charge of investigating computer crime and intellectual property crime and is specialized in the search and seizure of digital evidence in computers and networks.

The United States Cyber Command, also known as USCYBERCOM, is tasked with the defense of specified Department of Defense information networks and *"ensure US/Allied freedom of action in cyberspace and deny the same to our adversaries."* It has no role in the protection of civilian networks.

The U.S. Federal Communications Commission's role in cybersecurity is to strengthen the protection of critical communications infrastructure, to assist in maintaining the reliability of networks during disasters, to aid in swift recovery after, and to ensure that first responders have access to effective communications services.

The Food and Drug Administration has issued guidance for medical devices, and the National Highway Traffic Safety Administration is concerned with automotive cybersecurity. After being criticized by the Government Accountability Office, and following successful attacks on airports and claimed attacks on airplanes, the Federal Aviation Administration has devoted funding to securing systems on board the planes of private manufacturers, and the Aircraft Communications Addressing and Reporting System. Concerns have also been raised about the future Next Generation Air Transportation System.

Computer Emergency Readiness Team

"Computer emergency response team" is a name given to expert groups that handle computer security incidents. In the US, two distinct organization exist, although they do work closely together.

- US-CERT: part of the National Cyber Security Division of the United States Department of Homeland Security.

- CERT/CC: created by the Defense Advanced Research Projects Agency (DARPA) and run by the Software Engineering Institute (SEI).

International Actions

Many different teams and organisations exist, including:

- The Forum of Incident Response and Security Teams (FIRST) is the global association of CSIRTs. The US-CERT, AT&T, Apple, Cisco, McAfee, Microsoft are all members of this international team.

- The Council of Europe helps protect societies worldwide from the threat of cybercrime through the Convention on Cybercrime.

- The purpose of the Messaging Anti-Abuse Working Group (MAAWG) is to bring the messaging industry together to work collaboratively and to successfully address the various forms of messaging abuse, such as spam, viruses, denial-of-service attacks and other messaging exploitations. France Telecom, Facebook, AT&T, Apple, Cisco, Sprint are some of the members of the MAAWG.

- ENISA : The European Network and Information Security Agency (ENISA) is an agency of the European Union with the objective to improve network and information security in the European Union.

Europe

CSIRTs in Europe collaborate in the TERENA task force TF-CSIRT. TERENA's Trusted Introducer service provides an accreditation and certification scheme for CSIRTs in Europe. A full list of known CSIRTs in Europe is available from the Trusted Introducer website.

National Teams

Here are the main computer emergency response teams around the world. Most countries have their own team to protect network security.

Canada

On October 3, 2010, Public Safety Canada unveiled Canada's Cyber Security Strategy, following a Speech from the Throne commitment to boost the security of Canadian cyberspace. The aim of the strategy is to strengthen Canada's "cyber systems and critical infrastructure sectors, support economic growth and protect Canadians as they connect to each other and to the world." Three main pillars define the strategy: securing government systems, partnering to secure vital cyber systems outside the federal government, and helping Canadians to be secure online. The strategy involves multiple departments and agencies across the Government of Canada. The Cyber Incident Management Framework for Canada outlines these responsibilities, and provides a plan for coordinated response between government and other partners in the event of a cyber incident. The Action Plan 2010–2015 for Canada's Cyber Security Strategy outlines the ongoing implementation of the strategy.

Public Safety Canada's Canadian Cyber Incident Response Centre (CCIRC) is responsible for mitigating and responding to threats to Canada's critical infrastructure and cyber systems. The CCIRC provides support to mitigate cyber threats, technical support to respond and recover from targeted cyber attacks, and provides online tools for members of Canada's critical infrastructure sectors. The CCIRC posts regular cyber security bulletins on the Public Safety Canada website. The CCIRC also operates an online reporting tool where individuals and organizations can report a cyber incident. Canada's Cyber Security Strategy is part of a larger, integrated approach to critical infrastructure protection, and functions as a counterpart document to the National Strategy and Action Plan for Critical Infrastructure.

On September 27, 2010, Public Safety Canada partnered with STOP.THINK.CONNECT, a coalition of non-profit, private sector, and government organizations dedicated to informing the general public on how to protect themselves online. On February 4, 2014, the Government of Canada launched the Cyber Security Cooperation Program. The program is a $1.5 million five-year initiative aimed at improving Canada's cyber systems through grants and contributions to projects in support of this objective. Public Safety Canada aims to begin an evaluation of Canada's Cyber Security Strategy in early 2015. Public Safety Canada administers and routinely updates the GetCyberSafe portal for Canadian citizens, and carries out Cyber Security Awareness Month during October.

China

China's network security and information technology leadership team was established February 27, 2014. The leadership team is tasked with national security and long-term development and co-ordination of major issues related to network security and information technology. Economic, political, cultural, social and military fields as related to network security and information technology strategy, planning and major macroeconomic policy are being researched. The promotion of national network security and information technology law are constantly under study for enhanced national security capabilities.

Germany

Berlin starts National Cyber Defense Initiative: On June 16, 2011, the German Minister for Home Affairs, officially opened the new German NCAZ (National Center for Cyber Defense) Nationales Cyber-Abwehrzentrum located in Bonn. The NCAZ closely cooperates with BSI (Federal Office for Information Security) Bundesamt für Sicherheit in der Informationstechnik, BKA (Federal Police Organisation) Bundeskriminalamt (Deutschland), BND (Federal Intelligence Service) Bundesnachrichtendienst, MAD (Military Intelligence Service) Amt für den Militärischen Abschirmdienst and other national organisations in Germany taking care of national security aspects. According to the Minister the primary task of the new organisation founded on February 23, 2011, is to detect and prevent attacks against the national infrastructure and mentioned incidents like Stuxnet.

India

Some provisions for cybersecurity have been incorporated into rules framed under the Information Technology Act 2000.

The National Cyber Security Policy 2013 is a policy framework by Department of Electronics and Information Technology (DeitY) which aims to protect the public and private infrastructure from cyber attacks, and safeguard "information, such as personal information (of web users), financial and banking information and sovereign data".

The Indian Companies Act 2013 has also introduced cyber law and cyber security obligations on the part of Indian directors.

Pakistan

Cyber-crime has risen rapidly in Pakistan. There are about 34 million Internet users with 133.4 million mobile subscribers in Pakistan. According to Cyber Crime Unit (CCU), a branch of Federal Investigation Agency, only 62 cases were reported to the unit in 2007, 287 cases in 2008, ratio dropped in 2009 but in 2010, more than 312 cases were registered. However, there are many unreported incidents of cyber-crime.

"Pakistan's Cyber Crime Bill 2007", the first pertinent law, focuses on electronic crimes, for example cyber-terrorism, criminal access, electronic system fraud, electronic forgery, and misuse of encryption.

National Response Centre for Cyber Crime (NR3C) – FIA is a law enforcement agency dedicated to fight cybercrime. Inception of this Hi-Tech crime fighting unit transpired in 2007 to identify and curb the phenomenon of technological abuse in society. However, certain private firms are also working in cohesion with the government to improve cyber security and curb cyberattacks.

South Korea

Following cyberattacks in the first half of 2013, when government, news-media, television station, and bank websites were compromised, the national government committed to the training of 5,000 new cybersecurity experts by 2017. The South Korean government blamed its northern counterpart for these attacks, as well as incidents that occurred in 2009, 2011, and 2012, but Pyongyang denies the accusations.

Other Countries

- CERT Brazil, member of FIRST (Forum for Incident Response and Security Teams)
- CARNet CERT, Croatia, member of FIRST
- AE CERT, United Arab Emirates
- SingCERT, Singapore
- CERT-LEXSI, France, Canada, Singapore

- INCIBE, Spain

- ID-CERT, Indonesia

Modern Warfare

Cybersecurity is becoming increasingly important as more information and technology is being made available on cyberspace. There is growing concern among governments that cyberspace will become the next theatre of warfare.

In the future, wars will not just be fought by soldiers with guns or with planes that drop bombs. They will also be fought with the click of a mouse a half a world away that unleashes carefully weaponized computer programs that disrupt or destroy critical industries like utilities, transportation, communications, and energy. Such attacks could also disable military networks that control the movement of troops, the path of jet fighters, the command and control of warships.

This has led to new terms such as *cyberwarfare* and *cyberterrorism*. More and more critical infrastructure is being controlled via computer programs that, while increasing efficiency, exposes new vulnerabilities. The test will be to see if governments and corporations that control critical systems such as energy, communications and other information will be able to prevent attacks before they occur. As Jay Cross, the chief scientist of the Internet Time Group, remarked, "Connectedness begets vulnerability."

Job Market

Cybersecurity is a fast-growing field of IT concerned with reducing organizations' risk of hack or data breach. According to research from the Enterprise Strategy Group, 46% of organizations say that they have a "problematic shortage" of cybersecurity skills in 2016, up from 28% in 2015. Commercial, government and non-governmental organizations all employ cybersecurity professionals. The fastest increases in demand for cybersecurity workers are in industries managing increasing volumes of consumer data such as finance, health care, and retail. However, the use of the term "cybersecurity" is more prevalent in government job descriptions.

Typical cybersecurity job titles and descriptions include:

Security analyst

> Analyzes and assesses vulnerabilities in the infrastructure (software, hardware, networks), investigates using available tools and countermeasures to remedy the detected vulnerabilities, and recommends solutions and best practices. Analyzes and assesses damage to the data/infrastructure as a result of security incidents, examines available recovery tools and processes, and recommends solutions. Tests for compliance with security policies and procedures. May assist in the creation, implementation, and/or management of security solutions.

Security engineer

> Performs security monitoring, security and data/logs analysis, and forensic analysis, to detect security incidents, and mounts incident response. Investigates and utilizes new

technologies and processes to enhance security capabilities and implement improvements. May also review code or perform other security engineering methodologies.

Security architect

Designs a security system or major components of a security system, and may head a security design team building a new security system.

Security administrator

Installs and manages organization-wide security systems. May also take on some of the tasks of a security analyst in smaller organizations.

Chief Information Security Officer (CISO)

A high-level management position responsible for the entire information security division/staff. The position may include hands-on technical work.

Chief Security Officer (CSO)

A high-level management position responsible for the entire security division/staff. A newer position now deemed needed as security risks grow.

Security Consultant/Specialist/Intelligence

Broad titles that encompass any one or all of the other roles/titles, tasked with protecting computers, networks, software, data, and/or information systems against viruses, worms, spyware, malware, intrusion detection, unauthorized access, denial-of-service attacks, and an ever increasing list of attacks by hackers acting as individuals or as part of organized crime or foreign governments.

Student programs are also available to people interested in beginning a career in cybersecurity. Meanwhile, a flexible and effective option for information security professionals of all experience levels to keep studying is online security training, including webcasts.

Terminology

The following terms used with regards to engineering secure systems are explained below.

- Access authorization restricts access to a computer to group of users through the use of authentication systems. These systems can protect either the whole computer – such as through an interactive login screen – or individual services, such as an FTP server. There are many methods for identifying and authenticating users, such as passwords, identification cards, and, more recently, smart cards and biometric systems.

- Anti-virus software consists of computer programs that attempt to identify, thwart and eliminate computer viruses and other malicious software (malware).

- Applications with known security flaws should not be run. Either leave it turned off until it can be patched or otherwise fixed, or delete it and replace it with some other application. Publicly known flaws are the main entry used by worms to automatically break into a system and then spread to other systems connected to it. The security website Secunia provides a search tool for unpatched known flaws in popular products.

- Authentication techniques can be used to ensure that communication end-points are who they say they are.

- Automated theorem proving and other verification tools can enable critical algorithms and code used in secure systems to be mathematically proven to meet their specifications.

- Backups are a way of securing information; they are another copy of all the important computer files kept in another location. These files are kept on hard disks, CD-Rs, CD-RWs, tapes and more recently on the cloud. Suggested locations for backups are a fireproof, waterproof, and heat proof safe, or in a separate, offsite location than that in which the original files are contained. Some individuals and companies also keep their backups in safe deposit boxes inside bank vaults. There is also a fourth option, which involves using one of the file hosting services that backs up files over the Internet for both business and individuals, known as the cloud.

  o Backups are also important for reasons other than security. Natural disasters, such as earthquakes, hurricanes, or tornadoes, may strike the building where the computer is located. The building can be on fire, or an explosion may occur. There needs to be a recent backup at an alternate secure location, in case of such kind of disaster. Further, it is recommended that the alternate location be placed where the same disaster would not affect both locations. Examples of alternate disaster recovery sites being compromised by the same disaster that affected the primary site include having had a primary site in World Trade Center I and the recovery site in 7 World Trade Center, both of which were destroyed in the 9/11 attack, and having one's primary site and recovery site in the same coastal region, which leads to both being vulnerable to hurricane damage (for example, primary site in New Orleans and recovery site in Jefferson Parish, both of which were hit by Hurricane Katrina in 2005). The backup media should be moved between the geographic sites in a secure manner, in order to prevent them from being stolen.

- Capability and access control list techniques can be used to ensure privilege separation and mandatory access control. This section discusses their use.

- Chain of trust techniques can be used to attempt to ensure that all software loaded has been certified as authentic by the system's designers.

- Confidentiality is the nondisclosure of information except to another authorized person.

- Cryptographic techniques can be used to defend data in transit between systems, reducing the probability that data exchanged between systems can be intercepted or modified.

- Cyberwarfare is an internet-based conflict that involves politically motivated attacks on information and information systems. Such attacks can, for example, disable official websites and networks, disrupt or disable essential services, steal or alter classified data, and cripple financial systems.

- Data integrity is the accuracy and consistency of stored data, indicated by an absence of any alteration in data between two updates of a data record.

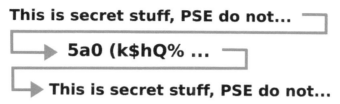

Cryptographic techniques involve transforming information, scrambling it so it becomes unreadable during transmission. The intended recipient can unscramble the message; ideally, eavesdroppers cannot.

- Encryption is used to protect the message from the eyes of others. Cryptographically secure ciphers are designed to make any practical attempt of breaking infeasible. Symmetric-key ciphers are suitable for bulk encryption using shared keys, and public-key encryption using digital certificates can provide a practical solution for the problem of securely communicating when no key is shared in advance.

- Endpoint security software helps networks to prevent exfiltration (data theft) and virus infection at network entry points made vulnerable by the prevalence of potentially infected portable computing devices, such as laptops and mobile devices, and external storage devices, such as USB drives.

- Firewalls are an important method for control and security on the Internet and other networks. A network firewall can be a communications processor, typically a router, or a dedicated server, along with firewall software. A firewall serves as a gatekeeper system that protects a company's intranets and other computer networks from intrusion by providing a filter and safe transfer point for access to and from the Internet and other networks. It screens all network traffic for proper passwords or other security codes and only allows authorized transmission in and out of the network. Firewalls can deter, but not completely prevent, unauthorized access (hacking) into computer networks; they can also provide some protection from online intrusion.

- Honey pots are computers that are either intentionally or unintentionally left vulnerable to attack by crackers. They can be used to catch crackers or fix vulnerabilities.

- Intrusion-detection systems can scan a network for people that are on the network but who should not be there or are doing things that they should not be doing, for example trying a lot of passwords to gain access to the network.

- A microkernel is the near-minimum amount of software that can provide the mechanisms to implement an operating system. It is used solely to provide very low-level, very precisely defined machine code upon which an operating system can be developed. A simple example is the early '90s GEMSOS (Gemini Computers), which provided extremely low-level machine code, such as "segment" management, atop which an operating system could be built. The theory (in the case of "segments") was that—rather than have the operating system itself worry about mandatory access separation by means of military-style labeling—it is safer if a low-level, independently scrutinized module can be charged solely with the management of individually labeled segments, be they memory "segments" or file system "segments" or executable text "segments." If software below the visibility of the operating system is (as in this case) charged with labeling, there is no theoretically viable means for a clever hacker to subvert the labeling scheme, since the operating system *per se* does not provide mechanisms for interfering with labeling: the operating system is, essentially, a client (an "application," arguably) atop the microkernel and, as such, subject to its restrictions.

- Pinging The ping application can be used by potential crackers to find if an IP address is reachable. If a cracker finds a computer, they can try a port scan to detect and attack services on that computer.

- Social engineering awareness keeps employees aware of the dangers of social engineering and/or having a policy in place to prevent social engineering can reduce successful breaches of the network and servers.

Shell (Computing)

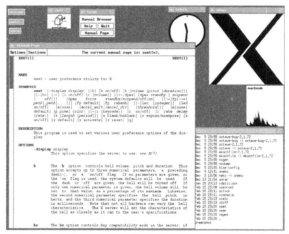

A graphical interface from the 1990s, which features a TUI window for a man page.
Another text window for a Unix shell is partially visible.

In computing, a shell is a user interface for access to an operating system's services. In general, operating system shells use either a command-line interface (CLI) or graphical user interface (GUI), depending on a computer's role and particular operation. It is named a shell because it is a layer around the operating system kernel.

The design of a shell is guided by cognitive ergonomics and the goal is to achieve the best workflow possible for the intended tasks; the design can be constricted by the available computing power (for example, of the CPU) or the available amount of graphics memory. The design of a shell is also dictated by the employed computer periphery, such as computer keyboard, pointing device (a mouse with one button, or one with five buttons, or a 3D mouse) or touchscreen, which is the direct human–machine interface.

CLI shells allow some operations to be performed faster, especially when a proper GUI has not been or cannot be created, however they require the user to memorize commands and their calling syntax, and to learn the shell-specific scripting language (for example bash script). CLIs are also easier to be operated via refreshable braille display and provide certain advantages to screen readers.

Graphical shells place a low burden on beginning computer users, and they are characterized as being simple and easy to use. With the widespread adoption of programs with GUIs, the use of graphical shells has gained greater adoption. Since graphical shells come with certain disadvantages (for example, lack of support for easy automation of operation sequences), most GUI-enabled operating systems also provide additional CLI shells.

Overview

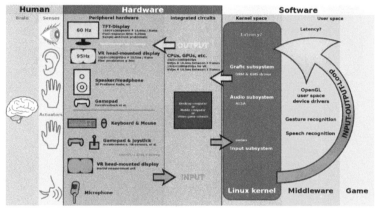

A particular view on the interaction between the end user, hardware and software

Operating systems provide various services to their users, including file management, process management (running and terminating applications), batch processing, and operating system monitoring and configuration.

Most operating system shells are not *direct* interfaces to the underlying kernel, even if a shell communicates with the user via peripheral devices attached to the computer directly. Shells are actually special applications that use the kernel API in just the same way as it is used by other application programs. A shell manages the user–system interaction by prompting users for input, interpreting their input, and then handling an output from the underlying operating system (much like a read–eval–print loop, REPL). Since the operating system shell is actually an application, it may easily be replaced with another similar application, for most operating systems.

In addition to shells running on local systems, there are different ways to make remote systems available to local users; such approaches are usually referred to as remote access or remote administration. Initially available on multi-user mainframes, which provided text-based UIs for each active user *simultaneously* by means of a text terminal connected to the mainframe via serial line or modem, remote access has extended to Unix-like systems and Microsoft Windows. On Unix-like systems, Secure Shell protocol is usually used for text-based shells, while SSH tunneling can be used for X Window System–based graphical user interfaces (GUIs). On Microsoft Windows, Remote Desktop Protocol can be used to provide GUI remote access.

Most operating system shells fall into one of two categories – command-line and graphical. Command line shells provide a command-line interface (CLI) to the operating system, while graphical shells provide a graphical user interface (GUI). Other possibilities, although not so common, include voice user interface and various implementations of a text-based user interface (TUI) that are not CLI. The relative merits of CLI- and GUI-based shells are often debated.

Text (CLI) Shells

Command Prompt, a CLI shell in Windows

Bash, a widely adopted Unix shell

A command-line interface (CLI) is an operating system shell that uses alphanumeric characters typed on a keyboard to provide instructions and data to the operating system, interactively. For example, a teletypewriter can send codes representing keystrokes to a command interpreter program running on the computer; the command interpreter parses the sequence of keystrokes and responds with an error message if it cannot recognize the sequence of characters, or it may carry out some other program action such as loading an application program, listing files, logging in a user and many others. Operating systems such as UNIX have a large variety of shell programs with different commands, syntax and capabilities. Some operating systems had only a single style of command interface; commodity operating systems such as MS-DOS came with a standard command interface but third-party interfaces were also often available, providing additional features or functions such as menuing or remote program execution.

Application programs may also implement a command-line interface. For example, in Unix-like systems, the telnet program has a number of commands for controlling a link to a remote computer system. Since the commands to the program are made of the same keystrokes as the data being sent to a remote computer, some means of distinguishing the two are required. An escape sequence can be defined, using either a special local keystroke that is never passed on but always interpreted by the local system. The program becomes modal, switching between interpreting commands from the keyboard or passing keystrokes on as data to be processed.

A feature of many command-line shells is the ability to save sequences of commands for re-use. A data file can contain sequences of commands which the CLI can be made to follow as if typed in by a user. Special features in the CLI may apply when it is carrying out these stored instructions. Such batch files (script files) can be used repeatedly to automate routine operations such as initializing a set of programs when a system is restarted. Batch mode use of shells usually involves structures, conditionals, variables, and other elements of programming languages; some have the bare essentials needed for such a purpose, others are very sophisticated programming languages in and of themselves. Conversely, some programming languages can be used interactively from an operating system shell or in a purpose-built program.

The command-line shell may offer features such as command-line completion, where the interpreter expands commands based on a few characters input by the user. A command-line interpreter may offer a history function, so that the user can recall earlier commands issued to the system and repeat them, possibly with some editing. Since all commands to the operating system had to be typed by the user, short command names and compact systems for representing program options were common. Short names were sometimes hard for a user to recall, and early systems lacked the storage resources to provide a detailed on-line user instruction guide.

Various Unix shells and their derivatives including the DOS shell exist.

Graphical Shells

Graphical shells provide means for manipulating programs based on graphical user interface (GUI), by allowing for operations such as opening, closing, moving and resizing windows, as well as switching focus between windows. Graphical shells may be included with desktop environments or come separately, even as a set of loosely coupled utilities.

Most graphical user interfaces develop the metaphor of an "electronic desktop", where data files are represented as if they were paper documents on a desk, and application programs similarly have graphical representations instead of being invoked by command names.

Microsoft Windows

Modern versions of the Microsoft Windows operating system use the Windows shell as their shell. Windows Shell provides the familiar desktop environment, start menu, and task bar, as well as a graphical user interface for accessing the file management functions of the operating system. Older versions also include Program Manager, which was the shell for the 3.x series of Microsoft Windows, and which in fact ships with later versions of Windows of both the 95 and NT types at least through Windows XP. The interfaces of Windows versions 1 and 2 were markedly different.

Desktop applications are also considered shells, as long as they use a third-party engine. Likewise, many individuals and developers dissatisfied with the interface of Windows Explorer have developed software that either alters the functioning and appearance of the shell or replaces it entirely. WindowBlinds by StarDock is a good example of the former sort of application. LiteStep and Emerge Desktop are good examples of the latter.

Interoperability programmes and purpose-designed software lets Windows users use equivalents of many of the various Unix-based GUIs discussed below, as well as Macintosh. An equivalent of the OS/2 Presentation Manager for version 3.0 can run some OS/2 programmes under some conditions using the OS/2 environmental subsystem in versions of Windows NT.

Unix-like Systems

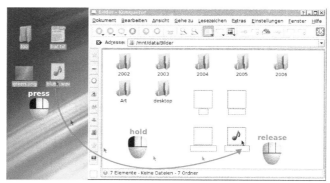

Drag and drop operation performed on a file between KDesktop and Konqueror in KDE

Graphical shells typically build on top of a windowing system. In the case of X Window System or Wayland, the shell consists of an X window manager or a Wayland compositor, respectively, as well as of one or multiple programs providing the functionality to start installed applications, to manage open windows and virtual desktops, and often to support a widget engine.

In the case of OS X, Quartz could be thought of as the windowing system, and the shell consists of the Finder, the Dock, SystemUIServer, and Mission Control.

Other Uses

"Shell" is also used loosely to describe application software that is "built around" a particular component, such as web browsers and email clients, in analogy to the shells found in nature.

In expert systems, a shell is a piece of software that is an "empty" expert system without the knowledge base for any particular application.

References

- Silberschatz, Abraham; James L. Peterson; Peter B. Galvin (1991). Operating system concepts. Boston, Massachusetts: Addison-Wesley. p. 696. ISBN 0-201-51379-X.

- Ball, Stuart R. (2002) [2002]. Embedded Microprocessor Systems: Real World Designs (first ed.). Elsevier Science. ISBN 0-7506-7534-9.

- Deitel, Harvey M. (1984) [1982]. An introduction to operating systems (revisited first ed.). Addison-Wesley. p. 673. ISBN 0-201-14502-2.

- Hansen, Per Brinch (1973). Operating System Principles. Englewood Cliffs: Prentice Hall. p. 496. ISBN 0-13-637843-9.

- Tanenbaum, Andrew S. (1979). Structured Computer Organization. Englewood Cliffs, New Jersey: Prentice-Hall. ISBN 0-13-148521-0.

- Baiardi, F.; A. Tomasi, M. Vanneschi (1988). Architettura dei Sistemi di Elaborazione, volume 1 (in Italian). Franco Angeli. ISBN 88-204-2746-X. Cite uses deprecated parameter

- Silberschatz, Abraham; Cagne, Greg; Galvin, Peter Baer (2004). "Chapter 4. Processes". Operating system concepts with Java (Sixth ed.). John Wiley & Sons. ISBN 0-471-48905-0.

- Vahalia, Uresh (1996). "Chapter 2. The Process and the Kernel". UNIX Internals: The New Frontiers. Prentice-Hall Inc. ISBN 0-13-101908-2.

- Hyde, Randall (November 2004). "12.10. Protected Mode Operation and Device Drivers". Write Great Code. O'Reilly. ISBN 1-59327-003-8.

Game Console Operating Systems

A game console operating system is a computer device or a digital device that is particularly used to display a video game. The operating systems of gaming that have been stated in this chapter are Linux for PlayStation 2, Wii U system software, Wii system software, Xbox One system software and otherOS. This section has been carefully written to provide an easy understanding of game console operating systems.

Linux for PlayStation 2

Linux for PlayStation 2 (or PS2 Linux) was a kit released by Sony Computer Entertainment in 2002 that allows the PlayStation 2 console to be used as a personal computer. It included a Linux-based operating system, a USB keyboard and mouse, a VGA adapter, a PS2 network adapter (Ethernet only), and a 40 GB hard disk drive (HDD). An 8 MB memory card is required; it must be formatted during installation, erasing all data previously saved on it, though afterwards the remaining space may be used for savegames. It is strongly recommended that a user of Linux for PlayStation 2 have some basic knowledge of Linux before installing and using it, due to the command-line interface for installation.

The official site for the project was closed at the end of October 2009 and communities like ps-2dev are no longer active. There is still a small group of enthusiasts that meets on Freenode in the channel #sps2.

Capabilities

The Linux Kit turns the PlayStation 2 into a full-fledged computer system, but it does not allow for use of the DVD-ROM drive except to read PS1 and PS2 discs due to piracy concerns by Sony. Although the HDD included with the Linux Kit is not compatible with PlayStation 2 games, reformatting the HDD with the utility disc provided with the retail HDD enables use with PlayStation 2 games but erases PS2 Linux, though there is a driver that allows PS2 Linux to operate once copied onto the APA partition created by the utility disc. The Network Adaptor included with the kit only supports Ethernet; a driver is available to enable modem support if the retail Network Adaptor (which includes a built-in V.90 modem) is used. The kit supports display on RGB monitors (with sync-on-green) using a VGA cable provided with the Linux Kit, or television sets with the normal cable included with the PlayStation 2 unit.

The PS2 Linux distribution is based on Kondara MNU/Linux, a Japanese distribution itself based on Red Hat Linux. PS2 Linux is similar to Red Hat Linux 6, and has most of the features one might expect in a Red Hat Linux 6 system. The stock kernel is Linux 2.2.1 (although it includes the USB drivers from Linux 2.2.18 to support the keyboard and mouse), but it can be upgraded to a newer version such as 2.2.21, 2.2.26 or 2.4.17.

Open-source Applications

Contents of the Linux kit; the hard disk is already installed inside the machine,
and the network adaptor is attached to the back.

The Linux kit's primary purpose is amateur software development, but it can be used as one would use any other computer, although the small amount of memory in the PS2 (32MB) limits its applications. Noted open source software that compiles on the kit includes Mozilla Suite, XChat, and Pidgin. Lightweight applications better suited to the PS2's 32MB of RAM include xv, Dillo, Ted, and AbiWord. The default window manager is Window Maker, but it is possible to install and use Fluxbox and FVWM. The USB ports of the console can be connected to external devices, such as printers, cameras, flash drives, and CD drives.

With PS2 Linux, a user can program his/her own games that will work under PS2 Linux, but not on an unmodified PlayStation 2. Free open source code for games are available for download from PS2 Linux support sites. There is little difference between PS2 Linux and the Linux software used on the more expensive system ("Tool", DTL-T10000) used by professional licensed PlayStation game programmers. Some amateur-created games are submitted to a competition such as the Independent Games Festival's annual competition. It is possible for an amateur to sell games or software that they develop using PS2 Linux, with certain restrictions detailed in the End User License Agreement. The amateur cannot make and sell game CDs and DVDs, but can sell the game through an online download.

Distribution

As of 2003, this kit is no longer officially sold in the USA due to the entire allocation of NTSC kits being sold out, but it is available through import or through an auction site, such as eBay. Some incorrectly speculate it was used as an attempt to help classify the PS2 as a computer to achieve tax exempt status from certain EU taxes that apply to game consoles and not computers (It was the Yabasic included with EU units that was intended to do that). Despite this, Sony lost the case in June 2006. The kit was released in the spirit of the earlier Net Yaroze. PlayStation and Sony ended their support of hobbyist programmers with the support of Linux on the PlayStation 3 being discontinued.

Model Compatibility

The original version of the PS2 Linux kit worked on only the Japanese SCPH-10000, SCPH-15000 and SCPH-18000 PlayStation 2 models. It came with a PCMCIA interface card which had a 10/100 Ethernet port and an external IDE hard drive enclosure (as there is no room inside the unit). This kit cannot be used with any later model PS2 (which includes all non-Japanese models) because these models removed the PCMCIA port.

Later versions of the PS2 Linux kit use an interface very similar to the HDD interface/Ethernet sold later for network play (the later released Network adaptor was also usable with the kit, including the built-in 56k modem.) This kit locates the hard drive internal to the PS2, in the MultiBay. With this kit, only the SCPH-30000 model of PlayStation 2 is officially supported. The kit does though work equally well with models newer than SCPH-30000 with the exception that the Ethernet connection tended to freeze after a short period of use. Thus the newer SCPH-50000 PlayStation 2 model will only work correctly with PS2 Linux with an updated network adapter driver, which must be transferred to the PlayStation 2 HDD by using either an older model PlayStation 2 to transfer the driver or a Linux PC with an IDE port. Both methods involve swapping HDDs. This is due to the inability to use USB Mass Storage devices with the relatively old kernel (version 2.2.1) shipped with the kit.

The slim SCPH-70000 PlayStation 2 model does not work with PS2 Linux at all, due to the lack of a hard drive interface, though a very few early models in this revision had solder pads of an IDE interface on the motherboard that could be used (but required modding of the console, thereby voiding its warranty.) Even so, it is possible to network boot from a PXE server

PS2 Linux install DVDs are region encoded, as are all other PS2 game discs. A European/PAL disc will be rejected by an NTSC PlayStation 2 game system, however this is only at boot time: if you have a mod that allows you to load a PAL disk, then the PS2 Linux boot loader supports both PAL and Linux (read the documentation to determine the button presses), so once you are past the "DVD not supported", you can boot Linux and then later start X Window in NTSC mode.

Unofficial Support

Ever since the discontinuation of the PS2 Linux Kit and some time before that there has been a large, less active group who have tried and succeeded to run the Linux operating system through other methods, most notably using the KernelLoader Linux loader developed by Mega Man since 2008 where they have copied the necessary kernel files onto removable storage or DVDs formatted as Video DVDs due to Sony's anti-piracy efforts which restrict any data DVDs and loaded them through the program.

Through this method it has become possible to use custom Linux distros and other UNIX-like operating systems compiled for the PlayStation 2 and this has enabled users to use more compatible Linux kernels with smaller footprints and programs specially designed for the console. These methods often require the use of PS2 exploits such as Free MCBoot which allows the end user to boot from the PlayStation 2 memory card and launch custom made homebrew applications packaged as ELF files and other exploits such as SwapMagic etc. however these tend to void the warranty as some require the opening of the PlayStation 2 console itself.

Wii U System Software

The Wii U system software is the official firmware version and operating system for Nintendo's Wii U game console. Nintendo maintains the Wii U's systemwide features and applications by offering system software updates via the Internet. Updates are optional to each console owner, but may be required in order to retain interoperability with Nintendo's online services. Each update is cumulative, including all changes from previous updates.

The system's official integrated development environment, named MULTI and published by embedded software engineering vendor Green Hills Software, is intended for use by Nintendo and its licensed developers in programming the Wii U. Details of the operating system's internal architecture have not been officially publicized.

Wii U Menu

The Wii U Menu is the main dashboard of the system, acting as an application organizer and launcher. It is a graphical shell similar to the Wii's "Wii Menu" and Nintendo 3DS HOME Menu. It allows launching software stored on Wii U optical discs, applications installed in the internal memory or an external storage device, or Wii titles through the system's *"Wii Mode"*. The WaraWara Plaza is displayed on the TV screen, while the Wii U GamePad screen displays the application icons available for launch; the two screens' display roles can be swapped with the press of a button. Like the original Wii, discs can also be hot-swapped while in the menu. The Wii U Menu may also be used to launch applications entirely beyond just gaming: the Miiverse social network which is integrated with all games and applications; the Internet Browser for the World Wide Web; play media through Netflix, Amazon Video, Hulu, YouTube, Nintendo TVii, and more; download Wii U software and content through the Nintendo eShop; and receive official notifications from Nintendo. System settings, parental controls and the activity log can also be launched through the menu.

WaraWara Plaza

The Wii U Menu is directly integrated with Miiverse and the Nintendo Network. When the Wii U powers on, the television screen shows the WaraWara Plaza in which user status and comments on Miiverse are shown. Each user is represented by their respective Mii and is often associated with a Miiverse community. Users can save any Mii on the WaraWara Plaza to their personal library, like their posts (with a "Yeah!"), write a comment, and send a friend request.

Home Menu

The Home Menu (stylized as HOME Menu) can be accessed during any game or application through the user pressing the Home Button on the Wii U GamePad, Wii U Pro Controller or Wii Remote. The Home Menu allows the user to launch certain multitasking applications, such as Miiverse, Nintendo TVii, Nintendo eShop and the Internet Browser while a game or application is running. It also displays various information such as date and time, the wireless signal status, controller battery life and controller settings. Current downloads can also be managed in the Download Manager, which downloads and installs games and applications and their respective updates, as well as downloading system updates in the background.

Pre-installed Software

Nintendo Eshop

The Nintendo eShop is Nintendo's online digital distribution service, serving both the Wii U and the Nintendo 3DS handheld console. The eShop provides downloadable Wii U software titles (both retail and download only), Wii games, Virtual Console games, trial versions (demos), and various applications. It also allows users to purchase downloadable content (DLC) and automatically download patches for both physical and downloadable games. All content obtained from the Nintendo eShop is attached to a Nintendo Network ID but can only be used in one system. The Wii U allows background downloading via SpotPass, either while playing a game or application or in sleep mode. Up to ten downloads can be queued at a time and their status can be checked on the *Download Manager* application. A pop-up notification will appear on the *Home Menu* section to notify the user that a download is finished.

Unlike past Nintendo digital stores, such as the Wii Shop Channel and the Nintendo DSi Shop which used Nintendo Points as its currency, the Nintendo eShop uses the user's local currency using a digital wallet system whereby funds are added to and debited from the wallet. The user can add funds to their wallet in a number of ways either by credit or debit card or by purchasing Nintendo eShop cards. It is also possible to purchase download codes from select retailers and later redeem the on the eShop. On July 22, 2014, the Japanese Nintendo eShop was updated to support digital money cards to add funds to the user account's digital wallet via near field communication (NFC) on the Wii U GamePad. These cards are embedded with IC chips and are typically used to buy train or bus tickets as well as make purchases at convenience stores.

The Nintendo eShop supports user software reviews. Users can submit a review with "stars" ranging from one to five, representing its quality in a crescent order. It is also possible to categorize the software on whether it is suitable for hardcore or for more casual players. Reviews can only be submitted after the software in review has been used for at least one hour. In the future, it will be possible to attach Miiverse posts to each review.

Miiverse

Miiverse (portmanteau of "Mii" and "Universe") is an integrated social networking service, which allows players to interact and share their experiences through their own Mii characters. Miiverse allows users to seamlessly share accomplishments, comments hand written and game screenshots notes with other users. Select games are integrated with Miiverse, where social interactions can also occur within the game. Miiverse is moderated through software filtering as well as a human resource team in order to ensure that the content shared by users is appropriate and that no spoilers are shared. In order to facilitate this, it was stated that comments posted could take up to 30 minutes to appear on Miiverse.

On April 25, 2013, Miiverse also became available on web browsers for internet-enabled smartphone, tablet and PC devices. It later became available for the Nintendo 3DS in December 2013.

Nintendo are also planning to release a specialized Miiverse app for smartphone and tablet devices in the future.

Internet Browser

Internet Browser allows users to browse the web on the Wii U GamePad and/or the television screen. It functions as a multitasking application on the Wii U, so it can be used while another game or application is suspended in the background. The browser is primarily controlled using the Wii U GamePad's touchscreen, or with the analog stick to scroll through web pages and the D-pad to cycle through links on the page, similar to using a keyboard. It can play HTML 5 video and audio in websites such as YouTube and various other social media. The user can choose to hide the browser's view on the TV screen for privacy, which contains presentation effects such as the opening of stage curtains. The user can also choose between the Google and Yahoo! search engines. There is a text wrap option to automatically wrap text to the width of the screen at different zoom levels. Users can also create bookmarks, with each user having its own set of personal bookmarks. The browser supports up to six tabs simultaneously. Up to 32 pages can be stored into the browser's history before the older items start being replaced.

Nintendo TVii

Nintendo TVii is a free television based service which allows users to find programs on Netflix, Hulu Plus, Amazon Video, and on their cable network. Nintendo TVii also allows users to control their TiVo DVR through the Wii U. Users are then able to select the source of the program they wish to watch and watch it on their television or on the Wii U GamePad. By default, the GamePad screen shows information on the show currently being watched. This information includes reviews, screenshots, cast lists, trailers, and other general information about the show provided by English Wikipedia, IMDb, Rotten Tomatoes, as well as other individual source services. Nintendo TVii also has a dedicated sports section where the user can view player positions and highlights of the match updated in real-time.

Each user has its own personalized settings on Nintendo TVii, such as their preferences, favorite shows and sports teams, personal Mii and social network account integration. Users can then interact with their friends and the community by sharing and commenting on reactions to live moments on the current show, on social networks such as Miiverse, Facebook, and .Twitter, through the GamePad while they watch their show on the television screen.

Nintendo TVii was made available with the Wii U's release in Japan on December 8, 2012. It was released in North America on December 20, 2012 and was scheduled to be released in Europe sometime in 2013, but was never fulfilled. Nintendo UK had since issued an apology and stated to expect further announcements in the "near future". However, on February 14, 2015, Nintendo Europe officially confirmed they cancelled plans for the service's release in European countries "[d]ue to the extremely complex nature of localising multiple television services across a diverse range of countries with varied licensing systems".

Other Streaming Service Apps

Nintendo is also working with YouTube, LoveFilm (United Kingdom and Ireland only), Nico Nico

Douga and YNN! (Japan only) to bring streaming movie and television content to the Wii U. Nintendo had initially delayed the deployment of some media capabilities for the Wii U as it delayed its online infrastructure. Late in the launch day, a firmware update deployed the Netflix app. Then, access to the Hulu Plus, Amazon Video, and YouTube apps gradually became active later in the launch week. On December 25, 2014, and without prior notice, Crunchyroll launched their eponymous app for the North American Wii U eShop, and was later released for PAL systems by January 8, 2015. Initially, despite being free to download, the content on the Crunchyroll app was only accessible to Premium account users, but this has since been fixed to allow access of all Crunchyroll members. After a long delay and without prior notice, as of May 28, 2015, users with access to the Nintendo eShop for the United Kingdom can download the BBC iPlayer app. On December 17, 2015, also without prior notice, the music streaming app Napster was released on the Wii U for eligible European countries, and the app was later released in the United States on March 11, 2016, under the Rhapsody name.

Wii U Chat

Wii U Chat is Nintendo's online video chat solution, powered by the Nintendo Network. The service allows the users to use the Wii U GamePad's front-facing camera to video chat with registered friends. While video chatting, only the Wii U GamePad is essentially needed, since the application is compatible with Off-TV Play. Users can draw pictures on the GamePad, on top of the video chat display. If there is a game or another application already running, the GamePad's HOME button ring will flash indicating that there is an incoming call.

Wii Street U

The Wii Street U logo

Wii Street U is a built-in map application developed by Nintendo and Google for the Wii U. During a Nintendo Direct, Satoru Iwata revealed that Google Maps will be integrated with the panorama feature of the Wii U. The player can choose any place from around the globe to look at, use the street view feature and can use the Wii U GamePad.

This application was available on Wii U eShop as a free download until October 31, 2013, after which it became a paid app. In January 2016, Nintendo announced the app will be discontinued on March 31, 2016. It has since been delisted off the Nintendo eShop as of January 31, 2016, albeit users who already acquired it could still download the app until its discontinuation date.

Wii Karaoke U

The Wii Karaoke U logo

Wii Karaoke U is a built-in karaoke app developed by Nintendo and Joysound for the Wii U. It licenses the Joysound online song library from Japanese karaoke service provider Xing. The game can use both the Wii U GamePad's microphone and any universal USB microphone connected to the Wii U console.

The game requires an Internet connection for players to access new songs to download. Buying tickets for songs from the Nintendo eShop, players rent the songs they want to sing for a limited period (from 24 hours to up to 90 days) from Joysounds's song library. Choosing a stage to perform on, players are able to select their own Mii characters to represent themselves. Players are also able to adjust options such as echo, key and speed of the song, and other players can use their Wii Remotes to accompany the singer by playing instruments such as cymbals and maracas. The game includes a lesson mode which trains and quizzes players on tone and rhythm.

It was released as a free app, titled *Wii Karaoke U by Joysound*, on the Nintendo eShop in Europe, on October 4, 2013.

Wii Mode

The Wii U's *Wii Mode* is a fully virtualized Wii system, with all of the limitations and privileges thereof. When a Wii game disc is inserted into the Wii U, an appropriate launchable icon appears on the Wii U Menu. Alternatively, the Wii U may be powered on while holding the B button. Either method will effectively relaunch the Wii U to entirely become a virtual Wii system until it is relaunched into Wii U mode. As with a native Wii system, the Wii Mode's internal storage memory is limited to 512 MB, and the SD Card Menu can utilize a card up to 32 GB in size.

There are a few slight differences between the Wii U's Wii Mode and a native Wii system. The data management settings are accessible, but the Wii System Settings are not. The Wii Shop Channel is fully available for the purchase of Wii software; however, its Netflix, Hulu Plus, and YouTube applications cannot be used. The system must be relaunched into Wii U mode, in order to utilize the native versions of these applications.

Other Software

- Health & Safety Information
- User Accounts
- Wii U optical disc launcher
- Activity Log
- Parental Controls
- System Settings

Multitasking Applications

In addition to running one primary game or application, the Wii U is capable of simultaneously opening select system applications. Once a primary application has been launched from the Wii U

Menu, the user can then push the HOME button to temporarily suspend that application. One of the following applications may then be launched, and may possibly interoperate with the primary application, such as screenshots and game scores.

- Miiverse

- Nintendo eShop

- Internet Browser

- Nintendo TVii

- Notifications

- Friend List

- Download Manager

History of Updates

The Wii U launched with its system software at either version 1.0.1 or 1.0.2. An update released on the same day added a web browser, Miiverse, a method of transferring data from a Wii, and a sandboxed way for owners to play Wii games, but not GameCube games. On April 25, 2013, a major new update at version 3.0 improved system loading times and added automatic installation of downloaded software. Version 4.0 released on September 30, 2013 added further features such as the ability to plug a headset directly into the GamePad for Wii U Chat, the ability to take screenshots and upload them through the web browser during gameplay, and supports for USB keyboards and surround sound for Wii games. On June 2, 2014, another major update with version number 5.0 was released, with added abilities to display a Quick Start Menu and Wii U GamePad Alerts in addition to other changes. The version that immediately followed (5.1.0) added the support for Wii U to Wii U System Transfer.

Wii System Software

The Wii system software is a set of updatable firmware versions, and a software frontend on the Wii video game console. Updates, which are downloaded via the system's Internet connection (WiiConnect24), allow Nintendo to add additional features and software. When a new update becomes available, Nintendo sends a message to connected systems notifying them of the available update.

Several game discs, both first-party and third-party games, have included system software updates so that players who are not connected to the Internet can still update their system. Additionally this can "force" an upgrade by requiring the player to perform the update, without which the new game cannot be played. Some online games (such as Super Smash Bros. Brawl and Mario Kart Wii) have come with specific extra updates, such as being able to receive posts from game-specific addresses, so, regardless of the version of the installed software, it will install an update.

Technology

Ios

The Wii's firmware is in the form of IOSes (thought by the Wii homebrew developers to stand for "Input Output Systems" or "Internal Operating Systems" and not to be confused with "iOS", the operating system of Apple's iPhones and iPads), which run on a separate ARM architecture processor to other Wii software (nicknamed Starlet by the Wii homebrew community, as it is physically located inside the graphics chip, the Hollywood, so it is a small part of Hollywood. The patent for the Wii U indicates a similar device which is simply named "Input/Output Processor"). These control input and output between the code running on the main processor (the PowerPC "Broadway" processor) and the Wii's hardware features that did not exist on the GameCube, which can only be accessed via the ARM.

When Nintendo releases a new IOS version, except for unusual circumstances (for example security updates to block homebrew), the new IOS does not replace any IOS already installed. Instead, it gets installed in addition to any current IOS versions. All native Wii software (including games distributed on Nintendo optical discs, the System Menu itself, Virtual Console games, WiiWare, and Wii Channels), with the exception of certain homebrew applications, have the IOS version hardcoded into the software.

When the software is run, the IOS that is hardcoded gets loaded by the Wii, which then loads the software itself. If that IOS does not exist on the Wii, in the case of disc-based software, it gets installed automatically (after the user is prompted). With downloaded software, this should not theoretically happen, as the user cannot access the shop to download software unless the player has all the IOS versions that they require. However, if homebrew is used to forcefully install or run a piece of software when the required IOS does not exist, the user is brought back to the system menu.

Nintendo created this system so that new updates wouldn't unintentionally break compatibility with older games, but it does have the side effect that it uses up space on the Wii's internal NAND Flash memory. IOSes are referred to by their number, which can theoretically be between 0 and 254, although many numbers are skipped, presumably being development versions that were never completed.

Only one IOS version can run at any given time. The only time an IOS isn't running is when the Wii enters GameCube backward compatibility mode, during which the Wii runs a variant of IOS specifically for GameCube games, MIOS.

User Interface

The system provides a graphical interface to the Wii's abilities. All games run directly on the Broadway processor, and either directly interface with the hardware (for the hardware common to the Wii and GameCube), or interface with IOS running on the ARM architecture processor (for Wii-specific hardware). The ARM processor does not have access to the screen, and therefore neither does IOS. This means that while a piece of software is running, everything seen on the screen comes from that software, and not from any operating system or firmware. This includes the home menu (a menu of uniform appearance that appears when the home button is pressed in any piece of official Wii software), and any error messages that might appear. Therefore, the version number reported by the Wii is actually only the version number of the System Menu. This is why some updates do not result in a change of the version number: the System Menu itself is not updated, only (for example) IOSes and channels. As a side effect, this means it is impossible for Nintendo to implement any functions that would affect the games themselves, for example an in-game system menu (similar to the Xbox 360's in-game Dashboard or the PlayStation 3's in-game XMB).

The Wii Menu (known internally as the System Menu) is the name of the user interface for the Wii game console, and it is the first thing to be seen when the system boots up. Similar to many other video game consoles, the Wii is not only about games. For example, it is possible to install applications such as Netflix to stream media (without requiring a disc) on the Wii. The Wii Menu let users access both game and no-game functions through built-in applications called Channels, which are designed to represent television channels. There are six primary channels: the Disc Channel, Mii Channel, Photo Channel, Wii Shop Channel, Forecast Channel and News Channel, although the latter two were not initially included and only became available via system updates. Some of the functions provided by these Channels on the Wii used to limited to a computer, such as a full-featured web browser and digital photo viewer. Users can also use Channels to create and share cartoon-like digital avatars called Miis and download new games and Channels directly from the Wii Shop Channel. New Channels include for example the Everybody Votes Channel and the Internet Channel. Separate Channels are graphically displayed in a grid and can be navigated using the pointer capability of the Wii Remote. Users can also rearrange these Channels if they are not satisfied with how the Channels are originally organized on the menu.

Network Features

The Wii system supports wireless connectivity with the Nintendo DS handheld console with no additional accessories. This connectivity allows players to use the Nintendo DS microphone and touch screen as inputs for Wii games. *Pokémon Battle Revolution* is the first example Nintendo has given of a game using Nintendo DS-Wii connectivity. Nintendo later released the Nintendo Channel for the Wii allowing its users to download game demos or additional data to their Nintendo DS.

Like many other video game consoles, the Wii console is able to connect to the Internet, although this is not required for the Wii system itself to function. Each Wii has its own unique 16-digit Wii Code for use with Wii's non-game features. With Internet connection enabled users are able to access the established Nintendo Wi-Fi Connection service. Wireless encryption by WEP, WPA (TKIP/RC4) and WPA2 (CCMP/AES) is supported. AOSS support was added in System Menu version 3.0. As with the Nintendo DS, Nintendo does not charge for playing via the service; the 12-digit Friend Code system controls how players connect to one another. The service has a few features for the console, including the Virtual Console, WiiConnect24 and several Channels. The Wii console can also communicate and connect with other Wii systems through a self-generated wireless LAN, enabling local wireless multiplayer on different television sets. The system also implements console-based software, including the Wii Message Board. One can connect to the Internet with third-party devices as well.

The Wii console also includes a web browser known as the Internet Channel, which is a version of the Opera 9 browser with menus. It is meant to be a convenient way to access the web on the television screen, although it is far from offering a comfortable user interface compared with modern Internet browsers. A virtual keyboard pops up when needed for input, and the Wii Remote acts like a mouse, making it possible to click anywhere on the screen and navigate though web links. However, the browser cannot always handle all the features of most normal web pages, although it does support Adobe Flash, thus capable of playing Flash games. Some third-party services such as the online BBC iPlayer were also available on the Wii via the Internet Channel browser, although BBC iPlayer was later relaunched as the separate BBC iPlayer Channel on the Wii. In addition, Internet access including the Internet Channel and system updates may be restricted by the parental controls feature of the Wii.

Backward Compatibility

The original designs of the Nintendo Wii console, more specifically the Wii models made pre-2011 were fully backward compatible with GameCube devices including game discs, memory cards and controllers. This was because the Wii hardware had ports for both GameCube memory cards, and peripherals and its slot-loading drive was able to accept and read the previous console's discs. GameCube games work with the Wii without any additional configuration, but a GameCube controller is required to play GameCube titles; neither the Wii Remote nor the Classic Controller functions in this capacity. The Wii supports progressive-scan output in 480p-enabled GameCube titles. Peripherals can be connected via a set of four GameCube controller sockets and two Memory Card slots (concealed by removable flip-open panels). The console retains connectivity with the Game Boy Advance and e-Reader through the Game Boy Advance Cable, which is used in the same manner as with the GameCube; however, this feature can only be accessed on select GameCube titles which previously utilized it.

There are also a few limitations in the backward compatibility. For example, online and LAN features of certain GameCube games were not available since the Wii does not have serial ports for the Nintendo GameCube Broadband Adapter and Modem Adapter. The Wii uses a proprietary port for video output, and is incompatible with all Nintendo GameCube audio/video cables (composite video, S-Video, component video and RGB SCART). The console also lacks the GameCube footprint and high-speed port needed for Game Boy Player support. Furthermore, only GameCube functions were available and only compatible memory cards and controllers could be used when playing a GameCube game. This is due to the fact that the Wii's internal memory would not save GameCube data.

Because of the original device's backward compatibility with earlier Nintendo products players can enjoy a massive selection of older games on the console in addition to hundreds of newer Wii game titles. However, South Korean units lack GameCube backward compatibility. Also, the redesigned Wii Family Edition and Wii Mini, launched in 2011 and 2013 respectively, had this compatibility stripped out. Nevertheless, there is another service called Virtual Console which allow users to download older games from prior Nintendo platforms (namely the Nintendo Entertainment System, Super NES and Nintendo 64) onto their Wii console, as well as games from non-Nintendo platforms such as the Genesis and TurboGrafx-16.

List of Additional Channels

This is a list of new Wii Channels released beyond the four initial Channels (i.e. Disc Channel,

Mii Channel, Photo Channel and Wii Shop Channel) included in the original consoles. The News Channel and the Forecast Channel were released as part of system updates so separate downloads were not required. As of 28 June 2013, some Channels listed below had been discontinued, which include News Channel, Forecast Channel, Everybody Votes Channel, Check Mii Out Channel (Mii Contest Channel) and Nintendo Channel.

Additional Wii Channels			
New Channels added	**Regions**	**Download**	**Release dates**
Amazon Instant Video Channel		✓	January 17, 2013
BBC iPlayer Channel		✓	November 18, 2009
Check Mii Out Channel		✓	November 12, 2007
Daigasso! Band Brothers DX Speaker Channel		✓	June 26, 2008
Demae Channel		✓	May 26, 2009
Digicam Print Channel		✓	July 23, 2008
Everybody Votes Channel		✓	February 13, 2007
Forecast Channel		✗	December 19, 2006
Hulu Plus Channel		✓	February 16, 2012
Internet Channel		✓	April 11, 2007
Mario Kart Channel		✗	April 10, 2008 - April 27, 2008
Metroid Prime 3 Preview Channel		✓	August 10, 2007
Netflix Channel		✓	October 18, 2010 - January 9, 2012
News Channel		✗	January 26, 2007
Nintendo Channel		✓	November 27, 2007 - May 30, 2008
Television Friend Channel		✓	March 4, 2008
Today and Tomorrow Channel		✓	December 2, 2008 - September 9, 2009
Wii Fit Channel		✗ (except ●)	December 1, 2007 - May 21, 2008
Wii no Ma Channel		✓	May 1, 2009
Wii Speak Channel		✓	December 5, 2008
YouTube Channel		✓	November 15, 2012 - December 10, 2012

History of Updates

This is a list of major system updates of the Wii.

Wii system update releases			
System version	**Regions**	**Release date**	**Note**
4.3		June 21, 2010	Final version
4.2		September 28, 2009	
4.1		July 16, 2009	
4.0		March 25, 2009	Notably SDHC support
3.5		March 1, 2009	First major update to Korean Wii models
3.4		November 17, 2008	
3.3		June 17, 2008	
3.2		February 25, 2008	
3.1		October 10, 2007	
3.0		August 6, 2007	
2.2		April 11, 2007	
2.1		January 9, 2007	
2.0		November 19, 2006	First major update
1.0		November 19, 2006	Initial release

Xbox One System Software

The Xbox One system software, sometimes called the Xbox OS, later on OneCore, is the operating system for the eighth-generation home video game console, Xbox One. It is a Windows-based operating system using the Hyper-V virtual machine monitor and contains separate operating systems for games and applications that can run on the console. It is located on the internal HDD for day-to-day usage, while also being duplicated on the internal NAND storage of the console for recovery purposes and factory reset functionality.

The Xbox One allows users to download applications that add to the functionality of the dashboard. From June 2014 onwards, entertainment apps no longer required the user to be signed into a valid Xbox Live Gold account in order to use the features advertised for the given app.

Since launch, Microsoft has been updating the OS monthly, with updates downloaded from the Xbox Live service directly to the Xbox One and subsequently installed, or by using offline recovery images downloaded via a PC. In November 2015, a major system update known as the New Xbox One Experience was released, which brought very significant changes to the design and functionality of the system. Notably, the Windows 10-based Core had replaced the Windows 8-based one in this update, and the new system is sometimes referred to as "Windows 10 on Xbox One".

Technology

System

The Xbox One console runs on an operating system that includes the Windows 10 core, although initially it included the Windows 8 core at the Xbox One's release. The Xbox One system software contains a heavily modified Hyper-V hypervisor as its host OS and two partitions. One of the partitions, the "Exclusive" partition is a custom virtual machine (VM) for games; the other partition, the "Shared" partition is a custom VM for running multiple apps. The Shared Partition contained the Windows 8 Core at launch until November 2015, where via a system update known as the "New Xbox One Experience", it was upgraded to the Windows 10 Core. With Windows 10, Universal Windows Platform apps became available on Xbox One. According to the current head of Microsoft's Xbox division, Phil Spencer, "The importance of entertainment and games to the Windows ecosystem has become really prevalent to the company". The program that Microsoft launched allows developers to build a single app that can run on a wide variety of devices, including personal computers and Xbox One video game consoles. According to *Polygon*, Microsoft is obliterating the distinction between Xbox One and Windows PC.

Starting in February 2014, Microsoft invited select users to join a preview program that enables them to receive early builds of upcoming system updates and experiment with the features prior to the public launch of the software. Once registered for the Xbox One Preview Program, participants will be able to test the early features included in the update and provide feedback on a private forum and can opt out of future waves. Through its Xbox Feedback website, Microsoft has been soliciting input from consumers on its features and taking requests for future additions to the console. Low battery notifications and Blu-ray 3D support are two examples of ideas that have been among the top vote-getters on the site.

User Interface

The Xbox One system software's interface uses a geometrical placement of squares and rectangular items that scrolls as a continuous horizontal line, using the Metro design language that is also seen in Windows 8, Windows 10, and other Microsoft products. The dashboard is divided into "Home", "Community", "OneGuide", and "Store" sections; the "Home" section contains a recent apps and games list, and shortcuts to "pinned" apps and games. The "Community" section allows users to view their friends' in-game activities and captures, post status updates, as well as view trending content. The "OneGuide" section aggregates television and online video content, while the "Store" section serves as a portal to the games, video, music, and app marketplaces. In general, the top level menu of the Xbox One feels a lot less cluttered than the Xbox 360's dashboard. For example, the friends tab has been removed and replaced with a dedicated app that users can load up to see what their connections are doing. There are a couple of columns for settings options and an area for "pinned" favorites, a "main" screen showing current and recent apps and games that the user played or used, and a small "What's New" section highlighting some recently added content.

In total, the interface is very clean and sparse. Microsoft also introduced a new way to multitask called Snap, which allows Xbox One users to open multiple panes in a single window.

When Microsoft upgraded the Windows 8-based Core to a Windows 10-based one, they made a tour of the new user interface up on Xbox Wire, promising faster, easier navigation, improved community features and, notably, the return of Xbox Avatars. The main feature on the home screen is a list of most recently played games. Selecting any given title will give users more information about announcements, achievements, social activity and so forth. It is also more focused on the actual games they are playing, which is part and parcel of the company's new direction under Phil Spencer, the current head of Microsoft's Xbox division.

Multimedia Features

While like other video game consoles the Xbox One is primarily designed for playing games, it is more than a game console. It is an entertainment hub for games, television, music, and videos. Mainly the console focuses on functionality and entertainment as a whole. At Gamescom 2014 Microsoft unveiled a new plan to remedy this and make earnest on the Xbox One's label as the "all-in-one entertainment" solution by way of expanding its media support. The Xbox One's media player is quite similar to the Xbox 360's playback suite in terms of form and function, however the newer console now supports more than 30 formats including the MKV container and GIF files. The Xbox One console also does some unique things. For example, its owners can control their television broadcasts using the device, as well as use it as a functioning DVR. Apart from streaming music and videos via Play (Charms > Devices > Play), there is also a networked approach. There are two primary ways to do this. The first is to stream media from a computer or tablet, and the second is to play it directly off of a USB flash drive. The advantage of this method over the Play system is that users can do it all from wherever they sit via the Xbox One, instead of sending the video from a PC to their console. Aside from multimedia files, Xbox One plays CDs, DVDs and Blu-ray Discs, and it also comes with DLNA and MKV support, which means that downloaded video files can be streamed via the PC or transported via external hard drive and USBs. Meanwhile, the interactive TV Guide allows users to turn on and control television with their voice. Furthermore, the system comes with a comprehensive range of applications related to multimedia features. In the United States, video channels include for example the Amazon Instant Video, Crackle, Hulu Plus and Netflix. Microsoft had announced that the Xbox One was awarded for its multimedia capabilities at the 66th Annual Technology & Engineering Emmy Awards in early 2015, and the prize was given for the Xbox One's television-on-demand functions.

Backward Compatibility

The Xbox One was not backwards compatible with either the original Xbox or the Xbox 360 console at launch, and Microsoft had admitted that attempts to use cloud streaming to allow Xbox 360 games to be played on Xbox One proved to be "problematic". However, during its E3 press conference on June 15, 2015, Microsoft announced plans to introduce Xbox 360 backward compatibility using the software method on the Xbox One. Supported Xbox 360 games are supposed to run within a software emulator provided by the updated system software, implementing both the hardware and software of the Xbox 360. Xbox One recording and broadcasting features are supported along with Xbox 360 multiplayer, achievements and cloud save access.

Unlike Xbox 360's emulation of the original Xbox, games do not have to be specifically patched but need to be repackaged in the Xbox One format. Users' digitally-purchased games will automatically appear in their library for download once available. Games on physical media will not be executed directly from disc; inserting the disc will initiate a download of a repackaged version. As with Xbox One titles, the disc must be inserted during play for validation purposes.

At least 100 Xbox 360 games are officially supported and available for the feature's public launch alongside the November 2015 "New Xbox One Experience" system update, and Xbox One preview program members received early access with a limited number of titles upon the announcement. Microsoft expects the number of supported games to increase significantly over time, but not all Xbox 360 games will be supported—this explicitly includes any games that require Kinect or access to USB peripherals.

Xbox division head Phil Spencer has stated that the idea of possibly adding support for games from the original Xbox was not "silly", but that the Xbox division is focusing on Xbox 360 compatibility first.

Development

At the 2016 Build conference, it was announced that all Xbox One consoles could be updated to include a development kit for universal Windows applications on Xbox One, with official support for the platform and Cortana coming in summer 2016.

History of Updates

Along with introducing improvements and fixes for native console apps and software, the monthly updates to the Xbox One system software introduce major features that are voted on or requested by the community, though some months have included more than one update. Starting in February 2014, beta releases of updates are tested before going live to check for unwanted bugs and stability.

On the day of the console's launch in 2013, a system update was released to remove the controversial always-online DRM announced at Electronic Entertainment Expo 2013. This DRM would have required the Xbox One to connect to the Internet at least once every twenty-four hours, or else games would cease to function. After a wave of backlash from gamers and press alike, Microsoft was forced to reverse its policies regarding this, but early users had to go online at least once to receive this patch.

The February 2014 update introduced the ability to see how much hard disk space is available. It also introduced support for USB keyboards, enabling users to plug a keyboard into their console, thus eliminating the need to use the on-screen keyboard. Over a year later, in July 2015, Phil Spencer, head of the Xbox team, vowed that mouse support would be added sometime in the future as part of cross-platform gameplay between Windows 10 devices and the Xbox One console.

The March 2014 update added support for video output at 50 frames per second rather than 60, allowing smoother video on 50 Hz displays common in Europe. In the United States, refresh rates on screens are higher (60 Hz) than in Europe.

In June 2014, support was added for external hard drives of 256 gigabytes or more, allowing two to be connected to the console at a time via USB 3.0.

As part of the July 2014 update, consoles could better understand voice commands spoken in different accents and dialects of English and German. A month later, purchases from the official Xbox website and the SmartGlass app were enabled, allowing for easier content purchasing.

In the October 2014 update, a media player app was added with support for many formats and codecs, including the Matroska container, as well as DLNA streaming from other networked devices.

In March 2015, a new screenshot feature was added to the console along with tile transparency, allowing owners to share game screenshots online or use one as a menu background.

In April 2015, due to criticisms of the power consumption needed for the Instant-On feature, a system update prompted users to select between Instant-On and an energy saving mode. Instant-On had been enabled by default in the U.S., drawing criticism from the Natural Resources Defense Council.

During the Electronic Entertainment Expo 2015 in June, Microsoft discussed three major features that later came to Xbox One consoles in November 2015: Windows 10 streaming, Xbox 360 backward compatibility, and an interface redesign known as the New Xbox One Experience. In advance of the public release of Windows 10, a July 2015 update let users stream games from their Xbox One to any device running Windows 10, a feature announced in January 2015. The service streams only to one device at a time.

In the February 2016 update, a slew of new features became available. For example, global leaderboards for each game and the ability to hide unused or expired beta games, and demos from a users game collection. More notably, the February 2016 update allowed users to rearrange their customized 'pins' via the controller, whereas previously users had to use the Xbox One SmartGlass application to use this feature.

The March 2016 update builds on the features that were introduced in the February 2016 update. New features that were included in the March 2016 update was the ability to purchase Xbox 360 compatible games on the Xbox One, party chat while broadcasting Twitch streams, customizable DVR recording lengths, which means that owners can now record a clip for up to 5 minutes long. Other improvements included the ability to track achievement progress from the Xbox One guide, video playback from the Xbox One activity feed, the ability to have 16 people in a party chat, the ability to track Xbox 360 achievements on the Xbox One activity feed. Further improvements in the March 2016 update include the ability to launch web links and YouTube videos directly from the Game Hubs and the ability for a user to compare their avatars to their friends. Additionally, the update also introduces the ability to factory reset the console without deleting installed games and applications.

On the 6th June 2016, the first preview update of the Windows 10 Anniversary update was made available to participants of the preview program. This included many new features and enhancements to the software. Build 14352 was one of the first builds to introduce Cortana. The main aim of this was to help users to undertake certain tasks, such as setting up a party using voice commands. Unlike the older Kinect voice commands, Cortana gives users audio feedback to the commands, similar to the PC and Windows Mobile versions. The update also included a refreshed design of the Xbox store, further cementing the relationship between Xbox One and Windows 10 PCs, as well as a redesigned 'My Games & Apps' interface, which includes a vertical design rather than the older horizontal design. The 'My Games & Apps' interface in build 14352 also gives the user more information when downloading games and apps such as the percentage completed, the current download size, total download size and the current download speed. The June 2016 update also includes a new 'Facebook Friend Finder', which allows users to find and add friends on Facebook on Xbox Live. The final release to the public was published on 30th July 2016 to coincide with the release of the Windows 10 Anniversary Update, which was released a few days later on 2nd August 2016. The final release introduced the newly redesigned universal store, as well as further integration of the Universal Windows Platform.

Version History

Microsoft aims to release frequent updates to the Xbox One console. To add features, and improve install/loading times for games, and apps. The largest of which was in November 2015, named the *New Xbox Experience* update.

OtherOS

Yellow Dog Linux booting up on a PS3

OtherOS was a feature available in early versions of the PlayStation 3 video game console that allowed user installed software, such as Linux or FreeBSD, to run on the system. The feature is not available in newer models and is removed from older models through system firmware update 3.21, released April 1, 2010.

Software running in the OtherOS environment had access to 6 of the 7 Synergistic Processing Elements; Sony implemented a hypervisor restricting access from the RSX. IBM provided an introduction to programming parallel applications on the PlayStation 3.

A class action lawsuit was filed against Sony on behalf of those who wished to pursue legal remedies but was dismissed with prejudice in 2011 by a federal judge. The judge stated: "As a legal matter, [..] plaintiffs have failed to allege facts or articulate a theory on which Sony may be held liable." However this decision was overturned in a 2014 appel-late court decision finding that plaintiffs had indeed made clear and sufficiently substantial claims. Ultimately, in 2016, Sony settled with users who installed Linux or purchased a PlayStation 3 based upon the alternative OS functionality.

History

A cluster of PlayStation 3's running a Linux operating system

Since 2000, Sony has used the fact that the PlayStation 2 can run Linux in its marketing. They promoted the release of the PS2 Linux Kit, which included a Linux-based operating system, a USB keyboard and mouse, a VGA adapter, a PlayStation 2 Ethernet network adapter, and a 40 GB hard disk drive (HDD).

The PlayStation 3 does not have Linux pre-installed. However, Sony included an option in the XMB menu soon after the PlayStation 3 launched that allowed booting into Linux from the hard drive or from a Live CD that the distributor's kernel would boot. The installation manual for the Yellow Dog Linux version for PS3 stated, "It was fully intended that you, a PS3 owner, could play games, watch movies, view photos, listen to music, and run a full-featured Linux operating system that transforms your PS3 into a home computer."

When Sony announced the upcoming release of the PS3 Slim in September 2009, they stated that it would not be supporting the OtherOS feature, without offering any explanation for this. In March 2010 Sony announced that the "Other OS" capability of the original PS3 models would be removed due to security concerns in PS3 Firmware 3.21 on April 1, 2010.

Several methods of bypassing the updating and retaining the ability to sign into PSN have been discovered, most of which involve using third party DNS servers.

George Hotz claims to have created custom firmware for the PS3 called 3.21OO that re-enables OtherOS and has published a video of his Custom Firmware as proof. Despite the release of a YouTube video which apparently demonstrates the use of his custom firmware, some in the online community claim that this custom firmware was in fact a hoax. On July 14, 2010, Hotz announced that he would not bring out his custom firmware to the PlayStation 3.

On April 27, 2010 a class action lawsuit was filed in California. The lawsuit claimed that the removal of the OtherOS feature was "unfair and deceptive" and a "breach of good faith". Most of the filing relates to violation of various consumer protection laws relating to the removal. Several other lawsuits were also filed and are somewhat similar in nature but are filed by other individuals.

In January 2011, Sony sued Hotz and members of failoverflow for their jailbreaking of the PS3. Charges included violating the DMCA, the CFAA, copyright law, and California's CCDAFA, and for breach of contract (related to the PlayStation Network User Agreement), tortious interference, misappropriation, and trespass.

In February, 2011, U.S. District Judge Richard Seeborg dismissed most of the class claims with leave to amend, finding the plaintiffs failed to state a claim. Seeborg stated: "While it cannot be concluded as a matter of law at this juncture that Sony could, without legal consequence, force its customers to choose either to forego installing the software update or to lose access to the other OS feature, the present allegations of the complaint largely fail to state a claim. Accordingly, with the exception of one count, the motion to dismiss will be granted, with leave to amend."

On May 4, 2011, Youness Alaoui from the PS3MFW team announced the release of a modified PS3 firmware that allows running OtherOS.

On December 8, 2011, U.S. District Judge Richard Seeborg dismissed the last remaining count of the class action lawsuit, stating: "As a legal matter, [..] plaintiffs have failed to allege facts or articulate a theory on which Sony may be held liable."

In January 2014 the U.S. Court of Appeals for the Ninth Circuit partially reversed the dismissal and have sent the case back to the district court.

In 2016, Sony settled with American users who installed Linux or purchased a PlayStation 3 based upon the alternative OS functionality. This settlement provided a payment of $55 to those owners who used an alternative OS and/or $9 for purchasing a PlayStation based upon the option.

Linux kernel

Linux supported PlayStation 3 with version 2.6.21. No patches or modifications are required. A simple Linux add-on CD for the PS3 includes support for Fedora 8 and other operating systems that already claim to install natively on the PS3. However, there is currently an issue with the latest kboot boot loader provided by kernel.org. Once the user selects the default action, the USB ports are de-registered on some systems. A work-around is available at PSUbuntu.

Distributions

Debian, Fedora 8, Gentoo, OpenSUSE (10.3 to 11.1), and Ubuntu run on the PlayStation 3. Yellow Dog Linux for the PlayStation 3 was first released in late 2006.

Ubuntu

Some versions of Ubuntu up to the release 10.10 have been ported to the PS3 platform. The installer cannot run in Live mode when running in 480i or 480p video resolutions, but it offers a text-based installer that installs fully functional Ubuntu. It is possible to mount an external USB hard drive as the home folder during install.

The LTS release 8.04 (Hardy Heron) of Ubuntu is incompatible with the PS3. However the 8.10 (Intrepid Ibex) release was ported to the PS3 on the same release date as the official main Ubuntu release.

Yellow Dog Linux

Yellow Dog Linux 5.0 was one of the first Linux distributions to run on Sony's PlayStation 3 platform. It is designed specifically for HDTV so users with SDTV will have to use the commands 'installtext' and 'ydl480i' to install and run.

Yellow Dog Linux is based on the Red Hat Enterprise Linux/CentOS core and relies on the RPM package manager. Digital audio has been verified to function properly, however, the Nvidia graphics card is not supported beyond framebuffer mode. In addition, some other hardware components will not function properly without modifications to the kernel. WiFi functionality via the Network Manager is also not fully supported and must be entered manually via the Network Configuration tool, or in some cases, through the command shell. A workaround is available to enable wireless to be configured via the Network Manager.

OpenSUSE

OpenSUSE 10.3 was the first version of OpenSUSE to run on the Sony PlayStation 3 platform. OpenSUSE is a free version of SUSE Linux, which is owned by Novell. There are PlayStation 3 specific installation instructions available for OpenSUSE.

Starting with OpenSUSE 11.2, support for the PowerPC (and therefore the PlayStation 3) has been dropped.

Fedora

Fedora also ran on the PlayStation 3. Fedora 7 works on a USB external hard disk but fails to detect the internal disk, Fedora 9 detects the internal disk but not the USB disk, Fedora 8 will not work due to video "card" detection problems. Fedora 10 installs on the internal hard disk without any issues and works fine without having to change any settings.

Fedora 12 only installs on the PlayStation 3 when running the 64 bit kernel and only when English is the chosen language.

RSX Homebrew

Linux on the PlayStation 3 allows for a range of homebrew programs to be developed. Although the Cell's performance is more than enough to handle most media requirements or render complex 3D graphics, it does lack the teraflops performance of a contemporary GPU's texture fetching hardware. For this reason many complex games aren't possible on the PlayStation 3 through Linux, as access to hardware acceleration in the RSX is restricted by a hypervisor.

There have been developments in enabling access to the RSX through the Linux kernel and the X Window System. It's possible to use the RSX memory as swap space. A trick to access some 3D functions was blocked with firmware 2.10.

AsbestOS

Reverse engineering advancements focused around a recently discovered USB descriptor parsing vulnerability in 3.41 firmware, which allowed running the Linux kernel on 3.41 firmware. The current state of the project is the ability to load the Linux kernel via TFTP and run it with access to all 7 SPE's (requires applying a small patch to the kernel). The rest of the system can run off an NFS share - hard disk access is currently not implemented, as well as some other features.

Also, since the exploit runs the kernel with game privileges, graphics acceleration is now available, although it requires reworking of the nouveau driver code.

FreeBSD

Support for PlayStation 3 was added to FreeBSD 9.0 in summer 2010. This support is limited to machines with OtherOS functionality still intact (firmwares 3.15 and earlier).

References

- Whitehead, Thomas (2015-12-16). "Napster is Coming to the European Wii U eShop on 17th December". Nintendo Life. Retrieved 2016-03-12.

- McFerran, Damien (2016-01-29). "Wii Street U Service Being Discontinued In March, Leaving eShop This Month". Nintendo Life. Retrieved 2016-03-12.

- [%= data.comment.created_on %]. "Starting today, anyone can turn their Xbox One into a dev kit for free". Polygon. Retrieved 2016-04-08.

- Rexly Peñaflorida. "Microsoft Transforms Retail Xbox One Into A Dev Kit, Adding Mods And Overlay To Windows 10 Gaming". Tomshardware.com. Retrieved 2016-04-08.

- Hryb, Larry. "Coming To Preview: Buy Xbox 360 Games On Xbox One, 16-Person Party Chat And More". Major Nelson. Retrieved 4 March 2016.

- Morris, Tatiana (2016-03-10). "Xbox One update brings new features to preview members". Gamezone.com. Retrieved 2016-04-08.

- Ybarra, Mike. "More Social, More Games, More Devices – What's in the Xbox Update Coming this Summer". Xbox Wire. Retrieved 7 June 2016.

- Ohannessian, Kevin (November 12, 2015). "How Microsoft Created A New Xbox Experience". Co.Design. Fast Company & Inc. Mansueto Ventures, LLC. Retrieved 29 March 2016.

- Kamen, Matt (February 18, 2016). "Xbox One gets biggest software update in months". Wired UK. Condé Nast Publications. Retrieved 8 April 2016.

Evolution of Operating Systems

The computers that were created initially did not have an operating system. Since the computers did not have an operating system, every program required full hardware specification to run properly and to perform tasks correctly. This section helps the readers in understanding the progress operating systems have made over a period of years.

History of Operating Systems

Computer operating systems (OSes) provide a set of functions needed and used by most application programs on a computer, and the links needed to control and synchronize computer hardware. On the first computers, with no operating system, every program needed the full hardware specification to run correctly and perform standard tasks, and its own drivers for peripheral devices like printers and punched paper card readers. The growing complexity of hardware and application programs eventually made operating systems a necessity for everyday use.

Background

The earliest computers were mainframes that lacked any form of operating system. Each user had sole use of the machine for a scheduled period of time and would arrive at the computer with program and data, often on punched paper cards and magnetic or paper tape. The program would be loaded into the machine, and the machine would be set to work until the program completed or crashed. Programs could generally be debugged via a control panel using dials, toggle switches and panel lights.

Symbolic languages, assemblers, and compilers were developed for programmers to translate symbolic program-code into machine code that previously would have been hand-encoded. Later machines came with libraries of support code on punched cards or magnetic tape, which would be linked to the user's program to assist in operations such as input and output. This was the genesis of the modern-day operating system; however, machines still ran a single job at a time. At Cambridge University in England the job queue was at one time a washing line from which tapes were hung with different colored clothes-pegs to indicate job-priority.

As machines became more powerful the time to run programs diminished, and the time to hand off the equipment to the next user became large by comparison. Accounting for and paying for machine usage moved on from checking the wall clock to automatic logging by the computer. Run queues evolved from a literal queue of people at the door, to a heap of media on a jobs-waiting table, or batches of punch-cards stacked one on top of the other in the reader, until the machine itself was able to select and sequence which magnetic tape drives processed which tapes.

Where program developers had originally had access to run their own jobs on the machine, they were supplanted by dedicated machine operators who looked after the machine and were less and less concerned with implementing tasks manually. When commercially available computer centers were faced with the implications of data lost through tampering or operational errors, equipment vendors were put under pressure to enhance the runtime libraries to prevent misuse of system resources. Automated monitoring was needed not just for CPU usage but for counting pages printed, cards punched, cards read, disk storage used and for signaling when operator intervention was required by jobs such as changing magnetic tapes and paper forms. Security features were added to operating systems to record audit trails of which programs were accessing which files and to prevent access to a production payroll file by an engineering program, for example.

All these features were building up towards the repertoire of a fully capable operating system. Eventually the runtime libraries became an amalgamated program that was started before the first customer job and could read in the customer job, control its execution, record its usage, reassign hardware resources after the job ended, and immediately go on to process the next job. These resident background programs, capable of managing multistep processes, were often called monitors or monitor-programs before the term "operating system" established itself.

An underlying program offering basic hardware-management, software-scheduling and resource-monitoring may seem a remote ancestor to the user-oriented OSes of the personal computing era. But there has been a shift in the meaning of OS. Just as early automobiles lacked speedometers, radios, and air-conditioners which later became standard, more and more optional software features became standard features in every OS package, although some applications such as database management systems and spreadsheets remain optional and separately priced. This has led to the perception of an OS as a complete user-system with an integrated graphical user interface, utilities, some applications such as text editors and file managers, and configuration tools.

The true descendant of the early operating systems is what is now called the "kernel". In technical and development circles the old restricted sense of an OS persists because of the continued active development of embedded operating systems for all kinds of devices with a data-processing component, from hand-held gadgets up to industrial robots and real-time control-systems, which do not run user applications at the front-end. An embedded OS in a device today is not so far removed as one might think from its ancestor of the 1950s.

Mainframes

The first operating system used for real work was GM-NAA I/O, produced in 1956 by General Motors' Research division for its IBM 704. Most other early operating systems for IBM mainframes were also produced by customers.

Early operating systems were very diverse, with each vendor or customer producing one or more operating systems specific to their particular mainframe computer. Every operating system, even from the same vendor, could have radically different models of commands, operating procedures, and such facilities as debugging aids. Typically, each time the manufacturer brought out a new machine, there would be a new operating system, and most applications would have to be manually adjusted, recompiled, and retested.

Systems on IBM Hardware

The state of affairs continued until the 1960s when IBM, already a leading hardware vendor, stopped work on existing systems and put all its effort into developing the System/360 series of machines, all of which used the *same* instruction and input/output architecture. IBM intended to develop a single operating system for the new hardware, the OS/360. The problems encountered in the development of the OS/360 are legendary, and are described by Fred Brooks in *The Mythical Man-Month*—a book that has become a classic of software engineering. Because of performance differences across the hardware range and delays with software development, a whole family of operating systems was introduced instead of a single OS/360.

IBM wound up releasing a series of stop-gaps followed by two longer-lived operating systems:

- OS/360 for mid-range and large systems. This was available in three system generation options:

    o PCP for early users and for those without the resources for multiprogramming.

    o MFT for mid-range systems, replaced by MFT-II in OS/360 Release 15/16. This had one successor, OS/VS1, which was discontinued in the 1980s.

    o MVT for large systems. This was similar in most ways to PCP and MFT (most programs could be ported among the three without being re-compiled), but has more sophisticated memory management and a time-sharing facility, TSO. MVT had several successors including the current z/OS.

- DOS/360 for small System/360 models had several successors including the current z/VSE. It was significantly different from OS/360.

IBM maintained full compatibility with the past, so that programs developed in the sixties can still run under z/VSE (if developed for DOS/360) or z/OS (if developed for MFT or MVT) with no change.

IBM also developed TSS/360, a time-sharing system for the System/360 Model 67. Overcompensating for their perceived importance of developing a timeshare system, they set hundreds of developers to work on the project. They ended up with a bloated, buggy project that took as long to boot as it did to crash, and ended the project without releasing it.

Several operating systems for the IBM S/360 and S/370 architectures were developed by third parties, including the Michigan Terminal System (MTS) and MUSIC/SP.

Other Mainframe Operating Systems

Control Data Corporation developed the SCOPE operating systems in the 1960s, for batch processing and later developed the MACE operating system for time sharing, which was the basis for the later Kronos. In cooperation with the University of Minnesota, the Kronos and later the

NOS operating systems were developed during the 1970s, which supported simultaneous batch and timesharing use. Like many commercial timesharing systems, its interface was an extension of the DTSS time sharing system, one of the pioneering efforts in timesharing and programming languages.

In the late 1970s, Control Data and the University of Illinois developed the PLATO system, which used plasma panel displays and long-distance time sharing networks. PLATO was remarkably innovative for its time; the shared memory model of PLATO's TUTOR programming language allowed applications such as real-time chat and multi-user graphical games.

For the UNIVAC 1107, UNIVAC, the first commercial computer manufacturer, produced the EXEC I operating system, and Computer Sciences Corporation developed the EXEC II operating system and delivered it to UNIVAC. EXEC II was ported to the UNIVAC 1108. Later, UNIVAC developed the EXEC 8 operating system for the 1108; it was the basis for operating systems for later members of the family. Like all early mainframe systems, EXEC I and EXEC II were a batch-oriented system that managed magnetic drums, disks, card readers and line printers; EXEC 8 supported both batch processing and on-line transaction processing. In the 1970s, UNIVAC produced the Real-Time Basic (RTB) system to support large-scale time sharing, also patterned after the Dartmouth BASIC system.

Burroughs Corporation introduced the B5000 in 1961 with the MCP (Master Control Program) operating system. The B5000 was a stack machine designed to exclusively support high-level languages, with no software, not even at the lowest level of the operating system, being written directly in machine language or assembly language; the MCP was the first OS to be written entirely in a high-level language - ESPOL, a dialect of ALGOL 60 - although ESPOL had specialized statements for each "syllable" in the B5000 instruction set. MCP also introduced many other ground-breaking innovations, such as being one of the first commercial implementations of virtual memory. The rewrite of MCP for the B6500 is still in use today in the Unisys ClearPath/MCP line of computers.

GE introduced the GE-600 series with the General Electric Comprehensive Operating Supervisor (GECOS) operating system in 1962. After Honeywell acquired GE's computer business, it was renamed to General Comprehensive Operating System (GCOS). Honeywell expanded the use of the GCOS name to cover all its operating systems in the 1970s, though many of its computers had nothing in common with the earlier GE 600 series and their operating systems were not derived from the original GECOS.

Project MAC at MIT, working with GE and Bell Labs, developed Multics, which introduced the concept of ringed security privilege levels.

Digital Equipment Corporation developed TOPS-10 for its PDP-10 line of 36-bit computers in 1967. Before the widespread use of Unix, TOPS-10 was a particularly popular system in universities, and in the early ARPANET community. Bolt, Beranek, and Newman developed TENEX for a modified PDP-10 that supported demand paging; this was another popular system in the research and ARPANET communities, and was later developed by DEC into TOPS-20.

Scientific Data Systems/Xerox Data Systems developed several operating systems for the Sigma series of computers, such as the Basic Control Monitor (BCM), Batch Processing Monitor (BPM), and Basic Time-Sharing Monitor (BTM). Later, BPM and BTM were succeeded by the Universal Time-Sharing System (UTS); it was designed to provide multi-programming services for online (interactive) user programs in addition to batch-mode production jobs, It was succeeded by the CP-V operating system, which combined UTS with the heavily batch-oriented Xerox Operating System (XOS).

Minicomputers

Digital Equipment Corporation created several operating systems for its 16-bit PDP-11 machines, including the simple RT-11 system, the time-sharing RSTS operating systems, and the RSX-11 family of real-time operating systems, as well as the VMS system for the 32-bit VAX machines.

Several competitors of Digital Equipment Corporation such as Data General, Hewlett-Packard, and Computer Automation created their own operating systems. One such, "MAX III", was developed for Modular Computer Systems Modcomp II and Modcomp III computers. It was characterised by its target market being the industrial control market. The Fortran libraries included one that enabled access to measurement and control devices.

IBM's key innovation in operating systems in this class (which they call "mid-range"), was their "CPF" for the System/38. This had capability-based addressing, used a machine interface architecture to isolate the application software and most of the operating system from hardware dependencies (including even such details as address size and register size) and included an integrated RDBMS. The succeeding OS/400 for the AS/400 has no files, only objects of different types and these objects persist in very large, flat virtual memory, called a single-level store. i5/OS and later IBM i for the iSeries continue this line of operating system.

The Unix operating system was developed at AT&T Bell Laboratories in the late 1960s, originally for the PDP-7, and later for the PDP-11. Because it was essentially free in early editions, easily obtainable, and easily modified, it achieved wide acceptance. It also became a requirement within the Bell systems operating companies. Since it was written in the C language, when that language was ported to a new machine architecture, Unix was also able to be ported. This portability permitted it to become the choice for a second generation of minicomputers and the first generation of workstations. By widespread use it exemplified the idea of an operating system that was conceptually the same across various hardware platforms, and later became one of the roots of the free software and open source including GNU, Linux, and the Berkeley Software Distribution. Apple's OS X is also based on Unix via NeXTSTEP and FreeBSD.

The Pick operating system was another operating system available on a wide variety of hardware brands. Commercially released in 1973 its core was a BASIC-like language called Data/BASIC and a SQL-style database manipulation language called ENGLISH. Licensed to a large variety of manufacturers and vendors, by the early 1980s observers saw the Pick operating system as a strong competitor to Unix.

Microcomputers

Beginning in the mid-1970s, a new class of small computers came onto the marketplace. Featuring 8-bit processors, typically the MOS Technology 6502, Intel 8080, Motorola 6800 or the Zilog Z80, along with rudimentary input and output interfaces and as much RAM as practical, these systems started out as kit-based hobbyist computers but soon evolved into an essential business tool.

Home Computers

While many eight-bit home computers of the 1980s, such as the BBC Micro, Commodore 64, Apple II series, the Atari 8-bit, the Amstrad CPC, ZX Spectrum series and others could load a third-party disk-loading operating system, such as CP/M or GEOS, they were generally used without one. Their built-in operating systems were designed in an era when floppy disk drives were very expensive and not expected to be used by most users, so the standard storage device on most was a tape drive using standard compact cassettes. Most, if not all, of these computers shipped with a built-in BASIC interpreter on ROM, which also served as a crude command line interface, allowing the user to load a separate disk operating system to perform file management commands and load and save to disk. The most popular home computer, the Commodore 64, was a notable exception, as its DOS was on ROM in the disk drive hardware, and the drive was addressed identically to printers, modems, and other external devices.

More elaborate operating systems were not needed in part because most such machines were used for entertainment and education, and seldom used for more serious business or science purposes.

Another reason is that the hardware they used was (largely) fixed and a need for an operating system to abstract away differences was thus not needed. They shipped with minimal amounts of computer memory—4-8 kilobytes was standard on early home computers—as well as 8-bit processors without specialized support circuitry like a MMU or even a dedicated real-time clock. On this hardware, a complex operating system's overhead supporting multiple tasks and users would likely compromise the performance of the machine without really being needed.

Video games and even the available spreadsheet, database and word processors for home computers were mostly self-contained programs that took over the machine completely. Although integrated software existed for these computers, they usually lacked features compared to their standalone equivalents, largely due to memory limitations. Data exchange was mostly performed though standard formats like ASCII text or CSV, or through specialized file conversion programs.

Operating Systems in Video Games and Consoles

Since virtually all video game consoles and arcade cabinets designed and built after 1980 were true digital machines based on microprocessors (unlike the earlier *Pong* clones and derivatives), some of them carried a minimal form of BIOS or built-in game, such as the ColecoVision, the Sega Master System and the SNK Neo Geo.

Modern-day game consoles and videogames, starting with the PC-Engine, all have a minimal BIOS that also provides some interactive utilities such as memory card management, audio or video CD playback, copy protection and sometimes carry libraries for developers to use etc. Few of these cases, however, would qualify as a true operating system.

The most notable exceptions are probably the Dreamcast game console which includes a minimal BIOS, like the PlayStation, but can load the Windows CE operating system from the game disk allowing easily porting of games from the PC world, and the Xbox game console, which is little more than a disguised Intel-based PC running a secret, modified version of Microsoft Windows in the background. Furthermore, there are Linux versions that will run on a Dreamcast and later game consoles as well.

Long before that, Sony had released a kind of development kit called the Net Yaroze for its first PlayStation platform, which provided a series of programming and developing tools to be used with a normal PC and a specially modified "Black PlayStation" that could be interfaced with a PC and download programs from it. These operations require in general a functional OS on both platforms involved.

In general, it can be said that videogame consoles and arcade coin-operated machines used at most a built-in BIOS during the 1970s, 1980s and most of the 1990s, while from the PlayStation era and beyond they started getting more and more sophisticated, to the point of requiring a generic or custom-built OS for aiding in development and expandability.

Personal Computer Era

The development of microprocessors made inexpensive computing available for the small business and hobbyist, which in turn led to the widespread use of interchangeable hardware components using a common interconnection (such as the S-100, SS-50, Apple II, ISA, and PCI buses), and an increasing need for "standard" operating systems to control them. The most important of the early OSes on these machines was Digital Research's CP/M-80 for the 8080 / 8085 / Z-80 CPUs. It was based on several Digital Equipment Corporation operating systems, mostly for the PDP-11 architecture. Microsoft's first operating system, MDOS/MIDAS, was designed along many of the PDP-11 features, but for microprocessor based systems. MS-DOS, or PC DOS when supplied by IBM, was based originally on CP/M-80. Each of these machines had a small boot program in ROM which loaded the OS itself from disk. The BIOS on the IBM-PC class machines was an extension of this idea and has accreted more features and functions in the 20 years since the first IBM-PC was introduced in 1981.

The decreasing cost of display equipment and processors made it practical to provide graphical user interfaces for many operating systems, such as the generic X Window System that is provided with many Unix systems, or other graphical systems such as Microsoft Windows, the Radio Shack Color Computer's OS-9 Level II/MultiVue, Commodore's AmigaOS, Atari TOS, Apple's classic Mac OS, and macOS, or even IBM's OS/2. The original GUI was developed on the Xerox Alto computer system at Xerox Palo Alto Research Center in the early 1970s and commercialized by many vendors throughout the 1980s and 1990s.

Since the late 1990s, there have been three operating systems in widespread use on personal computers: Microsoft Windows, Apple Inc.'s OS X, and the open source Linux. Since 2005 and Apple's transition to Intel processors, all have been developed mainly on the x86 platform, although OS X retained PowerPC support until 2009 and Linux remains ported to a multitude of architectures including ones such as 68k, PA-RISC, and DEC Alpha, which have been long superseded and out of production, and SPARC and MIPS, which are used in servers or embedded systems but no longer for desktop computers. Other operating systems such as AmigaOS and OS/2 remain in use, if at all, mainly by retrocomputing enthusiasts or for specialized embedded applications.

Mobile Operating Systems

In the early 1990s, Psion released the Psion Series 3 PDA, a small mobile computing device. It supported user-written applications running on an operating system called EPOC. Later versions of EPOC became Symbian, an operating system used for mobile phones from Ericsson, Motorola, and Nokia. In 1996, Palm Computing released the Pilot 1000 and Pilot 5000, running Palm OS. Microsoft Windows CE was the base for PocketPC 2000, renamed Windows Mobile in 2003, which at its peak in 2007 was the most common operating system for smartphones in the U.S.

In 2007 Apple introduced the iPhone and its operating system, iOS, which, like OS X, is based on the Unix-like Darwin. In addition to these underpinnings, it also introduces a powerful and innovative graphic user interface – later also used for the tablet computer iPad. A year later, Android was introduced, based on the Unix-like Linux, and its own graphic user interface, and Microsoft re-entered this market with Windows Phone in 2010, due to be replaced by Windows 10 Mobile in 2015.

In addition to these, a wide range of other mobile operating systems are contending in this area.

Rise of Virtualization

Operating systems originally ran directly on the hardware itself and provided services to applications, but with virtualization, the operating system itself runs under the control of a hypervisor, instead of being in direct control of the hardware.

On mainframes IBM introduced the notion of a virtual machine in 1968 with CP/CMS on the IBM System/360 Model 67, and extended this later in 1972 with Virtual Machine Facility/370 (VM/370) on System/370.

On Intel microprocessor personal computers, VMware popularized this technology with their 1999 product, VMware Workstation, and their 2001 VMware GSX Server and VMware ESX Server products. Later, a wide range of products from others, including Xen, KVM and Hyper-V meant that by 2010 it was reported that more than 80 percent of enterprises had a virtualization program or project in place, and that 25 percent of all server workloads would be in a virtual machine.

Over time, the line between virtual machines, monitors, and operating systems was blurred:

- Hypervisors grew more complex, gaining their own application programming interface, memory management or file system.

- Virtualization becomes a key feature of operating systems, as exemplified by KVM and LXC in Linux, Hyper-V in Windows Server 2008 or HP Integrity Virtual Machines in HP-UX.

- In some systems, such as POWER5 and POWER6-based servers from IBM, the hypervisor is no longer optional.

- Radically simplified operating systems, such as CoreOS have been designed to run only on virtual systems.

- Applications have been re-designed to run directly on a virtual machine monitor.

In many ways, virtual machine software today plays the role formerly held by the operating system, including managing the hardware resources (processor, memory, I/O devices), applying scheduling policies, or allowing system administrators to manage system.

History of IBM Mainframe Operating Systems

The history of operating systems running on IBM mainframes is a notable chapter of history of mainframe operating systems, because of IBM's long-standing position as the world's largest hardware supplier of mainframe computers.

Arguably the operating systems which IBM supplied to customers for use on its early mainframes have seldom been very innovative, except for the virtual machine systems beginning with CP-67. But the company's well-known reputation for preferring proven technology has generally given potential users the confidence to adopt new IBM systems fairly quickly. IBM's current mainframe operating systems, z/OS, z/VM, z/VSE, and z/TPF, are backwards compatible successors to operating systems introduced in the 1960s, although of course they have been improved in many ways.

Both IBM-supplied operating systems and those supplied by others are discussed here, if notably used on IBM mainframes.

Before System/360

IBM was slow to introduce operating systems: General Motors produced General Motors OS in 1955 and GM-NAA I/O in 1956 for use on its own IBM computers; and in 1962 Burroughs Corporation released MCP and General Electric introduced GECOS, in both cases for use by their customers.

In fact the first operating systems for IBM computers were written by IBM customers who did not wish to have their very expensive machines (US$2M in the mid-1950s) sitting idle while operators set up jobs manually, and so they wanted a mechanism for maintaining a queue of jobs.

The operating systems described below ran only on a few processor models and were suitable only for scientific and engineering calculations. Users with other IBM computers or other applications had to manage without operating systems. But one of IBM's smaller computers, the IBM 650, introduced a feature which later became part of OS/360: if processing was interrupted by a "random processing error" (hardware glitch), the machine could automatically resume from the last checkpoint instead of requiring the operators to restart the job manually from the beginning.

From General Motors' GM-NAA I/O to Ibsys

General Motors' Research division produced GM-NAA I/O for its IBM 701 in 1956 (from a prototype, GM Operating System, developed in 1955), and updated it for the 701's successor. In 1960 the IBM user association SHARE took it over and produced an updated version, SHARE Operating System.

Finally IBM took over the project and supplied an enhanced version called IBSYS with the IBM 7090 and IBM 7094 computers. IBSYS required 8 tape drives (fewer if the system had one or more disk drives). Its main components were: a card-based Job Control language, which was the main user interface; compilers for FORTRAN and COBOL; an assembler; and various utilities including a sort program.

In 1958, the University of Michigan Executive System adapted GM-NAA I/O to produce UMES, which was better-suited to the large number of small jobs created by students. UMES was used until 1967, when it was replaced by the MTS timesharing system.

BESYS

Bell Labs produced BESYS (sometimes referred to as BELLMON) and used it until the mid-1960s. Bell also made it available to others without charge or formal technical support.

FORTRAN Monitor System

Before IBSYS, IBM produced for its IBM 709, 7090 and 7094 computers a tape-based operating system whose sole purpose was to compile FORTRAN programs—in fact FMS and the FORTRAN compiler were on the same tape.

Early Time-sharing and Virtual Machine Systems

MIT's Fernando Corbató produced the first experimental time-sharing systems, such as CTSS, from 1957 to the early 1960s, using slightly modified IBM 704 and IBM 7090 mainframes; these systems were based on a proposal by John McCarthy. In the 1960s IBM's own laboratories created experimental time-sharing systems, using standard mainframes with hardware and microcode modifications to support virtual memory: IBM M44/44X in the early 1960s; CP-40 from 1964 to 1967; CP-67 from 1967 to 1972. The company even released CP-67 without warranty or technical support to several large customers from 1968 to 1972. CP-40 and CP-67 used modified System/360 CPUs, but the M44/44X was based on the IBM 7044, an earlier generation of CPU which was very different internally.

These experimental systems were too late to be incorporated into the System/360 series which IBM announced in 1964, but encouraged the company to add virtual memory and virtual machine capabilities to its System/370 mainframes and their operating systems in 1972:

- The M44/44X showed that a partial approach to virtual machines was not good enough, and that thrashing could severely reduce the speed of virtual memory systems. Thrashing is a condition in which the system runs very slowly because it spends a lot of its time shuffling virtual memory pages between physical memory and disk files.

- IBM learned from CP-40 and CP-67: how to make the thrashing problem manageable; that its other virtual memory and virtual machine technologies were sufficiently fast and reliable to be used in the high-volume commercial systems which were its core business. In particular IBM's David Sayre convinced the company that automated virtual memory management could consistently perform at least as well as the best programmer-designed overlay schemes.

In 1968 a consulting firm called Computer Software Systems used the released version of CP-

67 to set up a commercial time-sharing service. The company's technical team included 2 recruits from MIT, Dick Orenstein and Harold Feinleib. As it grew, the company renamed itself National CSS and modified the software to increase the number of paying users it could support until the system was sufficiently different that it warranted a new name, VP/CSS. VP/CSS was the delivery mechanism for National CSS' services until the early 1980s, when it switched to IBM's VM/370.

Universities produced three other S/360 time-sharing operating systems in the late 1960s:

- The Michigan Terminal System (MTS) was developed in 1967 by a consortium of universities led by the University of Michigan. All versions ran on IBM mainframes which had virtual memory capability, starting with the S/360-67. MTS remained in use until 1999.

- McGill University in Montreal started developing MUSIC (McGill University System for Interactive Computing) in 1969. MUSIC was enhanced several times and eventually supported text searches, web publishing and email as well as software development. MUSIC became an IBM Systems Product (MUSIC/SP or Multi-User System for Interactive Computing / System Product) in 1985. The last official version was released in 1999.

- ORVYL and WYLBUR were developed by Stanford University in 1967-68 for the IBM S/360-67. They provided some of the first time-sharing capabilities on IBM S/360 computers.

System/360 Operating Systems

Up to the early 1960s IBM's low-end and high-end systems were incompatible - programs could not easily be transferred from one to another, and the systems often used completely different peripherals (e.g. disk drives). IBM concluded that these factors were increasing its design and production costs for both hardware and software to a level that was unsustainable, and were reducing sales by deterring customers from upgrading. So in 1964 the company announced System/360, a new range of computers which all used the same peripherals and most of which could run the same programs.

IBM originally intended that System/360 should have only one batch-oriented operating system, OS/360. There are at least two accounts of why IBM later decided it should also produce a simpler batch-oriented operating system, DOS/360: because it found that OS/360 would not fit into the limited memory available on the smaller System/360 models; or because it realized that the development of OS/360 would take much longer than expected, and introduced DOS/360 as one of a series of stop-gaps to prevent System/360 hardware sales from collapsing - the others were BOS/360 (Basic Operating System, for the smallest machines) and TOS/360 (Tape Operating System, for machines with only tape drives).

System/360's operating systems were more complex than previous IBM operating systems for several reasons, including:

- They had to support multiprogramming, otherwise the faster CPUs in the range would have spent most of their time waiting for I/O operations (e.g. disk reads) to complete. This meant that the operating systems had to be the real masters of the systems, to provide whatever services the applications validly requested, and to handle crashes or misbehavior in one application without stopping others that were running at the same time.

- They had to support a much wider range of machine sizes. Memory ranged from 16 KB to 1 MB and processor speeds from a few thousand instructions per second to 500,000.

- System/360's operating systems had to support a wide range of application requirements, for example: some applications only needed to read through sequential files from start to finish; others needed fast, direct access to specific records in very large files; and a few applications spent nearly all their time doing calculations, with very little reading / writing of files.

This was one of the largest software projects anyone had attempted, and it soon ran into trouble, with huge time and cost over-runs and large numbers of bugs. So the company had to release a series of short-lived stop-gaps because:

- To develop and test the planned operating systems it needed to use System/360 hardware. So it first developed Basic Programming Support(BPS), which it used to develop the tools it needed for developing DOS/360 and OS/360 and the first versions of tools its would supply with these operating systems - compilers (FORTRAN and COBOL), utilities including Sort, and above all the Assembler it needed to build all the other software.

- Competitors took advantage of the delays to announce systems aimed at what they thought were the most vulnerable parts of IBM's market.

IBM released four stop-gap operating systems to prevent sales of System/360 from collapsing:

- BOS/360 (Basic Operating System), which loaded from a card reader and supported tape drives and a few disks. This system was supplied to beta test customers and may have been an early version of DOS/360.

- TOS/360, which was designed to provide an upgrade path for customers who had IBM 1401 computers with tape drives and no disks.

- DOS/360, which was built by the developers of BOS/360 and TOS/360 (IBM's small business computers division) and went on to become a mainstream operating system whose descendant z/VSE is still widely used.

- PCP (Primary Control Program), which was a very early option of OS/360 that didn't support multiprogramming.

When IBM announced the S/360-67 it also announced a timesharing operating system, TSS/360, that would use the new virtual memory capabilities of the 360/67. TSS/360 was so late and unreliable that IBM canceled it. By this time the alternative operating system CP-67, developed by IBM's Cambridge Scientific Center, was running well enough for IBM to offer it "without warranty" as a timesharing facility for a few large customers. CP-67 would go on to become VM/370 and eventually z/VM.

The traumas of producing the System/360 operating systems gave a boost to the emerging discipline of software engineering, the attempt to apply scientific principles to the development of software and the management of software projects. Frederick P. Brooks, who was a senior project manager for the whole System/360 project and then was given specific responsibility for OS/360 (which was already long overdue), wrote an acclaimed book, *The Mythical Man-Month*, based on the problems encountered and lessons learned during the project, two of which were:

- Throwing additional resources (especially staff) at a struggling project quickly becomes unproductive or even counter-productive because of communication difficulties. This is the "Mythical Man-Month" syndrome which gave the book its title.

- The successor to a successful system often runs into difficulties because it gets overloaded with all the features people wished had been in the earlier system. Brooks called this the "second-system effect", and cited OS/360 as a very comprehensive example.

DOS/360

DOS/360 became the usual operating system for processors less than 256 KB of memory. It had a good set of utility programs, an Assembler, and compilers for FORTRAN, COBOL, RPG and eventually PL/I. And it supported a useful range of file organizations with access methods to help in using them:

- Sequential data sets were normally read one record at a time from beginning to end.

- In indexed (ISAM) files a specified section of each record was defined as a key which could be used to look up specific records.

- In direct access (BDAM) files, the application program had to specify the physical location on the disk of the data it wanted to access. BDAM programming was not easy and most customers never used it themselves; but it was the fastest way to access data on disks and many software companies used it in their products, especially database management systems such as ADABAS, IDMS and IBM's DL/I.

Sequential and ISAM files could store either fixed-length or variable-length records, and all types could occupy more than one disk volume.

DOS/360 also offered BTAM, a data communications facility which was primitive and hard to use by today's standards. But BTAM could communicate with almost any type of terminal, which was a big advantage at a time when there was hardly any standardization of communications protocols.

But DOS/360 had significant limitations compared with OS/360, which was used to control most larger System/360 machines:

- The first version could run only one program at a time. A later enhancement allowed 3 at the same time, in one of 3 "partitions" whose size was set by each customer when DOS/360 was installed.

- The JCL it used for submitting jobs was designed to be easy for the low-end machines to process, and as a result programmers did not find it easy to read or write.

- There was no spooling sub-system to improve the efficiency of punched card and printer use. In the late 1960s an independent software company started selling a spooler called GRASP.

- DOS/360 had no relocating loader, so users had to link edit a separate executable version of each program for each partition in which the program was likely to be run.

- Executable programs were stored in the Core Image Library, which did not reclaim space when programs were deleted or replaced by newer versions. When the Core Image Library became full, it had to be compressed by one of the utility programs, and this could halt development work for as much as half a day.

- Its application programming interface was different from that of OS/360. Programs written in high level languages such as COBOL needed small modifications before they could be used with OS/360 and Assembler programs needed larger changes.

IBM expected that DOS/360 users would soon upgrade to OS/360, but despite its limitations DOS/360 became the world's most widely used operating system because

- System/360 hardware sold very well

- Over 90% of the 360 systems sold were Models 20, 30 & 40

- Most of these had far less core memory than required by OS/360.

DOS/360 ran well on the System/360 processors which medium-sized organizations could afford, and it was better than the "operating systems" these customers had before. As a result, its descendant z/VSE is still widely used today, as of 2005.

OS/360

OS/360 included multiple levels of support, a single API and much shared code. PCP was a stop-gap version which could run only one program at a time, but MFT ("Multiprogramming with a Fixed number of Tasks") and MVT ("Multiprogramming with a Variable number of Tasks") were used until at least the late 1970s, a good five years after their successors had been launched. It is unclear whether the divisions among PCP, MFT and MVT arose because MVT required too much memory to be usable on mid-range machines or because IBM needed to release a multiprogramming version of OS (MFT) as soon as possible.

PCP, MFT and MVT had different approaches to managing memory, but provided very similar facilities:

- The same application programming interface (API), so application programs could be transferred among PCP, MFT and MVT without even needing re-compilation.

- The same JCL, which was more flexible and easier to use than that of DOS/360.

- The same facilities (access methods) as DOS/360 for reading and writing files (sequential, indexed and direct) and for data communications (BTAM).

- An additional file structure, partitioned, and access method (BPAM), which was mainly used for managing program libraries. Although partitioned files needed to be compressed to reclaim free space, this seldom halted development work as it did with DOS/360's Core Image Library, because PCP, MFT and MVT allowed an indefinite number of partitioned files and each project generally had at least one.

- A file naming system which allowed files to be managed as hierarchies, e.g. *PROJECT. USER.FILENAME*.

- A spooling facility (which DOS/360 lacked).

- Applications could create sub-tasks, which allowed multiprogramming within the one job.

Experience indicated that it was not advisable to install MFT on systems with less than 256 KB of memory, which was a common limitation in the 1960s.

MFT

When installing MFT, customers would specify up to five "partitions", areas of memory with fixed boundaries, in which application programs could be run simultaneously. MFT Version II (MFT-II) raised the limit to 52.

MVT

MVT was considerably larger and more complex than MFT and therefore was used on the most powerful System/360 CPUs. It treated all memory not used by the operating system as a single pool from which contiguous "regions" could be allocated as required by an indefinite number of simultaneous application programs. This scheme was more flexible than MFT's and in principle used memory more efficiently, but was liable to fragmentation - after a while one could find that, although there was enough spare memory in total to run a program, it was divided into separate chunks none of which was large enough.

In 1971 the Time Sharing Option (TSO) for use with MVT was added. TSO became widely used for program development because it provided: an editor; the ability to submit batch jobs, be notified of their completion and view the results without waiting for printed reports; debuggers for some of the programming languages used on System/360. TSO communicated with terminals by using TCAM (Telecommunications Access Method), which eventually replaced the earlier Queued Telecommunications Access Method (QTAM). TCAM's name suggests that IBM hoped it would become the standard access method for data communications, but in fact TCAM was used almost entirely for TSO and was largely superseded by VTAM from the late 1970s onwards.

TP Monitors

System/360's hardware and operating systems were designed for processing batch jobs which in extreme cases might run for hours. As a result, they were unsuitable for transaction processing, in which there are thousands of units of work per day and each takes between 30 seconds and a very few minutes. In 1968 IBM released IMS to handle transaction processing, and in 1969 it released CICS, a simpler transaction processing system which a group of IBM's staff had developed for a customer. IMS was only available for OS/360 and its successors, but CICS was also available for DOS/360 and its successors. For many years this type of product was known as a "TP (teleprocessing) monitor". Strictly speaking TP monitors were not operating system components but application programs which managed other application programs. In the 1970s and 1980s several third-party TP monitors competed with CICS (notably Taskmaster, Shadow and Intercomm), but IBM gradually improved CICS to the point where most customers abandoned the alternatives.

Special Systems for Airlines

In the 1950s airlines were expanding rapidly but this growth was held back by the difficulty of handling thousands of bookings manually (using card files). In 1957 IBM signed a development contract with American Airlines for the development of a computerized reservations system, which became known as SABRE. The first experimental system went live in 1960 and the system took over all booking functions in 1964 - in both cases using IBM 7090 mainframes. In the early 1960s IBM undertook similar projects for other airlines, and soon decided to produce a single standard booking system, PARS, to run on System/360 computers.

In SABRE and early versions of PARS there was no separation between the application and operating system components of the software, but in 1968 IBM divided it into PARS (application) and ACP (operating system). Later versions of ACP were named ACP / TPF and then TPF (Transaction Processing Facility) as non-airline businesses adopted this operating system for handling large volumes of online transactions. The latest version is z/TPF.

IBM developed ACP and its successors because: in the mid-1960s IBM's standard operating systems (DOS/360 and OS/360) were batch-oriented and could not handle large numbers of short transactions quickly enough; even its transaction monitors IMS and CICS, which run under the control of standard general-purpose operating systems, are not fast enough for handling reservations on hundreds of flights from thousands of travel agents.

The last "public domain" version of ACP, hence its last "free" version, was ACP 9.2, which was distributed on a single mini-reel with an accompanying manual set (about two dozen manuals, which occupied perhaps 48 lineal inches of shelf space) and which could be restored to IBM 3340 disk drives and which would, thereby, provide a fully functional ACP system.

ACP 9.2 was intended, primarily, for bank card (MasterCard®, et al.) and other "financial" applications, but it could also be utilized for airlines reservation systems, too, as by this time ACP had become a more general-purpose OS.

Indeed, ACP had by then incorporated a "hypervisor" module (CHYR) which supported a virtual OS ... usually VS1, but possibly also VS2... as a "guest", with which program development or file maintenance could be accomplished concurrently with the on-line functions.

In some instances, production work was run under VS2 under the hypervisor, including, possibly, IMS DB.

System/360 Model 20

The Model 20 was labeled as part of the System/360 range because it could be connected to some of the same peripherals, but it was a 16-bit machine and not entirely program-compatible with other members of the System/360 range. Three operating systems were developed by IBM's labs in Germany, for different 360/20 configurations; DPS—with disks (minimum memory required: 12 KB); TPS—no disk but with tapes (minimum memory required: 8 KB); and CPS—punched-card-based (minimum memory required: 4 KB). These had no direct successors since IBM introduced the System/3 range of small business computers in 1969 and System/3 had a different internal design from the 360/20 and different peripherals from IBM's mainframes.

System/360 Model 44

This was another processor which used the System/360 peripherals but had a different internal design. The 360/44 was designed for scientific computation using floating point numbers, such as geological or meteorological analyses. Because of the internal differences and the specialized type of work for which it was designed, the 360/44 had its own operating system, PS/44. An emulator for missing System/360 instructions allowed the Model 44 to run OS/360. The 360/44 and PS/44 had no direct successors.

System/370 and Virtual Memory Operating Systems

When System/370 was announced in 1970 it offered essentially the same facilities as System/360 but with about 4 times the processor speeds of similarly-priced System/360 CPUs. Then in 1972 IBM announced "System/370 Advanced Functions", of which the main item was that future sales of System/370 would include virtual memory capability and this could also be retro-fitted to existing System/370 CPUs. Hence IBM also committed to delivering enhanced operating systems which could support the use of virtual memory.

Most of the new operating systems were distinguished from their predecessors by the presence of "/VS" in their names. "VS" stands for "Virtual Storage" - IBM avoided the term "memory", allegedly because it might be interpreted to imply that their computers could forget things.

All of today's IBM mainframe operating systems except z/TPF are descendants of those included in the "System/370 Advanced Functions" announcement - z/TPF is a descendant of ACP, the system which IBM initially developed to support high-volume airline reservations applications.

DOS/VS

DOS/VS was the successor to DOS/360. In addition to virtual memory DOS/VS provided other enhancements:

- Five memory partitions instead of three. Later releases increased this to seven.

- A relocating loader, so that it was no longer necessary to link-edit a separate copy of each program for each partition in which it was to run.

- An improved spooling component, POWER/VS.

DOS/VS was followed by significant upgrades: DOS/VSE and VSE/SP (1980s), VSE/ESA (1991), and z/VSE (2005).

OS/VS1

OS/VS1 was the successor to MFT, and offered similar facilities, with the addition of virtual memory. IBM released fairly minor enhancements of OS/VS1 until 1983, and in 1984 announced that there would be no more. OS/VS1 and TSS/370 are the only IBM System/370 operating systems that do not have modern descendants.

The *Special Real Time Operating System* (SRTOS), Programming RPQ Z06751, was a variant of

OS/VS1 extended to support real-time computing. It was targeted at such industries as electric utility energy management and oil refinery applications.

OS/VS2 and MVS

OS/VS2 Release 1 (SVS) was a replacement for MVT with virtual memory; while there were many changes it retained the overall structure. But in 1974 IBM released what it described as OS/VS2 release 2 but which was a major rewrite that was upwards-compatible with the earlier OS/VS2 SVS. The new system's most noticeable feature was that it supported multiple virtual address spaces - different applications thought they were using the same range of virtual addresses, but the new system's virtual memory facilities mapped these to different ranges of real memory addresses. As a result, the new system rapidly became known as "MVS" (Multiple Virtual Storages), the original OS/VS2 became known as "SVS" (Single Virtual Storage). IBM itself accepted this terminology and labelled MVS's successors "MVS/...".

The other distinctive features of MVS were: its main catalog *had* to be a VSAM catalog; it supported "tightly-coupled multiprocessing" (2 or more CPUs share the same memory and copy of the operating system); it included a System Resources Manager (renamed Workload Manager in later versions) which allowed users to load additional work on to the system without reducing the performance of high-priority jobs.

IBM has released several MVS upgrades: MVS/SE, MVS/SP Version 1, MVS/XA (1981), MVS/ESA (1985), OS/390 (1996) and currently z/OS (2001).

VM/370

VM/370 combined a virtual machine facility with a single-user system called Conversational Monitor System (CMS); this combination provided time-sharing by allowing each user to run a copy of CMS on his / her own virtual machine. This combination was a direct descendant of CP/CMS. The virtual machine facility was often used for testing new software while normal production work continued on another virtual machine, and the CMS timesharing system was widely used for program development.

VM/370 was followed by a series of upgrades: VM/SEPP ("Systems Extensions Program Product"), VM/BSEPP ("Basic Systems Extensions Program Product"), VM/SP (System Product), VM/SP HPO ("High Performance Option"), VM/XA MA ("Extended Architecture Migration Aid"), VM/XA SF ("Extended Architecture System Facility"), VM/XA SP ("Extended Architecture System Product"), VM/ESA ("Enterprise Systems Architecture"), and z/VM. IBM also produced optional microcode assists for VM and successors, to speed up the hypervisor's emulation of privileged instructions (those which only operating systems can use) on behalf of "guest" operating systems. As part of 370/Extended Architecture, IBM added the Start Interpretive Execution (SIE) instruction to allow a further speedup of the CP hypervisor.

Technical Notes

Time-sharing

Time-sharing (or timesharing) is based on the idea that computers are much faster than humans, so while one human user is reading what a computer has just displayed on a screen the computer can do some useful work for another user. Large time-sharing systems can have hundreds or even thousands of simultaneous users, and the memory required by their programs and data generally adds up to much more than the physical memory attached to the computer. Time-sharing systems solve this problem by various combinations of:

- virtual memory, described below.

- swapping, in other words while the OS is waiting for a response from one user, a Time slice has ended or the OS is trying to free up real storage, it saves that user's programs and data on a disk or drum and reads it all back into its memory when the user sends a response, resources free up or another user is swapped out due to time slice end. Swapping does not require virtual memory and was implemented before virtual memory. It transfers *all* of a user's programs and data between memory and disk, and is mainly driven by user's responses to information displayed by the system.

Virtual Memory

Virtual memory is a memory management technique by which programs are made to work as if they have more memory available to them than is actually attached to the computer. Running programs' code and data may be scattered over several areas of physical memory or even placed on a disk until needed.

The main components of an IBM virtual memory system are:

- Virtual memory, consisting of all memory addresses accessible by the CPU hardware. *Virtual memory* is an abstraction, so systems can easily have more virtual than real memory.

- Pages, fixed-size blocks into which all *virtual memory* is divided. Most IBM operating systems use 4 KB (4,096-byte) pages, although some older systems ran quite well with 2 KB (2,048-byte) pages. Newer IBM System z systems also support 1 MB large pages in addition to the normal 4 KB pages.

- Real memory, Random access memory (RAM) attached to the computing system.

- Page frames, realized by dividing all *real memory* into pieces equal to the system's page size. Virtual-memory *pages* must be placed into real-memory *page frames* before they can be used by the CPU and I/O channels.

- Page Tables track the location of every virtual-memory page, whether in a real-memory *page frame* or on disk, in a *paging file*. Critical to memory management, Page Table entries also record the last time each page was accessed.

- Dynamic Address Translation hardware (sometimes called a "DAT box" in early systems because of its separate enclosure) is integrated into the CPU itself and participates in every memory reference. If the Page Table shows the page in a real-memory page frame, DAT translates the virtual address to a real one and allows the memory access to complete. If, on the other hand, the referenced page is not in real memory, the DAT hardware generates an interrupt (internal signal) which calls the Paging Supervisor into action.

- The Paging Supervisor (part of the operating system) manages all memory, both real and virtual, moving pages between real memory and disk as needed, keeping the Page Table updated, servicing memory allocation requests, and cleaning up after itself. As the load on the system increases, a page can be referenced when all page frames are in use. When this happens, the paging supervisor typically identifies the page that has not been read or written for the longest interval of time (least-recently used), copies the page to the paging file (on disk), updates the Page Table, and uses the newly available page frame to satisfy the memory request.

When functioning properly, the virtual memory system keeps active pages in real memory, inactive ones on disk, and allows more efficient execution of the systems workload.

Virtual Machine

Virtual machine techniques enable several operating systems ("guest" operating systems) or other software to run on the same computer so that each thinks it has a whole computer to itself, and each of these simulated whole computers is called a "virtual machine". The operating system which really controls the computer is usually called a hypervisor. Two of the major components of the hypervisor are:

- Virtual memory management. Each virtual machine appears to have a complete range of addresses from 0 to some large number, and virtual memory techniques prevent different virtual machines from confusing each other.

- Simulating "privileged" functions on behalf of the "guest" operating systems. "Privileged" functions are those which enable programs to take over all or at least large parts of the computer, and usually operating systems immediately terminate any other program which tries to use them. But "guest" operating systems think they are entitled to use these functions, so the hypervisor detects their attempts to do so and runs the privileged functions on their behalf, using virtual memory techniques to prevent them from corrupting memory areas used by other "guest" operating systems.

References

- Brooks, F.P. (1995) [1975]. The Mythical Man-Month: Essays on Software Engineering. Addison-Wesley Professional. ISBN 0-201-83595-9.

- Pugh, E.W., Johnson, L.R. and Palmer, J.H. (1991). IBM's 360 and Early 370 Systems. MIT Press. ISBN 0-262-16123-0.

- Fiedler, Ryan (October 1983). "The Unix Tutorial / Part 3: Unix in the Microcomputer Marketplace". BYTE. p. 132. Retrieved 30 January 2015.

- "Snappy Ubuntu challenges CoreOS and Project Atomic on lightweight cloud servers", Dec 10, 2014, Steven J. Vaughan-Nichols, ZDNet.com

Permissions

Index

CPSIA information can be obtained
at www.ICGtesting.com
Printed in the USA
LVHW060904170921
698049LV00003B/320

9 781635 492040